KINDERGARTEN ≈
a Year of Learning

Marguerita Rudolph

Consultant in Early Childhood Education

Dorothy H. Cohen

Graduate Programs
Bank Street College of Education

KINDERGARTEN
a Year of Learning

 New York

Appleton-Century-Crofts

Division of Meredith Publishing Company

Acknowledgments for Photographs

2: California State Department of Education, Bureau of Audio-Visual Education, Sacramento 14, California
6: Office of the Superintendent of Schools, San Diego County, California
7: California State Department of Education
9: Los Angeles County Schools
10: U.E.S., U.C.L.A., Bob Vase
11: New York City Board of Education
12: Federation of Protestant Welfare Agencies, Inc., New York
13: Child Development and Parent Education Bureau, State Education Department, Albany, New York
16: San Diego City Schools
17: U.E.S., U.C.L.A., Gene Daniels
18: Bellflower School District, Bellflower, California
19: California State Department of Education
20: San Diego County Schools
21: New York City Board of Education
22: New York City Board of Education
23: California State Department of Education
24: California State Department of Education
25: New York City Board of Education
26: San Bernardino County, California
27: California State Department of Education
28: New York City Board of Education
29: California State Department of Education

Foreword

The remark is often heard today that kindergarten children are different now from what they were a generation ago. They talk more easily, use longer words, express more complicated ideas. They seem older, interested in more complex things. They are much less tractable, less docile, and much more likely to rebel against restrictions. Is this mid-century five-year-old really so different? On the surface yes; deep down to the core of him—no.

Of course the whole exciting drama of today—television, electric trains, war (cold and hot), mothers at work, fathers away, moving about, and space ships—has had its impact on five-year-olds as it has on twenty, thirty, and sixty-year-olds. We adults probably see how the five-year-old differs from his age peers of the past more clearly than we see how we differ from those of our own age group of a generation ago. Listening to him chatter in the lingo of today—*virus, stratosphere, jets, video, power steering, atoms*—doting adults are apt to think they have a wonder child in their midst. And unfortunately, they sometimes treat him as such. Then trouble begins. The chances are he is just a normal child picking up the vocabularly of his environment. Had he lived fifty years ago on a farm he would have been talking of silos, fertilizers, planting time, harvest, and shearing.

The differences are only superficial. Our child's potential—physical, emotional, and mental—has not changed. True, our better understanding of his physical needs has made him stronger and healthier on the whole; our increasing knowledge of his emotional and intellectual needs has made us somewhat more humane and more intelligent in our treatment of him. This means that his potential is being somewhat better realized. But it is still the potential of a five-year-old, not that of an eight or even a six-year-old. This we must not forget. The warning is needed, for we watch with increasing alarm the tendency of the kindergarten to take on more and more of the character of the first grade. Too often the kindergarten is looked upon as a means for pushing a child ahead more quickly, and even perhaps of enabling him to gain a year and get through school earlier. And the way to this goal is *reading!* "He doesn't want any more baby stuff." "Listen to his vocabulary." "He needs some real learning." On all sides we hear this. And we wonder how we can explain that we too want to make sure that the enormous capacity for learning during the first six years of life is realized as nearly as possible. But we also want to make clear that in spite of his complex vocabulary the kindergartener's bodily proportions are no different from those of the five-year-old of generations ago. Neither is his eye focus, his appetite, his curiosity, his willfulness, his need for play and rest, his affection, and most of all, his way of learning.

The way of learning of the five-year-old is today, as it has always been, the way of play and of absorption. The problem of the kindergarten teacher today, as always, is that of finding, largely through play, how best the children can be guided in their absorption of the "here and now" world of today. Of course, this "here and now" world is not that of yesterday. Hence, the materials and the experiences of the kindergarten will, in specifics, be different from those of yesterday. But the difference in their fundamental character will be no greater than the difference between the fundamental character of the problems we face today and that of the problems of yesterday.

The present book attempts, largely through the writers' experience, to show how teachers can teach today's children effectively in the kindergarten. In brief, as the incidents related in the book so well illustrate, two basic qualities of the teacher as a person are essential: understanding of, and respect for, children, and identity with today's world.

Of the first, little need be said. That a teacher must respect and understand children is generally accepted. Just one thought here might be pertinent; this understanding and respect can be fully realized only when the teacher has kept, along with her increasing wisdom, much of the child in her nature. She must be able to see with a child's eyes, hear with a child's ears, and above all feel with a child's heart.

The second, identity with today's world, may need some clarification. First, identity does not mean acceptance. Rather, it means a constructive relation with the problems of today, a critical evaluation of our way of life, and the effort to play the role of a good citizen on a local, national, and world basis. The teacher must be part of today's world if she would help children to live intelligently in this world. To guide children through its maze, the teacher needs to work toward the formulation of her own values. Otherwise her work with children will lack clearly defined goals, and, hence, become a mere hit-or-miss hodge-podge of activity.

To combine the two, identity with the children and identity with the world, is a supreme art. It is to the extent that the reader will note the interplay of these two elements in the experiences narrated, that the present book will be of value to him.

Agnes Snyder
Professor Emeritus
Adelphi College

Preface

This book had its beginnings in the years Marguerita Rudolph spent gathering the many episodes that run through its pages as live material. To the initial material Dorothy H. Cohen later added the particular insights and perspectives of her years spent in teacher education. In an unusual collaboration based on an essentially common point of view each of the authors was able to bring to bear special skills and strengths on the ultimate outcome. It is hard now for each to say which page is hers, which words the other's.

Because we both have faith in the possibilities for growth inherent in human beings—little ones at the preschool stage and older ones embarking on a professional career—we tried to develop a text in kindergarten education that would stress this human value. We sought to write a book for students and teachers that would bring children to life for them in such a way that they would inevitably empathize and sympathize with the challenges involved in growing up. At the same time we wanted the book to be as helpful as possible to the early childhood student or teacher herself as she goes through the difficult and often painful process of transforming her personal self into the more objective and knowledgeable professional self the teaching task requires.

We considered it most helpful to this process of growth in child and student to take a generally nondirective and nonjudgmental approach. There are few *musts* and no *shoulds* in our book, which may be a matter of concern to some people who will be looking for them. But it was our aim to illuminate possibilities, not restrict to one, stimulate thought, not prescribe it, because we believe that there are many ways to be a good teacher, and that each teacher or prospective teacher must find her own. We would go further and say that each teacher owes it to herself as well as to the children to actively seek the uniquely personal fulfillment of the teaching role in her own applications of the principles underlying sound education for children.

We have therefore tried to give understanding of the theoretical "why" in clear relation to the no less important "how" of practice. We are convinced that only a thorough grasp of the theoretical combined with a detailed knowledge of the practical can make a teacher sufficiently creative so that she can encourage similar creative living and thinking in children.

We are grateful to the many nursery and kindergarten teachers whose devotion in daily work with children is part of the substance and spirit of this book; to the professional friends who read portions of the manuscript and whose encouragement served us well; to the many responsive students on whom much of the material was tried; to Jessie Stanton for the use of her records on blockbuilding; to Rose Engel and the *Journal of Nursery Education* for the use of her episode on the snails; and to our indefatigable typist, Eleanor Mullins, whose stamina and patience helped carry us through.

M.R.
D.H.C.

Contents

I. THE TEACHER GETS TO KNOW THE CHILDREN

II. THE CHILDREN GET TO KNOW THEIR WORLD

III. THE CHILDREN COMMUNICATE FEELINGS AND IDEAS THROUGH ARTS AND SKILLS

1

the teacher gets to know the children

1

Relation of Early Childhood to Later Schooling and Life Itself

In many countries throughout the world, governments and educated leaders are struggling with the vast problem of bringing the skills
of reading and writing to wholly unlettered peoples. In the United States
we have long since climbed this first step of the educational ladder. Despite much unevenness in different parts of the country, despite teacher
shortages and building deficiencies, we are by and large a literate nation.
For us the major educational challenge is of another character, over and
above the mechanics of reading and writing. For us there is the challenge
of teaching people to use the tools of reading and writing for deepening
and expressing human experience and feeling. For us educating the un-
educated means adding quality to the mass production standards of lit-
eracy, stretching minds to embrace ideas with enthusiasm, and cultivating
tastes and even appetites for cultural and intellectual richness.

To fulfill this deeper meaning in education we must not only be
convinced of the worthiness and necessity of our ambition, but we must
analyze clearly the factors that facilitate or impede its realization. Within
this enlarged educational horizon a child's year in kindergarten takes on
strategic importance, for research has shown a clear relationship between
early childhood experience and formal learning.

The kindergarten year has for too long been appraised as a pleas-
urable entr'acte before the important business of skill learning that takes

3

place later. But the newer knowledge gleaned from psychology and the social sciences indicates that there must be serious meaning in the kindergarten experience even though in the eyes of the child kindergarten remains primarily a year of pleasure. We must not assume however, that seriousness of purpose simply means copying in diluted form the skill learning of the grades. Nor must we assume that there can be a mechanical acceleration of the existing curriculum by starting the skills in the kindergarten. On the contrary, we are strongly opposed to the proposals that kindergarten children start their preparation for advanced skills by handling specific aspects of the three R's at five. We have in mind something different, and to understand the basis for serious planning as we see it we ask you to step outside the school temporarily for a broader perspective of our children's lives and of society's needs. Only with this perspective can we determine what is good education at five.

IN WHAT KIND OF WORLD ARE TODAY'S CHILDREN GROWING UP?

At no time in history has it been more necessary that the average citizen be a well-educated person. Our time is one in which changes of all kinds occur so rapidly that only the most backward can enjoy the security and comfort of thinking they know what makes the world go around. Technical knowledge has increased man's leisure time and brought the far reaches of the earth close to the eyes and ears of the ordinary citizen. East and West face each other's customs and mores in wide-eyed wonder; concepts of time and space shift faster than all of us can adjust to easily. Although further advanced than ever, knowledge of man, of the earth he inhabits, and of the space in which the earth whirls becomes outmoded at a more rapid pace than ever before.

In such a world there is no question of the need for increasing areas of factual information. But there is no question either of the great need for agility and maturity in coping with new ideas. Children need not only facts; they must learn to think, and must be prepared to grow and learn continuously if they are to cope successfully with the coming eras of expanding research and knowledge. Such an educational goal is not really new. But our past understanding of how to achieve this goal must be subjected to critical analysis as we learn more about what affects the learning process itself. It is this relatively recent insight into how learning takes place that makes us say that the base on which school learning flourishes as well as the groundwork for original thinking and scientific problem solving needed in our time, are both laid in the preschool years. The kindergarten, first school experience for large numbers

of children, is the most logical place—almost too late for many children—
to begin.

ENVIRONMENTAL INFLUENCE ON LEARNING CAPACITY

Why have we suggested that kindergarten is almost too late? Research has shown that what happens to children long before they dream of entering school markedly influences their capacity to grow in school. Consider the implications of the following studies.

Knoblock and Pasamanick (1960) [1] tested some three hundred children, half Negro, half white. They found no difference in intelligence scores between white and nonwhite babies at forty weeks of age. But when tested again at age three the environmentally less favored Negro children showed less responsiveness and curiosity; their language intelligence scores were as much as sixteen points lower than those of the white children with whom they had been on a par as babies. On the other hand, Irwin [2] (1961) persuaded a group of mothers whose husbands were unskilled, semiskilled and skilled workers to read to their children ten minutes a day from the time they were one. Not only were the mothers, who ordinarily would not have read to their children, amazed to find a strong interest in books among their little ones, but Irwin found a measurable difference in the speech development of these children as compared with that of a control group of similar background. And this difference showed up when the children were as young as twenty months. Or consider Esther Milner's[3] study (1951) of three groups of Negro first-graders. This study revealed a definite relationship between children's ability to read in the first grade and two factors, a) the warmth of affectional relationship (parents and children chatted at meals together), and b) the degree of intellectual stimulation (not only were there books in the house but even the punishment was *verbal*).

What does all this mean? That learning, the precious birthright of curiosity and adaptiveness to new and changing phenomena, and the development of speech, which is so dependent on having something to say and on a model to imitate, can be encouraged or extinguished much earlier and more easily than we have ever believed. A child's life condi-

[1] Hilda Knoblock and B. Pasamanick, "Environmental Factors Affecting Human Development Before and After Birth," *Pediatrics*, Aug., 1960.

[2] O. C. Irwin, "Infant Speech: Effect of Systematic Reading of Stories," *Journal of Speech and Hearing Research*, Vol. 3 (June, 1960), pp. 187–190.

[3] Esther Milner, "A Study of the Relationship Between Reading Readiness in Grade 1 School Children and Patterns of Parent-Child Interaction," *Child Development*, Vol. 22 (June, 1951), pp. 95–112.

tion must offer stimulation and interest within an emotional climate of love and support, or he will not grow in capacity to learn.

It seems apparent, Pasamanick suggests, that while differences in inherited capacity for responsiveness and adaptiveness, which we might label intelligence, probably do exist, these differences are not as wide apart at birth as environment causes them to become. There are many studies of institutionalized children which support the theory that children who do not receive stimulation and love, as is often true in poorly-staffed orphanages, not only do not develop but actually regress in intellectual and social abilities. It is possible of course for the same deprivation to exist in families of poor and limited educational and cultural background, with the same depressing results.

Some researchers believe that such lack of opportunity in early childhood and its resultant damage, cannot be overcome. But others are inclined to the view that if a stimulating environment counteracts this void in the early years much can be done to reverse the downward trend. The fact that environment can play so dramatic a role in children's capacity to learn, and the frighteningly early state at which children can show the effects of inadequate experience, points up the responsibility of the teacher of young children in a way we have not fully recognized before. Kindergarten, the earliest school experience for large numbers of children, may be seen as strategic in relation to their future educational progress. In some cases it may be crucial.

ONE LEARNS FIRST FROM LIFE AND THEN FROM BOOKS

It is important to realize that under ordinary circumstances of daily stimulation and affection, children are capable of learning and growing intellectually long before they can read from books. Yet the common conception of learning assumes that it begins with books and therefore with reading. Educators must revise their conception of learning to recognize that whether ideas are gleaned from books, films, discussions, or firsthand observation the major consideration is that a mind is at work and insights are deepening. To assume that only reading skills offer information and provoke thought is a fallacy that underestimates the capacity for factual learning, generalization, problemsolving, and cause-and-effect thinking of the preschool child. The young child may be illiterate but he has a mind and a heart! Indeed the amount of learning many children do before they come to school, about customs, people, animals, natural phenomena, the industrial world they live in, and the more abstract conceptions of what they may or may not do, is enormous. Of course books do in time become a major source of learning. But they are secondary sources and as such cannot be used beneficially without suitable and adequate preparation in firsthand learning.

EXPERIENCE AND SYMBOLIC LEARNING

What children learn on their own, if the opportunity is there, is real enough. But without adult guidance what they learn may be inaccurate, since they tend to substitute parts for the whole; inadequate, since they may be limited in the use of data from which to draw generalizations. Misconceptions and misinterpretations are then inevitable. Children need adults if their natural bent for wanting to know is to be rooted in a solid base of accurate facts and clear concepts. A child, for example, learns at the beach that sand can crumble into seemingly endless grains, pack into a specific shape when wet, be scattered by the force of water, absorb water and change color, be soft, dry, and warm as the sun shines on it, and cold, wet, and clammy when it is in the shade of rocks. But the adult teaches him that sand is made up of disintegrated rock, mainly quartz which is a specific kind of rock, and geology beckons. The adult tells him that sand was once used to dry ink and to tell the passage of time, and history opens up. The adult introduces him to Shakespeare's allusion, "the sands are numbered that make up my life," and the child is introduced to literature. Naturally knowledge which the adult presents to the child should be comprehensible to him and at his maturity level, and some of the above is beyond the understanding of a five-year-old. The important thing here is that the child's own learning from life serves well as an introduction and springboard to the accumulated heritage stored in books.

It is this relationship between "natural" learning and "book" learning that makes the kindergarten experience so valuable for later school learning. Let us use an illustration closer to the life of a young child.

EXPERIENCE AS A BASE FOR READING

Natural learning is experience. Experience is the underpinning of symbolic learning, which is what reading is. Suppose you saw *dog* on a billboard, in a neon light, or in a book. You would recognize this particular configuration because you have been taught to identify it. Moreover you could interpret it because that particular four-legged creature is commonplace enough in most people's lives. But suppose you had been bitten by a dog. Would you recognize the word faster or be reluctant to recognize it at all? Suppose your family made their living through kennels; would *dog* mean hated chores or quick response to variety in breed and temperament? Suppose *mutt* was the word you ascribed to the animal, and dog meant a frankfurter or referred to putting on airs. A configuration, the word in and of itself, is easy to identify and recognize. Read *lomt, fevu, taw, sko, pildin, brunsil, nart.* You can read them easily but can you understand what they mean? It happens that they mean nothing because they have never been used to apply to any aspect of human experience. The symbol without the experiential foundation is meaningless. This means that for children the learning of symbols without enough general background of experience to comprehend what the symbols stand for is so much wasted effort. Reading is the recognition and interpretation of written symbols. The written symbols are in turn symbols for the spoken word, and a word is a symbol for a thing, an action, or an idea—something experienced, felt, known. The combination of understood experience and expressed reaction (verbal or nonverbal) is indispensable if any child is to relate one symbol (the spoken word) to another symbol (the written word) and know that behind it all there is the real thing.

A very young child can be taught to recognize words, and theoretically, to read. But he will not become a *reader of books* unless he can use the skill of recognition to absorb the ideas that the symbols represent. For this he must have lived a while in order to be ready to share ideas and communicate through symbols, verbal as well as written ones. It is no accident that there is a high correlation between language facility (verbal intelligence) and school learning. But language facility means having something to talk about and knowing how to say it. This depends heavily on opportunity to experience.

Kindergarten must therefore be seen as a significant aspect of school life in its own unique way, stretching the minds of children but holding off on the tools for book learning, developing the broad qualities necessary for scholarship but not demanding the specific skills that eventually will enhance scholarship.

An article by William D. Sheldon, Director of the Syracuse Reading Laboratory, deals with research related to teaching kindergarten children to read.[4] Dr. Sheldon quotes one study done in Great Britain, where children start reading earlier than ours do. The results showed that eight-year-old Scottish children who were taught to read at the age of five were not significantly more able in reading comprehension than a comparable group of English children whose reading instruction began at the age of six. It is true that a small percentage of five-year-olds are ready to read, and indeed learn before they enter kindergarten. But this

[4] William D. Sheldon, "Research Related to Teaching Children to Read," *Reading In The Kindergarten,* (Washington Association for Childhood Education International, 1962).

does not alter the truth about the majority of five-year-olds—that premature reading instruction can lead to confusion and failure. Even the very bright child may profit from waiting to read by himself, especially if he is the kind of child who reads in order to escape facing the challenge offered by other children. It is conceivable that a kindergarten teacher, aware of individual differences and carefully blocking out her time, would help some children learn to read. But what would be served? Five is a time of great intellectual curiosity but it is also a time of important social learning. Are we sure that it is wise to run the risk of cutting a child off from the give-and-take with his peers so soon? Is reading the only road to intellectual stimulation at five?

The confusion about what is intellectual seems to lie in historical tradition rather than in a true analysis of the problem. Traditionally reading has been associated with the educated and has been the road to learning. But knowing the technique of reading does not make one educated nor does it necessarily lead to learning. The truth of this is apparent in the large numbers of nonreaders in America, a country that prides itself on being practically one hundred percent literate. Secondly, readiness for reading is not like readiness for other subjects; French 1, for example, *must* precede French 2. One cannot take the elements of comparing, seeing likenesses and differences, discriminating sounds, and all the other aspects of reading skill, and deal with them in isolation as though they alone precede reading the way French 1 precedes French 2. The workbook approach to reading readiness does this, overlooking completely the fact that reading involves above all the conceptualization of what reading is—a statement of experience through symbols. And by stressing the *parts* of the reading process before a child has even grasped the concept of the *whole*, the entire experience becomes meaningless, is performed by rote to please the teacher, and does not become the helpful tool for unraveling ideas that it can be when a child knows how and why the analysis of parts is helpful. Since a child must comprehend fully what he is doing, this emphasis on the mechanics at the wrong time is probably responsible for much of the resistance to reading that we have among people who can read but do not.

It is not wise to introduce reading formally in the kindergarten because most five-year-olds have neither proper eye-hand coordination nor the patience to sit still for too long in an imposed program of sequential learning. It is certainly not wise as a matter of policy because too many of the children who enter our elementary schools are simply not ready. The few who are will not be harmed by waiting; the many can be soured on reading for life by being pushed too soon. Unhampered by a tightly prescribed course of study, the kindergarten teacher is in a position to concentrate on the quality of experience in a child's life and on the stretching of his mind so he will be ready to read later. Kindergarten is the time to find out that wanting to know is exciting, stimulating, and fulfilling. It is a time to ask questions, seek answers wherever they are to be found, and exchange ideas, knowledge, and impressions; it is a time to learn that mistakes and confusions can be turned into clarification and enlightenment. The kindergarten teacher makes it possible for the children to explore, examine, test, and understand that which is reality to a five-year-old. Only in this way, by building understanding of what his senses contact, will the child truly be ready for the symbolic learning that will come in time. There is no more important teacher in the educational structure than the teacher of the young child.

EDUCATION IN THE KINDERGARTEN AND MENTAL HEALTH

Understanding the world in which he lives does more for a child than strengthen his intellectual powers. There is a tremendous sense of security in understanding what goes on around one, a sense of security not too easily won by a child in our highly complex, industrial civilization. This idea may be seen more clearly if we think back to the life of a young child in our agricultural society of one hundred years ago. Reality stared such a child in the face, as he observed the step-by-step procedures by which his mother and father arranged for the basic necessities of food, clothing, and shelter. From the first plowing of the earth through seeding, weeding, and harvesting, he saw the cycle a product followed from the field to the table. He saw animals born, reared, and slaughtered; he saw clothing cut from cloth, and perhaps cloth itself made first. With his own eyes he saw the cutting of trees, the planing of wood, the erection of barns and houses. The five-year-old in that economy suffered the gaps in comprehension of all five-year-olds at any time. But he understood the one-to-one relationships that he saw—fruit on a tree to fruit in a jar, lamb to chops, hen to eggs, and milk to cow. He might not have been able to say it, but he knew just how man was dependent upon the earth's resources for survival. This *knowing*, this comfortable feeling of comprehension about the processes of life, unfinished to be sure, was nevertheless a solid underpinning to what we call security.

Let us contrast this with the situation of the young child in our complex way of life. He does not see firsthand one original source of the things he learns to identify from his earliest days. Water, which he so enjoys, comes from a tap; light and dark are effected by buttons and switches; bread is taken from a wax wrapper; telephones are just there, like trees, and to top it all, a world of people he cannot touch, voices he cannot answer, and actions he may not comprehend are an integral part of his home life through television. We would not go back to the simpler way of life for the sake of the children in society, but we must remember that today's children need the same sense of knowing and understanding that offers comfort and security as did children in a simpler society. The kindergarten teacher, in making the reality around them comprehensible, is helping to clear away some of the confusion so likely to appear in our apparently more sophisticated, but somewhat overwhelmed, preschoolers. This *is* a contribution to mental health.

The comfort that comes from understanding one's environment is itself only part of a total feeling of security, albeit an important part. Life includes people as well as processes and things, and interaction with people calls for a variety of emotional response. Much research and observation has gone into our understanding of the part emotions play in living and learning. The child who feels he is unloveable acts unloveable; the child who feels inadequate acts inadequate; the child who is afraid withdraws from the challenge of trying. By five, attitudes affecting one's relations with others and one's capacity to cope with what life offers (even with a good kindergarten program!) are indicated in fairly clear trends. By five, the potential delinquent can often be spotted by the astute teacher.[5]

But fives are still tender and pliable. Fives still respond to adults whose affection and approval are eagerly awaited. Even the predelinquent can still be steered into another course if he is only five. And the "normal" child, whose responses to life can be strengthened to become more healthful and positive, is certainly amenable to direction towards good mental health.

Unrestricted by a precise course of study, the kindergarten teacher has a clearer and more direct involvment with the development of human beings than is apparent in the upper grades of school. Children's emotions are still not concealed behind poker faces and polite formalities as they tend to become later. The many admonitions from home and community that "good children do not behave that way" have made kindergarten children aware of what adults approve and disapprove of, but they have not closed off entirely the relatively uninhibited expression of feeling, including the "unacceptable," in social behavior. Kindergarten children show their anger, their jealousy, hate, pique, fury, envy, rage, and bitterness. They also show tenderness, loyalty, affection, admiration, respect, and compassion. The teacher concerned with mental health has a golden opportunity in the kindergarten, not to hasten the repressing of emotional responses earlier than ever, but to help children know where and when feelings are fitting, their own and others', and to guide them toward tech-

[5] Eli M. Bower, "A Process for Early Identification of Emotionally Disturbed Children," *Bulletin of Calif. State Dept. of Education,* Vol. 27 (1958), No. 6.

niques of social behavior which will not destroy the honesty of their feelings and yet will take other people's feelings into account. This is not easy. But it is very important.

Our entire nation is concerned with the problem of mental health. There is beginning to be evidence that the school plays its part, for good as well as for bad, in the mental health of the nation.[6, 7] We have long known that early childhood experiences throw a far shadow, although not an unchangeable one over later behavior. While it is true of course that the home plays the primary role in this regard, school is the next single largest influence in any child's life, and school begins in the kindergarten. For many children, kindergarten can be a strategic emotional experience, as well as the strategic intellectual one pointed out earlier.

KINDERGARTEN IS REAL SCHOOL

It becomes apparent then that the role of the kindergarten teacher is fully professional in scope. It is not enough that she be charmed and intrigued by the wide-eyed naïveté, the trust and dependence on adults, and the unexpected independence and even cockiness of the five-year-old. It is not enough to be loving and kind and offer friendship and activity. The possibilities for intellectual development of these youngsters call for careful analysis of their capacities for comprehension and for just as careful analysis of which aspects of the environment will be built into curriculum. These may well be different for different groups of children. The teacher is called upon to know more about human behavior and learning than her own personal experience gives her, because she is responsible for children who are at a stage of growth when they are particularly impressionable and still quite susceptible to change. And growth in both of these areas, the intellectual and the emotional, is basic to children's adaptation to the more formal demands of grade school and of life itself.

[6] Carl R. Rogers, "The Criteria Used in a Study of Mental Health Problems," *Educational Research Bulletin*, Vol. 21 (Feb. 18, 1942), No. 2.

[7] Carl R. Rogers, "Mental Health Findings in Three Elementary Schools," *Educational Research Bulletin*, Vol. 21 (March 18, 1942), No. 3.

Bibliography

Biber, Barbara, *Schooling as an Influence in Developing A Healthy Personality,* Bank St. Publication 85 (New York, Bank Street College, 69 Bank Street).

Bower, Eli M., "A Process for Early Identification of Emotionally Disturbed Children," *Bulletin of California Dept. of Education,* Vol. 27 (1958), No. 6.

Heffernan, Helen, "Significance of Kindergarten Education," *Childhood Education,* March, 1960.

Irwin, O. C., *Speech Development and Added Verbal Stimulation.* (Unpublished manuscript, Iowa City, State University of Iowa, Iowa Child Welfare Research Station, 1961).

Knoblock, Hilda, and Pasamanick, B., "Exogenous Factors in Infant Intelligence," *Pediatrics,* 1960.

Milner, Esther, "A Study of the Relationship Between Reading Readiness in Grade 1 School Children and Patterns of Parent-Child Interaction," *Child Development,* Vol. 22 (1951).

Rogers, Carl R., "Mental Health Findings in Three Elementary Schools," *Educational Research Bulletin,* Vol. 21 (March 18, 1942), No. 3.

————, "The Criteria Used in a Study of Mental Health Problems," *Educational Research Bulletin,* Vol. 21 (Feb. 18, 1942), No. 2.

Sheldon, William D., "Research Related to Teaching Children to Read," *Reading in the Kindergarten* (Washington, Association for Childhood Education International, 1962).

Witmer, Helen, and Kotinsky, Ruth, eds., *Personality in the Making* (New York, Harper & Row, Publishers, 1952).

Institutions dealing with early childhood education:

Association for Childhood Education International, 3615 Wisconsin Ave., N.W., Washington 16, D.C. Publishes *Childhood Education* monthly, Sept. through May, and many timely pamphlets.

Bank Street College of Education, 69 Bank St., New York, N.Y. Publishes many significant pamphlets and lists of books for teachers and children.

National Association for Nursery Education, 155 East Ohio Street, Chicago, Illinois. Publishes quarterly *Journal.*

2

What Is Kindergarten and Kindergarten Age?

According to figures of the National Kindergarten Association, only about fifty percent of five-year-olds in the United States go to kindergarten. The reason is that not all states or all counties within the state have kindergartens in their public schools. Furthermore not many parents can afford private kindergartens, some children are served by the different church-supported schools that provide kindergartens, and not all communities are able to maintain parent cooperatives. However the number is growing, even if slowly.

VARIETY ON THE KINDERGARTEN SCENE

In our existing kindergartens there is great variation in goals and standards from state to state and district to district. Even within one district there are considerable differences from school to school. Some kindergartens may have more than fifty children in a class, others not more than twenty. Some kindergartens in public schools have their own specially-equipped playgrounds, others have access only to a playground which must be shared with older classes and which has only limited, stationary equipment. There are many kindergartens which have an ample supply of building blocks and art materials and good, new books; others have only dump boxes with a haphazard collection of blocks, broken crayons, and torn, ill-suited books. Some kindergarten teachers are happy in

14

their work, are properly educated, and appreciative of young children's capacities. Unfortunately there are also kindergarten teachers who are inadequate or to whom teaching is only an ill-paying chore. As on all levels there are also those who are apt to take out their own troubles on the children.

Throughout this book we will look at different kindergartens, meet different teachers, and try to analyze what makes them good or bad. But now we will focus on the children themselves and on their entrance into kindergarten.

HOW DOES KINDERGARTEN DIFFER FROM FIRST GRADE?

In these times of emphasis on scientific progress there is a feeling of urgency on the part of educators and lay people, particularly parents, about rushing children into school and "real" learning. Although, as we pointed out in Chapter 1, it has been well established that early childhood years *are* very important for learning in the basic, most general sense, the common concept of school is that it starts with Grade 1. The kindergarten is generally regarded as a preliminary of debatable necessity, a year spent pleasantly enough in games but adding little to what the child has already had at home or in some cases in nursery school. Therefore, if a child could somehow skip kindergarten and go directly into the first grade he would be ahead by a whole year. In view of the long years of schooling involved in the American trend towards higher education, and especially in technical and professional training, it is often felt that a year saved could be very worthwhile.

Mrs. Albert, a mother of a five-year-old, held such views. First, since her son was bright she wanted to know if the kindergarten program would be advanced enough to interest him. Second, Mrs. Albert wanted to know if the teacher was qualified enough to appreciate and channel a child like hers, who, though not a problem, was full of energy and imagination. Third, she thought that since her child was practically old enough for first grade, perhaps it would be best if he were tested for first grade readiness, a common practice in many communities. Before pressing the issue however, she thought it might be wise if she observed the kindergarten and the first grade for herself. Mrs. Albert called the principal and obtained permission to visit both the kindergarten and the first grade.

The kindergarten class was in a separate and especially attractive wing of the new public school, with its own separate play yard. The room was large and bright with children's work on the walls. The freedom and independence with which the children engaged in various activities and the informality of conversation and conduct quickly won Mrs. Albert's sympathy and respect. One child asked her to button his smock, another showed her drawings made by several children; she watched a small group of boys and girls experimenting with magnets and discussing their findings and opinions in a lively and intelligent way. With equal earnestness and imagination another group was managing a family dinner in the well-equipped housekeeping section of the class. Two were thoughtfully "reading" books taken from a well-stocked book rack. The teacher circulated among the children and was easily accessible to them. At that time she was in charge of a word-and-picture game which fascinated the group engaged in it. Everybody else in the room was working with zest, and as far as Mrs. Albert could see, without being told what to do or make. Equally impressive to Mrs. Albert were the respect and consideration which the teacher showed to the children; she listened to them as though she really believed that what they had to say was important. This teacher was so much a part of the children's lives that she appeared quite unconcerned about the impression she might be making on the visitor. At one point for example, she cheerfully admitted being wrong and said to the children, "I made a mistake. I bought turtle food instead of fish food," and she laughed spontaneously with them! Mrs. Albert had not really expected the kindergarten teacher or the program to be so sensitive to children's feelings and ideas.

However, since she wanted to compare the alternatives before making a decision on whether or not skipping kindergarten would be wise, Mrs. Albert went on to observe the first grade. The first-grade room was adjacent to the kindergarten and the two teachers had sufficient communication to be aware of each other's programs and problems. The room was as large, bright, and sunny as the kindergarten. The walls were attractively hung with children's original paintings and drawings, as well as charts, pictures, and interesting notices. The piano was laden with much-used music books, the teacher's desk was piled with work materials, and there was a sense of important activity in the room. There was informality here too, with children and teacher speaking naturally and several kinds of work going on in small groups—art work, experimentation with magnets, writing in workbooks, and taking turns reading aloud to the teacher.

Some dissimilarities however, soon became apparent. For one thing, there was a definite physical difference between the kindergarten and first-grade children. Mrs. Albert was astonished to see how much bigger the first-graders were. Although her son was of average size for his age she now saw that he was quite small in comparison to these children and that at his age being the youngest in a class would make him look and feel noticeably smaller. Also on the physical side, there was more sitting still in first grade. The children sat in groups for reading and individually for writing, for art work, and for discussion. They also seemed more controlled in their movements. A boy raised his hand and waited quite a while before the teacher called on him to make his comment; although he wiggled he still seemed to take the necessary waiting in stride and he spoke coherently and to the point. Mrs. Albert could not help wondering whether her restless, active Robert would not have difficulty doing this. She realized too from her past experiences at the playground and from these observations at school, that little boys seemed more charged than little girls and might find the going rougher in the more demanding first grade. Perhaps Robert did need more time to settle down!

Continuing her observations Mrs. Albert saw that there was a degree of seriousness and even responsibility in what the children were doing and in following through on a project; this was subtly different from the kindergarten. Individual children were given assignments for seat work and they were expected to carry these out independently. The teacher mentioned in passing that this class had been on one topic of a unit for several weeks; this would never be suited to the rapidly-changing interests of the kindergarten children. These six and seven-year-olds as a group were definitely more mature and advanced in ways that Mrs. Albert could see often had little to do with brightness.

Although the accomplishments in the first grade impressed Mrs. Albert she was no longer sure that her son would benefit fully from an immediate introduction to formal learning. As a result of her visit and her talk with both teachers Mrs. Albert felt that although Robert was indeed a bright boy and could no doubt learn the required first-grade reading and writing without the year in kindergarten, he would be handicapped by being less mature and less experienced in learning in a group, if he entered first grade that fall. Impulsive and impatient Robert, whose interests shifted frequently, still had difficulty waiting even for a short time for what he wanted. The more flexible kindergarten structure would give him a better chance to test and try and more time to mature and gain in control over himself. Indeed, Mrs. Albert decided, a year of growing and learning in a stimulating kindergarten would be a wonderful opportunity for Robert and a sound start of real schooling.

WHAT ARE KINDERGARTEN CHILDREN LIKE?

Kindergarten Children May Be at Different Levels of Maturity

All kindergarten children are young children but not all who attend kindergarten are the same age chronologically or in terms of maturity. The chronological age for entry may be anywhere from four to six depending on the district laws, the child's birthday, or the type of school. A kindergarten teacher is thus just as likely to start in September with children not yet five, as to have sixth year birthdays in February. She may expect to encounter occasional wet pants among the fours and fives or toothless gaps in the smiles of the sixes. Furthermore there are tremendous individual differences in development at even the same chronological age. Since a child's home life and environment have important bearing on his development and abilities the children may differ greatly in their readiness for group living, their use of school materials, their receptivity to teacher authority, and their responsiveness to ideas and possibilities for creativity.

Thus Jackie, five years and two months, can hang by his heels from a jungle gym and is striving to accomplish more advanced tricks, while Jimmie, the same age, exerts caution and effort in slow climbing and steady descent, happy to land with both feet on the ground. Alice, not yet five, is wearing size six clothes, while Mary, the same age, is comfortable in size four. Ruthie picks up scissors and uses them matter-of-factly, while Timmy is hesitant and helpless in using such a tool. Jean speaks fluently and freely at five-and-a-half but is sometimes hard to understand, as her *r*'s and *k*'s do not come through; Debbie, two months younger, enunciates very clearly although she does not have as much to say.

Some General Characteristics are Typical of Kindergarten Children

Despite the wide range of individual differences so common at this and all ages, there are some characteristics kindergartners share that are worth bearing in mind. The contrasts in behavior are the most startling. These children are no longer babies, as they will tell you in no uncertain terms; yet they need affection and support and will break down under excessive stress as though they *were* babies. They are eager for information, yet they cannot concentrate for too long on any one area.

Kindergartners may use such advanced technical terms as *injection,* and of course atomic-age vocabulary; yet they may also use such baby words as *boo-boo* to denote a bruise, or *wee-wee* for urinate. They are creatures of feeling and they laugh and cry with remarkable ease. Yet they love to be philosophical and attack such weighty concepts as the meaning of life and death. They are concrete, direct, and full of lusty humor, yet not always sure of the difference between reality and make-believe in the grown-up world. Children of this age are also very limited in experience and may lack knowledge which is commonplace to adults.

The teacher in a class of four-and-a-half to five-year-olds told the children that she would be leaving them because she was going to have a baby. After she had gone out of the room for a few minutes and returned, some of them asked her, "Did you have the Baby?" Practically all of them had younger brothers or sisters and supposedly knew that it takes a while for a baby to be born; also the teacher had stated that it would take a while after she stayed home and "got ready," and until the baby grew big enough inside her to be born. Yet the children's lack of experience, their sense of immediacy in important matters, and their limited concept of time at this age made it natural for them to ask this question. Claudia Lewis describes the kindergarten child this way:

He comes with active feet, investigating hands. In these early years it is the concrete world around him that challenges him—the noisy, moving world of things that he can see and hear and touch. Only later on, with his growing powers of conceptualization, will his curiosities carry him into explorations of the abstract world, the distant universe, the historical past.

At five or six, every hallway, every street, every passing train or truck lures him. 'How does it work? Where does it go? Where did it come from?' These are his insistent questions. The wonderful workings of machines and engines and wheels, the ways of things that move above ground and under ground— from planes to subways, from clouds to rivers—he must find out about them all, touching, handling, watching.[1]

Young Children are Physical in Their Responses

We cannot help noticing that physical activity is the first characteristic of healthy young children. They are always ready to run and climb and reach and grasp and shout. Watching them in the playground we marvel at their energy as they race at full speed, climb over self-imposed obstacles, and screech with delight when propelled into the air on a see-saw.

We sedate adults must remind ourselves that a five-year-old's power is not only exciting to him, but its full strength may even be unknown to him. When he pushes a large crate with his arms and chest he surprises himself by causing the crate to turn upside down. His coordination is still to be refined. He therefore finds it necessary to do a great deal of practicing of such interesting skills as jumping from or over moderate heights, suspending vertically by hands or by feet, or climbing swiftly up and slowly down. Kindergarten children often choose to do something the hard way just to give themselves interesting exercise!

[1] Claudia Lewis, Prologue, *Know Your Children in School* by Lucy Sprague Mitchell, ed. (New York, The Macmillan Co., 1954), p. 18.

Fives Love to Talk

With their keen ears, good memory, and flexible tongues five-year-olds grow astonishingly in language power and in vocabulary. At this age they can pick up a foreign language, they can use accurate intonations and inflections when portraying a certain character in dramatic play, they can learn many verses of a song, and they delight in acquiring new words, especially appealing ones like *manhole, sycamore,* or *trillion.*

To exercise their expanding speech power kindergarten children need to experiment and be inventive with language, to engage in rhyming, and to indulge in joking. They need to have opportunity for easy conversations with each other and with teachers, to do some arguing, and to express their ideas.

Fives Are Eager Learners

Intellectual growth is most noticeable in the kindergarten child throughout the school year—his constantly increasing power of reasoning, his deep and often unanswerable questions, his love of guessing games or riddles, his absorption in problem solving, his fascination with a variety of mathematical concepts, and his spontaneous interest in symbols. The children in the kindergarten need and want a chance to exercise their fast growing minds. Yet they do not learn primarily by passive attention to the teacher or mere listening to information. Exercise of the mind at this age comes about as part of the total activity of the child and is accompanied by a sense of urgency to find out *now, on the spot.*

Tony is typical of kindergartners as he says excitedly and earnestly, "I have an idea, I have an *idea.* If one of us could sit in the wagon and hold the milk, then the milk won't spill. Okay?" Observe the concentration of a little boy digging to the depth of a root and calling excitedly, "I see how far it goes, I see it!" Or look at the attention to detail with which a group of five kindergartners are playing bus. They are oblivious to all other activity in the room and are concentrating on the proper bodily positions of the "passengers," on representing the bus itself by sounds of the engine and wheels, on portraying the driver by appropriate movements of shoulders, arms, and hands, on keeping track of the people getting on and getting off the bus, on the financial transactions involved, and on the definite and rhythmic calling out of the stations. Or see what happened the day Marcia brought lemons to school for making lemonade and the children at once began to investigate the lemons intently by smelling them and fingering the skins. They speculated on the color and quantity of juice. When the teacher cut the lemons and let the children squeeze them with ordinary hand squeezers there was excitement over the possession of a special muscle in the palm of the hand which had to be put to use.

"See how my muscle works!"

"I am squirting out a *lot* of lemon juice!"

"Let me squeeze the juice out with my muscle without the squeezer."

Then those four-and-a half to five-year-old children enjoyed the experiment of tasting the plain lemon juice and the bitter rind.

"Look at Johnny making a sour face!"

They added a measured amount of water and the right amount of sugar. They judged and differentiated among degrees of sweetness and sourness and noted how grimacing reflected taste sensations.

"I don't make any face—you want to see?"

Fives Love Feeling Grown-up

Young children also want to experience being trusted with responsibility. They want the chance to practice some "real grown-up" work. That is why they appreciate going on errands, helping the teacher with responsible tasks, using proper tools, taking a legitimate part in such grown-up work as cooking, cleaning, shopping, or suggesting solutions to practical problems.

Growth in Personality is a Continuing Process

The emotional growth and personality development of a kindergarten child are not as obvious as his getting bigger, stronger, and smarter. You can easily see the increases in height and weight, and the loosening teeth. But if you look closely you will also see that a kindergarten child develops noticeably in personality too. He may change from a youngster who seems to have no initiative and who only imitates what another child does, into a child who asserts his preferences, expresses his ideas, and carries them out so that both teachers and children have a genuine respect for him.

Harry, according to his teacher, "became a different child in six months." He seemed frightened and confused at first, hitting children impulsively for no apparent reason and disturbing other children's work. His classmates referred to him as "the bad boy." In the course of the year he learned to be constructive and satisfied with many materials. He made contributions to the children's play. Although he still demanded extra attention from the teacher once in a while and still had occasional outbursts of destructiveness, the teacher and the class, including Harry himself, knew that he had changed.

Kindergarten Children Need Each Other

Just as kindergarten children are ready for all kinds of experience they are ready for each other. They are hungry for companionship and will go to any length to seek it. "He hasn't anybody to play with" is a common complaint one hears from parents, and it constitutes one of the important reasons the children are registered at kindergarten. At three years of age a child can take or leave the companionship of others. But by five the ability to identify with the world beyond his immediate self, curiosity about what lies beyond himself, readiness to share, and the diminishing dependence on adults for direction and companionship make children indispensable to each other. Although the road to balanced give-and-take is not smooth and the friendships bloom and wither with amazing rapidity, this need goes on.

Teachers often say that when the kindergarten class has less than fifteen children in it life seems dull. To satisfy the continuing experimentation in relationships, twenty to twenty-five children seems to be a good number. This offers sufficient opportunity for each child to choose friends and change partners. The other children in class are an important reason why fives like school so much.

SCHOOL ENTRY AND ADJUSTMENT

The child's formal introduction to a public kindergarten comes at the initial registration when his mother produces the certificate of his birth, showing not only the date of his entry into the world and his family, but his legal name—William Henry Howell or Mary Elizabeth McCarthy. Up to this time a child may have heard himself called only Billy, Betsy, or Junior. Katherine Ann Porter [2] describes this experience in the reaction of one little boy:

School was easy. Teacher was a square-shaped woman with square short hair and short skirts. She got in the way sometimes, but not often. The people around him were his size; he didn't have always to be stretching his neck up to faces bent over him, and he could sit on the chairs without having to climb. All the children had names like Frances and Evelyn and Agatha and Edward and Martin, and his own name was Stephen. He was not Mama's 'Baby,' nor Papa's 'Old Man'; he was not Uncle David's 'Fellow' or Grandma's 'Darling' or even Old Janet's 'Bad Boy." He was Stephen.

Some schools ask for the child's nickname along with his given name. Even so, there is much that is unfamiliar in the new surroundings

[2] Katherine Ann Porter, "The Downward Path to Wisdom," in *The Leaning Tower* (New York, Harcourt, Brace & World, Inc., 1934), p. 93.

which causes a child some worry. For instance, in a large school, which to a child's eyes seems even larger than it is, there may be many doors to open and go through; sometimes the doors all look alike. What if one opens the wrong door? How can one be sure which is right? Children worry about bathroom facilities that appear unfamiliar or whether they have the right to use all the toys. Worries about getting home safely and finding home and family intact are not uncommon for children of this age. Many a kindergarten child has questions which he cannot bring himself to ask in the early weeks because he does not feel sure yet that he can fully trust the teacher. Many children do not function to the best of their ability in the beginning weeks of school because they feel uncertain about some aspect of the new experience.

A great help in the initial adjustment to school is acquaintance with the teacher beforehand, and this can be accomplished in several ways. One way is for the teacher to visit each child at his home in the few days allotted for preparation before the official opening of school. Facing his teacher in his own home, surrounded by the familiar and protective, a child finds it easier to fit the teacher into his world and then to make the transition to hers. Obviously the teacher cannot visit too many children even for brief greetings. She either cannot get around to all or the visits become perfunctory and mechanical. Nevertheless it remains desirable for a child to feel close to his teacher in a more intimate fashion than the initial impact of the total class will allow. Therefore, if individual home visits are impractical, small groups of children, and even individuals, can come visiting at the school on a planned schedule before the formal opening. Some schools also encourage such visiting in the spring before admission. Other schools stagger the entry of children during the first week so that the teacher can get acquainted with no more than a handful of fresh and eager faces each day. Her closer attention to these few makes them feel especially noted and accepted. However it is done, it is wise to allow for a one-to-one relationship between the teacher and each individual child before plunging into the overwhelming confusion of faces, materials, and regulations involved in school entry.

Make Haste Slowly

Most children start kindergarten having very little experience with rules, and the teacher's introduction of various necessary class rules may seem confusing to some five-year-olds at the beginning. It is best during the opening weeks to be gradual in introducing new rules as well as new materials to a kindergarten child. He needs to take a while to absorb the first new impressions, new ideas, and experiences before being confronted with more newness. He will show pride in remembering and chagrin in forgetting what is expected of him. And he is sure to have much experience with both of these feelings! Adjustment may be slow for some children, painful for others, and no problem at all to still others. This depends not only on age, for there are "young" and "old" kindergartners, but on previous experience with adults, children, materials, and learning. There is no precise time schedule for adjustment of any one individual child, but a sympathetic, helpful teacher can make the period shorter and in some cases smoother. For most groups two to three months is the reasonable time span in which full acquaintance with the program can be realized.

KINDERGARTEN IS AN OPPORTUNITY

The child under six goes to school as a matter of special advantage rather than legal requirement. Yet the special ways in which kindergarten can be profitable make it worth our while to urge expansion of such opportunities for all young children, particularly in such an affluent and democratic country as the United States.

As we have pointed out, the five-year-olds' curiosity and eagerness for information, their hunger for companionship, their readiness to grow in independence and competency, their ability to reason and think, make it desirable that such potential for growth be nurtured by professional, planned guidance within our schools. Such professional guidance can be given in good kindergartens, kindergartens that promote health, stimulate many interests, and provide a year of learning.

Bibliography

Children's Bureau, U.S. Dep't. of Health, Education, & Welfare, *Your Child From 1 to 6* (Washington, Superintendent of Documents, 1962).

Hymes, James L., *Three to Six: Your Child Starts to School* (Public Affairs Pamphlet, No. 163, 22 E. 38th St., New York 16, N.Y.).

————, "What Makes a Good Kindergarten?" *Parents' Magazine,* January, 1960.

Jenkins, Gladys G., and others, *These Are Your Children* (Chicago, Scott, Foresman & Co., 1953).

Lewis, Claudia, prologue to *Know Your Children in School,* Lucy Sprague Mitchell, ed. (New York, The Macmillan Co., 1954).

National Society for the Study of Education, Forty-sixth Yearbook, Part II, Early Childhood Education (Chicago, University of Chicago Press, 1947).

New York State Council for Children, *Good Living for Young Children* (N.Y.S.C.C. Publications Center, The Carousel School, 173–53 Croydon Road, Jamaica 32, N.Y., 1960).

Porter, Katherine Ann, "The Downward Path to Wisdom," in *The Leaning Tower* (New York, Harcourt, Brace, & World, Inc., 1934).

3

Individuals Within the Group

GROUPS ARE UNIQUE IN COMPOSITION

Teachers appreciate the unique charm of children's faces, so open and expressive, without the masks and pretenses which all but few adults have. The beauty of children's faces was a source of special joy to one of the authors when working at the United Nations International School a number of years back. The delicacy and transparency of the skin color of the Scandinavian children, the velvety textures, and deep, warm eyes of the Indians, the subtle shades of color and sculpture of features among the Oriental, and the marvelous combination of dark skin and straight look of the African child, were stunning to behold.

Yet in their behavior, these children were like children everywhere, teasing and testing, physically active and exploring, having sudden bursts of tears, and giving in to abandoned laughter. Of different ethnic background, they were nevertheless all spontaneous and childlike. The special individuality of each shone clearly through the outer coloration, and this uniqueness of the individual holds true for all groups. Let us therefore focus on the individual child in a kindergarten class.

THE SIZE OF THE GROUP AFFECTS THE EXPERIENCE OF THE INDIVIDUAL

Clearly, education in a democratic society puts primary emphasis on the worth of the individual. But children attend school in groups, and there's the rub. A group may consist of fifty, which can seem like a herd, an undifferentiated mass, and the teacher will find it difficult to maintain contact and give guidance on an individual basis to the Tommys and Marys who make up the fifty. Gwen W. McConkie and Marie M. Hughes [1] found, in a study of two groups of kindergarten children—one composed of thirty-seven and the other of twenty-six—that the quality of interpersonal relationships was related to the size of the group. In the large group, forty-three percent of the children who asked questions were not answered. In the small group, only thirteen percent of the questions went unanswered. In the large group one-fourth of the children were not greeted on arrival during the period under observation. In the small group no child was left ungreeted.

It is easy to see the educational and human advantages of smaller kindergarten classes, and theoretically that is our national goal. At this point each state and community is working in its own way on expanding and improving school facilities in general, and on reducing the overcrowded conditions of kindergartens in particular.

But although they will not be as effective, we maintain that there are ways in which a teacher can reach and communicate with the individual child even under the adverse conditions of overlarge classes.

AN INDIVIDUAL CHILD NEED NOT BE LOST TO VIEW IN A CROWDED CLASS

Here is a public school kindergarten with forty-nine children in the class. Mrs. Rand, the teacher, is concerned with the limitations and frustrations that such crowded conditions impose on her and on the children, and is looking forward to improvement. But she is more concerned with the immediate and considerable challenge of reaching each individual child. Mrs. Rand has a firm belief that each child is worthy of her attention. Her twelve years of working in crowded classes have not diminished that belief. What does Mrs. Rand do?

First, whenever possible she avoids speaking to the children en masse, and therefore impersonally to some degree. She does not have an entrance line into class nor does she say one impersonal "Good morning, children." Instead, she allows informal arrival by groups and individuals and therefore has the opportunity for informal, spontaneous greetings and pleasantries, even if these are reduced to a wave of the hand and a smile for some. Although this takes a few more minutes of her time each day it gives her in return some measure of genuine communication with each child, and a chance to notice any special needs.

[1] Gwen W. McConkie and Marie M. Hughes, "Quality of Classroom Living Related to Size of Kindergarten Groups," *Childhood Education*, May, 1956.

Later in the session when the children are settled in work activities, attending independently to painting, working with clay, building, puzzles, housekeeping play, and other activities, Mrs. Rand resists the temptation to bury herself in clerical tasks and keep only a perfunctory order in the free play. Instead she often works on a special private project with one, two or three children, such as sewing, carpentry, storytelling by the children, or reading by the teacher. The ten minutes of such meaningful, fully personal attention coming regularly, albeit not often enough for each child, help to establish a sense of the worthiness of the individual which is readily appreciated by the children in the class.

In many other situations Mrs. Rand shows her awareness of the feelings likely to be felt by each of the many children, just because they *are* children. She speaks of these to the group with the confident assumption that the feeling is known to each individually. While reading a story one day she was called out of class on official business. The children had to wait for her return to hear the end of the story. When Mrs. Rand did return she spoke to the class as a whole, but included all in her glance as she said warmly and sincerely, "Children, you were wonderful to wait quietly so long while I was talking on the telephone. I know it was hard." And it *is* hard for any five-year-old to exercise such control. Despite the size of the class Mrs. Rand's honest pleasure and her understanding of the strength of the achievement helped each child feel appreciated for his efforts. This pervasive understanding, growing out of a teacher's knowledge of the age group, becomes particularly important when not enough attention can be given to individuals.

In another crowded class the teacher confides cheerfully that she looks forward to days when winter colds and spring epidemics cut her class of fifty to practically half. On those days she makes a point of establishing closer contact with the children present, and especially of getting to know the overlooked ones who were previously lost in the shuffle. Somehow teacher and children are never strangers to each other after that.

In still another crowded class the teacher evolves her special system of attending to individual children; each day when the forty children are distributed in about six working groups, she spends twenty minutes or so with one working group. Thus she concentrates one day on the children who draw, then on those who build, or on those who finger-paint. By focusing on small groups she increases her knowledge of individual children.

The teacher working under crowded conditions must strive to reach each child and not be discouraged by only partial success. She can do this in the following ways: keeping her program and routines informal so that advantage can be taken of every possible opportunity for communication; speaking to children personally and separately as much as possible; listening to at least some individuals every day; discerning individuals within small groups.

ONE CAN SEE INDIVIDUALS MORE EASILY IN THE GROUP OF REASONABLE SIZE

When the enrollment in a kindergarten group is in the neighborhood of twenty or twenty-five children, with a sufficiently large room and adequate equipment, the teacher has many opportunities to know and enjoy each child, to help each one in different ways, and to communicate to each child her knowledge and appreciation of him.[2] When the organization of the classroom materials and program is flexible enough to meet particular children's interests and needs, the teacher can even more effectively focus on individuals and small groups.

Here is a teacher of 24 five-year-olds in a Child Care Center reading to her children at the end of a long rainy day. All nineteen children who are present want to hear the story and sit in front of the teacher on the floor. First she tells the children that she has gotten this particular book (*The New Pet*)[3] from the library because it is about babies and about pets, "and," she says, looking at the close, friendly circle of faces, "because Susie and Linda have new babies, and because Walter told us about his pets." Information about additional pets is promptly added by other children and the teacher gives full recognition to that. During the story she relates some details from the book to individual children and some situations to the experiences the children have had. The children ask questions and make comments about their babies at home; they surround the teacher, both to look at the pictures and for the personal contact. She speaks to the children without sentimentality or even endearments, yet weaves personal and individual considerations into the ordinary process of reading a book. Each child feels the teacher's interest and devotion.

SOME CHILDREN STAND OUT IN ANY GROUP

In any group, whether large or small, one is always conscious of the dramatically different child. A teacher of a class of fifty speaks readily about Glenn because "he is extremely bright and can answer any ques-

[2] Helen K. Mackintosh (Asst. Chief, Elementary School Section, Office of Health, Education and Welfare), "The Recommended Maximum," *Childhood Education,* March, 1954.

[3] Marjorie Flack, *The New Pet* (Garden City, N.Y., Doubleday & Co., Inc., 1943).

tion quicker than anybody else in the class." Another teacher in a class of twenty-five tells how Bobby is her "biggest challenge; he is very aggressive so that other children always have run-ins with him." A teacher in a class of forty is aware of Roslyn who has defective muscular coordination, yet "sticks to her work and is so cheerful!" No teacher can overlook bouncy Jimmy (literally bouncy). His overabundance of energy, his constant mobility and activity, his exciting ideas and lively talk, and the unique zest with which he does everything, are magnetic points of focus.

SOME CHILDREN MUST BE SOUGHT OUT

But what about the less demanding, the not so aggressive, not brilliant, not dramatically attractive child? What about the overlooked "good" child about whom the teacher will say to an inquiring mother, "She is getting along just fine, Mrs. Smith." What does the teacher know concretely about that "just fine" child? How much helpful understanding or stimulating appreciation does the child get from the teacher?

Let us look at two children who are not easily distinguished from the group. Are such children as uninteresting as the appearance indicates? Jill, almost five, a seemingly placid child who takes school for granted, complies with routines and busies herself in the doll corner or with materials. She is never heard in the room nor is she distinguished by any special contribution. Jill allies herself with only a few children and takes her place matter-of-factly among the others for group games or projects without saying much, if anything. She is also merely on looking terms with the teacher: looking when the teacher reads a story, looking when she carries on some communication with other children. One day the teacher realizes that for the past week Jill has been insisting stubbornly on wearing a special little wool hat with a bow in the back while indoors; if she is persuaded to remove it and place it in her cubby, she invariably will get it back on her head later during the morning. So the teacher asks about it.

"This is a pretty hat, Jill—is it new?" Jill laughs gleefully at this and makes a sweeping motion with her hand at the teacher's absurdity.

"It's not new. It's my *mommy's* hat."

"Oh?" the teacher raises her eyebrows.

"She even gave it to me . . ." (whatever the word *even* means). Now the teacher is surprised and curious about Jill; she watches Jill's motherly and managerial play in the doll corner, her independent kind of conversation, and her relations with the other children. And perhaps responding to the teacher's new notice of her, Jill herself begins to confide in the teacher. Other times Jill dares to test the teacher's authority and thus commands the teacher's further attention. Jill has come alive.

Jackie, just five, simply blends into the group. One not only does not hear Jackie, but one does not see him. A small child, he usually works quietly by himself, smiling amiably when approached by the teacher and looking on casually at the livelier children and activities in the room. The only time the teacher really becomes aware of Jackie is when a sliding block bruises his ankle during clean-up time. Jackie then becomes frightened and clings silently to the teacher for protection and comfort, looking up at her appealingly. So the teacher becomes aware of Jackie's baby quality but she knows practically nothing about Jackie as a growing, active school child.

Then Nina, in many ways also a gentle child, suddenly notices Jackie and goes after him. Exactly that! "Will you build with me, Jackie?" Jackie nods. "I want to sit next to Jackie," she tells the teacher at snack time, and Jackie smiles at this—clearly a smile of being favored. "Let's wrestle!" she proposes to Jackie outdoors and the two of them (similar in size and with similar spirit of fun) push and pull each other and laugh and fall on the ground, rise and chase each other all over the yard. The teacher, thanks to Nina, at last sees Jackie's humor, his physical power, his ingenuity with materials, his tractability, and certainly his response to friendship and affection.

TAKING CHILDREN AS THEY ARE

Appreciating the individual child means appreciating him not only for what the teacher or the parents *want* him to be or are helping him to become ("more mature," "better skilled," "more outgoing"), but for what he is *at present*. Perhaps a negative example will make the point clearer.

Here is a little kindergarten boy showing his teacher a drawing he has just made. He has written his name on it. "Oh," says the teacher with exaggerated admiration, but ignoring the drawing proper, "you wrote the letter *l* in your name straight! That's just like a big first grader, did you know that? Like a big first grader!" The response of this little boy who had labored long and hard on his drawing can only be described as noncommittal.

Why did the teacher give this little kindergartner such uncalled-for recognition for becoming a first grader when he still had eight months to go before he would be in the first grade? What is wrong with being a relaxed, spontaneous, struggling five-year-old kindergartner?

Similarly, when Marilyn went to a kindergarten she struggled valiantly to produce various daily prescribed constructions from boxes and cardboard and paper. However, she was not as handy as some other children with those constructions and thus disappointed the teacher and herself. The teacher unfortunately had no opportunity to know how skillful and responsible Marilyn could be with other activities. Marilyn complained philosophically at home, "The teacher wants us to *make things* all the time. I like nursery school better 'cause in kindergarten it's only what you make that counts; but in nursery school, it's what you are that counts." That is educational philosophy, even if uttered by a child barely six, and it does confirm our contention that it is of basic importance to children to be recognized for what they are as individuals.

How does a teacher come to realize this uniqueness? She does it by looking closely at each youngster to see what she can see, by observing him as he reacts to the life about him.

PHYSICAL APPEARANCE AND MOVEMENT

The most striking first impression of any child is given by his outward appearance and quality of movement. Closer observation without prejudice reveals not only how different children are in looks, but how different children are. See how a first look at their outward appearance led to further investigation of the behavior of the following children.

In the first month of school the teacher noticed that Sammy was different physically from the other children. He had a heavy sluggish walk and a slight stoop; his hands hung down idly most of the time. With his rather small face and thin mouth, he looked like a little gnome. There seemed to be a minimum of inflection in Sammy's speech and never any shouting. How different from the other boisterous four-and-a-half-year-olds! His glance shifted uncomprehendingly from one object to another and his smile in response to the teacher or children was not fully formed. The teacher felt impelled to discuss Sammy's rate of development with his mother, and was not too surprised to learn that he had been slow in developing. This knowledge served her well as a teacher to this little boy, who, in spite of his slowness, wanted very much to come to school, liked being among the children, and responded to the teacher even if in a limited way.

The same teacher noticed Paul. Paul was conspicuously big in size with a heavy, middle-aged type of figure which was most obvious when he wore long pants and a tight belt which revealed his bulges. He had a large face illumined by shiny, black, twinkly eyes. Just five, Paul was not the oldest, although he was the biggest child in the class. His mother said with a mixture of pride and worry that he wore size eight clothes. When Paul entered the room even close to the middle of the year, when surely he ought to have felt comfortable enough to know what there was to do, he stood hesitantly by the door. He answered the teacher with a charming smile and ready talk about what he had done at home, or about a trick that he was going to play on someone. But still he stood there, as if he were not sure he really belonged in the class.

There he is sitting down because he got a bump. Such an alert looking child, with a mobile sensitive face; he has such a friendly eager manner with everyone who approaches him. Yet he often sits lonely and apart, with discouragement revealed in the curve of his little boy's mouth. When the teacher and the mother talk together, the teacher learns that Paul's size is a burden for him at home. His mother tells sympathetically that when Paul cries or acts naturally babyish, there is always someone who makes fun of him. "A big boy like you" someone will say in a shaming tone. He has no place to hide from such hurting and confusing remarks. Why is Paul uncomfortable? Is it because he is big? Children all *like* to be "big." Paul, too, often boasts about being the biggest. But then, Paul's boasting does not exactly mean satisfaction with being big . . . What does being big mean to Paul, the teacher asks herself. Understanding his problem assures Paul that she is on his side, that he does not have to act big for her or be ashamed of his occasional babyishness; he can be himself.

In the same class there is Lenny, also a young five, a handsome little boy with shiny black hair, sunny brown eyes, a quick expressive face, and a quick body. He is of average height and all his movements show fine strength and zest, but he looks quite thin when he removes his padded snow pants and heavy sweater—a predominance of knees and elbows. Lenny's grandmother complains about his being "so skinny," and tells Lenny's mother to "fatten him up." "I tried everything, even changed doctors, but he is still a very poor eater," the mother acknowledges. The teacher tells the mother that Lenny shows plenty of strength and energy and alertness in school, so that she *must* have succeeded in feeding him pretty well after all. "I'll tell that to his grandmother!" the mother jokes with evident pleasure. The teacher watches Lenny some more. He has a ravenous appetite at snack time, stuffs his mouth with as many crackers as he can grab in his hands, and making a pecking motion with his finger he picks up the scattered crumbs from the basket on the table. Lenny usually has something in his mouth that he chews on, such as a mitten thumb, a wad of paper, sometimes the upper part of his shirt. Yet his attention is always on some activity; building or woodworking, or construction with table materials. Lying on the floor for a rest, Lenny is almost perpetually wiggling, stretching, or drawing himself up to different positions. When sitting on a chair, Lenny's appearance may be caught by a movie camera, but not by a still; he always either tips the chair, or taps or scuffs his feet. Yet with all this bodily activity that seems disruptive

Lenny concentrates fully on the task at hand. The teacher is impressed simultaneously by his bodily mobility, his busy mouth, the wealth of interest and feeling shown in his face, and his constant mental activity. There is so much more to Lenny than his elbows and knees.

We can see how in the case of all three children, slow Sammy, big Paul, and wiry Lenny, their physique and appearance led to further inquiry on the teacher's part, and even to conferences with parents. Inquiry and conferences lead to further observation and further understanding of the individual child in the group.

OBSERVING THE CHILD'S USE OF MATERIALS

As the children choose and use the materials made available by the teacher, getting whatever help and guidance they may need, the teacher has the opportunity to observe the individual child's approach to materials and the quality of his performance with them. She can observe one child's hesitation and tentativeness with everything new. She sees the emergence of confidence in another child as he gains experience with some material. In still another child she may see the complete assurance and skill that comes with success. She may also notice in her class a child who is so attracted to new things that he rushes and grabs them, and in his haste indeed makes waste, or even causes damage. The teacher soon learns to keep an eye on such a child and help him learn healthy caution, whether with water at the sink or with a saw at the work bench.

The teacher will also observe that some five-year-olds may use school materials as if they were weapons; they hit with the crayons on the paper, they jab the paintbrush on the easel, they pick up a building block as if it were a gun. She may squirm inside at first, but if the jabbing painter operates with paintbrush on paper and even compares his sharp strokes with the large curly ones or little squiggly ones of his nearby friends, she simply watches and learns. She may be wary of the block gun but if the "soldier's" attention is shifting to construction of a jet port or barn (just as likely as a fort) and if his activity invites participation of others, the teacher again watches and learns about the individual child.

She notices also the difference in the way children regard the results of their work. Some want to make sure that their name is properly affixed to the painting; some are concerned about taking home anything they make; some are eager to produce as large a number of objects as possible. "I did *six* paintings, didn't I, teacher? And I am going to make more!" Although children generally enjoy the results of their work, some child may find his building or clay work wanting and wish to destroy it. The teacher then encourages that child to try again. Still another child may appreciate the work of others even more than his own. An individual child may show modesty, nonchalance, concern, pride, or possessiveness in the results of his efforts.

OBJECTS MAY HAVE PERSONAL MEANING

Some five-year-olds may still depend on a special toy. They either bring something from home to hold on to or stake a claim to something attractive on a shelf at school. Such a child likes to have this possession— a little wooden horse perhaps, a rubber ball, or a small metal car—in his pocket or hand or by his side, for security, support, or some private need. At school there are generally rules about where play things must be kept, or rules about not bringing toys from home. But a sensitive teacher can make temporary exception to such rules where it is obvious the child has a definite need for the little inanimate friend. In time, she may tell him that the toy car which belongs in school will be on the shelf for him *and* the others, with whom he will eventually take turns. She may in time encourage the child to let others hold and touch it, leading to the eventual suggestion that personal treasures might be left at home to wait for him and brought only if they can readily be shared by all in the way a record or a book can. At the same time, by noting what other materials he prefers and what use he makes of them, she tries to extend his field of activity and satisfaction.

OBSERVING THE CHILD'S BEHAVIOR IN ROUTINES

The time when all children in the class do the same thing according to the teacher's plan is during routines: getting outer clothing on before going out; cleaning up after work period; washing hands; preparing for a snack; settling for rest. Teachers sometimes think that routines should run smoothly and expediently, for in group living conformity makes sense. Actually however, in spite of the sameness of procedure this is a good place to notice individual behavior, especially at the beginning of the term.

During dressing time the teacher can observe that some children are helpless and give up easily, others are independent to the last stubborn button, and still others are able and happy to help friends with sleeves and scarves and attend to themselves as well. Fearfulness or shyness about the body or excessive fastidiousness are not infrequent among fives when you observe them in the bathroom; a child may even have total resistance to using the toilet all the time that he is in school, although most five-year-olds have a healthy matter-of-factness in this area.

When it comes to cleanup the children are especially apt to show differences of behavior. There are always children who show resistance in various degrees. Some may simply refuse to take any part; some will invent devices to get out of work; some will cooperate only on a minimum level. Yet other children the same age will respond to cleanup with gusto, loading their arms with blocks from the floor, swooshing a brush across a table, stuffing the waste basket to capacity. And some child will become so fascinated with removing wetness with a sponge that he will squeeze the sponge out over the table in order to do the work over again several times. Observing the children's individual behavior at cleanup enables the teacher not only to plan her routines realistically, but to assess the capabilities and the needs of each child more concretely.

OBSERVING INDIVIDUAL RESPONSES TO CHILDREN AND ADULTS

A child's way of approaching and responding to others is such an important area of human strength and growth that we are devoting a separate chapter to the subject. Our immediate concern is the teacher's observation of the child's behavior with others so she can understand him better as an individual and be able to guide him.

Although five-year-olds are by and large sociable beings who need and seek each other out, a teacher can readily see tremendous individual differences in the way they do it. Within a kindergarten group there may very likely be some who pick fights and push others around (especially fearful ones). The teacher might well ask: What do these children want? What could make them happy? What and whom do they like? She could ask too about the fearful one who gets pushed around (this can be boy or girl). Such a child does not dare stand up for his rights, yet he may go into the midst of the rougher children and *prefer* playing with the very ones who abuse him. What does *this* child really want? What are his *strengths?*

A quiet child who usually chooses to play by himself comes to school one day with a package of bubble gum and offers it to the four most aggressive and extroverted children in class. The next day he brings some charm trinkets and distributes them to the same potential friends. "This is bribery," the teacher thinks. She feels impelled to tell Randy: "this is not the way to make friends." Yet apparently this is the only way that gives Randy the confidence to approach others and actually win friends.

Many children have difficulty in getting along with others their own age and at the same time are able to get along beautifully with older children and adults. They do not hesitate approaching a visitor in the room, and love to play host; they speak politely and well with adults and are content in adult company.

Finally there may be a child in the class—again either boy or girl— who can be characterized as a "goody." Among candid, outspoken, impulsive preschoolers a "goody" is a pathetic phenomenon! He does everything to please the teacher, he is conspicuously polite, he uses adult phrases, even cliches ("I always eat vegetables—they are *good* for you."); and he is ridiculously righteous ("I *never* cry"). A veritable apparition in the midst of flesh-and-blood five-year-olds! Yet some teachers encourage "goodies" by citing their behavior as exemplary. One sometimes confuses "goodiness" with straight-forward goodness. The one shows watchful, currying, and even fearful responses to adult appraisal. The other is friendly, cooperative, positive, and natural with adults.

Thus individual children reveal themselves in many different ways. Their appearance and quality of movement tell us some things about them, their responses to people and objects tell us other kinds of things. Each child is responding to the life around him in his own unique way. A sensitive teacher notes the details that add up to a fuller understanding of the individual.

CHILDREN ARE NOT THE SAME AT ALL TIMES

A teacher may find that a child is assertive in one situation and quite different in another. Thus big, boisterous, and bold Howard, who intimidated several smaller children in class, surprised the teacher during a trip to the neighboring fire house. While the other children, including the quieter, more cautious ones, were excited by the adventure of touching the shiny equipment and ringing the loud bell, Howard was too scared even to go in.

In another class Linda, a silent, uncommunicative, tense child who refrained from using materials most of the time, joined some children one day at the work bench where there was a big coconut which the class had been trying to open for several days with the teacher's help. The teacher soon came over to the three children who were taking turns whacking the coconut with the hammer. To the teacher's surprise Linda grasped the hammer forcefully and, warming up to the activity, this normally passive little girl became genuinely excited. As part of the outer hard shell of the coconut broke off, a layer of very tough brown hairy fiber was revealed. The other children were fascinated with snipping "the hair" off the coconut with scissors, but Linda was determined to get hold of "the hair" and pulled it hard. She actually succeeded in pulling off a wad of the tough fiber. "There! I am pulling the skin off!" she exclaimed eagerly and squealed, "Ooh, ooh, ooh!" Noting that Linda really enjoyed such rough materials and work, the teacher encouraged her to try the tools at the work bench, which she had hitherto shunned.

CAREFUL LISTENING AS WELL AS LOOKING

Young children like to talk, and a teacher can take the comments as clues to knowledge about individuals. Mary says to the teacher, "I'll better not even have any milk and cookies because I'm going to have dinner at my grandmother's! She is going to wait for me!" On another day Mary exclaims: "You know what my mother and I did? We made a cake together. I'll even bring some to school." And again, "Guess who is coming for me today! My daddy—yes. You don't believe it, but he is!" It is easy to see how important family life and family members are to Mary, and she to them.

DO NOT INTERPRET TOO READILY

Alive and responsive to children, a teacher is often intrigued by the different personalities in her class. It seems only human to indulge in interpretations of the causes for children's behavior or misbehavior. It is easy to label a thumbsucker insecure or to conclude that a child who does not like painting is inhibited. And it seems especially easy for teachers to "diagnose" a questioning child as an attention-seeker and a whiner as spoiled. Quick judgments and superficial "diagnosis" may prove quite incorrect after a more careful examination of the total situation.

Mrs. Bryan, a kindergarten teacher, told a visitor in an instructive aside that Neil, the slight blond boy in the plaid shirt, was immature, and to "just notice how way behind the others he is." At first glance it seemed that way. While all the other children distributed themselves in groups for woodworking, playing in the housekeeping corner, climbing, constructing an elaborate truck from large blocks, or drawing, Neil was operating a wooden train all by himself, making soft sounds and contentedly arranging passengers and freight on the little cars. He was crawling on the floor bending over his train, but occasionally looked up to take a peek at what the others were doing or to watch the teacher hovering over some child's drawing or paper construction.

During the music period however, Neil joined all the others readily in rhythms. In the excitement of the children's dancing a number of books were knocked off the shelves. It was Neil who left the dancers, put all the books back in place, and rejoined the others as soon as he finished. Later that morning the children sat down on the floor and chose job assignments for the following week—sweepers, bird feeders, plant waterers, table setters, and juice pourers. The teacher either called on a child or read the job from the large chart and asked for raised hands. The children then wrote their names in a space corresponding to the job. Neil told the teacher that he wanted to be the sweeper. "Good!" the teacher praised loudly, and then offered, "Shall I write your name for you, Neil?" "I know how to write my name," Neil answered with calm assurance, as he stepped over some children, took a pencil from the teacher, and slowly and crookedly wrote his name in capitals. "Well, that's just wonderful. You can really write your name!" the teacher said emphatically and with surprise in her voice.

Why had Mrs. Bryan labelled Neil "immature"? Neil's behavior actually shows us a gentle and nongregarious child, but one who is active and functioning in his own unique way. He is obviously aware of others and shows interest and initiative in undertaking the responsible task of putting scattered books back on the shelf. He responds to good music and dancing. He writes his name with reasonably developed coordination and definite interest. He may be different from the other children in one respect, but if Mrs. Bryan had observed Neil's behavior in greater detail and over a wider range of interests she would have hesitated to judge him immature.

THE TEACHER PERCEIVES THE INDIVIDUAL IN MANY WAYS

Thus the warm, perceptive kindergarten teacher will put herself to work getting to know the individual children, and will strive to understand each one. On the physical side she will notice the different expressions, the individual features, the distinguishing gait, the particular pace, and quality of mobility or passivity. She will see the different sizes, stamina, and physical skills, and be moved by the many kinds of beauty among children. The perceptive teacher will look beyond the external appearance too. She will observe the caution in approaching materials on the part of one, the hostile use of the same materials by another, and the happy easy way of a third. She will observe each child's way of approaching others, of settling differences, and of sharing and exchanging ideas. She will be conscious of the special way each youngster responds to life, what causes him frustration, and what gives him satisfaction. She will get as full a picture as she can of each child's patterns of response. And she must refrain from hasty interpretations and judgments, recognizing that each child is a growing, changing human being at a point in time. Knowing her children better, she can be more useful in guiding their growth. Understanding each child, she can win his confidence and his trust in the wisdom of her leadership.

Bibliography

Amrein, Polly, *The Blind Child in Your Kindergarten* (South San Francisco, Paragon Publications, 1951).

Cohen, Dorothy H., and Stern, Virginia, *Observing and Recording the Behavior of Young Children* (New York, Bureau of Publications, Teachers College, Columbia University, 1958).

Hymes, James L., *A Child Development Point of View* (Englewood Cliffs, N.J., Prentice-Hall, Inc., 1955).

————, *Listen, Teachers, the Children Speak* (pamphlet, N.Y. State Committee on Mental Hygiene, 105 E. 22nd St., New York).

Isaacs, Susan, *The Children We Teach* (London, University of London Press, Ltd., 1950).

Mackintosh, Helen K. (Asst. Chief, Elementary School Section, Office of Health, Education and Welfare), "The Recommended Maximum," *Childhood Education,* March, 1954.

McConkie, Gwen W., and Hughes, Marie M., "Quality of Classroom Living Related to Size of Kindergarten Groups," *Childhood Education,* May, 1956.

Stone, Joseph L., and Church, Joseph, *Childhood and Adolescence* (New York, Random House, Inc., 1957).

4

Relationships Within the Group

THE IMPORTANCE OF FRIENDSHIP IN THE KINDERGARTEN

Andy, just five-years-old, was invited to visit the kindergarten after he had registered. He spent almost twenty minutes in the class touching different materials on tables and floor, finding himself in the midst of playing, working children. To his surprise he noticed Bob, a neighborhood friend in the class. "Hi," Andy said, somewhat shyly but gleefully. To his joy, Bob responded.

At home that evening Andy's father, mother, and older sister were eager to hear about the kindergarten visit. Andy answered "yes" or "no" quite casually to various questions, but reserved his enthusiasm for, "And you know what—I saw Bob there, and I said 'hi' to him, and he said 'hi' to me." He repeated this information several times. The parents were perplexed. They regarded their son as quite a bright and perceptive child. Yet here, on a first visit to the kindergarten, to the "big school," as he had been referring to it, the most important thing to him was seeing his friend Bob there. Why should that be so important?

When Andy entered the kindergarten room for the first time he was interested in seeing familiar toys and materials and he did notice the teacher. But he could not unify and relate the brief experience to give it personal meaning. What made the strongest impression on Andy was to see Bob, whom he knew well, perfectly at ease there in the kindergarten—doing things, speaking to people, responding with a "hi" to him. So kindergarten was a place where you could speak to friends and do what they do! This concrete promise of being able to maintain or to create relationships was of first importance to Andy, as it is to all healthy children.

Creating relationships in class requires opportunities to practice different techniques of winning friends and apprehending enemies; opportunities for actually helping others, for choosing and changing friends, and for forming different alliances.

RELATIONSHIPS FOLLOW AN EXPANDING
PATTERN OF INVOLVEMENT

In any kindergarten class several stages of social development are usually present. The intimacy of one friend at a time is all some children can manage. Little twosomes play in the doll corner, chat at the swings, crayon together, or play dominoes. Three to five children join together in other parts of the room or outdoor play area, sometimes staying together as a unit, sometimes forming and reforming around one central dominating figure or strong pair. Relations within these larger units range all the way from the smoothest kind of cooperative effort applied to the completion of a commonly agreed upon task, to constant bickering and quarreling over every detail.

Still larger than the groups of three, four, or five which may be forming (often along sex lines) is the unit of the entire class. To this larger unit each child must somehow make reference and within it he must find his niche. At first the size of the class can be quite confusing. But in time identification with the class as a whole gives a child the assuring comfort that feelings are universal, and the special sense of power that comes only with being one of many who are tied in common interests. A child who has experienced intimacy for the first time with a friend and enrichment of play interests in a group of friends feels that he belongs to something that is part of a big world indeed. "That's my teacher," he says with pride. "Those kids are in *my* class."

EXPERIMENTATION WITH FRIENDSHIP

When children work together in small groups there is spontaneous conversation, there is exchange of ideas, there is acquaintance with one another's interests and performances, there is the experience of liking others and of being liked. Special friendships or lasting attachments may thus be formed. There is also clashing and conflict and sharp differences that have to be resolved. A teacher has to be aware of the children's need to *practice* relating.

Here are three five-year-old girls at a table with play dough. Jeannie, for no *apparent* reason, snatches pieces of dough from the other girls; she does not heed their demand that she return their dough, and to make sure that the two girls do not get the dough back by force, Jeannie throws it on the floor and steps on it. When Jeannie persists in trying to snatch more dough from the table, one of the two girls, Mary, restrains Jeannie by grasping and pinching her shoulder. Jeannie's defiance weakens and she bursts into the classic face-saving song:

> It-doesn't-even-hu-urt,
> It-doesn't-even-hu-urt.

As she sings she keeps pulling away. Now there is a triumphant expression on Mary's face as she magnanimously stops pinching Jeannie and says, "Well, if it doesn't hurt, why do you try to get away?" Jeannie shrugs, then just as magnanimously gives all the dough back to the other two girls!

Sometimes kindergarten teachers admonish children not to "jabber," or they arbitrarily stop arguments, forgetting that arguments can be a satisfying way of getting to know another person as well as a way of testing language power. An argument can be quite as civilized among children as among adults. And surely learning to resolve disagreements plays an important part in becoming friends. The best friends in the kindergarten often have the most arguments.

To be able to argue well, or to dare to argue at all, a child needs a chance to practice good techniques. A teacher would do well then to listen to and appraise a children's argument before arbitrarily stopping it out of a fear that it will get out of hand. She might also remind herself that children's arguments, quarrels, and fights are short-lived and not as dangerous as they may appear.

CHILDREN ARE NOT UNIFORMLY PREPARED FOR ESTABLISHING RELATIONSHIPS

Some children at five are still very dependent on grown-ups and unable to make decisions on their own. Such children can hardly have the best relationship with other five-year-olds if they are not sure of their own likes and wants. Other children have been so indulged by adults that they are startled and unbelieving when they are crossed. Children make short shrift of the child who thinks he is entitled to special consideration as a matter of course.

Children at five already have some concept of their inner worth and this affects their relationships with others. One child is friendly, warm, and relaxed. It never occurs to him that someone will not like him, because people have always liked him. Approaching others with an expectation of friendly response, he gets it more often than not. Other children are not so fortunate. Scolded and berated too often at home they may be on the defensive outside, and attack without provocation simply because they do not trust people. Still others have been overprotected with constant admonitions, such as "be careful," "you'll fall," "watch out" to the point where they no longer trust themselves to act, and approach all situations with an anxious fear that something will go wrong if they do act. How can they abandon themselves to the carefree, physical activities of their peers if they are so afraid?

Experiences differ for children, of course. But some have far more to share or contribute than others. The "idea man" in the group is frequently sought out. The child who can see the sense in a variety of play themes is better off than the one who thinks playing ball is the only form play can take.

The causes for the very normal difficulties involved in forming relationships are many; the stage of development of the children is the outstanding one. But experience with other children, relative independence from adults, concept of self, and scope of general experience all play their part too. The poignancy of how much some children have to overcome before they can finally make contacts that eventually lead to good relationships is clearly seen in the year-end report below.

Writing about five-year-old Randie, his teacher became strongly aware of how he had struggled to be noticed and accepted and how he had thrived and rejoiced after winning recognition. A painfully shy child all his life, he spent weeks of school time clinging to his mother, then more weeks standing stiff and silent in one spot most of each session. He shrank when approached by teacher or children, who did not force themselves upon him. Then Randie began watching the teacher's expression as she dealt with children in the group. He seemed particularly fascinated by how she disciplined them. He then moved about the room watching one group of children and then another, coming closer and closer each day. More weeks went by and Randie still did not engage in any activity or take part in dancing or games, but he watched with a vicarious pleasure that shone on his face. Whenever possible he endeavored to sit next to the teacher. When spoken to he made no audible reply and when asked a direct question he either nodded or shook his head. When pushed or punched he did not resist, but neither did he run away. As time went by he began coming into the very midst of children's active play, and began doing remarkable tricks with his body, although he was still not talking.

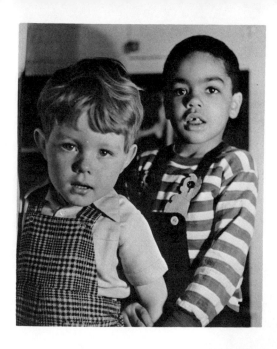

*so unique in spirit and
varied in physique*

2

*through confidences shared
and intimacies exchanged—
relationships slowly evolve*

He climbed in an intricate way to the top of the jungle gym and made the highest, most daring jumps; he balanced on one foot on a walking board, and he carried heavy boards by himself. All the time he was doing this he watched from the corner of his eyes to see the reaction of the nearby children. The teacher's sincere praise and the children's genuine admiration made Randie glow and exert further effort in other areas, such as construction work at the tables and blockbuilding on the floor.

After four months Randie only said a word here and there although he sometimes talked to himself (practicing perhaps, the teacher thought). He did communicate through facial expression, calling the teacher's attention to his work by a persistant look of expectancy as he hovered around it. He also showed delight and curiosity as he began to smile more frequently and actually join other children. By this time he was defending himself physically quite effectively. What gave him a real thrill was being chosen for a game by a leader in the class. This happened after five months of school and by this time he was responding more and more to the attention paid him by the class in the natural course of activities. He began speaking more and more freely—first only to the teacher but eventually to the children.

As Randie found himself and his activities acceptable in the eyes of others and as he spoke his thoughts, a change took place. In what looked like an attempt to raise his importance in the eyes of classmates, he bragged, "We have trees in our yard too. Bigger ones." And again, "My dog is even stronger than that." When shouting was in order as part of an outdoor game originated by a group of children, Randie shouted the loudest. During the last three months of the school year he felt so happy and so much a part of school that he told his mother, "I wish I could live in school—all the time."

In summarizing Randie's year the teacher could see that what continued giving him the greatest joy and stimulation was the recognition of his contribution in class projects and work and particularly other children's full acceptance of him. With this acceptance he evinced a perceptible growing sense of confidence in his ability to handle every kind of material and to take part in every kind of activity,—completely new courage to assert himself as an individual.

FORMING FRIENDSHIPS IS A STRUGGLE FOR SOME

Donny well illustrates how awkward some children are in forming friendships. He went along without apparent zest in various activities, evincing a minimum of involvement with others. Then suddenly he singled out a little girl for attention. But she did not respond to his direct

"Will you play with me?" After a while he tried something different; he followed her and aped whatever she was doing—puzzles, clay, water play. But Nancy remained indifferent to his efforts. Still Donny did not give up. He tried another method of gaining response. He gave her a poke— affectionately perhaps, but still a poke. Well! He got a negative response, but at least it was a reaction! Seeing that Nancy could well cope with this the teacher did not interfere. Donny however, delighted that Nancy was at last responding even if negatively, continued to follow his excit- ing pursuit and the consequent learning. He went on talking, persuading, poking, showing preference (when passing cookies he passed them to Nancy first), inviting her to look at a book with him, and sometimes dis- rupting her building. He persisted in this difficult relationship until he finally met with some success and satisfaction. At the same time he began to respond to an approach from another child, a little girl full of initiative and adventure. Donny rather lacked those qualities himself, yet stimu- lated by Kathy he gained courage. Through Kathy's leadership Donny engaged in exuberant physical activities, including wrestling; in joyful and experimental use of different materials; in seeking new ways of co- operating and of testing relationships. The two were sharing various de- lights not only with each other but with others, now including Nancy. Through his relationship with one, then finally with several children, Donny grew in his interests, developed initiative, and began to express humor. His relationships with others gave meaning to the word *school*.

CHILDREN WANT TO MAKE FRIENDS BUT MAY NOT KNOW HOW

Kindergarten children are eager for friendships outside their fam- ilies. There are good reasons why it is hard for them to develop these smoothly. Kindergarten children are very inexperienced in the art of re- lating. During their first two or three years of experience they were on the receiving end of affection and attention. Whatever they have learned of giving was learned primarily in response to and in imitation of the grown-ups who showered them with love. Even their feelings for siblings are still mixed and rarely do they take the same tender and protective view of little brothers and sisters that their parents do. Young children are still very much involved with themselves. *Their* feelings are far more im- portant to them than anyone else's. Indeed they are not too certain about the nature of other people's feelings, although they are carried away by their own. Yet as growth proceeds they inevitably plunge into relation- ships with eagerness. But they may have had limited experience with children their own age and may not know what to do. An adult after all recognizes that a child is "only a child," and makes concessions. But no child can see another child with the eyes of an adult. At five, concessions to someone else still carry overtones of unwanted deprivation to one's self. Experience teaches a child to barter, and trial and error gives him further techniques. Necessary as this trial and error learning is, it is certainly not easy.

CHILDREN NEED A TEACHER'S HELP IN DEVELOPING RELATIONSHIPS

A kindergarten class houses a group of human beings unquestionably aware of each other, actively influencing each other, and constantly relating on different levels. When a young child is noticed by the teacher he feels he has a place in the class which makes it worth coming to school. When he has an opportunity to be heard by the teacher and the children the child feels the security of being among friends. When he enjoys their response he does not hesitate to take part in activities or to try again if he fails. On the other hand fear of a bully can inhibit his participation and a teacher's indifference can squelch a child's fresh enthusiasm for school.

The teacher's role in helping children form relationships must be based on reality. A teacher must be neither overly idealistic in her expectations of children's behavior nor fearful of direct action when necessity calls for it. She needs to be helpful without being didactic, and the nature and extent of her help must be different in each situation. Above all the teacher must be aware of the constant challenge to stimulate and guide the growth of positive human relations in her classroom.

THE TEACHER HELPS CHILDREN UNDERSTAND THEIR OWN AND OTHER PEOPLE'S MOTIVES

Children's motives are as varied as adults' but are more readily apparent to the careful observer. Young children feel strongly, with a black-and-white approach that sometimes makes them seem quite stubborn and unreasonable. The saving grace is that feelings pass quickly and five-year-old children are intelligent enough to understand a teacher's guidance in the handling of their feelings. The basic human emotions motivate children—they love someone or hate him; they admire freely and envy easily; they are tender to each other and jealous too. They are afraid of being put upon but enjoy leadership. Above all it is important to them to save face, and self-esteem thus is vital. As the following episode shows, it is completely possible for a teacher to appeal to kindergarten children for understanding in time of troubled relationships.

Victor had worked painstakingly on a "skyscraper" building when Charles inadvertently caused it to collapse by removing a box next to it. Victor was enraged and quickly reached out to hit Charles. Unaware of any wrongdoing, Charles felt the sting of injustice even more than the hurt of Victor's punch. He retaliated in kind. Stepping right into the battle the teacher called for an immediate cease fire. But she did not leave it there; she called each child to account and challenged each to think. "Victor," she asked, "why are you so mad at Charles?"

"He made my building break down! Don't you know?" Victor answered.

"No," the teacher explained, "he only took the box which was near and empty; Charles didn't realize you needed it for support." Victor thought this over.

"And Charles," the teacher continued, "why are you so mad at Victor?"

"He got after me *first!*"

"But you can understand why Victor was upset," the teacher said, clarifying the matter without scolding.

"Yes, his building broke. But I just took the box. I didn't know the building would crash," Charles explained.

"Explain that to Victor," the teacher advised confidently. Charles did this gladly and graphically. Both boys after talking a bit even saw something funny in the episode.

The teacher recognized that indirectly there *was* an implication of apology on the part of Charles and an expression of silent understanding on the part of Victor. More than a truce had been established between the children. Helped to understand each other's motives, the two boys furthered their friendship.

A TEACHER INVITES CHILDREN'S TRUST

Children can sense the feelings teachers have about them. They know when a teacher accepts them as they are or when a teacher likes only certain kinds of children. It is perfectly true that no teacher can love all children equally. Children are different, and teachers are human. But all children should feel they have an equal chance in the eyes of the teacher, and this they will feel if she accepts each one for what he is without judgment or prejudice.

When the teacher is genuinely friendly in the way she talks to children and works with them, she will invite their trust and encourage their friendship. When she makes it a practice to listen to children every day as well as to speak to them even the shy ones will want to talk to her. When she makes only the promises she intends to keep ("We will go to the farm next Wednesday if it doesn't rain," or "The five children who missed the trip will be the ones to bake the cookies tomorrow"), the children will believe and trust her.

A teacher of young children should be a motherly person—warm, caring, attentive. Yet she must not expect such response and devotion from the children as she might if she *were* their mother. Because kindergartners can be helpless and dependent a loving teacher may become possessive in her maternal attitude and speak strongly of "*my* children." She may even compete with the real mother for status with the child! The teacher must never forget that the children are not hers; her devotion is expressed through service to them, not possession of them; her affection as their teacher consists of building security and promoting learning in the children. She can derive great satisfaction from fulfilling such a role without taking full possession.

The most loving teacher however is definitely not a paragon. She may at times be tired and cranky or too busy to hear a child out. She may face realistic interferences and fail sometimes to notice something important. But if she is basically friendly the children will readily forgive her. And she can try to compensate for a failure. ("I didn't come over to see your building yesterday when you asked me to but I will today. I was too busy with the woodworking.") In such a teacher the children will not lose their trust. Knowing that she is on their side they continue their faith in her and accept her as a fellow human being with human foibles. With this mutual acceptance an emotional climate is established in which good relationships can flourish.

Some adults feel superior to children and unwittingly show condescension. This was the case with Mrs. Imrie who genuinely felt she loved children. Stroking the hair of a wiggling little boy one day she asked him good-naturedly but with tongue-in-cheek, "What's the matter? What happened when they gave you a haircut? Did they inject you with something?" The child answered her perfectly seriously, glad to have the chance to talk. Excitedly he described the kind of haircut his mother had requested and the funny surprise of the short crew cut that resulted. As he talked on Mrs. Imrie shrugged her shoulders in boredom and loss of interest. The child continued for a while, then his voice trailed off and he gave up. Watching this little drama the student-teacher present laughingly said in surprise, "He took you literally, you know." Both adults felt that they had missed out on something—as they had—but could not tell what. Teasing and condescension have no place in the growing relationships of a young child.

TEACHERS BUILD RELATIONSHIPS WHEN THEY
HELP CHILDREN IN TROUBLE

A young kindergarten teacher working for the first time in a child care center in an impoverished neighborhood was full of her impressions when she met former classmates at a professional conference.

"The thing about these children that really bothers me," she said, "is that when they get hurt, instead of coming to me for help they hide behind the door or in an out of the way corner, crouching and silent."

For this young teacher helping children who get hurt seemed like the most natural thing in the world. And it should. But children who have known harsh treatment from grown-ups learn to fend for themselves early. It is a sign of their trust and confidence in a teacher when they do turn to her for needed help. Let us see how Miss Gaye handled one such incident, when the help needed was more than a band-aid.

One morning Eddie fell during some rough play outdoors and scratched and bruised a small area on his leg. The pain and the sight of blood upset Eddie enormously although another child might not have been bothered by it at all. Eddie sobbed and clung to the teacher and resisted in a rigid panicky way the usual painless first aid medication. "I want my mommy, I want my mommy!" Eddie wailed. The teacher of course remained calm, repeating her need to inspect the bruise, to treat it, and then if necessary to call the mother. Meanwhile six or seven children gathered around Eddie and the teacher, offering sympathetic suggestions to each. "Do it to me teacher, do it to me, then Eddie will know it doesn't hurt," said Ellen. The teacher put the antiseptic solution on her while Ellen looked on with self-conscious bravery and Eddie with genuine curiosity. But again he insisted, "I want my mommy, you call her." Knowing that Eddie was not suffering seriously, and knowing too that he did have a good sense of humor and that all the other children were beginning to be amused by the situation of Eddie's exaggerated fussing, the teacher resorted to humor without, of course, making fun of him. "Okay, Eddie, I will go and call your mother. I'll say, 'Hello, Eddie's mother? I'm calling about Eddie.' 'Well,' your mother will say, 'what about Eddie? Is he hurt?' 'I don't know,' I'll answer, 'I just don't know . . .'" Eddie followed the imaginary conversation with intense interest and he burst out laughing at the teacher's silly answer. Eddie as well as the other children requested a repetition of the telephone dialogue, and the teacher obliged them. The laughter relaxed Eddie enough so that he held still and cooperated with the teacher in examining the scrape. But he was still irritable about medication and since the scrape was superficial and it was very close to dismissal, the teacher did not persist about treating it. She wrote a note to the mother and for Eddie's sake made it humorous. "Dear Mrs. G.: Eddie hurt his leg in school, but he has *already* cried so all he has to do now is wash it and put on a band-aid." She let him take a band-aid from a box and put it in his pocket. At home he repeated to his mother, "Show me where it says 'he has already cried' —that's funny." Both he and his mother were thoroughly amused by the note.

A TEACHER SHARES THE CHILDREN'S INTERESTS

Sometimes the teacher participates in the children's special enjoyments and play. At midmorning snack time Miss Wayne does not merely serve the children efficiently but she partakes of the snack herself and often joins in the children's conversation and humor. "I didn't have any milk. See, my glass is empty," says Tommy, clanking onto the table a freshly emptied milk glass. His lively five-year-old companions restrain themselves from correcting Tommy. They are bursting to know what the teacher will say; maybe Tommy really fooled Miss Wayne. To their great delight she goes along with the joke: "Oh, poor Tommy, you must be so thirsty! Pass Tommy the milk pitcher Annie!" The children all burst out laughing at this, and although they reveal the truth to Miss Wayne another child immediately repeats the same prank. Everybody laughs together once again. The children have a close feeling with this teacher who is able to share their kind of fun.

Similar participation by the teacher is appropriate in many activities. "Watch out, watch out, Miss Bell," commands a kindergartner bus driver while "steering" from a pile of large hollow blocks. "Oh goodness," says the teacher jumping out of the way. "Want a ride, Miss Bell?" The driver motions to a "seat" and Miss Bell actually perches for a minute. As she gets off to attend to other business the driver waves with one hand, keeping the other on the steering wheel. The teacher's sharing in class activities and going along with their imagination is rewarding for her and fun for the children. But some delicacy, diplomacy, and restraint may be necessary if the potentially good relationship is not to deteriorate into one in which the teacher replaces the child leader. And of course the teacher is always firmly rooted in reality. She may agree to be put in jail by an eager jailer, but on no account should the ropes be real in a misguided effort to prove her sincerity to the children. In joining children's play a teacher never compromises her basic freedom to attend quickly to some real "teacher" task.

A TEACHER SHARES HER TASTES AND
LOVES WITH CHILDREN

Every teacher has her own tastes and her special enjoyments. She can share these with the children in a spontaneous way. She may love garden flowers and may bring them to school once in a while to let the children help her in arranging, placing, and watering them. Or she may have among her treasures a piece of beautiful material which she would bring for the children to touch and admire and wear in costume fashion.

One teacher shared her husband's carpentry skill by having him build a bird feeder for her class, and shared her own bird watching hobby with the children by placing the feeder so they could see the brave, persistent winter birds. A student-teacher, noticing the children's lively interest in the small, caged guinea pig that was kept in the classroom, decided to bring to the children the animal she had raised on her family farm—a strong, uncaged goat with a big appetite. She went to some trouble transporting the goat and returning it to the farm, but she was amply rewarded by the joy the children showed as they shared her beloved pet with her.

Presents less unusual and less exciting, such as a teacher's own favorite childhood book, can still be very impressive. *Any* object actually valued by the teacher and freely shared with the children for their benefit enhances good relationships and promotes a communal feeling in the group.

GOOD RELATIONSHIPS THRIVE ON
GOOD COMMUNICATION

Perhaps an observer's first impression of the teacher's relationship with the children in her kindergarten class comes from the content and manner of her speech: the familiarity to the children of her vocabulary and allusions, the naturalness or formality of her voice, the quality of talking *at* or *with* children. Sensitivity to the children's comprehension and range of interests, and explanation of new words on their own level of understanding strengthen the relationship of trust and sharing so necessary to good teaching.

Miss D. gathers the children together one morning after an indoor work period. Bobby seems uncontrollably eager to talk. "Bobby wants to tell you about his building, since he was the principal architect of it," announces Miss D. Immediately a couple of children turn their heads. "Principal?" one child murmurs. Miss D. realizes that the word *principal* could mean only one thing to these children—the principal of the school who pays pleasant visits to the class. And so Miss D. hastens to explain. "That means, children, that Bobby was the *chief builder,* even though others worked with him."

A teacher often takes for granted that five-year-old children understand words which she has used most of her life. Let us look at Miss A. as she sits with her kindergarten class, holding up an attractive book she is about to read. The children look with rapt attention, not wanting to miss a picture or a word. Miss A. turns the title page and then starts reading.

"You skipped a page!" a child calls urgently.

"No, this is the beginning of the story," Miss A. answers.

"But what does it say *there?*" the child persists, pointing to the turned page. The other children follow the question too.

"That's just the title page," Miss A. answers quickly and perhaps a little impatiently. No evidence of recognition of the word "title" appears on the faces of these five-year-olds. But they understand that the teacher is ready to read them a good story and that she has had enough interruptions. They do not press the issue. In the brief casual phrase "That's just the title page," Miss A. has lost an opportunity to capitalize on the children's interest at the time. In her adherence to the task at hand she failed to note their curiosity as well as their lack of comprehension of the word she used so casually. All too often children simply have not had enough experience to comprehend what seems so apparent to an adult.

GOOD RELATIONSHIPS MEAN A GOOD LIFE TOGETHER

Good relationships in class provide both an incentive and a stimulation to good learning. Whether good relationships are developed and maintained in a classroom depends heavily on the teacher, not only on what she does, but on what kind of a person she is.

Lucy Sprague Mitchell writes:

The teacher-child and the child-teacher relationship is a close one in a more significant way than spending hours each day together in the same room. There must be a sharing of interest, a sharing of planning, a sharing of putting interests into action. The teacher remains an adult though she becomes a member of the group. Her role is different from the role of the children. But it remains true that teacher and children must have a good life *together,* or neither will have a good life.[1]

[1] Lucy Sprague Mitchell, *Our Children and Our Schools* (New York, Simon and Schuster, Inc., 1951), p. 17.

Bibliography

Cohen, Dorothy H., and Stern, Virginia, "Recording Children's Behavior With One Another," Chapter 6, *Observing and Recording the Behavior of Young Children* (New York, Bureau of Publications, Teachers College, Columbia University, 1958).

Freiberg, Selma, *The Magic Years* (New York, Charles Scribner's Sons, 1959).

Isaacs, Susan, *Social Development in Young Children* (London, Routledge & Kegan, Paul, Ltd., 1932).

Mitchell, Lucy Sprague, Our Children and Our Schools (New York, Simon and Schuster, Inc., 1951).

Read, Katherine H., *The Nursery School* (Philadelphia, W. B. Saunders, 1960).

5

The Meaning of Play
in Children's Lives

Susan Isaacs, British educator and psychoanalyst, once made the following very penetrating statement about play: [1]

If now we compare . . . the more adaptable and intelligent animals with the less, for instance, the reptiles and fishes with the mammals, we notice something which throws much light on human childhood—viz: the fact that the animals which are able to *learn* more are also able to *play* more. Those with fixed and inherited instincts play not at all; the young behave as the old from the beginning, and there is nothing to add to the wisdom of the species. But the playing animals, and in proportion as they play, gain something of an individual wisdom. They are the curious, the experimental animals. The young lamb skips, but only for a short time, and soon settles down to sheep-like stolidity. Whereas the kitten plays on, and tries its way about the world with playful paw and nose, long after its size might lead us to expect a sober maturity. Those animals nearest of all to ourselves, the monkeys and the ape, are like us in keeping the will to play even into maturity: but no animal young play so fully, so inventively, so continually and so long as human children.

Play has long been considered a natural part of childhood. But it was not always understood to have the significance we see in it today. "Child's play" has been a term denoting something trivial and not to be taken seriously. "A way of releasing energy" has been another appraisal. Yet serious investigation has revealed meaning in play that kindergarten

[1] Susan Isaacs, *The Nursery Years* (London, Routledge & Kegan Paul, Ltd., 1932).

teachers would do well to understand and interpret to the public. Hartley, Frank, and Goldenson [2] have formulated eight functions of play in their studies of children's activities: (1) to imitate adults, (2) to play out real life roles in an intense way, (3) to reflect relationships and experiences, (4) to express pressing needs, (5) to release unacceptable impulses, (6) to reverse roles usually taken, (7) to mirror growth, (8) to work out problems and experiment with solutions. These conclusions grew out of hundreds of observations in nursery schools and kindergartens, and we strongly urge any student of kindergarten education to read the book in its entirety.

Susan Isaacs spent many years recording episodes of play and relating these episodes to the total growth in intellectual and social development of the children she observed.[3, 4] Her findings fall into three major areas of functioning: (1) play leads to discovery, reasoning, and thought, (2) play is a bridge to social relations, and (3) play leads to emotional equilibrium. Let us examine each of these in detail.

PLAY LEADS TO DISCOVERY, REASONING, AND THOUGHT

As a child plays he reaches out to all materials available (we are not talking now of store-bought toys) and examines them, handles them, observes changes and possible uses, pulls things apart, and puts them together again. How does this lead to discovery? Let us take a simple common experience: playing with water. Every youngster loves to dabble in water. He spends more time at the sink than efficient washing calls for, he splashes in puddles with a fine disregard of his clothes, he pokes his fingers into the opening of the faucet to see what will happen to the flow, he pours water back and forth into containers of different size and shape, he adds ingredients to it, he sucks it up with a straw, and he luxuriates in a tubful of water when he tires of floating toy boats and ducks on its surface. This is all play, truly childlike play. But what does a child discover? He discovers the properties of water; it can flow and take on the shape of any container, it can act with force and push things away, it has weight and some things can rest on it comfortably while others cannot, it can be mixed with some ingredients to make substances of different color or texture, it has no color by itself but it appears to be blue or green when you see lots of it in some settings, it can form little drops, or it can spread

[2] R. Hartley, L. Frank, and R. Goldenson, *Understanding Children's Play* (New York, Columbia University Press, 1952).

[3] Susan Isaacs, *Social Development in Young Children* (London, Routledge & Kegan Paul, Ltd., 1933).

[4] Susan Isaacs, *Intellectual Growth in Young Children* (London, Routledge & Kegan Paul, Ltd., 1930).

flat over a surface. Is not this discovery in an important sense? Do not all children learn this without adult help through play? How many other discoveries they make in this way depends of course on the number of things they may observe, touch, and experiment with.

Let us see what happens beyond discovery in the play with water. On a little mound of sand or dirt a child carefully pours his bit of water. It runs downhill. Another time he spreads water just as carefully at the base of his mound and it spreads out and away, or remains in a puddle. It does not go upwards. He learns not only to recognize this as a phenomenon but to reason for himself that water apparently does not have an inner force of its own to carry it upward. After a few attempts he no longer expects that it will go up. Through trial and error and experimentation he arrives at a conclusion; he reasons.

Normally any child will have a good deal of experience not only with water but with other fluids as well. He pours milk or watches it being poured; he spills it and mops it up. At some time or other as every mother knows, he plays with it; he makes bubbles in his glass, he pours it from a small glass to a large one, and he puts his finger into the little milk puddle on the table and makes designs. Or exploring elsewhere, he pretends he is a painter and stealthily slips a brush into his father's can of paint and quickly dabs at an empty spot on the fence; he helps his older brother make lemonade for an outdoor stand, adds sugar and watches it dissolve, and cautiously pours lemonade into a paper cup and sells it. He is playing all the time, but generalizations begin to form. Apparently many things flow, take on the shape of their containers, can be mixed with other ingredients, will spill, and so on. He learns to generalize about fluids although he may not know the word *fluids*. He learns how to handle fluids for maximum efficiency and begins to admonish younger children to be careful. He *knows* from his experience, and he can think and talk about what he knows.

Here is a record of play taken by a kindergarten teacher in which one can clearly see discovery, reasoning, and thought taking place:

Richard put some water in the bottom of the wagon in the yard. He deliberately *shook* the wagon by pushing the handle, and a little water spilled on the pavement. He was very intent about this activity and rushed inside to get another pitcherful, then shook the wagon again by pushing it back and forth. "I'm making waves," he said (informatively) and eagerly got more water, with a bucket this time, and filled the wagon practically full; now his wave-making was recognized by several children who also wanted to do the same. Richard was ecstatic, pushing the wagon and causing what seemed enormous splashes to rise up in the wagon and spill all around. His pushing of the wagon and his wave-making was quite rhythmic and he planned to replenish the water as soon as it diminished. Apparently he was discovering that it takes a certain quantity of water to produce a satisfactory wave.

PLAY IS A BRIDGE TO SOCIAL RELATIONS

Much of the above dealt with play from the point of view of an individual youngster. He may or may not be involved with other children as he plays with water or a wagon, stones and sticks, or cans or paper plates. But a time comes when any child wants children to play with because only children can communicate within the same dimension of thought that is meaningful to him. Only another child can see dishes in broken pieces of glass or coffee in the seeds of wild flowers; only another child can understand that a big rock or an empty box is obviously a boat, or a plane, or the top of the Empire State Building. The world of imagination and make-believe can only be peopled by members of the same generation.

The world of make-believe has an almost real quality for children and they can pretend within a wide range of possible behavior. They can wish themselves anything they like, and play that it becomes a reality. They can pretend to be big and powerful and authoritative, even if they really are only little children with very little power indeed. They can pretend that they are angry tigers, growling dogs, and fierce lions, even if in reality they are gentle and well-mannered boys and girls. They can try on for size the feeling of being a mother, a father, a street cleaner, or a truck driver. They can go back to babyhood or forward to adulthood, they can frighten others or be the thing they are themselves afraid of. This inner life of children we call their fantasy life and it represents an integral part of children's efforts to comprehend themselves and the world around them.

The combining of inner need and outer reality is beautifully illustrated in the play of Freddie, who in a short span of time had to understand two very different environments—the Nazi Germany of his babyhood and the democratic America to which he came at age four. Freddie had the inner need to feel big and important, a leader and a force. His expression of it in play reflected his effort to understand his environment in terms of his personal need. He would roll a piece of paper, toot-toot forcefully into it, and march around and around. Or he would take a long block, place it across his shoulder, raise his chin, and with undeviating glance march, march, march. One day, with a few children following him, he suddenly stopped before a keg and stood upon it. Then with a commanding glare he laid down his "gun" and made a short bombastic speech. Abruptly he climbed down and resumed marching.

After several months at an American school and the acquisition of some English vocabulary and American values, Freddie expressed that inner need in new terms.

"Look, I am so big now!" said Freddie with pride and purpose in his bigness. He stretched his body and placed one hand on his hair to indicate his height. He made a line on the teacher's waist, just where his head reached. Finally, to explore still further his own size, he stood back-to-back then nose-to-nose with other children to see how much bigger he was than they.

"I am a big boy now, yes," he reiterated. That started other children measuring their bodies and discussing their size.

Freddie watched them, listened, and continued the subject. "Next month when I am big," he said, tiptoeing, stretching his hand as high as possible, "so big, then—I be a father."

That was undisputably the ultimate in growth. Nothing that the other children offered came up to it. Yet to Freddie even being a father was not all. He was reaching out for other concepts of manliness.

"I am strong," said Freddie flexing his muscles on arms and legs. "See?" There was a new look in Freddie's eyes now as he expanded his chest, held his head high, and smiled. "I am Joe Loui." He made heroic gestures with his arms and body. "I am Joe Loui."

This drew an immediate response from two other boys. "And I am Joe Loui!"

"Me, too. I am strong." And all three Joe Louises walked around with powerful steps.

It was brave and good to be Joe Louis. The children carried chairs on their heads and tried to carry some protesting children. Finally they moved a couple of tables in preparation for lunch. "I carry it! I carry it myself," said Freddie. "I am strong. I am Joe Loui."

Freddie's concepts of American heroes and men challenged even Americans of longer years than Freddie. He was successively Santa Claus, truck driver, and "union man." But the most significant thing occurred the day after Lincoln's birthday. Freddie came to the school yard and immediately made an announcement: "I am Lincoln."

He poked with his foot in the snow, contemplated a while, and was ready for action. He picked up a stick lying nearby and began digging in the snow with it, saying, "I am Lincoln. Lincoln is working now."

In due course this stick became a gun. Freddie put the gun across his shoulder and began marching briskly with it, saying, "I am Lincoln. Lincoln is a soldier." All his movements were simple and clear and integrated with his thoughts. There was seriousness in his face but lightness and change were in it too.

When the soldiering was done the "gun" was transformed into a "banner." Gayly now, Freddie carried it in front of him singing "Happy Birthday." His air of festivity and pleasure made the other children join him. They all sang "Happy birthday, dear Lincoln."

An hour later inside the large nursery school room a teacher was at the piano with the children gathered about her. They were whispering and hesitating with their requests for songs. Then came Freddie's request in an open, confident manner. "I want to sing happy birthday, happy birthday to Lincoln," he cried.

There was joy on his face as he listened to the music, to the children's chorus, to his own lusty voice. "Happy birthday, dear Lincoln," he sang.

The Lincoln idea grew as the day progressed. Before settling down for a nap, Freddie warned, "Don't call me Freddie. No. My name is Lincoln. Abraham Lincoln." The earnestness in his voice made one not dare to do otherwise.

When everything became quiet in the sleeping room, Freddie lifted his head and confided in an audible whisper, "Lincoln was a very good man. I am Abraham Lincoln."

Adults frequently assume that because absorption in fantasy at an adult level means escape from reality the same thing is true in childhood. But in 1935 Ruth Griffiths did an analysis of the fantasies of fifty children of five years of age and found that the most important effort involved in their fantasy was problem solving! [5]

Friendships Develop Out of Need

Working out fantasies through play is extremely important to preschool children. But they need each other to be most effective. How can a child feel she is a "real" mother without a "real" baby? How can a child be a "real" pilot without passengers? How can a child feel powerful if he has no one to intimidate or subject to his power? Thus the search for playmates begins and the play is often a hodge-podge of different children's fantasy needs meeting, crossing, conflicting, or merging into the ideas of the theme they are pursuing.

As Harry [6] tries to incorporate children into his play ideas he faces frustration and must finally modify the form, but not the essence, of his relationship with the children! At first Harry pushes and shoves several children who scream and attract the teacher's attention. She discovers three children cornered behind a table and box in the housekeeping area, pleading to her in a chorus of complaint. Harry, standing guard over them, is now on the defensive.

"But they are in *jail*—I have to keep them in jail!" Harry asserts. The teacher must see both sides, including this jailer's.

[5] Ruth Griffiths, *A Study of Imagination in Early Childhood and its Function in Mental Development* (London, Routledge & Kegan Paul, Ltd., 1935).

[6] Marguerita Rudolph, *Living and Learning in Nursery School* (New York, Harper & Row, Publishers, 1954), pp. 53–55.

She says to Harry, "When you want to play jail, get people who *want* to play jail with you," and she watches Harry carry out this advice as he continues his game. He promptly turns to the imprisoned children in a matter-of-fact manner:

"Do you *want* to be in jail?"

"No," they answer grumblingly.

"Let's let them out then," says the teacher, and together with Harry she pushes the table and box away and releases the victims. Harry continues playing jail and follows the teacher's suggestion for a way of obtaining prisoners. He comes over to every active group of children in the different areas of the room as well as to Brad, a released prisoner who is working on a puzzle by himself, and asks:

"Do you *want* to go to jail?" And the children, scattered as they are in the room—some painting, some building, some listening to a story—all hear Harry's question and answer definitely "No." They are expressing their preferences. And Harry is finding out personally that other people have interests and wishes as well as he.

"They all don't want to go to my jail," he says to the teacher. The teacher looks interested. "Should I ask them again?" Harry asks. Such naive persistence in a child constitutes vital learning of social techniques. As he goes around canvassing the room this time, Harry changes his approach. He adds an appealing note to his voice and manner and qualifies his question with an implied promise: "Do you want to go to jail? *It's nice.*" Though not as decisively this time, the children still decline—all except Linda. She is such an easily led person that she cannot say no. Harry grins with a sense of victory as Linda looks hesitant but follows him. When she gets to the jail area however, she suddenly changes her mind, turns around, and escapes from jail before even entering it! Harry is now really distressed; after all that work—defeat. He makes a plea to the teacher and they face reality together.

"Nobody wants to be in jail," the teacher points out simply. "Why don't you ask them to play something else?" she suggests, since it is apparent that Harry has an urgent need to play with a group of children and to lead them in some way. He cannot manage such social activity himself and accepts the teacher's help.

"Okay," Harry agrees promptly, "I'll ask them to be cowboys on my ranch."

"Fine!" The teacher is very hopeful about Harry.

"Who wants to be a cowboy?" he asks, with confidence in his voice and an appropriate swagger. Nickey and Billy and Johnny promptly come up with a "Yip-pee!" And Harry shouts "Yip-pee!" swatting an imaginary horse and leading the others to the ranch, which is on the site of the former jail and is indeed the same structure slightly altered.

The Pursuit of Friends Goes On

One of the reasons five-year-olds change their friendships through the year has to do with their outgrowing old needs and discovering new ones for which different companions are suitable. Thus Susie, who was content to be Binney's baby for weeks, wants very much to be mother. If Binney agrees they reverse roles. But if Binney still must be mother Susie goes off to find a willing baby. When Jack no longer feels the need to prove his strength by bossing timid children he finds the courage to share ideas with other strong members of the group, and changes his choice of play partner. As Meredith gains confidence from her relationship with a compassionate and gentle Cora she extends her friendship to include Lydia, who is crisper and more brusque but stimulating in her relationships.

Thus, by sharing both their outer and inner lives in play and by exchanging ideas about the world as well as acting out feelings about their place in the world, children learn from each other. They become sensitive to how far they may go with different children; how much of their own needs they give up for the sake of holding on to companions; which techniques work and which do not. In short, their play inevitably leads them to people and to ways of getting along with people. That is why Susan Isaacs described play as a "bridge to social relations."

PLAY LEADS TO EMOTIONAL EQUILIBRIUM

Few adults remember in detail the play experiences of early childhood. But most do remember the play of their middle childhood years. Since in this period the self-directed unsupervised play of children leads to the same sense of well-being and satisfaction that it does earlier, an adult's own experiences of that period help him understand this feeling.

Think back to when you were in elementary school. You came home from school with an eagerness to change clothes, have your milk, and get out to your friends on the street as quickly as you could. To paraphrase Robert Smith, "Where are you going?" your mother asked. "Out," you said. "What will you do?" "Nothing." [7] "Nothing" meant skipping double-dutch, playing jacks, playing hide-and-seek. "Nothing" meant skating, ring-o-levio, playing movie stars and princesses. "Nothing" was the delicious sense of being irresponsible without any trace of guilt, of losing oneself completely in the wonderful world of childhood with its magic and make-believe, its special rules, and its cooperative and competitive games. Do you remember how you felt when you returned home? You probably had forgotten to pick up the loaf of bread your mother had

[7] Robert Paul Smith, *"Where Did You Go?" "Out." "What Did You Do?" "Nothing."* (New York, W. W. Norton & Co., Inc., 1957).

asked you to get on the way back. You were a little reluctant to go home but not actively unhappy about it. Inside you felt quiet, relaxed, and content, unless you had had a fight just before coming in! In general though you probably remember those experiences with nostalgia. They were satisfying in a peculiarly thorough way.

This is what happens to younger children too. Of course they argue and become upset as they work things out with others. But in general there is release of tension and a deep sense of satisfaction as one is successful in leading, planning, arguing, sharing, demanding, giving, hating, and loving.

PLAY REFLECTS KIND AND AMOUNT OF EXPERIENCE

Just as we know that the capacity for play varies with the level on the evolutionary scale, so there is evidence that the quality of play is related to the quality of total life experience. Play is a means of expression, both of feeling and of thought. If one's feelings and thoughts are few there will not be much to express. A dramatic illustration of this was given many years ago in the experience of a New York City nursery school teacher [8] who left her job among children of professionals, artists, and business people to work with the children of Tennessee mountain folk, whose lives were spent within the narrow confines of their meager shacks in an impoverished community. She came with materials and ideas that had proven useful with the city children. But she found that the mountain children were not as responsive to the materials, not as richly imaginative in the themes of their play, and not so intensely and eagerly involved in play as the city children had been. Although they were friendly children and loving to each other, their play remained locked within a few simple themes of the comings and goings of adult preoccupations. This barrenness can appear in a city neighborhood too. A little girl we know came back from a session of play with neighborhood children whose home lives were considerably emptier than hers. She was obviously cross and frustrated. "I don't want to play with them anymore," she told her mother. "They always wake up the dolls, dress them, and take them to church." "They *never* want to take the children to the doctor or to the library or on a hike or *anything!*

PLAY REFLECTS MEANINGFUL EXPERIENCE

Linda's teacher was aware that there were complications at home for Linda and that the family had moved recently. The following play episode came as no surprise.

[8] Claudia Lewis, *Children of the Cumberland* (New York, Columbia University Press, 1946).

One morning while no one was in the housekeeping area, Linda came in and took charge. First she very busily pretended to cook some fried eggs on the stove and told another child who came in, "You've *got* to eat them. You eat it all up." She was forceful and insistent. The other child first complied, but soon refused and finally escaped from the scene. Linda then pulled at the teachers, saying, "*Sit* down and eat those eggs— I cooked them for you." Her eyes blazing with power, she was flinging her arms and snatching things up in a managerial fashion. She seemed really at work doing something terribly important. "We've got to move," she suddenly announced, "get everything out of the house." And with considerable strength she began pushing furniture into the room proper, throwing boxes and doll-clothes after them. Everyone in the classroom stopped to look at the unusual commotion in that area and the teacher approached Linda with words of restraint: "Don't take everything out. It will be hard for us to put it all back." But Linda's zeal and imagination were in full operation as she answered: "I said, everything out—this is moving. Everything is coming out and I am not putting it back!" How much in earnest she was about doing a thorough job of moving!

Several other children promptly, almost automatically, took it up and came to Linda's aid and support. "Let's get going with the moving, men," came from Larry and Peter as a bed was carried out. "I see," the teacher said, "I'd better get the broom and mop ready to clean as everything is moved out." Another child wanted to clean the strangely empty area. The teacher and the children commented on the completeness of the moving. "Linda did it." "Linda wanted to move." "It's a real moving day." There was understanding and respect of the whole situation and of Linda. While the teacher was helping with the cleaning the movers were at work bringing furniture back into the housekeeping corner. Alice became particularly interested in a different distribution of furniture than they had before, and some other children gave advice on where to put things. Linda took some part in arrangement of pots on the stove, but without much interest. Her special play, her particular satisfaction, came from having *done* the moving, for she had at the same time done something about a deep concern.

PLAY CAN BE STIFLED BY EMOTIONAL INTENSITY

Sometimes play is unimaginative or even nonexistent, and yet one could not say that the external stimulation has been inadequate. Often the cause is the strength of emotion which overwhelms a child and which is too much for him to understand or express. He cannot play. Some light was thrown on the relation between play and emotions during World

War II when large numbers of displaced and orphaned children were studied for their responses to deprivation.[9] In one residential nursery in England a fairly young child, both of whose parents had been killed in a bomb shelter, was placed under the care of a warm and friendly matron. The child did very little, did not speak, and betrayed no emotion in his facial expression for eighteen months. One memorable day after tentative play with building blocks he constructed a shelter. Suddenly he ceased his building activity and turned to the matron to speak at last. "Does it hurt to die?" he asked.

It is not often that a child is overcome by such tragedy that he loses all capacity for expression, even the normal urge to speak and play. But it does happen that children who are distressed beyond the ordinary find it hard to lose themselves in the world of children and materials outside themselves. Absorbed with their inner problems, they either do not play or tend to play out repetitively the one theme which absorbs them so fully. Where the problem is obviously not paucity of experience and where sufficient time has elapsed to assume that the lack of play is more than a cautious adjustment to a new environment, the careful teacher does well to note which of the children in the kindergarten are participating only minimally or not at all in the play activities. This is often a major clue to maladjustment, which can only be better understood by further observation of the child and examination of his life situation outside of school.

TEACHERS CAN HELP CHILDREN'S PLAY BE MEANINGFUL

Quality of play then, is a reflection of the quality of experience children have undergone. To the watchful teacher the themes that crop up and the way in which the themes are developed in play give clues to two important aspects of curriculum development: one, what the children are interested in, how much understanding they have, and what confusions and misconceptions they reveal, and two, what leads there are to teacher planning of trips, stories, pictures, accessory materials for play, discussions, and use of human and other resources in the community to further and enhance their knowledge and understanding.

Lucy came to school one Monday morning clutching a "bouquet" of feathers she had gathered over the weekend on a visit to a State Fair. The children surrounded her and had much to say about the variety of color, size, and texture.

"This shiny is the prettiest one."

[9] Anna Freud and Dorothy Burlingham, *Infants Without Families* (New York, International Universities Press, Inc., 1944); *War and Children* (New York, International Universities Press, Inc., 1943).

"Ooh, I like this long one best."

"Feel how soft this one is."

The children played with the feathers, discovering their tickling qualities and their strength for brushing and dusting. When water spilled on a bunch of feathers a little girl looked very distressed. Surely the feathers would be ruined now, she surmised. This stimulated comments from children as well as teachers on how creatures with feathers get wet and then get dry again; there is a similarity between the way feathers cover birds and the way clothes cover people. Maybe feathers keep birds from getting wet. The teacher deliberately encouraged the children to immerse the feathers in the sinkful of water so they could see that feathers float. Maybe the feathers help the birds swim. Soon an interest in the lightness of feathers arose and the teacher, noticing the children's interest, shared the fun of investigating at the same time.

"I wonder how much a feather would weigh," she said jokingly.

"Ha-ha—nothing!" asserted Allen.

"Yes, it would weigh nothing!" echoed another child, regarding the answer as a big joke.

"All right Allen," the teacher went on, "you close your eyes and open your hands; I'll put a feather in one hand and Nothing in the other hand. See if you can tell what's in each hand."

"Let me see how you put Nothing in."

"Let *me* put the Nothing in Allen's hand," several children begged. The expression on the faces of all the children was full of curiosity, imagination, and humor! But Allen as well as several children who followed him in the test, concentrated most seriously on discerning weight, on trying to feel lightness, and also on trying to get a concept of Nothing.

Exploring the lightness of feathers with the children, the teacher blew a stray feather towards a child. Delighted, the child directed the landing of the feather in a similar manner, with his breath. Needless to say this kind of controlled and satisfying mouth and breathing activity appealed to many children and there were many feathers put to motion." The proverbial expression "light as a feather" which the teacher used deliberately was no longer an academic one to these children. After this interest subsided and the feathers were put in a decorative arrangement on a mound of plasticine on the window sill, Marjie began fingering the feathers and pressing them together in her hand.

"If I had a big *bunch* of feathers in my hand I bet they wouldn't be as light as just one." It was a thoughtful question, based on the lasting impression of that weighing game of one feather.

"Did you ever hold a big bunch, or a bagful of feathers?" the teacher asked.

"No," answered Marjie.

"I didn't either," other children added.

"Well, I have a bag of feathers at home, and I sleep on it!" the teacher said. Most of the children did not know that the teacher was talking about a pillow. The teacher realized that some modern homes do not have any feather pillows since the advent of foam rubber and other synthetics, so she brought an old feather pillow to school. She carefully cut an incision in it, slowly pulled out some feathers, and stitched up the hole —all in the children's presence. She did this to add further to the children's tangible and relevant experience with feathers, to answer their questions concretely, and to stimulate curiosity in a sensory as well as intellectul way. The pillow, which was borrowed for a few weeks, was especially interesting and popular in the class. The children squeezed it, carried it, rested their heads on it, and compared its weight with various other objects. On their level they were genuinely studying physics and mathematics!

VARIETY IN CHILDREN'S PLAY IS ENCOURAGED BY A SENSITIVE TEACHER

Children in the kindergarten have been noted to base their play on as wide a variety of topics as their communities and contacts embrace. Typical themes include: house, doctor, cowboy, space travel, trains, ships, bus, circus, zoo, dentist, store, rabbi, going to church, weddings, parents' meetings, animals, firemen, garbage collectors, and too many more to enumerate. Lack of variety, poorly-embroidered play, conventionality, and endless repetition, are signs that children need rich exposure to first-hand experience that is comprehensible to them. This is where a teacher's sensitivity to what might truly interest children and spark their imagination becomes crucial to the development of curriculum. The choices must be made in terms of child values however, not necessarily of adult tastes. This concept is further developed in later chapters.

Children take what they are ready for from their environment, absorb it, and then give it back through play in the form they best understand. It is because of the personal meaning involved that we must be so careful to protect children's right to free play without imposing adult organization of prescribed games and activities for too great a block of time in the kindergarten. The teacher's role however, is not a minimal one, even if not direct and controlling. It is the teacher who makes it possible for the children to play at all by allowing time for it in the program, providing space indoors and out, supplying materials to aid the children in carrying out their ideas, and creating an emotional climate in which feelings can be honestly expressed.

It is the teacher's role to keep children from going out of safety bounds as they play and to assist them with useful techniques for playing together. A teacher can clarify the misconceptions that children reveal in their play and give them information to enrich their activity where this seems necessary. Most of all a teacher must not intrude unless she is wanted. Play is a child's way of experimenting, and if he is required to conform too much and too soon to adult molds he will miss the joy and particular learning experience that only play activities offer.

Bibliography

Bacmeister, Rhoda, "Why Play is Important to Your Child," *Parents' Magazine*, November, 1952.

Baruch, Dorothy, "Doll Play," *Mental Hygiene*, Vol. 24 (1940).

Biber, Barbara, *Play as a Growth Process* (pamphlet, New York, Bank Street College, 69 Bank Street).

Conn, Jacob H., "Child Reveals Himself Through Play," *Mental Hygiene*, Vol. 23 (1939).

Freud, Anna, and Burlingham, Dorothy, *Infants Without Families* (New York, International Universities Press, Inc., 1944).

————, *War and Children* (New York, International Universities Press, Inc., 1943).

Gesell, Arnold, and Ilg, Frances L., "Play and Pastimes," Chapter 17, *The Child From Five to Ten* (New York, Harper & Row, Publishers, 1946).

Griffiths, Ruth, *A Study of Imagination in Early Childhood and Its Function in Mental Development* (London, Routledge & Kegan Paul, Ltd., 1935).

Hartley, Ruth, Frank, Lawrence, and Goldenson, Robert, *Understanding Children's Play* (New York, Columbia University Press, 1952).

Isaacs, Susan, *Intellectual Growth in Young Children* (London, Routledge & Kegan Paul, Ltd., 1930).

————, *Social Development in Young Children* (London, Routledge & Kegan Paul, Ltd., 1933).

————, *The Nursery Years* (London, Routledge & Kegan Paul, Ltd., 1932).

Kepler, Hazel, *The Child and His Play* (New York, Funk & Wagnall Co., Inc., 1952).

Lambert, Clara, *Play, a Yardstick for Growth* (pamphlet, Play School Association, 120 W. 57th St., New York 19, N.Y.).

Lewis, Claudia, *Children of the Cumberland* (New York, Columbia University Press, 1946).

Rudolph, Marguerita, *Living and Learning in Nursery School* (New York, Harper & Row, Publishers, 1954).

Smith, Robert Paul, *"Where Did You Go?" "Out." "What Did You Do?" "Nothing."* (New York, W. W. Norton & Co., Inc., 1957).

II

the children get to know their world

6

Science Experiences for Children and Teachers

Mid-twentieth century children live in a world where science determines their way of life. Every citizen must be, if not a scientist, at least appreciative of scientific progress. The kindergarten is not too early to start developing such citizens, and many kindergartens do have science programs. But there is much confusion on the part of teachers as to how science is best learned by young children.

PLAY REVEALS THE NATURE OF CHILDREN'S INTEREST

Let us look into one kindergarten classroom where the teacher takes science learning seriously, to see how effective she actually is. Mrs. Bascom is an enthusiastic teacher, conscientiously aware of her kindergarten class of twenty-two children and always ready to offer information and give advice.

At the moment there is a group of six children on a sturdy indoor jungle gym playing ship. This ship has people on it but even more important is the fact that it has cows. And the most distinguishing characteristic of a cow, according to the actions of the children, is the deep but rather loud mooing. As the mooing improves with practice it also becomes too noisy and Mrs. Bascom approaches the cattle ship cheerfully. Since the group has gone on a farm trip a week ago, she is glad to see them play-

73

ing cows. "Good, but how much do cows really moo?" The children, who
have good observation and memory, admit that the cows at the farm did
not moo much. Satisfied, the teacher leaves them. After a short while
however, the cows again moo with unrestrained and noticeable frequency.
Perhaps even the few moos which the children heard for the first time
emanating suddenly from the throat of a silent, stationary cow clamped in
a stanchion seemed more noisy and important than it really was for these
city children. And in their play the children reflect their feeling and impression of the mooing rather than the bare facts.

Hearing the noise Mrs. Bascom once again comes over to remind
the children that the cows really did not moo much on the farm.

"But this is a *ship*," answers a little boy, defending and explaining
the cows' distressing mooing.

"But what else do cows do?" the teacher prods. She believes it
proper at this time to bring in a discussion of cows and to add scientific
content to the game.

"They milk," respond the children. Whether "milk" means independent action on the part of cows or passive service is not clear.

Left alone again, the children continue playing cows aboard ship
but in a quieter manner, since they are now milking, as can be gathered
by the stage asides, vague squatting postures, and manual motions intended to symbolize this procedure. Before long it becomes apparent that
the bulls are getting as much milking as the cows. The teacher hears this
and calls the entire crew and cattle to attention. "Just a minute, children;
do you know what bulls are?"

"A bull is a daddy," a child answers.

"Right! And do daddies give milk?" These bright, articulate five-
year-olds who talk so easily with their teacher are now at a loss for an
answer.

"Well," the teacher persists, "does your daddy give milk?"

"Yes," one little boy answers in a straightforward manner. "My
daddy gets milk, too," says another child with complete assurance. The
teacher immediately corrects the children's misinformation by saying,
"No, only mommies give milk." In her eagerness to inform and give scientific facts she fails to hear what the children are saying and thinking.
These modern five-year-olds have of course seen daddies giving milk;
they have given a bottle to the baby or a glass to the child, and they have
been observed to get milk from the store or the refrigerator. They are
clearly not thinking of lactation and breast milk as Mrs. Bascom is. Neither the children nor the teacher however, seem unhappy about it. The
children have no difficulty leaving the game for an efficient and satisfying
clean-up period, then going over to a quiet, library period, and finally
coming to the news time and show-and-tell.

They all slide smoothly into a circle on the floor, facing Mrs. Bascom who has a friendly and interested expression in her face and manner. After three children have a turn telling personal news and showing attractive objects they have brought, the teacher has a turn. She recalls the earlier game of cows and the children's trip to the farm, and in this connection holds up a clear picture in a book, showing a cow family with bull and calf. The children point to the similarities in looks of each member of the family and one child says, "On our ship we had a grandpa and a daddy bull." The teacher acknowledges this with a nod and then tells the children about cows giving milk, pointing to a picture of a cow's udder. Continuing with the subject of biology the teacher asks the children, "And what makes good milk?" One child answers promptly, "A lot of cream makes good milk!" This time the teacher tries to clarify her question by changing the wording: "What does a cow have to *do* to make good milk?" The answer this time is, "Eat grass." This pleases the teacher. But does Mrs. Bascom herself know how grass makes good milk? Do the children really understand it? Is the success of a science lesson determined by the children's repetition of the teacher's answer to the teacher's question?

CHILDREN LEARN FROM EXPERIENCE

Preschool children do not gain concepts primarily by following a teacher's thinking and by answering a teacher's questions. A child may observe, handle, and use ice many times during a school year before knowing that water will become ice when frozen and that melting ice will produce water. A four-year-old saying that a cup of melted ice contained "ice juice" meant it without trying to be cute. The logic of his experience told him that if orange juice comes from oranges, ice juice comes from ice; as far as he could see water comes from the faucet and has no connection with ice. To build a generalized *concept* of the propensity of water to freeze and melt, there must be many physical contacts, related experiences, thinking and expression, and sharing all this with others. Being told the facts is not always enough. Furthermore science concepts in early childhood are gained gradually, over a long period of time and through repeated and related experiences. This point is well brought out by John G. Navarra.[1] Presenting and discussing a case study of a preschool child, Dr. Navarra shows the gradualness of concept formation which involves various irregular stages of limited comprehension, erroneous thinking, acquisition of reliable knowledge, and finally expression of scientific principles.

[1] John G. Navarra, *The Development of Scientific Concepts* (New York, Columbia University Press, 1955).

FACTS AND CONCEPTS ARE LEARNED DIFFERENTLY

The confusion in teachers' minds lies in their mistaking *facts* for *concepts*. Traditional schooling has been based for centuries on the acquisition of facts, and our present uncertainty about how to teach concepts is understandable. Yet facts unrelated to each other or to general principles become isolated items that by themselves may not lead to thinking at all. Science learning and especially scientific thinking are heavily dependent on the understanding of concepts. Facts are included in concepts but they are not the same. Let us clarify this.

A fact is a statement which is regarded as true, accurate, final, and therefore unchangeable. The sun rose at 5:32 is a fact; the rising of the sun is a concept. Two and two make four is a fact; addition is a concept. A fact is unitary but a concept is an abstraction, formed out of the essentially common features of a class of objects, events or situations, which may even appear dissimilar. Sometimes a concept is close to the phenomenon represented, as in the example of the rising sun. Sometimes concepts are difficult to relate to the concrete world, as the concepts of morality, dependency, democracy. A concept is not necessarily accurate, final, or even true. A concept is flexible and subject to change. It also depends on facts, and for a young child, pretty much on observed events in the concrete world. But although facts and concepts are interrelated and interdependent, they are not the same and are not taught in the same way.

Any child can be taught facts if he can memorize. Enough repetition fixes the fact; nonuse over time causes him to forget the fact. How many dates do you remember from history? How many names of capital cities do you remember from geography? How many labels on rocks and plants do you recall from geology and botany? Names and dates are facts.

But if you study the causes behind the actions on a certain date, that is conceptual; if you know why a city arose at a certain spot, that is conceptual. The nature of plant growth, the possibility of change in rock formation, these too are conceptual. For all of us, but for children especially, facts make sense when they are related to a concept, a principle, an idea. Concepts in turn are enriched and broadened by facts.

In teaching science it is all too easy to state the facts and expect them to be remembered. Facts by themselves, unrelated to others, unclassified and uncompared, need the larger perspective implied in a corresponding concept if they are to serve a scientific purpose. Thus, before the children in Mrs. Bascom's class could understand the cause-and-effect relationship between the ingestion of grass and the producing of milk, they would have to understand the concept of chemical change, the relation between female physiology and milk production, and the relation between nutrition and functioning of the mammary glands. Obviously as words these are beyond a child. Adults are not necessarily too clear about these relationships either. Yet we go on repeating "cows need grass to make good milk."

Some things have to be taken on faith by children and learned by rote. But there must be a conscious effort to keep such rote learning to a minimum, especially in science, if a love and appreciation of the significance of science in our lives is to result. Children learn best by concrete and firsthand experience. With a little thought a teacher can develop concrete application of a surprising number of scientific concepts, such as the relation of parts to the whole, as in the human body; the transforming of matter from one physical state to another, as in ice and water; the relation of speed of an object in motion to the surface on which it travels. Let us take as an illustration the scientific concept of change which may seem remote and abstract. Yet one teacher recognized the concept itself when an unexpected occurrence in her classroom made it possible for the children to draw the desired conclusion themselves.

ABSTRACT CONCEPTS ARE LEARNED THROUGH CONCRETE EXPERIENCE

A bottle of milk left over from snack time in a kindergarten class was discovered on the sunny windowsill the next morning. The teacher told the children that the milk was not fresh any more for drinking. "Let's see it 'not fresh'," said one child. The teacher poured some milk into a bowl but the child could not tell that this milk was different by either looking at it or smelling it. Another child volunteered to taste it; the teacher did too, pronouncing it "a little bit sour." She might have left it at that but instead she put the bottle with spoiled milk back on the windowsill to really become sour and thick, "so we can make cheese from it."

"Cheese?" This did not make much sense to the children, as they could not visualize without previous experience how liquid milk could possibly change into soft but solid cheese. Many of the children were curious enough to make sure an adequate sign was placed on the souring milk bottle to protect it from being thrown out by another class or by the cleaning man. In a few days distinct curds appeared in the milk and a distinct and repellent odor emanated from the bottle when the lid was removed. Practically all the children were curious to see the sour milk and to observe any evidence of cheese, although none of them really expected anything the least bit edible to come from it.

"Smell it—pe-euw!"

"I'm not going to eat that!"

"Me neither."

The teacher had made cheese with such city-bred children before and this was the reaction that she anticipated. But she also counted on these four to five-year-olds' genuine interest in the origins of familiar things. Does cheese really come from milk? How? They would see, she promised them. She then heated the lumpy soured milk to complete the curds and whey separation, and provided a cheesecloth bag for draining off the whey. The children were surprised at the name "cheesecloth." (Some of them identified the cloth as polishing cloth). Several brave children followed the teacher's example and drank some whey; they said it was a little like lemonade. The mechanical process of squeezing the cheese bag between boards, finding heavy objects to facilitate the squeezing (blocks, stones, and filled cannisters) and obtaining appropriate receptacles for collecting the whey drainage was fascinating to all the children. There was, of course, constant curiosity to *see* if the curds had already turned to cheese. When in about an hour and a half the cheese bag was emptied into a bowl and the children took turns stirring it with a little seasoning and salt and a touch of cream, everyone was curious to taste it. When the cheese was served on crackers with a dot of red jelly it was a proven success. Even those children who did not want to eat it because they had remembered the smell of the soured milk or because they felt hesitant about any strange food were interested in the whole process and enjoyed vicariously the other children's pleasure in eating. When later in the year a new student-teacher in that class remarked, "Don't shake the milk when you are carrying it—it might turn to cream," the children who heard her answered: "Oh, no. Milk doesn't turn to cream. Milk turns to cheese after you keep it on the warm window."

Change in taste, change in shape, change in substance, change in color, and change in volume can be carefully observed by children in their concrete forms. A quart of hardly-moist, firm, leafy spinach, when cooked a few minutes in a glass pot, can diminish to a cupful of juicy, limp pulp before the children's eyes. And children see that heat releases water from broken vegetable fibers. Conversely a cupful of rice will swell to a potful when cooked with water. And here children see that heat causes expansion. Seeing a dripping wet shirt become perfectly dry hanging on a line in the sunshine is good preparation for children's learning the concept of evaporation later. Sometimes children make note of these things themselves; sometimes phenomena need focusing. Maggie, watching a crayon on the warm radiator cover, may have to be helped to see the cause of its gradual change from a hard cylindrical crayon to a soft shapeless thing, and finally to a colored liquid. A discarded apple section observed to change from white to brown may lead to curious questioning. How did it happen? Why? Would any apple change in color? In the refrigerator? If you cover it up would it still change? Questioning is a first step to exploration and exploration is the true basis of scientific learning. We might say that any concept which can be illustrated in concrete terms can be understood by a child.

Some concepts however, cannot be made concrete. Government, democracy, liberty, are among these, and it is not until long after kindergarten that children can understand such concepts. But many other concepts that seem as abstract actually can be illustrated in ways children can see, hear, touch, taste, or smell. Children are then able to generalize and draw conclusions from what they perceive through their senses.

In teaching any fact a teacher must always ask, "What concepts must the children understand in order to realize the significance of this fact?" In teaching concepts one asks, "What facts underpin and support this concept?" The above will become clearer as we illustrate the concrete experiences through which children learn.

SCIENCE LEARNING REQUIRES SKILLS OF DISCRIMINATION AND CLARIFICATION

We see then what a profound challenge there is to a kindergarten teacher who wants children to enjoy scientific knowledge. She must learn how much knowledge the children already have, help correct misconceptions, and then plan on the basis of children's interests and available sources to extend their knowledge. The variety of backgrounds and environments in kindergarten classes would make a precise guide or a specific formula much too limiting.

A first approach to science teaching is exploratory, one that says "Let us find out." A second is the one that uses children's observations to heighten their powers of discrimination and strengthen their ability to classify data. Children have a natural propensity to learn this way in any case. The teacher's job is to provide opportunities and encouragement. The following materials and activities are presented as examples from the authors' experiences and observations that convey this approach. Scientific effort in a classroom may begin with some collection of natural objects—an arrangement of autumn leaves, an assortment of acorns and nuts, a collection of rocks, or a display of differently-shaped sea shells. Feathers, birds' eggs, and seeds are some of the more unusual collections. The scientific validity of any collection in the kindergarten lies not only in the perfection of specimens or in their variety but in their meaning to children. A dazzling collection of pinned butterflies behind a glass, prepared by the teacher, is hardly better than a picture to be merely admired, a passive decoration. But a collection which children continue inspecting and handling is alive in possibilities. A box of shells brought in by one teacher was not a scientific collection in the technical sense; it was made by the teacher chiefly on the basis of eye appeal and appreciation of the shells' abundance and variety. The shells were familiar to the children, since most of them had had seaside vacations; yet gathered in an open box and brought by the teacher for the children, the shells aroused considerable interest and inspired further contributions. Several children brought additional collections and as a few children at a time played with the shells, arranging them as to size or shape, they began to differentiate them. "What kind is this purplish shell?" "A mussle," the teacher answered.

"This one looks like a saucer; I want to drink out of it," said Jill.

"Oh, I saw millions of those," said Johnny. "What do you call them? I forgot."

"Clam shells," the teacher helped out, and she permitted Jill to use them for "tea" in the housekeeping section.

"What's the name of this one? That's a beauty!" Johnny asked the teacher, showing her an intricate snail shell.

"Let me look in the book to make sure," the teacher answered.

"Let me look too. I want to see the picture." The teacher opened an old picture book, "Beachcomber Bobbie," [2] and Johnny promptly identified the picture of his shell, observing both the shape and the special "eye" design in the middle; he laid the shell directly on the picture. Three more children followed suit and picked up moon shells and scallops and clams and cockles. They were particularly impressed with the similarity between the actual starfish shell and the picture of it. For a few minutes the children used the book with studious concentration, the way one uses a laboratory manual. A great majority of the twenty-two children that year showed curiosity about the shells, sometimes pocketing a few, breaking some, or using them for dishes or as a block-building decoration. A few children referred to the pictures of shells constantly, asked about names, and inquired about the whereabouts of the former inhabitants of the shells. The teacher did not quiz these five-year-old children for names and facts. She was sure however, of the children's initial enjoyment in handling the shells, of their discerning appreciation of shapes, sizes, and colors, of the sparking of their curiosity about sea life from the tangible shells at hand,—all a good beginning toward further study at some future time in their lives.

A collection of stones can provide an analogous experience in investigation through observation, touch, and feel, and can lead to practical and intellectual inquiry. Using a heavy stone and finding out how its crushing weight cracks an especially hard black walnut, a child wants to know: "Can one stone break another stone?" And he spends considerable

[2] Florence Bourgeois, *Beachcomber Bobbie* (Garden City, N.Y., Doubleday, Doran & Company; out of print, may be available in libraries).

time testing the stone for size and weight, hardness and durability. Another child becomes fascinated with the doughnut shape of the stone in the collection and stimulates several other children to speculate on the causes of its odd shape. The teacher accepts the children's own imaginative spontaneous names for the stones, such as "potato stone" because of its shape and color, or "hand stone" because it fits especially nicely in a child's hand. This kind of naming of stones sharpens the children's direct perception.

Here is another class of suburban children, enjoying spring flowers. Dandelions in their bright abundance appeal to all the children, so they pick handsful and pocketsful and "a bouquet for my mother." At this point they are much interested in distinguishing the dandelion plant from a cluster of grass or weeds. The teacher demonstrates to the children that the tender dandelion leaves are tasty and they have a new experience in discovering an edible to be had for the mere picking (unusual indeed in modern living). Some children, though curious, are reluctant to taste the leaves, and some definitely do not like the taste. Others eat them out of interest rather than enjoyment, but the teacher does not expect a uniformity of response, and the children react freely.

When the teacher mentions that there may be some wild mustard in bloom all the children become fascinated.

"*Wild* mustard?"

"Can we eat it?"

"No, this is only the *flower* part of the plant."

"Will you pick me some?"

"Me, too."

"But you can pick it yourselves," the teacher tells them. The children look hesitant. "I'll show you where it grows," the teacher assures them. The children still look reluctant. Then Helen asks reflectively:

"Will *wild* mustard sting you?" So it is the term "wild" that is bothering these four and five-year-olds. Listening, a teacher learns what children need to know. Apparently the children are familiar with the term "wild" in its application to untamed animals and know its connotation of danger, but they do not know the term as it is used to classify uncultivated flowers and free growth.

CHILDREN ARE BIOLOGISTS

They Are Attracted to Anything Alive

A boy of four-and-a-half, playing with a can full of acorns which he has collected on the way to school, decides to poke one acorn open to see the nut inside. The teacher encourages him by advising the use of a hammer at the work bench. Instead of finding a nut inside the shell the boy finds the acorn full of soft, dry, brown matter and some small pale grubby worms.

"Look!" This is news indeed. Not only the boy who discovered the acorn worms, but everyone in the class becomes fascinated with the looks, movements, diet, and family life of the worm. Every child grabs an acorn and eagerly hammers or cracks it open looking for worms. For days the children collect acorns, excavating the worms and giving them acorn meat to eat. How disappointed Debby is when her three acorns prove empty, and she begs for a worm from "lucky" Stevie who has a "whole bunch."

"See, see, this acorn has a little hole. Here. I bet a worm lives in this acorn." Fascination with a living thing that moves and feeds and has a peculiar secret shelter is characteristic of all four to six-year-olds. They are true biologists.

Children Feel Possessive and Protective Toward Living Things

A similar excitement about finding something alive and a similar regard for a small creature is shown by a group of six-year-olds. This group of children, all of them ready for first grade in the fall, are in a play group in a city park. Peter finds a furry yellow caterpillar on a milkweed plant.

"Look what I found!" He picks it up as if it were a treasure. Immediately there is a cluster of boys and girls around Peter.

"Oh, look at the black feelers."

"Let him come on me!" Then one little girl pats the caterpillar as if it were a kitten.

"Don't. You might squash him," Peter cautions. "He needs a good twig to hold onto so he can spin a cocoon." And Peter finds a large enough forked twig. When the caterpillar is securely placed on it Peter carries the twig around. Several children follow him wanting to know, "What's the caterpillar going to eat?" "Milkweed leaves," says Peter, and adds enthusiastically to the teacher, "I saw him eating it before and I know it's milkweed because when I broke it off there was milk in the stem!"

"Where, where? Show me!" children ask eagerly and Peter shows the children the milkweed. Then he sticks some leaves on the twig for the caterpillar's meal. A little later one boy notices that a few leaves are floating in a shallow puddle. "They look like ducks swimming in the water," he says with amusement; then he gets an idea. "Hey! If I make a little boat then your caterpillar can have a boat ride in the water here. Right Peter?" Peter is concerned about the effect of wetness on his pet, but somehow a boat is constructed with scraps of wood and string and launched with the caterpillar aboard.

Children Draw Living Creatures Into Their Personal Experience

In one class the teacher accepted three yellow baby ducks for Easter as a present from a parent. She kept them partly in the classroom and partly in the adjacent yard. The children loved watching the ducks huddling together; they noticed particularly the shape of their feet and commented on the ducks' rapid growth and on how they sit and swim. As they watched the yellow-turned-white ducks in the large tub the children observed the water rolling off the ducks' backs as they splashed around; one child deliberately poured cold water on the ducks' feathered bodies to see the water rolling off. The children observed minutely as the ducks ate, drank, and excreted. They loved especially having the ducks as their own and requested that the teacher include the ducks in the attendance record as rightful members of the class. Thus, Lucky, Ducky, and Charlie provided a social experience as well as a scientific one. But when, after a month, the hygienic difficulties of caring for the animals in the confines of a city classroom became too much, the teacher gave them away to a farm in spite of the fact that this was a loss to the children and a cause for some sadness.

In another school children from several classes came in daily contact with a mother rabbit and her five tiny babies residing in a cage in the corner of the school lobby. The children noticed how at first the mother protected and concealed the babies and they were quickly convinced by the mother not to touch them. Next they saw how some of the babies "peeked around" and others hopped on big soft feet across the cage. They then noted when the rabbits were old enough and strong enough to be allowed by their mother to be taken out and to "play alone." The greatest satisfaction came a few weeks later when the rabbits were old enough to graze in the yard and to eat from the children's hands.

CHILDREN OBSERVE FACTS OF LIFE—AND DEATH— IN THE CLASSROOM

A teacher who allows the children experiences with living creatures must be prepared for consequences that may not always be pleasant but are entirely possible.

Mrs. Clark could not resist some baby chicks which were available in the local pet shop. She bought six of them and installed them in a proper wire cage. After attention to food and shelter several children had an enjoyable discussion about naming them, and finally decided upon: Chicky, Nicky, Ricky, Picky, Squeaky, and Petunia. After only two days there was an unexpected loss. One chick died, possibly from cold. After an inspection it was established that there was a draft in the classroom; after the maintenance man was consulted an electric bulb was attached to the cage to provide warmth, which the children understood was necessary for baby chicks' health. "It's a good thing the electricity works," one child observed. And with the interest in providing vital warmth for the five lively, growing chicks the death of the sixth did not arouse more than passing concern. Then another loss occurred which provided a different science lesson. Picky became droopy and would not eat. The children had watched the chicks so closely that they quickly noticed that "something is wrong with this one." This time another member of the school staff, who had had experience on a chicken farm, was consulted and her advice of isolating the sick chick so that others would not succumb was promptly followed. The next day there was intense interest in preserving the health of the four chicks and also in observing the dying chick which could no longer run or rise or take the eagerly proferred drinks of water.

Before the chick stopped breathing the children made plans for burying him. Richard took a box and put it next to the chicken to see if he would fit in it. The children on the whole were quite matter-of-fact about the death and burial of Picky. They did however, seem extra watchful and more protective towards the others than they had been before. But one emotional little girl, five-year-old Helen, was upset by the chick's death, cried a little in class, and watched the other chicks anxiously, saying frequently, "I hope *they* don't die." During that week she dreamt of another of the chicks dying and conveyed her worry to her family. The teacher was sympathetic towards Helen and assured her that the other chicks were healthy and would receive good care; she kept herself from becoming sentimental and from contributing to Helen's distress. Helen soon became particularly happy and devoted to the four chicks who grew to be fast-running young chickens and were transferred to a large enclosure outdoors. There the chickens provided endless entertainment by trying to take worms away from one another. Before the end of the year the surviving chickens were returned to the pet shop owner as originally agreed.

Were the deaths a shocking exposure to the children? And should the teacher have concealed them or at least prevented the children from observing dying animals? This teacher herself was not so shocked by the incident of infant mortality among baby chicks and she felt confident that reasonably good care was provided for the animals. It seemed to her that the natural death of an animal does provide children with important facts of life and that handling such a situation as it occurs, without denying the feeling of loss or regret, or the knowledge of pertinent facts, will provide a wholesome rather than a morbid or worrisome experience for children.

If a pair of animals is in school for a long enough time to grow, mature, and breed, this provides an opportunity for a true biological study for the kindergartners. Animal parents are both protective and destructive of their young, and children need help in assessing such behavior as it appears. A teacher must be prepared for all eventualities, ready to tackle with clarity and honesty the children's questions and observations.

Selecting "Livestock"

But how can a teacher decide what kind of animal offers most to children, or which requires the simplest care as well as scientific value?

Perhaps the general answer would be that any animal can be worthwhile if it can be safely cared for and if it evokes no revulsion on the part of the teacher. Classroom pets will invariably stimulate scientific observation and provide infinite pleasure as well. Hamsters, guinea pigs, and mice are small enough to be cared for in a cage in class and are easy to feed and clean. What is also important is that their breeding cycle is of short enough duration for a five-year-old to be able to observe it in its entirety.

Turtles are probably the most enduring of any pets, and in spite of their hardness and clumsiness seem both fascinating and endearing to children. Their slowness of locomotion, deliberateness in eating, and struggle in turning right side up invite such patient observation from the often impatient four and five-year-olds!

The children can have the satisfaction of patting or holding the animals; they can take the responsibility of giving them food and water and can observe their anatomy and particular style of family life. Of course you cannot really rely on children to carry this responsibility without some reminders and supervision. But they grow in responsibility in time and the total experience is too rich to miss.

Animals can be obtained from pet shops or laboratories. Advice and information concerning their care is usually offered in pet shops, zoos, and museums of natural history, or may be found in the library either under titles concerning the single animal or in larger volumes dealing with care of small pets.

Uninvited Guests Make Good Subjects for Study

Valuable as it is to provide particularly suitable animals to care for and to enjoy and study in the classroom, no less valuable is it to welcome or to take notice of animals that may appear uninvited.

A young, well-dressed mother brings her four-year-old Billy to school and notices with horror that Billy tries bare-handed to catch a lingering autumn fly.

"Don't you touch that dirty fly! Go wash your hands right away." She shudders and then smiles at the teacher as if to say "you are a saint to put up with children and flies," and she clicks out of the room on her high heels.

The teacher, seeing how completely fascinated Billy is with the fly, allows him to capture it and helps him place it in a jar. He feeds it, watches it wash itself, listens to its droning sound, and examines its wings. The teacher explains to Billy and the children why flies are unsanitary and objectionable. She makes it clear that they must be kept away from food and homes. Several children promptly attest to the flies' unpopularity. But, the teacher adds, in a jar at *school* a fly can be watched safely.

When a mouse appears in the waste basket the teacher at first has an impulse to dispose of it, but seeing the children's interest she transfers the animal to a cage. Soon the children name it "the little grey school mouse—because it came to school." They also observe that it is "too big to be a baby mouse . . . and it's too little to be a mommy mouse." They then conclude that just as they are children, this pet has to be "a child mouse." Furthermore, when the children watch it in a cage they quickly notice that this child mouse likes doing the same things they like doing, namely running, climbing, jumping, and eating cheese and crackers. The little grey school mouse, the child mouse, makes such an impression on the children with its agility, speed, and bright-eyed expression, that the teacher and the other staff members and parents all catch some of the children's genuine appreciation. When eventually the mouse escapes outdoors the children remember and reminisce about it the rest of the year.

Part-time Visitors Have Their Uses

Children feel enriched by acquaintance with an animal and by a certain sense of kinship that comes from caring for it. This can be true when an animal comes to the class for a much shorter time than the "child mouse," as long as the animal is in the children's midst and they have an opportunity for individual contact and spontaneous reaction and observation. When a freshly-caught green frog was brought to class and the children watched it sitting on a lily pad and met it face to face, feeling it on their hands, or on the tips of their fingers—even a week's visit was profoundly impressive. (The frog eventually escaped from an outdoor tank). "Hoppy has soft claws," Michael observed. How true, and it was independently discovered with his own sensitive little hand.

And when a neighbor's goat, Josephine, came to visit the class for only one hour practically all of the twenty children spoke about her to their incredulous parents. The animal's size in relation to the children, its manner of eating (they loved feeding it), the feel of its hide (they patted and rubbed it), the goat's face and separate features, the tail, and the detailed anatomy under the tail were not overlooked by the five-year-old investigators.

The Teacher Is Master of the Scientific Method

The value of having animals in the classroom depends very much on the teacher's own willingness and ability to take advantage of the learning possibilities which living creatures offer. Overcoming squeamishness is a major first step, but only a first step. Beyond that must be the unimpeachable honesty of genuinely scientific inquiry, which may just as often lead to unforeseen and even unexpected results as to predicted ones. Here is an account of the adventure in science that was experienced by a group of handicapped young children because their teacher brought an honest spirit of inquiry into her classroom. What happened was as amazing to the teacher as to the children.[3]

I teach in the Upper Preschool group at Lowman School. The children range in age from four-and-a-half through five-and-a-half. The group is made up of five girls and eight boys. Five of the children spend a large part of the time in wheel chairs. Eight of the children are cerebral palsied and the others have other orthopedic handicaps.

Because of their physical handicaps, many of these children have not had the opportunity to observe and enjoy the everyday things we too often take for granted. Bringing such experiences into the classroom is particularly important.

Our room is equipped with jars and small improvised cages for more than the usual number of crawling and wiggling things.

One day our attendant found two snails on the ground near the bus ramp and brought them into the room. We put them down on the floor and the children crowded around to see. With their noses close to the floor—and to the snails—they observed:

[3] Rose Engel, "Learning About Common Everyday Things: Snails," *The Journal of Nursery Education,* Vol. 16 (1960–61), No. 1.

The slowness of their movements.

The shell into which each disappeared when touched or when there was a loud noise.

The set of what looked like feelers on each side.

The mucus left as they moved along the floor.

Their habit of crawling over something rather than around it.

Even the children who usually sat in wheel chairs were placed on the floor on their stomachs so they could see for themselves. All of the youngsters touched the shell and the retractable horns but only a few wanted to touch the soft "foot" part. At the end of the period, the snails were reluctantly put into an open jar with a few leaves.

Second Day

The jar was empty! We had a "snail hunt," crawling around on our hands and knees until both snails were found, attached to the underside of the small table where the jar had been left. One of the children said, "Let's let them race again." We watched and a child said "He's a slow-poke."

I asked the children if they thought it was easy to move along that way. There were different answers of "yes" and "no."

I suggested that we find out and asked one young fellow to lie on the floor on the stomach and, without using his hands and feet, to move along the floor. Of course it was slow. Several other children wanted to try it so we had our own snail race with much wriggling and laughter and very little progress across the floor.

Third Day

On this day the Harriet Huntington Book, "Let's Go Outdoors" * was left opened to the section with pictures of snails. The children noticed the pictures when they came in.

I read the section and we looked at the pictures and the snails themselves. We talked about what they needed to stay alive and added a few drops of water to the jar. Some of the children said they would bring leaves to feed them. The findings of the first day's close examination were strengthened by the information in the book. Some of the children continued their watching and discussion among themselves. We set up a circle of chairs so neither the children nor the snails would be stepped upon by children engaged in other activities.

Fourth Day

Craig, a young fellow who is always bringing in leaves (which I suspect he has picked from the bushes near the bus ramp), brought a plastic bag with

---

* Harriet E. Huntington, *Let's Go Outdoors* (Garden City, N.Y., Doubleday & Co., Inc., 1959).

a "surprise" to share. "I brought a fresh snail," he said. The plastic bag also contained a few leaves. When I said that we had better keep the bag open, he informed me that plastic bags are dangerous and that is why he had made holes in the bag so the snail could breathe.

We came into the room and Craig went to put his snail into the jar. At this time we met two problems. The jar was empty again. The children began immediately to crawl around to look under the table and there they found our wandering pets again attached. The second problem was not so easily solved. The corner of the snail page in the Huntington reference book looked as if it had been chewed. The holes went through five pages, becoming smaller on each page.

We wondered what had caused this. One of the children suggested that perhaps one of the younger children in the morning class had chewed it. This idea was rejected by the rest of the group.

When an attendant came to pick up one of the children for therapy, the child pointed out the book damage. She asked what had happened and the children told her that we didn't know. She suggested that it might be a mouse. This idea was rejected also, as the book had been propped up on a table and the children thought no mouse would go there when the shelf holding other books was so close to the floor.

I felt sorry that the book had been damaged and put it back in the closet. Then I found another book entitled "Look" by Zhenya Gay which has a snail picture on the cover. The children watched as I turned the pages until we found the same snail picture on the inside. One of the children then set this book on the rack near the jar of snails.

Fifth Day

I was the most surprised of all when we found the new pages had been damaged in the same ways—as if they had been sandpapered. But this time there were some tell-tale glistening marks around the holes. We examined the markings and I asked the children what might have left a shining trail like that. Most of them knew that it was the snail but it seemed as incredible to me as to them that snails would eat paper.

Friday is our day to visit the library. I told the children I would look in the reference books there to see if snails were known to eat paper. In the meantime we put a cover over the jar to keep our wandering, gnawing snails out of the books—should they be the guilty ones.

While at the library I searched the encyclopedias and other references but found nothing indicating that snails eat paper.

We returned to the room still faced with the problem. In discussing the situation with the children, we came to the conclusion that we wouldn't take the chance of letting the snails out to see if they would "chew" any more books, but we could put some paper in the jar and see what might happen. So we put a sheet of regular writing paper into the jar, covered it with cardboard and left it over the weekend.

Sixth Day

On Monday we had our solution. The sheet of paper was our proof. It had a large half circle eaten away. We took out the sheet and put in a new one. While we watched we saw one snail edge its way slowly up the sheet of paper and eat a hole through the center. In a short time he had made a hole large enough that his body was all the way through and the shell section hung on the opposite side. He certainly looked odd suspended on both sides!

Seventh Day

I searched in our home encyclopedia and found a picture of a snail's mouth, highly magnified, and some information on its file-like construction. But there was no mention of the paper diet. Several of the children were interested in the picture. They also found a picture of a snail hanging over the edge of a razor. I had a cutting knife with a razor blade, used for art work.

We tried this experiment and found the foot of the snail tough enough that he could hang over the sharp edge without injury. After this there was less interest in the snail. Almost a week later, during lunch, one of the children said he was going to take his paper napkin to feed the snails. He put it into the bowl but the snail didn't seem to like it as well as the other kind of paper. The children examined the napkin later and decided that the snail had tasted it because there were a few tiny holes but it seemed to prefer writing paper.

It is now four weeks since the snails were brought to our room. They are still living in the jar on a diet of paper and a few drops of water daily. Believe it or not!

Even a very simple animal drew from children—and handicapped children at that—sustained interest, persistent inquiry, careful observation, and exciting, independent discovery. Inquiry, observation, gathering data, and formulating conclusions from evidence are clearly scientific approaches and techniques. It should be obvious that it was the teacher's interest and sensitivity that played an important part in that learning drama without in any way dominating the stage.

CHILDREN ARE NATURAL SCIENTISTS

Although children in nursery schools and kindergarten generally play with water for sensory pleasure and relaxation we shall focus here on the value of this pastime in promoting scientific inquiry. A resourceful teacher can find many ways to heighten children's appreciation of ordinary water supplies and uses and stimulate a search for knowledge. For example rain water can be collected by children in clean pails and investigated with great interest. This will bring up questions about measurement of quantity, analysis of taste, wonders about source of rain, speculation about and prediction of rain, and figuring out ways of gathering rain water. During one period of local water shortage many preschool children proved to be most conscientious about saving water when the problem was explained to them. There is also water that can be obtained from solid, stationary ice in a room. This will arouse interest and bring up questions of relative volumes of ice and of water and of measurement of temperature and effect of temperature on ice.

"Don't *touch* the ice!" Peter admonishes his classmates, "I want to see what happens." His patience in watching a glistening large sheet of ice, which he had brought in from outside, while it slowly thinned itself out into liquid, can only be compared with the patience of another child who watched an open pot of water on the stove steaming, bubbling, and finally turning into a rolling, noisy boil.

Children observe the dramatic behavior of water as it disappears as a result of evaporation, appears in drops as it condenses, and as it is transformed into ice.

There is also water pressed or mashed from soft snow that children find through play and experimentation which stimulates questions about temperature or cleanliness. And there is water discovered from a smooth shiny icicle that a child is "saving."

Let us now see a rather special experience with water. Here is a small group of bright five-year-olds from a privileged suburban community. They are in school a short afternoon session and their playing time outdoors in cold midwinter weather is brief. Inevitably several children find little islands of brittle ice on the ground. They squash it with their feet, splinter it with sticks, and characteristically pick up pieces to suck surreptitiously. The teacher smiles at the children's happy and carefree activity but suddenly wonders; they seem to take the ice so much for granted. How much do they know about ice?

"Where do you think this ice comes from?" she asks Sandy and Billy who are both chopping away at it.

"It comes from the ground," says Sandy, looking at the ice on the ground.

"It came from the cold," says Billy, feeling a piece in his hands.

"How do you get ice cubes at home?" The teacher is curious about how much children understand about cause-and-effect relationships.

"We get it from the freezer part of the refrigerator."

"From the ice cube tray."

There is no sign of recognition that ice is the same substance whether it is in large lumps in the school yard or small cubes served at the table. Nor do the children seem to see the connection between water, freezing temperature, and the formation of ice, whether caused naturally outdoors or by electricity indoors. Here then is an opportunity to help the children see the relationship.

"Let's make some ice cubes," the teacher offers. There is an immediate response and some puzzlement from the whole group.

"In the refrigerator?"

"No, outdoors. It's cold enough now." The children are more curious and puzzled.

"You need an ice cube tray," Vicki offers.

"All right. I'll bring one." And the teacher obtains an empty ice cube tray from the school kitchen.

"There is nothing in it," a child observes.

"We'll have to fill it up then," the teacher says.

"Will you fill it with ice?" Vicki asks.

"*I* won't put the ice in it . . ." the teacher cannot resist sounding a bit mysterious. "But I'll fill the tray with something. Or you can fill it."

"Fill it with water," several children say, and everybody runs inside, coming back with paper cups of water and filling all the spaces in the sectioned tray.

"Now put it in the refrigerator," says Sandy automatically. No one challenges that.

"Why in the refrigerator?" the teacher questions.

"To make ice cubes."

"Yes, the water in the tray would freeze in the refrigerator. You know that. But *it is freezing cold* outdoors. Do you want to see if there will be ice cubes in the tray after we leave it in the freezing cold, outdoors?" An enthusiastic, unanimous "yes" is followed by concern for the protection of the tray against tipping and being blown, and an appropriately heavy covering is secured.

"Will there be really ice cubes in the tray?" several children ask unbelievingly. "When? When?"

"If it doesn't get much warmer there will be ice in the tray by tomorrow," the teacher answers.

The children now watch the outdoor thermometer with serious concern. The next day when there actually are ice cubes, these sophisticated five-year-olds who speak knowingly about jet flights and space ships and dinosaurs, show astonishment and jubilation. Each child in the group reports the exciting event of making ice cubes to the parents. Several children want to make their own ice cubes and repeat it several times. There is real testing of, and inquiry about, conditions and results. Will a big and little dish of water freeze the same way? Will a rock freeze in the water? Unexpectedly, there is the discovery that ice makes objects adhere. There is repeated questioning about the time required for freezing and for unfreezing. When, on a day with thirty-five degree temperature the water in the ice tray remains liquid, the children see the connection. "It's not freezing cold to make ice."

CHILDREN ARE PHYSICAL SCIENTISTS

A subject like physics seems quite outside children's ken. Yet the common phenomena of velocity, leverage, balance, and gravity are observed and investigated by children all the time. Listen to Donald making his observations about gravity although he may never have heard the word.

"See what I've got," Donald says, digging into his bulging shirt and producing a collection of old paper plates. "What will happen if I throw them all up at once?" He does so and laughs hilariously. "Ha-ha, they fly right down! I *thought* they would."

Steven propels himself downward on a low slide devised from a long board and a saw horse. Noticing a round coffee can on the ground he picks it up and puts it on top of the slide, watching intently as the round can rolls down the full length of the board. He smiles broadly and promptly and eagerly retrieves the can, repeating and studying the downward process seriously. He also experiments with retarding and accelerating the speed by manual propulsion and by introduction of obstacles. Then he lets the can roll down, watching to see how far it will go. He is thrilled when the can rolls onto the pavement after coming down the slide and across a grassy area. When the can whirls at the end of the roll Steven watches it in motion most intently until it comes to a dead stop. Soon several other children want to roll the can down the slide and they line up for a turn at this curious activity which, besides being fun, involves investigation of velocity, inertia, speed, and space.

Or watch any two five-year-olds of different weights at opposite ends of a see-saw. Both the huskier and the lighter one will jiggle forward and back, studying the relation of weight to the distance from the fulcrum until balance is obtained or until they solve the problem by looking for a partner of the same size.

Five-year-olds love handling and using ropes, which of course requires supervision. With the addition of pails and wooden or metal pulleys, experimenting with ropes can help children understand concepts of weight, strength, force, and basic mechanics. Together with ropes, poles or trees or similar heavy secure equipment outdoors can become vehicles for studying distance and space in general. Playing with ropes, children consider ways of reaching or connecting particular areas or points.

Often, modern five-year-olds may well have more mechanical interest and aptitude than the kindergarten teacher! To provide suitable, safe, and functional mechanical items which the children can handle and operate, the teacher can employ ordinary household utensils. Manual grinders, graters, sifters, strainers and squeezers, beaters, mashers, and whisks are all fascinating to children for studying construction and mechanical operations. What is even more interesting is making some crude utensils: a funnel from paper (like a cornucopia); a strainer from a milk carton with holes on the bottom; a grater from a metal can with nail-holes rough side out; sandpaper made by spreading glue on thick paper and coating it with clean sand. And as the children show readiness or interest the teacher can bring in a silent three-minute egg timer, an exposed ticking mechanism of an old clock, and an alarm clock requiring winding. All these devices would lead to firsthand experience with the mechanical measurement of time.

Five-year-olds also love playing with magnets, electric lights, switches, bells, and buzzers, all of which can be made available by the teacher who herself understands the scientific principles and is respectful of the child's level of comprehension. A five-year-old who loves ringing an electric bell may simply enjoy pushing the button and hearing the noise. Yet some child may be ready for understanding electricity in its more complicated aspects or for exploring other areas of physical science not discussed here.

CHILDREN ARE CHEMISTS

It is a curious paradox that the modern home, a veritable display of scientific advances with its mechanical gadgets and labor-saving devices, actually deprives children of basic learning about sources of common products and of opportunities for stimulating firsthand experiences, manual and intellectual. Bottled juices, canned seasonings, packaged desserts, and frozen foods of all kinds give small children no direct and active acquaintance with the sources, processes of preparation, or even with the distinguishing characteristics of many common edibles. It would therefore be particularly valuable for kindergarten teachers to have some actual preparation of food as part of the science curriculum.

In the authors' own experience cooking provided the most valuable source of science learning on many levels and in many areas for children of all ages, but particularly for preschoolers. Cooking has an immediate appeal to all the senses; it arouses curiosity from children and invariably leads to questioning and investigation, particularly in the field of chemistry; it brings tangible results and personal and social satisfactions for many children. Cooking materials can either be purchased at nominal cost or brought by children from home.

In one four to five-year-old class the children took considerable interest in the fast-growing green carrot tops and in the winding vines of a rooting sweet potato. The teacher perceived that the children were interested in the plants not only as a biological phenomenon and a popular decoration, but that frequently they made such comments as, "Let me taste this carrot," or "My mommy bakes the sweet potato." Thus she suggested that the children bring from home different kinds of vegetables to make a vegetable soup. More than half of the children brought some fresh vegetables and there was an ample supply for a large pot of fresh vegetable soup.

Children Examine, Test, and Observe Changes in Different Materials Used

The different vegetables were weighed, washed, scrubbed with a brush, peeled (with finger nails to remove onion peels, and a safe metal peeler—not sharp knives—for carrots). Some vegetables were popped open, some were cut with butter knives and with blunt-edged scissors into slices, cubes, strips, and shreds; all were tasted and even eaten raw. The children either had never seen or heard of several common vegetables, or had no idea how a specific one felt to the touch, tasted or smelled, or even more, what was inside. No one knew for example that the large, oddly-shaped, heavy, hard, tan-and-yellow, mild-tasting Thing was a turnip.

"Turnip? Turn-up. Turn-*up*. Does it turn up?" The very name was strange and interesting and amusing. The parents were indeed incredulous when they heard their children speak of eating raw turnips.

It was a delightful surprise to find how many peas fit in a pod.

"I found five in mine! Let's see how many in *this* one."

"Eight? Let me count." Lima bean pods were found to be quite tough. "How do you open it? Show me," one boy asked after squeezing with his hand, tearing with his finger, and attempts at biting failed to fully open the lima bean pod. "Ooo, look, some are little and some are big." When the teacher cut a red beet in half a little boy exclaimed: "Look, it's bleeding." Several others echoed him and tinted their fingers. "See the blood." Other children used scissors to cut celery in small chunks, parsley into shreds, and a cabbage leaf into strips and "ribbons." One boy used his fingers to break off layers of an onion. When the teacher noticed his tears she asked: "Why are you crying?" and the boy was so intrigued by the phenomenon that he was not at all distressed by the minor irritation and continued with the onion to the amusement of the others. One child was especially challenged by the effect of onions and said daringly: "This little onion isn't going to make *me* cry." And oddly enough no tears appeared to mar his determined glance while he snipped and cut a raw onion!

Different seasonings were added with spoons and sprinkles and pinches. The soup was cooked on an electric burner. Some children were particularly interested in the cooking itself: watching the pyrex pot with the boiling broth (beef bone, water and seasoning), the globules of fat, the "dancing" of bubbles, and the appearance of color with the addition of vegetables. They observed the rising and spreading of the steam as the lid came off and talked about how hot the soup was ("so hot you couldn't touch it"). The nature of heat, the cause of heat, and the danger of heat were mentioned spontaneously by the children and picked up and clarified by the teacher. The soup was ladled, cooled, and eaten. All this took two days: one day to prepare as much as time allowed, including washing and cutting and all incidental investigation, and the other day for final additions, the cooking, and the eating. Not every child did everything of course. The two teachers designated and defined each activity: there is a technique as well as a purpose in tasting which is different from eating; seasoning requires caution and small amounts, different from pouring a pitcherful of water or dumping dozens of rolling peas. The teachers controlled quantities, guarded the necessary safety measures with respect to fire, heat, and use of utensils, and were arbiters in the division of labor.

Making vegetable soup was not a formal lesson or an official class project for the five-year-olds. The activity however, unmistakably dominated the classroom because it went on for hours with "workers" coming in shifts all during the two days. If any visitor had walked into the room he would hardly have noticed the blockbuilding, the water play, or the housekeeping play, because of the central attraction of the cooking. Yet all these other enterprises were going on. Nevertheless every child considered himself an important part of the big cooking event and shared the enthusiasm, wonder, intense curiosity, and the eager activity evident throughout the entire group. The event was important because making vegetable soup from different vegetables instead of opening a can was an unusual procedure for these modern children.

But children's personal observations and discoveries are equally impressive and important. The teacher needs to watch closely, for "discoveries" usually have to do with what seems commonplace to adults. Thus, a little girl who cut a potato was astonished that the dry potato was wet on the inside.

If the vegetable soup seems too elaborate and messy a cooking project for the average kindergarten teacher there are simpler recipes, such as applesauce, cocoa, or jelly which can be used profitably too. No matter how simple a cooking experience is it is impressive to young children.

CHILDREN ARE PHYSIOLOGISTS

What could be more familiar to a child or more important than his own body? His body with its inexhaustible source of powers and some very useful tools, and weapons when necessary, is a perfectly valid subject for scientific stimulation and knowledge. Such activities as the closing of ears to control sound reception, feeble flexing and boastful inspection of arm muscles, experimental holding of the breath and blowing of air, and deliberate tapping of fingers and pounding of feet, all test the variety of reactions possible in a child's body. The following examples might illustrate the extent of children's involvement in such activities.

Identifying and Exploring Parts of the Body

Four-year-old Michael, hearing the familiar folk song about bones (". . . shoulder bones connected to the arm bones/arm bones connected to the hand bones" etc.), became so interested in the anatomical connections and the variety of human bones that he persisted in sharing this interest with individual children, the teacher, and the whole group. He was not only interested in singing the song but in actually locating all the bones mentioned. The teacher picked up Michael's interest, learned all the words to the song herself, and sang it with the children. Thus Michael and several of his friends who caught the interest from him continued for a good part of the year to make their own kind of investigation of the various bones, the connections between the bones, and "the tough skin" covering the bones.

In the same spirit five-year-old Nancy touched the somewhat loose skin of the upper underarm of her teacher. "What's the matter with your skin, Mrs. R?" Nancy inquired. "It's too big on you. It doesn't *fit* you any more."

Although Nancy's approach was certainly not as scientific and as precise as Michael's she was nevertheless motivated by the same sense of exploration and slowly-awakening interest in the human body that is typical of kindergartners.

Discovering Body Powers

Here is an example of an experience with muscular strength. A group of children finds twigs and sticks and a limb in the yard after a storm. With the teacher's help they break the twigs and sticks, employing the strength of their arms and hands. When they fail with the muscles and strength in the upper part of the body the teacher and the children use the strength in their feet and legs. They place branches and stout sticks at a certain angle for stepping on and for snapping and breaking.

Testing the power of breath is fascinating to all children. This can be done by blowing up balloons for a party or special game or blowing up paper bags for particularly effective sound or for some experiment with paper and air power. Cooling hot food by blowing on it in a certain way and warming cold hands by a special kind of warm breathing stimulate persistent personal experimentation and discovery. The teacher's intellectual awareness, open-mindedness, and resourcefulness in response to children's manifest needs is essential if the children's curiosity and growth are to be encouraged.

Appreciation of the growth and vitality of the body through such activities as occasional measurement of height, noticing weight, or observing repeated cutting of hair and nails and the healing of cut skin and scraped knees, can lead to discussion with focus on growth and health and general good feeling about the body.

The Body as a Tool

Five-year-old Mark needed a piece of string to make a handle for some paper construction. He indicated vaguely, with the fingers of two hands, the length he wanted. The teacher complied with the child's request and then thought about the children's interest in measurement. At first she was going to bring out a ruler and introduce a scientific, reliable way of measuring, but decided instead to try a more primitive way. She believed that measuring by arm's length would be more meaningful to children at this level. When Mark asked for another piece of string the teacher said, "Let me measure you an arm's length" and she measured out the string against the full length of her stretched arms and chest. Immediately other children found need for string and requested a precise measure. Mark was delighted to obtain a sizeable length of string measured out against his own two arms and chest. Most of the boys and girls in the class were very much impressed with the dimensions of their arm's spread and some noted its relation to the person's height. Some commented on conditions to insure uniformity of measure and one child detected a way of possible "cheating." The entire concept and the practice of such measurement was completely new to these modern children, yet they were clearly ready to try it and enjoy it since it meant use of their own bodies.

The same children showed a similar response when the teacher showed them how to cup their hands to make a water receptacle when they were washing their hands outdoors, and the teacher poured water out of a pitcher into each child's hands. They all practiced diligently until each one was able to make a fairly leak-proof hand-cup, and to make most use of the rationed water.

CHILDREN ARE INTERESTED IN BODY PROCESSES

Unlike adults, children observe various parts of the body and the body products quite uninhibitedly and objectively. This is a typical observation of a five-year-old: [4] "How funny! I drink milk and water and cocoa and tea; but all that comes out of me is tea." Such observations sometimes lead to other than scientific investigation.

Fives are not too far away from the babyhood years of undifferentiated responses to the environment. Nor have they yet learned completely that some subjects are not generally suitable for public discussion. While the kindergarten teacher will want to help them become discreet in their expressions, she will not want to encourage prudery or squelch normal healthy interest. Sometimes a group of fives shows exaggerated interest in excretion, to the point of embarassing teacher and visitors, and more importantly, of diverting themselves from constructive activity. Such a high pitch of excitement over body processes generally means overstimulation growing out of unsatisfied curiosity or exaggerated concern. A down-to-earth discussion and answering of questions matter-of-factly often brings about a change in perspective.

Children Learn Through Bodily Senses

Recognizing five-year-olds' keen sensory equipment, a teacher can take full advantage of opportunities that allow children to make use of sensory perceptions. There can be simple blindfold games requiring recognition of objects by smell, taste, or hearing alone. Children show surprise in hearing the difference in the sound of tearing paper and tearing cloth, in the distinct odor of pine wood, and in the unique taste of raw potato. Special boxes with materials can be provided to stimulate children's investigations of textures and surfaces through tactile perception. Perceiving metallic hardness, textile roughness, plant smoothness, or animal softness by instinctive fingering on the part of a child can lead him not only to heightened sensory perception but to stimulation of artistic and intellectual perception.

[4] Kornei Chukovsky, *From Two To Five* (Berkeley, University of California Press, 1963).

CHILDREN ARE BOTANISTS

Plants usually appear on the kindergarten windowsill to add color and attractiveness to the room. Yet geared to the natural interests of five-year-olds, plants may offer more than mere decoration if handled with understanding. But this is something which some teachers fail to do.

I'll Do It For You

Mrs. Meyer is very fond of plants. She comes to school earlier than the prescribed time so she can personally inspect the buds on the geranium, remove the dry leaves from the sweet potato, and water the tall, branching avocado plant. Later she tells the children that she has already watered the plants and that they can do other work. Now and then Mrs. Meyer asks them with real pride, "Isn't the avocado plant growing beautifully?" or "Doesn't the geranium look gorgeous?" She takes the plants home with her during vacation and in school she often consults other teachers and parents about the plants.

Do It My Way

Next door Miss Campbell is deliberately trying to fit a scientific study of plants into her program. She has planned a discussion and the children are already seated facing her on the floor, waiting for her instructions and questions.

"Now children, you know what our center of interest is," she begins in a friendly manner. "So what then are we supposed to be talking about?"

"Flowers!" Donald offers the precise answer.

"Now what kind of flowers?" she again questions academically. There are many answers and each time the teacher asks "what color?" One girl contributes more than the teacher asked for.

"My mother was sick and she got tulips." The teacher nods to that. Another girl adds: "I saw some flowers on the way to school."

"What kind?" the teacher asks in a prodding tone. The child hesitates. Is she trying to remember what she saw, or is she figuring out what the teacher expects her to answer?

"Uh, . . . daffodils."

"That's right, Mary; daffodils are out now. What color were they?"

"Uh . . . red!" Mary exclaims. But the teacher shakes her head and corrects her.

"No, daffodils are not red; tulips are red." Then the teacher summarizes the discussion: "Tulips and daffodils are all *flowers* and that's our center of interest."

Watch Me Closely

Miss Sobel however, made definite plans for planting a real garden with and for her kindergarten class. She had discussed this garden project with the children on several occasions. The day of the planting she checked on the children's readiness.

"What will we have to do first?" she asked. The children knew about digging up the ground, and answered, "Turn the soil over." The garden had already been plowed and the children knew about raking the ground smooth, gesticulating appropriately as they spoke of it.

"And then we sprinkle seeds in the little ditch," explained Janet, making delicate dancing finger movements to express sprinkling. The teacher saw that the class was prepared for the activity, and collecting tools and seeds she conducted the group to the garden area beyond the playground. The children waited by the wire fence while the teacher inspected the garden. She then explained to them that because of rain the previous night the ground was unusually wet and that therefore she would rake the soil and plant the seeds herself. She instructed the children to stand and watch her. They could be in the garden area but Miss Sobel cautioned them to step only on the paved space so they would not get their shoes muddy.

It was a beautiful warm day with the ground just the right wetness for planting, and the children's eager hands waiting to do it. They were anxious to finger and manipulate the dark, soft, crumbly, clingy, wet garden earth. Apparently the teacher was unaware of such needs in children. She herself dutifully raked the ground and did not give them a chance either to enjoy that activity or to feel that good soil. As she was raking Miss Sobel explained about the ditch she was making. She deliberately called the ditch a furrow and several children repeated "furrow" with interest.

Then she took a handful of corn seed and said, "Watch. I am going to drop the seeds now."

As an afterthought Miss Sobel handed each child a kernel of corn while she herself planted the corn seed. The children held the corn kernels somewhat self-consciously and crowded tightly on the edge of the garden where the teacher was doing all the work and keeping an eye on their behavior. Because they were either pushed in the crowding or could not resist the temptation, two children from the group of thirty managed to step on the soil. They were told to stand outside the garden area.

Later Miss Sobel explained to a colleague that the children would have been disappointed if the planting had been postponed because of the wet ground, and that they could still see *her* planting very well. She concluded that they had learned a great deal from their garden project, and they had also learned the word "furrow."

Let's Do It Together

In order for children really to learn from gardening they must feel that it is *their* garden; that they use their ideas and choices, discover texture and shape, and hardness and softness with their own hands.

Mark asks his teacher about planting in school as a result of the story *The Two Little Gardeners*.[5] The teacher, Miss d'Angelo, suggests that the children bring some seeds to school. The next day she is deluged with children's contributions of seeds—seeds in fancy packages, slippery pits from fruit, seeds clustered in matted fibers of the interior of a pumpkin, and a pocketful of capped pointy acorns. And the children, who have talked about and seen and done planting before in the class and at home, show concern with the moisture and soil and sun. Then Mark declares he wants to plant a potato seed. At the teacher's suggestion he brings an entire potato, cuts a chunk, feels the bumpy potential sprouts, and stuffs it into the soil of a deep flower pot. Mark is possessive about the potato. He waters it, looks at it frequently, and tells children and adults confidently that the small piece of potato will grow. Happily enough a tall leafy plant does come up and after a while delicate purplish blossoms emerge. Then the stalks sprawl and seem to weaken and wither. Mark worries; he peeks to see the roots and makes an exciting discovery of the recognizable grape-size potatoes. Mark looks on with a sense of pride and even a touch of wisdom. "My potato did grow."

At the teacher's suggestion the potato crop is allowed to mature further. Mark is so excited about the phenomenon of invisible, underground growth that he advises his father to pull up a sturdy grapefruit plant to look for grapefruits among the roots!

Mark is actually the only one who is so involved and impressed with the potato, but the other children are all aware and interested and therefore share the experience. Mark's enthusiasm, his genuine intellectual curiosity, and his independent observations naturally stimulate the children and constitute science learning by contagion, which can be the most effective kind of all. Although Mark's project was rather individual the quality of his experience can occur in a group project too. Miss Birch brings in a package of string bean seeds. "We will plant them in our new window box," she tells the class.

[5] Margaret Wise Brown, *The Two Little Gardeners* (New York, Little Golden Book, Simon and Schuster, Inc.; out of print).

"Yes! Our new window box!" the children chant.

"I know where it is," one child offers. "I saw it in the closet." The large empty window box promptly appears on the table. Miss Birch throws the sealed package into it and about ten children surround the table to take part.

"What's in the package?" some children ask, and some answer, looking at the picture, "String beans." The teacher asks Candy to tear open the package and the children rush to pick up a hard white bean.

"These are not string beans. String beans are long and green."

"These are seed beans," the teacher points out.

"Can we eat them?" one child asks, and another promptly bites into a bean and ejects it, making a wry face.

"We could cook these beans and then eat them, but we will plant these seed beans in soil," the teacher explains. "And after they grow they'll be plants with string beans like those in the picture."

"Let's plant them!" the children say. Practically the whole class of twenty-one children is around the table by this time. The teacher lets five children at a time go out with shovels, empty milk cartons, and coffee cans and bring in dark soft soil. Some fifteen children have a chance to experiment with the soil in the window box. Some children pat it down, making hand impressions, others fluff and raise the soil, still others sift it through their fingers. They moisten the soil, thumb holes, drop a bean in a hole, cover the seed gently, and then water their garden as a final touch to planting. Every one of the children looks curiously at the solid smooth dark soil and the picture of string beans which a child has taped to the box at the teacher's instruction. There is an enigmatic expression on their faces.

"Can we see it grow?"

"After a while," the teacher answers. "The sunshine through the window here and the moisture from your watering will help the beans to grow; and in about a week you'll see some green sprouts come out from the dark earth."

The passage of time defies the children's comprehension and tries their patience. Every day they enumerate and name the days of the week, and every day they ask to see the beans grow. The teacher allows them to uncover one or two concealed mysterious seeds and they are impressed to see that they have changed. They continue watering the window box abundantly and watching the seeds' slow sprouting and the plant's gradual growing. They are observant of the changes that come with growing, the emergence of the blossoms, and finally the plant's bearing of scrawny pods.

"Look! *Now* there is a bean pod," Candy is the first to notice.

The biological fact of the forceful action of a quiet little seed as **it** pushes, expands, changes, and produces fruit takes on some meaning for the children.

"These are real string beans. Taste them . . . they came from the seeds that were in the package. We planted them." So the children have a harvest feast; they cook and eat their beans. They experience tangible proof of the intangible progress of the seed from the nourishing earth to the hungry mouth.

WHAT ELSE IS SCIENCE?

Don't kindergarten children ask questions on space travel and satellite orbit? Of course. Even three and four-year-old children talk about hydrogen bombs, men in space, and planned (as well as executed) trips to the moon. But such *talk* on the part of young children represents neither true readiness for a body of abstract knowledge nor ability to absorb technical information through words alone. The teacher will of course want to share the important news of scientific advances with the children, but more to include them in the adult community than to teach them science. Such news has immediate excitement and attraction for children, whether it involves medical discovery, mechanical invention, or space exploration.

But young children do not have the background of underlying facts and concepts for genuine understanding. Even the kindergarten teacher herself is not required to understand the engineering intricacies of a satellite's ascent or descent or the mathematical formulas for speed of planets in order to advance the kindergartner's scientific development. But she must indicate to the children that man does indeed have answers to many questions and that there also are an infinite number yet unanswered. What is particularly important for the teacher to realize is that she must herself appreciate and think about science. Above all she must maintain her own curiosity and courage to find out. She must exert effort to look up information and obtain materials. It is always best if a teacher has some firsthand knowledge, whether it be with baking pancakes, feeding ducks, lighting a bunsen burner, or testing for density of rocks. And she needs to understand that there must be tangible materials and experiences for the children so they can study them for themselves. The children must know the firsthand joy of all explorers and discoverers.

Herbert S. Zim [6] explains that "the approach to elementary science education advocated from our consideration of the nature of science and the child *lays more stress on the attitudes* and aptitudes it develops in the child than on the content learned . . . The development of attitudes

---

[6] Herbert S. Zim, *Science for Children and Teachers* (Washington, D.C., Association for Childhood Education, 1953), p. 8.

involves continued participation . . . if children are to develop scientific attitudes they must have *personal* science experiences. Furthermore these must be enjoyable experiences."

The world renowned scientist, the late Albert Einstein, made the observation that young children engage in thinking and investigation that are truly scientific and that the fresh naïve approach of children and their strong curiosity are the same as those on the part of great scientists. Dr. D. W. Bronk, President of the National Academy of Sciences, deplored the prevalent practice of discouraging the development of that curiosity and contended that "only the exceptional parent welcomes it in his child instead of thwarting it as a threat to his peace of mind [and] only the wisest teachers foster it (curiosity) in their students." [7]

What then is the legitimate scope of science in the kindergarten? And what is the teacher's role? Science learning enters into all the children's activities. The teacher must be constantly aware of the many opportunities that exist in the most commonplace ordinary experiences of life. The teacher must use the children's natural affinity for observation to develop keener powers of discrimination and comparison. She must help children formulate hypotheses about things they wonder about naturally and must make it possible, by planned experimentation or by logically expanding experience, for them to test the accuracy of their hypotheses. She must utilize both the firsthand knowledge with which they come to school and the further firsthand knowledge she introduces, as a basis for generalization and classification. She need not be afraid of technically precise language but she must guard against using words as a screen that conceals true understanding of the concepts involved. Sensitive to children's interests and to the concrete character of children's learning, a world of challenge and stimulation is open to her and the children for truly scientific exploration.

[7] *New York Times*, Science Meeting Report (Jan. 10, 1958), p. 342.

Bibliography

Blough, Glenn O., and Campbell, Marjorie H., *Making and Using Classroom Science Materials in the Elementary School* (New York, Dryden Press, 1954).

Bourgeois, Florence, *Beachcomber Bobbie* (Garden City, N.Y., Doubleday, Doran, & Company. (Out of print; may be available in libraries.)

Bronk, D. W., *New York Times* (Jan. 10, 1958), p. 342.

Brown, Margaret Wise, *The Two Little Gardeners* (New York, Little Golden Book, Simon and Schuster, Inc.; out of print).

Chukovsky, Kornei, *From Two to Five* (Berkeley, University of California Press, 1963).

Clemons, Elizabeth, *Shells Are Where You Find Them*, illus. Joe Gault (New York, Alfred A. Knopf, Inc., 1960).

Craig, Gerald S., *Science for the Elementary School Teacher* (Boston, Ginn & Company, 1947).

Engel, Rose, "Learning About Common Everyday Things: Snails," *The Journal of Nursery Education*, Vol. 16 (1960–61), No. 1.

Freidman, David Belais, and others, *Water, Sand and Mud As Play Materials* (The Journal of Nursery Education, 155 E. Ohio St., Chicago 11, Ill.).

Hochman, Vivienne, and Greenwald, Mildred, *Science Experiences in Early Childhood Education* (New York, Bank St. College, 69 Bank Street).

Huntington, Harriet E., *Let's Go Outdoors* (Garden City, N.Y., Doubleday & Co., Inc., 1939).

Navarra, John G., *The Development of Scientific Concepts* (New York, Columbia University Press, 1955).

New York City Board of Education, *Operation New York* (110 Livingston St., Brooklyn 1, N.Y.).

Parker, Bertha M., *Science Experiences: Elementary School* (New York, Harper & Row, Publishers, 1952).

Rudolph, Marguerita, *Toward Science* (Early Childhood Education Council of New York, South Bldg., 43 W. 4th St., New York 3, N.Y.).

Sheckles, Mary, *Building Children's Science Concepts* (New York, Bureau of Publications, Teachers College, Columbia University, 1958).

Zim, Herbert S., *Science for Children and Teacher* (New York, Association for Childhood Education, 1953).

7

Exploring the Environment

Eager-eyed and hungry for information, fives stop to stare at everything on their way to and from school as though trying to capture the essence of the civilization that surrounds them. Inside the classroom fives dramatize signs of the outside world in their persons, in the peaked caps of the boys, and the swinging pocketbooks of the girls. During a work period their spontaneous conversation is concerned with people and materials in the environment they know. They are very conscious of the world beyond themselves and seek to unravel its mysterious doings all the time.

Fives are constantly seeking answers to the question *"How?"* "How does it work?" "How did it get there?" "How do you know?" Some of the answers they uncover by themselves, some come to them through television, and some are given by parents. The haphazard character of finding answers is considerably decreased in the kindergarten classroom, where the teacher consciously answers children's questions, reads them a story that gives answers, shows them a picture, or takes them to see the actual thing or person they are curious about.

A good kindergarten curriculum inevitably makes wanted or needed information accessible to children. Although the best way to do this is by offering opportunity for firsthand investigation, this is not always possible or always necessary, and vicarious experience must be substituted. In either case any source of information to which a teacher deliberately exposes children must be simple, clear, and of course, accurate. Firsthand experiences in gathering information, such as trips and personal contacts, or vicarious experiences such as pictures and books, must be carefully chosen and developed so that they are completely comprehensible. Otherwise these sources will not prove useful in the special learning style typical of young children described in the chapter on play. Children must be able to pinpoint details, apply the knowledge which they learned in their play, and deepen their understanding through exchange with others.

TRIPS HAVE AN IMPORTANT PLACE IN ANY KINDERGARTEN CURRICULUM

As children leave the classroom to see the actual processes by which workers perform their tasks and as they recognize the distinctive uniforms or other marks of a trade, they use in their play the bits and pieces they pick up, digesting, assimilating, and raising further questions once they understand simple beginnings. The more obvious the nature of a person's performance the more dramatically fascinating it is to a young child. Imitable, it therefore can become comprehensible. This is why kindergarten children pretend to be garbage collectors, mechanics, bus drivers, or nurses rather than lawyers, judges, or accountants. From the nature of the play a teacher can gauge how much children actually understand, and she can plan for further intake experience which leads to further dramatization through play and thus to an increasing comprehension of the world.

CHILDREN'S INTERESTS ARE A STARTING POINT IN PLANNING TRIPS

The first thing that concerns the teacher in planning trips is the range of children's interests and preoccupations. She needs some evidence to show her which things the children themselves might want to know, and which they would enjoy if their attention was attracted.

A teacher learns to know this about her group by listening and watching. The children's comments and questions offer direct leads to possibilities for further exploration. But these direct comments and questions point only to areas children are articulate about. Dramatic play offers less direct but equally potent clues to children's interests, degree of knowledge, and concerns. Together, the direct and indirect expression serve as prolific sources of ideas for curriculum enhancement through trips or similar projects. Groups differ of course in the number and quality of their interests. Sometimes a teacher quite deliberately takes the lead of the more advanced children as a starting point for pursuit of knowledge. Sometimes she may cater to two or three dominant interests in turn. Since kindergartners are not usually likely to remain vitally interested in one topic (boats, trains, rodeo, farm, zoo, firemen) for more than one week, it is possible to enlarge their horizons in many directions.

Since we are suggesting that kindergarten curriculum should be influenced in large part by children's interests and needs, we should like to consider here one added factor in their growth that affects these. This is the newly-learned sex roles that tend to divide five-year-olds into areas of interest that society dubs masculine or feminine.

Teachers will find that in many communities the girls only play "house," while boys act out "manly" occupations. But society's concept of what is masculine and what is feminine is changing, and often boys and girls will play house together and share several hitherto masculine roles. A group of student-teachers who took an informal survey of kindergarten children's interests found that most of the girls they saw did in fact confine themselves to domestic roles and to such feminine occupations as teacher, nurse, dancer, actress, piano player, car driver, and cowgirl. The boys participated to a limited extent in the domestic play and then covered a wide range of occupations held by men in our culture: butcher, postman, fireman, truck loader, policeman, pilot, sheriff, cowboy, builder, and plumber. Both sexes enjoyed being animals, Indians, and storekeepers. Occasionally some boys were barbecue cooks and some girls were taxi drivers or ticket ladies. The fact that the boys tend to play the more stimulating and physically active occupational roles and the girls the more limited, passive ones, does not necessarily mean that boys and girls do not share interests as a matter of course. It does mean that five-year-olds are already seeking identification for themselves in the grown-up world. They understandably ape the grown-ups of their own sex and accept without question the divisions of labor they find. But occupational divisions along sex lines are becoming less and less rigid, and today's little boys and girls are growing up into far more fluid social relationships than their grandparents or even their parents did. Girls as well as boys need to have a good deal of the same kinds of socially useful information. A teacher might well ask, "But which of these many lines of interest shall I develop?" The answer is, as many as possible. It is important however, that ideas gleaned from the children should develop further along lines of concern for society's needs and how these are met, rather than along the narrower lines of which sex does what job.

The first task of the teacher then is to know what interests, misconceptions, and misinformation her children have. The next task is to decide the best way of satisfying interests, clarifying misconceptions, and correcting misinformation. Since children do learn best from the evidence of their own senses, trips planned to allow them to see, listen, smell, and perhaps touch, become a significant means by which their horizons are extended.

TAKING A TRIP

Let us at this point accompany a class on a trip and see just what happens. Here is a class of four-and-a-half-year-olds, quite excited about a train trip. They are driving a short distance from school to the railroad station, buying tickets, and traveling about fifteen minutes to a familiar neighboring town. How did it come about? What made the teacher decide on this particular trip?

According to her notes Mrs. W. noticed Stevie's special interest in playing with the interlocking wooden trains and asking questions about the caboose (an intriguing word to children). The teacher's response to Stevie attracted several other children, which in turn prompted the teacher to show the class pictures of trains and of a caboose. This stimulated Donald to tell the group about his visit to the Pennsylvania Station. The interest in trains mounted over a period of days, so that the whole class was talking and thinking about trains. Donald and the teacher brought in pictures of trains which were inspected by many of the children. Songs about trains and cabooses which the teacher had selected from her music books were especially enjoyed.

Two side interests developed. There was a thoughtful group discussion about transportation in general; this is a universal concern of modern children. They mentioned and commented on various vehicles including the horse and buggy and jet plane. There was also personal talk about the way daddies go to work, in connection with which the book *Here Comes Daddy* [1] was read.

The teacher could see that something had to be done about the interest. It was logical enough for the teacher and the children to decide on an actual train trip on the Long Island Line. Before long the teacher realized that many modern children have never ridden in a train, although they may ride in cars or school buses, be familiar with taxis, and have had experience with plane travel. Some of the children in the group knew that their fathers travelled to work on the Long Island train, and this added to the incentive of the trip.

As a matter of expediency and out of consideration for the ticket

---

[1] Winifred Milins, "Here Comes Daddy," *Read To Me Story Book*, compiled by Child Study Association of America (New York, Thomas Y. Crowell Co., 1947).

seller Mrs. W. purchased all the tickets herself, but the children all watched her intently. If this had been an older group, closer to six perhaps, it would have been wise to take enough time for all or several of the children to have the experience of buying the train ticket,—to transact business with the ticket seller.

The children in Mrs. W.'s class observed the entire station with care and Joan exclaimed, looking at the telephone booth, "That's where my daddy calls my mommy to say which train he is taking."

"Where are the tracks?" Danny asked anxiously, since they were still in the station building and no tracks were visible.

Waiting on the train platform the children continued their scrutiny of the surroundings.

"I think that man is waiting for a train."

"And we are waiting for a train, too."

"There is the station."

"And there is the bridge we came over."

"When is the train coming?"

"I see the track!"

"Choo-choo-choo!"

"Do you know what all those signs are?" the teacher questioned.

"Advertisements," Joan answered immediately.

"Oh! Here comes the train!"

Now the fourteen children boarded the train excitedly and each wanted to sit by the window in order to have the double pleasure of knowing what goes on inside and not missing anything passing on the outside. Luckily the midmorning suburban train was quite empty and it was possible to accommodate the children. Through the windows they were pointing to and identifying schools, lumber yards, and parks. Then Donald shouted, "I just passed my friend's house." Whereupon Danny started looking not only for *his* friend's house, but also for his friend. He finally conceded, "My friend isn't playing out today."

The children were indeed watching, listening, and thinking about every detail of train travel. Stevie asked the teacher, "Why does a train whistle?" And he listened seriously as she explained the signal.

A group of them sitting together watched the conductor's gestures and expression delightedly as he punched tickets.

"Where are you going?" he asked the group.

"To Port Washington!" the children answered in chorus, and Madelyn asked the conductor:

"Is the next stop ours?"

When the class of small children and their two teachers arrived the conductor helped each one step off the train onto the platform, and this pleased the children greatly. As they stood on the platform they all waved heartily and smiled at him. Thus they gathered an impression of him as a real person, a specialized worker, and a representative of the responsible, orderly, safe, and fascinating grown-up world.

CHILDREN DO NOT SEE THE SAME THINGS AS ADULTS

It is hard for teachers to resist making a trip a thoroughly academic experience, telling the children in advance what to look for and pointing out the important things to see when they are actually at the site. Yet this is neither necessary nor completely effective. Children are eager learners, but they learn at their own pace what is important to them. For example, children tend to see what is on the ground, to which they are physically closer than we are; in general, they concentrate on what is at their own eye level. Children are interested in the active and dramatic; adults tend to be sober and formal. Children have a limited capacity for absorption; adults have a far wider grasp.

Given their own orientation and their unique backgrounds, they may not see at all what the more sophisticated eye of the adult recognizes as important. How often has a group of young children been taken to see something "significant," and remembered only a kitten that they played with on their way! For this reason it is wisest to let the children learn in their own style and at their own pace. If subsequent discussion or the content of the dramatic play reveals that they have missed important aspects, then the trip can be taken a second time and even a third, for the children will see more and different things each time if they are really ready to absorb what is there waiting for them.

Learning cannot be forced and real understanding has to be directed towards something a child already knows. It is better for children to learn a little at a time than to be overwhelmed with too much and anxious about pleasing the teacher as well. Fortunately the kindergarten curriculum can be largely a self-stimulating, creative experience for every class and teacher. It is entirely possible to be relaxed about the quantity children learn if the quality of experience to which they are exposed is continuously rich and appropriate.

In the following thank-you letter sent by a teacher after a trip to an agricultural school farm, the teacher expressed her feelings and included some of the children's discussion of the trip to give life and meaning to the letter. Notice the differences in what adults and children chose to stress as a result of the same trip, and the difference in their mode of expression.

Dear Mr. C.:

Our class trip to the Farm last Wednesday was enormously interesting and pleasant to *all* of us—the twenty children and the five adults, including two parents, two teachers and one student teacher. I'd like to mention some of the things that were especially impressive and were talked about. First and most impressive was Jimmy, the high school student guide whom you assigned to us. His natural enthusiasm about every aspect of farming, and his knowledge about the soil, the fields, the trees, the orchard, the planting, the harvesting, every bit of machinery and even the costs and all the agricultural timing were fascinating! He answered every question—and we were asking them all the time! His friendly way with all the small children, and his tender yet practical regard for the animals were very important to the children. The grown-ups were very impressed with Jimmy's concern with cleanliness and order on the farm.

The children certainly enjoyed coming back laden with stalks of rye, handsful of colored chicken feathers, and most especially, with the freshly laid, still warm egg which every child felt. Everybody also appreciated tasting little chunks of asparagus which Jimmy cut for us. "Tastes like raw peas," one of the children said.

The next day we were, of course, talking about the farm, and what each person liked. These were the children's comments:

"I liked the rooster best."

"I liked to see the bunny—he was sleeping."

"I liked everything on the farm," several children said.

"I liked the horses."

"Remember the horses' teeth!" (Jimmy's explanation of how *healthy* the horse Bill's teeth were in spite of the grass stains, was very interesting and amusing! Jimmy had obligingly pulled the horse's lip up so the children could see the large teeth.)

"The horse has such a long tail."

"I remember the great big tree-bush with the roots. The boys had to dig it up to plant it" (referring to a transplanting job that was in progress and which Jimmy had explained to the children).

I told the children I was going to write a letter to the farm and they said, "Tell the farmer that we are going to *eat* the egg we brought from the farm—we'll have it hardboiled and cut up in little pieces."

"You should say in the letter 'thank you for the egg!'"

They all had fun playing with the feathers, brushing and tickling each other and themselves with them. So you see that for these four and five-year-old children, who have not seen and *handled* farm products on a farm, this was a very tangible and stimulating experience. I am very glad we have taken this trip, and we are all grateful to you for your kindness and interest in having us. Please convey our thanks and cordial greetings to Jimmy.

Sincerely yours,
M. R., Teacher

A TRIP MUST SERVE A SPECIFIC PURPOSE

Despite the fact that it is common practice to take children on trips, there must be attention paid to the kind of need any trip is meant to fulfill. Obviously one major purpose for going on a trip would be to seek answers to the direct questions of how, why, what, where. There are many things which are commonplace to grown-ups but full of mystery and novelty to children, and which they would do well to see for themselves.

On the other hand children may have been so involved many times in a personal experience, such as getting a haircut or seeing the doctor, that they were too close to the situation to be objective. Taking a fresh look from the vantage point of a school trip can really broaden the perspective of a five-year-old.

A second major purpose for taking a trip is to examine the *processes* underlying many activities that are taken for granted in our lives. How is a house built? How is bread baked? How is milk bottled? How is merchandise brought to town? In our industrial civilization there are so many steps between the sources of food, clothing, and shelter and ourselves that it is not until a heavy snowstorm or a similar emergency paralyzes transportation, power lines, and communication that we get a sense of the mysterious doings behind the neat packages we buy ready-made.

A third purpose might be to see behind-the-scenes people or operations related to familiar everyday things. A fourth purpose for taking a trip is to get something needed by the class or a group of children to accomplish some special task. It may just as well be a trip to the lot for stones to weigh as a trip to the store for a pumpkin for Halloween. If needed materials and supplies are available only outside the classroom the teacher and her class go out to get what they need.

Still another reason for going on a trip, and one not to be slighted, is for fun and adventure. Learning my indeed occur but it is incidental to the initial purpose. A picnic, a walk to smell the first spring smells, a trip to the park for some good running—these are important to a program and should not be neglected. One must be sure however, that the fun envisioned is the kind young children enjoy.

COMBING THE COMMUNITY FOR SUITABLE TRIPS

Once she has decided that a particular trip can best serve the needs of a class a teacher must uncover the opportunities actually available in any given locale.

Every community and neighborhood has its resources or its special places to provide exciting trips for children. There may be a bakery with white-aproned, high-hatted workers handling stretchy dough and producing hundreds of delicious smelling loaves. Children love a trip to a bakery, especially when they can bring back a fresh sample! There may be a shoe repair shop with black-aproned men handling hundreds of worn shoes, hammering and polishing and finishing them off with the help of noisy machines. Children notice the little mounds of leather scraps and the sour leather smells pervading the shop. On such a trip perhaps one or two children can have their shoes repaired while waiting in the special booths with low doors, or the children can purchase shoeshining materials to use in class the next day.

Another kind of trip can be taken when there is road construction or pavement repairs or work on some underground pipes or cables going on within walking distance from school. A trip to such a place provides real adventure for four to six-year-olds. The children see big men with powerful tools, elaborate devices, and varied instruments, performing fascinating operations—causing hard pavements to split, the earth to open, and huge caverns to become closed. Men wearing dark goggles equipped with wires descend into mysterious depths in the midst of drowning, drilling noises and come up again safely. Heavy rocks, enormous pits, and deafening roar and clatter are all interesting, and as the children watch and ask questions, touch and hold with their own hands bits and pieces from the construction, there is a dawning of comprehension and some of the mystery is cleared.

In some neighborhoods there may be a pet shop or a veterinarian's office where special kinds of workers provide food and care, protection and cure to different kinds of animals. Other neighborhoods are near ferries or fishing activities, major highways and bridges, or a network of transportation lines. It is a good idea for the teacher to walk around the school neighborhood before the term starts to see what the possibilities are.

Within the school building itself there is much to intrigue little children and clarify impressions for them. Where is the source of the heat? Who cleans up after school and where are his supplies kept? What is a principal and where can he be found? Where are the older children's rooms and what staircases do they use for getting to their classes? All this comes under the heading of orientation to be sure, but to little children it is pure adventure, research, and discovery. And how reassuring it is when one knows what is really going on around him!

ORGANIZING A TRIP INVOLVES THOUGHTFUL PLANNING

Early in October, when Mrs. Barnes' class had been in session only a few weeks, she decided to take a trip to the produce market to purchase pumpkins. Her concern was to have the classroom look ready for Halloween and to get a head start on her year's curriculum, which included a number of trips. "It is nice weather now, and I have parents to help me, so I am taking a class trip early," she reasoned. But although there were three adults to supervise the trip, walking six long blocks each way in a crowd (eighteen preschool children is a crowd) proved to be tiring and distracting. Since this was early in the year the children did not know each other well, they were not settled as a group and they were testing each other's powers and reactions as well as the teacher's authority and patience. Scattered children in a crowded market had to be collected, guarded, and hastily steered back to school. Although some of the children noticed the variety of fruits and vegetables and commented on the size of pumpkins, the trip proved to be an ordeal for all. The major feeling of the teacher was that of relief that it was over safely. Actually all Mrs. Barnes accomplished was an errand. And the children did not accomplish much more than bringing a pumpkin from the market.

The Class Must Function as a Group
Before Trips Are Undertaken

Children enter kindergarten as many separate individuals, each with different preparation for group life and group functioning. It takes a while for them to know each others' names, for the many individuals to respond as one to a suggestion or command made to all, and for the disparate interests to merge into any one common task or goal. Yet on a trip outside the building it may become necessary to demand and expect immediate and absolute obedience if any emergency should arise. Children have to be prepared to respond to a teacher in that way even if seldom called upon to do so.

There must be a sense of belonging on the children's part that will cause them to stay together and not be drawn off into individual pursuits of their own. A kindergarten teacher in a low-income area where children are quite accustomed to independence on the streets, returned from a trip to the nearby zoo with two of the five-year-olds unaccounted for and missing. She was in tears and kept repeating, "They simply disappeared. I can't understand it." Before a general alarm could be sent out the two missing youngsters strolled blithely into their classroom. "Where were you?" the teacher, principal, and children shouted at them. The two raised their eyebrows in surprise. "We know the way home. We don't need no teacher to show us how to get back!" This degree of individualism, commendable in some ways, needs channeling before so responsible a group action as going somewhere together can be undertaken. Children who have shifted considerably for themselves find it hard to learn group controls. On the other hand overprotected children may be afraid to try anything so new as an excursion away from the familiar classroom. Since groups differ so, a teacher has to look for the telltale signs in daily living that reveal enough cohesion for a trip. Are the routines fairly well carried out by most of the children? Is there communication between teacher and class so that she really feels she can reach them whenever she has to? Is there enough contact among the children in play so that there is something of what we grown-ups call *esprit de corps?* Only if the class has reached this level is it ready to take a trip. For some kindergartens this may be true in early October, for others not until April or May. Teachers sense when this has happened and they say, "My class has jelled. You can *do* things with them."

The Time of the Trip and the Distance From School

The attention span of kindergarten children, as we have indicated elsewhere, is not too long. On the other hand susceptibility to fatigue and overtension is high. Trips must be planned to capitalize on the best concentration period and to avoid the unpleasant aftermath of tired, overwrought children. Actual viewing time can be held safely to one half-hour except in situations that include opportunities for free running around and release from tension, or where attention is obviously keen and high. Little children have lots of growing time ahead of them and do not have to get everything in at once. A trip down the hall to see the fire extinguisher might only last seven minutes, yet be very meaningful to the children and therefore considered successful. Most walks in the neighborhood can thus be nicely managed under an hour, from the time of leaving to the time of return. If it is desirable to travel with the children and arrangements for buses or cars can be made, travel time should be no more than twenty minutes each way. Of course when one plans a picnic or a stay in the park, the time can be extended, but should include some restful activities, such as a story or quiet game.

When Are Trips Best Undertaken?

If weather conditions are suitable it is advisable to go on a trip at a time in the day when the children are fresh and rested. Obviously a trip should not be preceded by an active rhythms or game period. Since children become quite excited over the prospect of any excursion it is wise to plan to leave soon enough in the day to avoid exhaustion from sheer tension.

The Teacher Previews and Adds Final Touches to the Trip

A careful teacher knows exactly where the class will be going ahead of time, and may even make an advance visit herself. In some cases a short chat ahead of time with the people the class will see helps brief these adults on what to expect from kindergartners. Most adults are happy to welcome visiting children but some feel they owe children long involved explanations, some are afraid that the very things children enjoy most are too banal, and others worry excessively about the children getting hurt. The teacher can know better for herself what to include and what to avoid if she looks the scene over without the children present. She may also find that some hours are better for a visit by a whole class or that something special is going to occur at a certain hour. It is wise to know ahead of time if the children will have good vantage points for observation, considering their height and numbers, and where any danger spots may be. It always helps to know where the nearest bathroom facilities are since at least one child will surely have to use the bathroom.

A box of tissues and some band-aids in the teacher's purse are proven items of usefulness. With all this it is also necessary to have the parents' permission and notify the principal. Transportation arrangements must be fixed and definite well in advance. It is imperative to have more than one adult with any group of children, and safest to have three. There is always one child who needs help at a bathroom or comforting of one kind or another. There are always stragglers who need watching by an adult who brings up the rear. There may be cause to pursue a special line of inquiry that arises unexpectedly. And of course one has to keep counting heads, which is more reliably done when several do it together. Consequently efforts must be made to involve parents or older youngsters as aids. In most communities unless the mothers are working or tied down with infants there is little problem in enlisting parent assistance on trips.

Preparing the Children

The children of course have to know that they are going on a trip, although they need not know the exact date more than a few days in advance. They will have to know something of what is expected of them when they travel as a group. Interestingly enough most children have a real sense of "company manners" and are likely to be well behaved on a trip. It is desirable however, to discuss with them not only their manners ("Let's not all ask our questions at the same time.") but the safety considerations that are absolutely essential. Procedures for crossing streets, signals for starting and stopping, awareness of staying together and keeping an eye on the teacher, leaving space between people on stairs so no one gets pushed or bumped—these must be spelled out clearly. Sometimes it is even advisable to do a little acting out of how to behave on a trip. But a teacher's anxiety about the children's safety and welfare may cause her to create anxiety in the children and defeat her purposes. Therefore consideration must be given not only to the mechanics of conducting a large group but to the ways of conducting them with composure and self-assur-

ance. The question of how straight the line should look or of how strict
the maintenance of buddies and holding hands should be, becomes timely
here. To the anxious teacher, especially the inexperienced one, a compact,
orderly line of children brings security and the comfortable feeling of
having everything under control. But five-year-olds are orderly in only a
general way; it is not at all easy for them to maintain absolutely straight
lines and even spaces. They may not even be able to hold a partner's hand
consistently. Many a trip has been spoiled for the teacher and the children
by a misguided overinsistence on perfection in an area where it is impossible and not even completely necessary. The custom of the straight line
is in our tradition and is one with which most of us were brought up. But
there is a median between the absolute rigidity of a straight line, which
means a constant, unrewarding struggle, and utter chaos, which can be
unnerving and dangerous. By all means a teacher should set a standard of
group order which provides for safety and reasonable efficiency. But she
should not demand or expect army efficiency in the kindergarten.

Controls Are Necessary

The safety of the children on a trip of course calls for techniques
of handling numbers which may not be necessary in a simple one-adult-
one-child excursion. Staying together with no wandering off is a must.
Adults strategically placed at the front, middle, and end of a group can
supervise the entire group quite comfortably, especially if each adult is responsible for a small cluster of six to ten. Conversation is part of the
pleasure and value of doing something together, and children should be
permitted to talk to each other freely. However, because of the nature of
the experience it may at some point be necessary for an adult to communicate with all children at once, and here is where a teacher's original
rapport, the agreement on a preplanned signal, and the cohesion of the
group become important. It is not necessary to keep children constantly
quiet in order to have them available for a possible instruction. But they
must know what it means to stop talking and listen to the teacher when
she has something of importance to say. Instructions need to be broken
down into comprehensible units and made very specific. "When the first
people reach that lamppost we are going to stop and wait for the others."
"Hold each other's hands and do not talk at all when we cross the street."
"Does anybody have a question to ask?" Young children actually have no
idea of how to behave in large groups and no comprehension of the possible consequences of thoughtless behavior. Teachers, especially responsible ones, are often so worried about possible consequences that they
fail to enlist the children's understanding and cooperation as aids. In trying to do the whole job alone they often defeat their purposes. You can-

not go anywhere with a group of children as fast as you can go alone. Build the extra time for straggling and awkwardness into the planning; be reasonable and realistic about the demands you consider necessary and try to enjoy the trip with the children. In crossing streets you will find policemen most cooperative, but if there is not a policeman at the crossing have an adult stand out in the middle of the street to stop traffic while the children cross with the other adults. Most adults in the community, including motorists, feel protective and kindly towards little children and will not resent your expectation of help from them.

HOW MANY TRIPS DO YOU TAKE?

There is no mechanical answer to the question of how many trips are suitable for a kindergarten class. If the trips grow out of the children's needs, as we have indicated, then the number and kind of trips will be completely related to the total curriculum development. The quality and rapidity of the group's socialization which is so dependent on the maturity of the individuals in the class, will also play a part in determining how many trips can be made in the course of the school year. The backgrounds of the children are equally a determining factor, as is the availability of suitable places to visit. For example, there may be an excellent zoo not too far from school to which the children have been taken by their parents on innumerable occasions since they were toddlers. A trip to the zoo for such children would hardly have the significance it could have for another group to whom it would be a novel and eye-opening contact with animals they had so far seen only in picture books. Delightful as the zoo is, the importance of going there for the former group would lie in the sociability of the excursion, unless one followed up a specific interest aroused by a story or some dramatic play or went to focus on a specific procedure, such as the milking of the cows at a particular hour (which does occur at the Farm of the Bronx Zoo in New York). Trips have to be regarded as a teaching method and should be used when that particular method is the best one for accomplishing a curriculum goal. In chapter 12 we will discuss how neighborhood trips followed by blockbuilding resulted in a rich social studies project on an early childhood level.

THE OUTSIDE WORLD COMES IN

Another way of acquiring basic learning about the grown-up world of work can take place right in school or even in the classroom if the teacher is alert to it. The nurse who lets the children listen to the hearts of others on her stethoscope, the cook who demonstrates the enormous pots and ladles, mashers and grinders, the custodian who shares the mysteries of his separate cavernous quarters, the principal, clerks, school bus drivers, —all these people can help to interpret the world and the way it works to the youngest members of the school family.

A worker commonly in sight in a school building or a classroom is the repairman. He too is apt to be taken for granted and ignored. Yet a repairman is of great interest to children and can offer much understandable, practical knowledge about work. The children are fascinated by the jangling tools at his side and by the skill and confidence with which he uses the different tools. Jessie Stanton, the well-known specialist on preschool education, tells a story about a little boy who watched with greatest admiration a grimy plumber operating a rubber plunger. With a sense of awe and envy in his voice the little boy asked: "Mister . . . did you get that thing for Christmas?"

Most five-year-olds are more sophisticated than that, but not necessarily much more. One group of five-year-olds watched a carpenter fixing a wooden enclosure under the sink. They said this about him when he left: "A Man came. He is a Carpenter. He had a saw and an electric saw. He made lots of noise. He plugged in the plug and he buzzed so much noise, we had to close up our ears. He made a square hole." A precise account. The teacher's recognition of this stimulated the children's further observation and discussion of squareness and dimensions and depths of holes.

A man coming into a female-dominated room is indeed impressive to children, and a little teacher guidance can add significantly to the children's knowledge and appreciation of plumbers, porters, photographers, window-washers, and doctors as workers and as people.

Invited Visitors Can Make a Contribution

Sometimes a visitor to the class can provide adventure, bringing in the outside world in an importantly personal way. The visitor must of course have a significant reason for coming and the visit must bear relation to the children's interests.

When Mrs. Morrow heard the children's argument about the name of the friendly traffic policeman on the corner she suggested to the children that they invite him to visit in their class.

"Would a policeman come to our *class?*"

"Will you be scared, Jimmy?"

"What will he tell us?"

"What should we say to him?"

Mrs. Morrow had no doubt that the visit would not only be interesting but exciting. When the visitor came it was a memorable experience! Although the children had seen the policeman daily, had watched him respectfully and admiringly, and had responded to his smile, the contact had been only of a prescribed and routine nature. There in their own class, as hosts and hostesses, the children talked to him face-to-face and watched him sit on one of their small chairs and eat the same kind of cookie they were eating. They heard his manly laughter when a child asked if dogs could be put in jail and they listened to him tell them about his baby at home. They tried on the policeman's official hat and counted his shiny buttons. The most daring ones touched the holster. Mrs. Morrow was sure that this informal visit to the class of a formal guardian of law and order gave security to the children's experience within their society.

Mrs. Dillon on the other hand was not sure how to handle a visitor, and almost spoiled a valuable experience for her class. Learning that the mother of one of her children was a professional pianist, and believing it to be a wise step both for home-school relations and the cultural advancement of her class, she invited the mother to give the children a "little concert." Unfortunately Mrs. Dillon was so concerned about the children's behavior that she embarrassed the sensitive woman. Mrs. Dillon promptly called the class to attention and gave an extravagant introduction to the modest visitor. The children responded with slightly curious and self-conscious glances.

"And now, children," Mrs. Dillon stated admonishingly, "show our guest, Mrs. Genovese, how quietly you can do your work, and how quickly you can clean up so we can sit down and hear the *concert,* which I am sure you will all enjoy." The children proceeded with constrained movements and surreptitious glances at each other, but did attend to their routine tasks with unusual dispatch. With equal dispatch they settled on the floor in exact places and looked (some of them unmistakably smugly) towards the teacher, expecting praise. Mrs. Dillon did hand out words of praise and said to the visitor, "See how wonderful they are, Mrs. Genovese," as if implying of course that this was how she trained them to be. Mrs. Genovese played three short lively appealing pieces. But anxious Mrs. Dillon could not wait for the children's response. She initiated clapping at the end of each piece and made forceful comments *for* the class. "Wasn't that simply beautiful, children?" The children did not have a chance to ask questions or show their own reaction and the visitor was made uncomfortable by the ordeal of rigid politeness. She was therefore not able to communicate her special skill fully, and the whole experience was consequently of limited benefit.

Resources of a worthwhile kind are frequently available among the children's families. One kindergarten class had the benefit one year of visits from a tympanist father who brought six different drums for the

6

a science program calls for exploration and independent discovery

7

9

8

10

*often raw material for
stimulating play lies
beyond the classroom*

children to test for loudness and timbre, a ten-year-old brother who brought three snakes in a pillow case and talked about them, and an African visitor in colorful costume.

SELECTED CURRENT NEWS HAS INTEREST FOR CHILDREN

Up to now we have been considering direct firsthand experiences and contacts with people and work processes interesting to young children. But a secondhand contact can also be impressive, stimulate the imagination, and enlarge children's knowledge of their environment. Such a contact can come from occasional accounts in daily newspapers.

Here is one from a Chatham, New Jersey newspaper of Jan. 18, 1958: "Grandparents Help Teach Other People's Children." It shows photographs of a grandmother and a grandfather each helping in a class with young children. Grandmother is weaving a potholder and grandfather is adhering paper figures to a flannel board. Simplifying the adult article and sharing it with kindergartners can enlarge the children's awareness and interest in grandparents' work and worth and may result in direct contact with the grandparents of a particular class.

And here is a *New York Times* story about an incident in Perth, Scotland, with an incongruous photograph of a medium-sized horse pulling a large modern automobile; it happened when the car ran out of fuel on a lonely road and the British motorist engaged the horse.

"That's funny," the children say, looking at the clipping.

"Can a horse do that? He is a strong worker!" says Jimmy. And the children talk about horses' work and horses' virtues.

Another newspaper story about a beast of burden comes from Catskill, New York (*New York Times,* June 20, 1955). Although there are no pictures the story is quite graphic. It has to do with a mule-drawn, wooden covered wagon carrying a family of six children, and stopping at the toll gate at the end of a bridge. This stumps the toll collectors who for twenty years collected tolls only from drivers of motor vehicles! But they do collect tolls for the mules and wagon from the wagon-builder father of the family. Children hearing this story had a great deal to say about toll collection as well as many questions about making wagons and caring for mules!

If one looks for them one can find newspaper picture stories of firemen's rescues, of farmers' herds and harvests, and of people in far parts of the world producing goods for us right here. Stories of builders, hunters, fishermen, stories of big merchants and little pushcart peddlers are all quite newsworthy, authentic, and quite appropriate for young children.

PICTURES ARE A VALUABLE RESOURCE

There is another resource available to teachers for bringing stimulation and depth of interest into children's lives, and that is pictures. Every kindergarten room has wall space or separate bulletin boards on which pictorial displays can be hung. Pictures are easy to procure and no teacher should be without a classified file which she builds and can add to as the years go by. However, acquisition of pictures requires constant examination of magazines, newspapers, display material, industrial advertising, and any other source of pictorial representation generally available. Pictures must of course fulfill certain criteria to be useful. It is important that they be large and clearly printed so as to be easily "read" by young children. Naturally they must be mounted at the children's eye level. Aside from the clarity and size (9 x 12 is a good average), details must be accurate and true to life. As with trips, pictures too can serve several purposes in the kindergarten.

Pictures Are Full of Information

The first of these purposes is of course informational. This means that any picture that appeals to the general range of young children's interests or illustrates some aspect of adult work processes, has a place on the kindergarten bulletin board provided it is clear and easily comprehended. Coming after a trip, following a discussion, or put up to add meaning to some theme developed in dramatic play, such pictures bring added content into children's lives.

Children Enjoy Recognizing the Familiar

A second purpose is to give children the opportunity to recognize something familiar and known, and thus feel the glow of identifying their world. "Look, a highway!" "That lady's pushing a shopping cart like my mommy does." "There's a dog like Butch!"

Pictures Can Help Release Emotions

A third purpose is to allow children to identify with situations and scenes common to their lives, not with the pretty pictures that show only smiling, clean, good children but also the range of real experience, good and bad, known to every child. Such pictures may include the child and adult in the pleasant circumstance of storytelling or a picnic, but also the envious little fellow who watches his daddy toss the baby and is not sure he likes it; the child who successfully rides the high end of the see-saw as well as the child who lands in an ignominious lump at the foot of the slide; the child who is an eager and cooperative helper along with the child who creates a mess or breaks something; the proud child with the missing front tooth and the child in tears at the receiving end of an injection needle. Pictures put up for emotional identification free children to express the range of their feelings and often stimulate discussions in which a teacher can be very helpful and reassuring. There is much she can learn about individuals in her class as a result of reactions to pictures that capture a typical childhood experience.

Pictures Bring the Adult World Close to Children

Then of course there are the pictures illustrating some current event resounding in the environment and familiar to the children: a holiday, the new President, the man who made a unique science contribution, a snowstorm, a new store that opened in the community, or any other much talked about occurrence of which children are likely to be aware. And there are the pictures for pure aesthetic pleasure: a colorful design, a painting, a seasonal nature illustration, or anything else which is lovely in and of itself, regardless of the specific content.

In selecting pictures it is wise to be aware of the socioeconomic level and ethnic background of the characters portrayed. Children should be able to see illustrated the people and kinds of activities they know best before they are asked to learn about people and activities unfamiliar to them. Children of minority races should see similar children pictured on the walls of their classroom. A child in a slum neighborhood is not likely to respond to the illustration of a suburban child raking autumn leaves off the lawn.

Pictures Serve Special Purposes

Sometimes one acquaints children quite deliberately with peoples different from themselves in a conscious effort to foster intercultural understanding. Scenes showing the activities that are familiar but are performed by children of another race or nationality help to underline the essential oneness of humanity without discussing it verbally. There is a set of illustrations sold by Unesco of children attending school in many different countries. All are learning, all have a teacher, all are in groups. Yet some are clothed differently from Americans and some are clothed hardly at all. Some are in big buildings, some meet outdoors. Some are brown skinned, some black, some white. But all are children engaged in a common task familiar to all—going to school.

Pictures are a form of communication. Before any picture goes up on the wall a teacher should ask herself, "What does this picture say? Do I want this said to these children?"

WAYS OF HANDLING PICTURES

Pictures should be changed frequently enough so that the children do not learn to ignore the displays as part of the fixtures. Pictures can be a live and meaningful experience to children if they are thoughtfully chosen and changed regularly.

Illustrations cut and mounted can be filed according to a classification system, for example, animals, wild and tame; workers; transportation; children's activities; holidays; machinery. The right picture will then be readily available as it is needed. Some libraries and museums also have picture files from which teachers may borrow. Many of the big industrial companies supply pictures as part of their public relations program, if they are requested on school stationery.

A last essential prerequisite for any meaningful picture in a kindergarten room is that it capture a bit of life rather than depict a posed, highly romanticized, sentimental portrait. The question raised before, "What does it say?" is a good one to remember.

These then are the nonreading sources of information for a kindergarten class available to an alert teacher: trips out into the world to see what there is to see and hear what there is to hear; people and materials brought into the classroom for closer contact with someone or something which is generally remote; representational materials, especially pictures, as a constant exposure to features of the world which one cannot always examine directly.

Bibliography

Bank Street College Pamphlets (New York, Bank Street College, 69 Bank Street).
  Beyer, Evelyn, and Stanton, Jessie, *First Hand Experiences and Sensory Learning.*
  Hochman, Vivienne, *Trip Experiences in Early Childhood.*
  Mitchell, Lucy Sprague, *Geography With Five Year Olds.*
  ———, *Research on the Child's Level.*
  Stall, Dorothy S., *Being Six in the City.*
Mitchell, Lucy Sprague, *Our Children and Our Schools* (New York, Simon and Schuster, Inc., 1951).
New York City Board of Education, *Operation New York* (110 Livingston St., Brooklyn 1, New York).
Wann, Kenneth D., Dorn, Miriam S., and Liddle, Elizabeth, *Fostering Intellectual Development in Young Children* (New York, Bureau of Publications, Teachers College, Columbia University, 1962).
Ward, Muriel, *Young Minds Need Something to Grow On* (New York, Harper & Row, Publishers, 1957).

Sources of free and inexpensive materials:
Field Enterprises, Educational Division, Chicago, Ill.
George Peabody College for Teachers, Division of Surveys and Field Services, Nashville, Tennessee.
Miller, Bruce, Box 369, Riverside, California.

8

Exposure to Literature

FIVES ARE READY FOR LITERATURE

The field of literature has a prominent position in the landscape of
our culture. Children's literature, to be deserving of the designation, must
have the same artistic standards, the same power to affect the spirit, and
the same inherent stamina to survive changing generations as adult literature. The difference is only in degree of complexity of ideas, of subject,
and of language to allow for the children's limited experience and comprehension. Kindergartners have the emotional power however, to be
deeply moved by the feeling and the beauty of literary works, and although thy are illiterate they can become acquainted with good literature
by being read to. They also have the intellectual capacity to respond to
ideas, to learn new words and concepts, and to follow a story and catch
the humor from books properly presented to them. Like art and music,
true literature with style, originality, conviction, and valid content illumined with artistic insight, has something vital to say to preschool
children who are not yet able to read. And how fortunate and rich we
are in all the available children's literature that increases with each
year's literary harvest.

ABUNDANCE REQUIRES SELECTIVITY

Hundreds of excellent children's books come out annually and
hundreds of mediocre ones are just as sure to appear. In addition there
is an unlimited amount of printed matter on the market that unfortunately

passes for children's books, as well as scores of very good books still available that were published in the last few decades. There are also the classics: some of the traditional sturdy, stylized folk tales, and the rich rhymes of Mother Goose.

At first glance so many children's books may seem like a surfeit of goods presenting an insurmountable problem in selection for a conscientious teacher. On second thought this abundance can be regarded as an advantage; it gives the teacher a personal as well as a professional choice and thus gives individuality to the library of each kindergarten. Furthermore teachers can more easily change or add to volumes on the accessible or reserved shelves. There can be enough books to appeal to changing moods and curiosity and to provide for the many directions taken by growing minds.

Quality Rather Than Quantity in Children's Books

The kindergarten teacher cannot possibly be expected to know all the good books that are available but she definitely bears the responsibility of knowing how to evaluate what is good in young children's literature. Desirable as it is to have enough books and sufficient variety in a classroom, we must not succumb to the lure of large quantity or pride in sheer numbers. Filled book racks and shelves may seem to indicate ample exposure to literature in the class, but are valueless if they contain many unsuitable volumes. It is not uncommon to find books on school shelves that are so uninteresting that neither the teacher nor the children ever pick them up. ("It's been here ever since I can remember," is the usual explanation.) Children given a steady diet of poor books will be impeded in the development of literary interest and taste. If there is no way immediately to replace discarded books it would certainly be more functional and more interesting if those full shelves were only half full. A *few* good books may not satisfy a teacher's standards but she can enlarge her library if necessary by borrowing from the public library, provided she knows what to choose. Let us consider some of the basic essentials in books of literary merit suitable for young children.

Knowing Children and Knowing Appropriate Books

"Knowing children and knowing books are two sides of the same coin in good book selection." [1] Knowing children means understanding general principles of child development, especially preschoolers' capacities and the directions in which their interests lie as they try to get to

[1] Charlotte S. Huck and Doris A. Young, *Children's Literature in the Elementary School* (New York, Holt, Rinehart & Winston, Inc., 1961), p. 15.

know their world. Huck and Young attempt in the following table [2] to show the relation between developmental characteristics of children and their interests in books.

Pre-School and Kindergarten

Characteristics	Implications	Examples
Rapid development of language	Interest in words, enjoyment of rhymes, nonsense and repetition.	*Mother Goose* Krauss, *A Very Special House* Gag, *Millions of Cats*
Continuous activity, short attention span	Requires books which can be completed "in one sitting." Enjoys participation through naming, touching and repeating phrases.	*Three Billy Goats Gruff* Kunhardt, *Pat the Bunny* Munari, *Who's There? Open the Door!* Francoise, *The Things I Like*
Concepts and behavior are egocentered.	Likes stories in which he is clearly identified. In telling a story, teacher or parent may substitute his name for the main character.	Brown, *Good Night Moon* Krauss, *The Growing Story* Rand, *I Know a Lot of Things*
Curious about his world.	Stories about everyday experiences, pets, playthings, home, people in his immediate environment are enjoyed.	Flack, *Angus and the Ducks* Lenski, *Papa Small* Simon, *The Daddy Days* Marino, *Where are the Mothers?* Yashima, *Umbrella*
Enjoys imaginative play.	Likes stories which personify the inanimate. Talking animals are appreciated.	*Goldilocks & the Three Bears* Burton, *Mike Mulligan and*

[2] *Ibid.*, p. 9. By permission of the publisher.

		His Steam Shovel Gramatky, *Little Toot* Will-Nicholas, *Finders Keepers*
Seeks warmth and security in relationships with adults.	Enjoys the individual attention of storytime. Requires poetic justice and happy endings. The ritual of the bedtime story begins literature experiences.	Potter, *Peter Rabbit* Minarik, *Little Bear* Flack, *Ask Mr. Bear* Flack, *Wait for William* Zolotow, *The Night When Mother Was Away*
Beginning to seek independence from adults.	Books can help children to adjust to new and frightening experiences.	Brown, *The Runaway Bunny* MacDonald, *The Little Frightened Tiger*

Knowing children also means knowing the specific children with whom you as a teacher are now working. You may have children with advanced language development and wish to use stories of greater length and complexity than you otherwise would.

You may have children of low language development and may wish to rely on picture books with simple words or on brief, dramatic poems, until their language develops more. Surely in a class predominantly Negro in composition you will wish to have some books whose protagonists and illustrations are Negro.[3] This would apply to Puerto Rican, Mexican, Oriental, or any other predominant ethnic group. Or if many fathers of the kindergartners are coal miners, you would like to read to the children an interesting book dealing with this occupation.[4] There may be children in class with a strong interest in mechanics or special devotion to their pets, in which case books may be selected that

[3] L. and J. Beim, *Two Is a Team*, illus. Ernest Crichlow (New York, Harcourt, Brace & World, Inc., 1945). Eva K. Evans, *Araminta*, illus. Erick Berry (New York, G. P. Putnam's Sons, 1935). Eva K. Evans, *Jerome Anthony*, illus. Ernest Crichlow (New York, G. P. Putnam's Sons, 1935).

[4] Patricia Mahoney Markum, *First Book of Coal Mining*, illus. Mildred Walter (New York, Grolier, Inc., 1959).

would be particularly meaningful to them. In any event the children to whom you will read stories must influence your choices. The best piece of literature is worthless if the audience cannot appreciate it.

CRITERIA IN SELECTION OF BOOKS

Aesthetic Values—Illustration, Format, Lettering

One of the outstanding values of books, if not *the* outstanding value, is the overall aesthetic appeal. Children, emotional and artistic as we know them to be, respond to the aesthetic although they may not be able to express their feeling in words. Let us think for a moment of our childhood memories of books. Isn't one of the first books you remember one that you loved for its total effect, one that brought you visual delight from the illustrations, the special designs and decorations among the pages, the distinctive letters perhaps or the shape of the book, and one in which the story was itself part of the complete beauty? There are so many outstanding books that are beautiful in their entirety; they have an original, well-told, inspiring story (whether plotted or patterned), beautiful pictures, attractive design and printing, attractive format. In fact the difficulty is similar to the one felt by the old man who was seeking the most beautiful kitten and kept finding one more with distinctive and different characteristics of beauty till he selected millions and billions and trillions of cats! [5]

Illustrations and format. Since so much of the beauty of children's books comes from the illustrations, let us look at several kinds. *Make Way for Ducklings,*[6] an award-winning book of great popularity, captivates children with its detailed realistic scenery of the domestic activities of a family of ducks at the Boston Commons Gardens. Excitement, amusement, and warmth come across clearly in the McCloskey illustrations.

A more recent book, illustrated by another artist of distinction, is *Little Bear.*[7] A special kind of humor, whimsy, and originality in rhythmic designs and a spirited depiction both of characters and fantasy themes, all contribute to the total impression of beauty in Sendak's pictures in the life of a boy-like bear.

Very different from the large McCloskey book and the Sendak

[5] Wanda Gag, *Millions of Cats* (New York, Coward-McCann, Inc., 1928).

[6] Robert McCloskey, *Make Way for Ducklings* (New York, The Viking Press, 1941).

[7] Else H. Minarik, *Little Bear,* illus. Maurice Sendak (Harper & Row, Publishers, 1957).

book is the slim little volume by Leo Lionni.[8] Its boldness and simplicity of colored abstract forms are very effective and rather surprising. Children have no difficulty in perceiving Little Blue (a mere roundish blue blob) and Little Yellow (an equally crude roundish yellow shape) as thoroughly animate and important friends, by virtue of their proximity and position.

A book such as the one by the Rands [9] invites admiration of its distinctive printing, beautiful lettering, and quality of paper. Although the book is beautiful for its pictures and content as well, the beauty of the format can be appreciated separately by five-year-olds who like handling, feeling, and inspecting different books.

There is aesthetic stimulation in the variety of artistic styles in illustrations and in the general format and design of books. If, in a classroom, one particular type of book predominated, such as the uniformly-designed Golden Books, the children would be presented with dulling monotony in spite of the different stories and pictures inside the books. It is far more stimulating to have books of different size, shape, and construction, books with durable cloth-like soft covers, books with spiral binding that open and close differently from standard ones, books with full page pictures, and those with little scattered decorations.

When children inspect such books as those by the ingenious Bruno Munari [10] they are fascinated by the unique effect of exposing concealed objects and by finding out how the book "works."

Literary Merit

Literary value, intrinsic to the aesthetic character of a book, deserves serious attention and separate focus. What is the quality we call "literary" when applied to books for the young?

Reality in young children's literature. The reader probably has heard the expression "here and now" but may not have had an opportunity to learn its origin or application to children's literature. The phrase actually originated from Lucy Sprague Mitchell's famous first *Here and Now Story Book* and was reinforced by the second.[11] These col-

---

[8] Leo Lionni, *Little Blue and Little Yellow* (New York, Ivan Obolensky, Inc., 1959).

[9] Ann and Paul Rands, *I Know a Lot of Things* (New York, Harcourt, Brace & World, Inc., 1956).

[10] Bruno Munari, *Jimmy Has Lost His Cap* (Cleveland, The World Publishing Co., 1959); Bruno Munari, *The Birthday Present* (Cleveland, The World Publishing Co., 1959).

[11] Lucy Sprague Mitchell, *Here and Now Story Book*, illus. H. W. VanLoon (New York, E. P. Dutton & Co., 1921). Lucy Sprague Mitchell, *Another Here and Now Book*, illus. Rosalie Slocum (New York, E. P. Dutton & Co., Inc., 1937).

lections of stories of the familiar and the everyday are actually anthologies of original literary works of different forms, themes, and levels of language reflecting children's own development. The stories deal with the truly significant in a child's life as seen from the child's point of view. Whether the stories are personal episodes set in rhythmic pattern (as in the younger nursery section of the book) or the structured tales of adventures and pursuits in the exciting world of the fours, fives, and sixes, they are all treated with imaginative realism, uncanny insight into childhood, and with a vigor and delight that are never sentimental. The range of subjects and themes in the two *Here and Now* books is literally as large as life. Houses, horses, trees, city life, country life, and various forms of transportation are dealt with concretely and poetically. As important as the stories themselves are, the books are especially valuable for their sections dealing with children's language and receptivity to literary forms at different ages during early childhood. These stimulating and still timely chapters should be read for further thought and study of children's literature.

Contemporary works in the here-and-now tradition continue to take cognizance of children's feelings as well as interests; indeed they take children themselves seriously too. One of the best known modern children's writers, the late Margaret Wise Brown, was a student and close associate of Lucy Sprague Mitchell. Experimenting with literary styles, exploring exhaustively all the senses and perceptions, reveling in the riches of the here-and-now genre, Miss Brown carried forth the early influence of Mrs. Mitchell in creating literature of high calibre for children. All of her many works show great originality and a genius for evoking deep feelings. One of the best known of Miss Brown's books is *The Noisy Book*.[12] The purely sensory element in this book was so loved by children that the author followed this book by a whole series of *Noisy Books*; indoor, outdoor, city, country, and even *The Quiet Noisy Book*. The essence of the *Noisy Book* is the exciting exploration of pure sound. Muffin the dog gets a bandage over his eyes after the doctor takes a cinder out, and so he cannot see. But Muffin can hear. Does he know what he hears and who makes the particular, the peculiar noises? Intensely responsive to the guessing and recognizing of different, familiar, everyday noises, young children not only identify with Muffin but they take the story over and become co-authors.

Another modern author, Betty Miles, also bears the influence of the here-and-now philosophy in conveying the deep meaning and poetry of the intimate surroundings and patterns in a child's life, as in *A House*

---

[12] Margaret Wise Brown, *The Noisy Book*, illus. Leonard Weisgard (New York, Harper & Row, Publishers, 1939).

for Everyone.[13] There are different sizes and shapes of houses; some "reach up high," some "stretch sideways." And different kinds of families live in houses. People leave their houses to go places (school, store, place of work) and of course they come home to their houses where they belong and where "the children are tucked warm and soft in their beds." The author reaches out into the environment and comes back with a cozy place for the child.

Morality—literary portrayal of struggle comprehensible to young children. Although there was a time when only goodness and sweetness were the appropriate subjects for children's books, there is recognition today that young children face many realities in life and must resolve frustrations, fears, and conflict. Consequently many of today's books have adventurous heroes who undergo considerable struggles of a type familiar and comprehensible to the young. Heroes may be represented by human or animal characters. But the problems fall within the experience of preschoolers.

Timothy,[14] a heavy turtle, slides down a river bank and lands upside down, unable to turn over. The physical struggle for desirable bodily position in Timothy is very understandable to young children, and when Timothy's condition invites the struggles and unique cooperation of his numerous friends the children understand that too, and share in the ultimate victory.

In another book [15] struggle of a different kind is experienced by a nameless little boy who plants a carrot seed. In spite of all the doubts and discouragements from every member of the family and the continued days when "nothing came up," the little boy persists in watering and weeding; he does not give up until one day a carrot comes up, "just as the little boy thought it would." And the reader, who most likely also thought so, experiences the same struggle and faith vicariously.

In another work of children's literature [16] we see a little boy, Willie, struggling to keep up determination and courage no matter what.

> He came to a hill.
> It was a very high hill.
> Should he turn around?
> No. Not Willie.

[13] Betty Miles, *A House for Everyone,* illus. Jo Lowrey (New York, Alfred A. Knopf, Inc., 1958).

[14] Alice Davis, *Timothy Turtle,* illus. Guy Brown Wiser (New York, Harcourt, Brace & World, Inc., 1940).

[15] Ruth Krauss, *The Carrot Seed,* illus. Crockett Johnson (New York, Harper & Row, Publishers, 1945).

[16] Margaret Wise Brown, *Willie's Adventures* (New York, William R. Scott, Inc., Publisher, © 1954, Estate of Margaret Wise Brown. By permission of the publisher).

> He walked up the hill backwards
> So as not to see how high it was.
> Then he walked down the hill
>   backwards,
> So he could see how high the hill had been.
> And Willie whistled as he walked on to
>   Grandma.

Children have no difficulty understanding the need to be brave and resourceful.

Identification with the literary character. In their response to literature children, like adults, identify with certain characters. Such characters need not necessarily be representative of the children's own way of life but they must have believable and meaningful experiences and communicate universal human feelings artistically.

Ferdinand [17] is a hero of an old story book which enjoyed a best-selling career in the thirties. Although the book has a background of Spanish bullfight ritual and regalia and the hero is a shy, flower-smelling bull (what an unusual subject for American preschool children), it is immediately understood by children; they identify with the idiosyncrasies of the bull and with his being different from the other bulls, and they feel his plight when the very important grown-ups misunderstand him. The direct style and physical earthy humor and drama, as well as the outstanding illustrations, contribute to the intensity of the children's response.

> He didn't look where he was
> sitting, and instead of sitting
> on the nice cool grass in the
> shade he sat on a bumble bee.
> Well, if you were a bumble bee
> and a bull sat on you, what
> would you do? You would sting
> him. And that is just what this
> bee did to Ferdinand. Wow! Did
> it hurt! . . . . .

And the children listening to the story *do* empathize with Ferdinand!

Another literary character of great appeal to children is a curious, questioning little raccoon.[18]

"How dark is the dark tonight?" asked the little raccoon.

"Not so dark," said his mother. "There is a new moon tonight, thin as the curve of a raccoon's whisker in the sky above the tree tops."

---

[17] Munro Leaf, *Ferdinand the Bull,* illus. Robert Lawson (New York, The Viking Press, Inc., 1936). By permission of the publisher.

[18] Margaret Wise Brown, *Wait Till the Moon is Full,* illus. Garth Williams (New York, Harper & Row, Publishers, 1945). By permission of the publisher.

"Can I see it?" asked the little raccoon.

"No," said his mother. "You must wait. Wait till the moon is full."

"How big is the night?" asked the little raccoon.

"Very big," said his mother.

"How big is Big?" asked the little raccoon.

"Wait," said his mother. "Wait till the moon is full."

The children identify with him not because he is a raccoon and lives in the woods but because he expresses the urgent wish to see the hidden, the as yet forbidden; because he has a compelling curiosity and has to endure the inevitability of waiting for what he wants to know.

Fantasy Appropriate for Young Children

Many of the books we have referred to in this chapter as well as others with which the reader must be familiar have an important element of imagination and fantasy: the old man brings millions of cats as a present for his wife, a little bear takes a trip to the moon, and a raccoon asks questions about the night. Yet the fantasy is within the bounds of real sense. The characters do have genuine physical attributes appropriate to their kind; animals may talk in human language but what they say is relevant and right for them and for the story. There is some contact between the story's fantasy and the world children know as real. For children who are still unsure about the difference between fantasy and reality, fantasy that creates an entirely new world where nothing is familiar can be an unsettling experience. In this connection the beautiful fairy tales one always thinks of when talking about fantasy in children's literature seem by and large to be unsuitable for children under seven years of age. The great heroes performing elaborate symbolic deeds in distant places are out of the intellectual range of young children and such themes as revenge, prophesy, jealousy, and wickedness which often appear in the fairy tales constitute too heavy and confusing an emotional dose for them.

Five-year-olds appreciate the presence in story characters of negative as well as positive feelings. But the envy, greed, anger, and mischief they understand are aspects of normal human behavior and not the epitome of evil as they appear to be in the fairy tales. Good and evil as abstract concepts are beyond the kindergarten child. Yet some years later when the same child goes through the developmental struggle of strengthening his moral sense his own conflict about right and wrong makes the issue in the fairy tale, or T. V. western for that matter, a very personal one indeed. At that time fairy tales can be enjoyed for their literary quality and their emotional impact taken in stride.

The popular classic folk tales however, are in a different category. With a durable literary structure, simple pattern rather than complicated plot, and colorful language, they have a literary vigor all their own. The fantasy in the folk tales can be enjoyed by five-year-olds and we shall discuss samples of these later.

Fantasy, appropriate for young children, is a common ingredient in many beautiful modern books. It is quite clear in *The Giant Story*.[19] The title alone suggests a removal from, or at least a natural manipulation of, reality. And once established the book's make-believe is consistent. The once-little-boy-now-giant performs purely gigantic deeds till the end of the day. At that point, to satisfy the young reader who is not too secure in his distinction between a story and the truth, the author has the one-day-giant-now-little-boy get back home to his mother.

The two playful furry rabbits in the picture book, *The Rabbits' Wedding*,[20] live in a lovely world of hills and fields of flowers. With great simplicity of scene and action Mr. Williams conveys a deep mood, and through an easy dialogue he unfolds a pastoral tale of joyous companionship and fulfillment of wishing, of sadness, and of longing, ending with a wedding of the two rabbits wearing golden dandelions in their graceful ears. Of course the beauty of the story is heightened by the harmonious mood in the illustrations and the soft contrasts in the pictures of the black and the white rabbits.

The reader's appreciation of a particular fantasy story and the meaning gained from the story will depend on his imagination and taste. Some will like one kind of story, some another. Some may appreciate the poetic treatment of Margaret Wise Brown's fantasy, as in *The Runaway Bunny* [21] and some will enjoy more the narrative folktale style of Wanda Gag.[22] Others may choose the rhyming hilarity of Dr. Seuss' well-known fantasy tales, such as *Horton Hatches An Egg*.[23]

Mother Goose. And for a brief excursion into fantasy one can always resort to the rhyming *Mother Goose*. Here is one dealing strangely enough with a modern adventure, that of going to the moon! [24]

> There was an old woman tossed up in a basket,
>   Seventy times as high as the moon.
> And where she was going, I couldn't but ask it;

[19] Beatrice Schenk de Regniers, *The Giant Story*, illus. Maurice Sendak (New York, Harper & Row, Publishers, 1953).

[20] Garth Williams, *The Rabbits' Wedding* (New York, Harper & Row, Publishers, 1958).

[21] Margaret Wise Brown, *The Runaway Bunny*, illus. Clement Hurd (New York, Harper & Row, Publishers, 1942).

[22] Wanda Gag, *Nothing at All* (New York, Coward-McCann, Inc., 1941).

[23] Dr. Seuss, *Horton Hatches An Egg* (New York, Vanguard Press, Inc., 1940).

[24] *Mother Goose*, illus. Gustaf Tenggren (Boston, Little, Brown and Co., 1940).

> For in her hand she carried a broom.
> "Old woman, old woman, old woman," quoth I,
>   "Whither, oh whither, oh whither so high?"
> "To sweep the cobwebs out of the sky!
>   And I'll be with you by and by."

But perhaps a modern child would consider this tale as reality rather than fantasy, interpreting the broom to be a space rocket and "I'll be with you by and by," to mean terrestrial landing! *Mother Goose* is fun for its rhythm and rhyme. It should not be the biggest part of children's literary fare because on the whole it is incomprehensible.

The folk tale. In the long-lived classic folk tales the fantasy seems well established; it is taken for granted that "The Three Bears" [25] or "The Little Red Hen" [26] are "just stories," which means they are make-believe and thus free the children's imagination. The rhythmic refrains of folk tales accentuate the magic. "And I can run away from you, too. I can, I can," fulfills the reader's expectations of the "Ginger Bread Man." [27] Different versions of the same folktale can be found in various collections and there are so many collections and beautiful, wise, or highly entertaining folktales that teachers can choose favorites to read to children. The humorous ones are usually most favored. A good example is *Caps For Sale.*[28] Keeping his wares on his head in a precise order of colors, a traveling peddler sits down beneath a tree. On waking the peddler misses all but one of his caps and naïvely looks for them to the right and the left. When he discovers that the tree is full of monkeys and each monkey is wearing one of his caps, the peddler's anger grows in stages; each stage of anger is expressed with different gestures which are copied by the monkeys. In final fury the peddler throws his cap from his head onto the ground. When the monkeys copy him this time the peddler picks up the caps and puts them all back on his head in the precise order of colors. So the monkeys' cleverness that seems to give them the upper hand with the man becomes their downfall and brings the man an advantage. The ending of the funny story is a happy one and the children want it read all over again.

Some folk tales fascinate and amuse children (and adults) with their fantastic but fitting exaggerations in portraying a hero. Such a hero is the unique and gorgeous, dark-skinned, *Little Black Sambo* [29] who works up an appetite to eat 169 pancakes and without any weapon battles

---

[25] *The Tall Book of Nursery Tales,* illus. Feodor Rojankowsky (New York, Harper & Row, Publishers, 1944), p. 37.

[26] *Ibid.,* p. 79.

[27] *Ibid.,* p. 16.

[28] Esphyr Slobodkina, *Caps For Sale* (New York, William R. Scott, Inc., 1947).

[29] Helen Bannerman, *Little Black Sambo,* illus. Gustaf Tenggren (New York, Golden Press, Inc., 1947).

tigers in the jungle and comes home safe and successful. *Little Black Sambo* is a folk tale that comes to us from India. Unfortunately this little dark-skinned hero has been misrepresented; in the original illustrations the little boy Sambo is pictured as a stereotyped caricature of a Negro, which makes the whole story appear offensive to many people. Such pictures are of course wrong and have no place in the story. The story has to do with the little boy Sambo who gets all dressed up in different stunning, colorful items of clothing to go for a walk in the jungle, where naturally enough he meets a tiger. And he meets another and still another tiger, each threatening "I am going to eat you up." Appealing to the vanity of each tiger little Sambo forfeits his clothing one piece at a time, so that even when he is without trousers he remains prudently intact. At this point the terribly envious and vain tigers engage in a deathly struggle, each trying to assert his "grandness." And the patient, always polite, practical, and capable little Sambo comes home glorying in the results of his courageous adventure; indeed he has something to show for all his pains—a big brass potful of melted tiger-butter or " 'ghi' as it is called in India." This is just the thing to use in pancakes, of which triumphant little Black Sambo has naturally had his share. If the reader should think that this story with man-eating tigers is frightening to all children because they might worry about being eaten up themselves, think again! What is the story really about? *Not* about the horrors of being eaten! One of the authors read *Little Black Sambo* many times to children approximately four to seven years of age, and only once was there an expression of worry on a child's face.

"But-but-but . . ." five-year-old Mike stammered excitedly as he was following the diminution of Sambo's wardrobe. "What will Sambo's *mother* say when he comes home without the beautiful new clothes she just got him?" So tigers were not the cause of worry to Mike after all. It was his own mother; Sambo's mother is a very generous and trusting one. Children not only take what the fantasy story has to offer but give to it of their particular experience and sensitivity. Preschool children generally are more robust and unsentimental than adults regard them, and they will not be easily hurt by exposure to literature that touches on strife, danger, and even death, providing such themes are treated as part of living, presented artfully and briefly, and end with a sensible and secure resolution.

Structure and Plot in Children's Books

All good children's stories have an orderly arrangement of content; an understandable and satisfying pattern, an interesting intriguing plot. Order is as basic to children's literature as to all art. Let us consider some well-tested and much demanded stories for the merit of their plot.

In "Poppy Seed Cakes" [30] the plot springs from the nature of the characters in the separate stories in the book. Among the characters are a boy who would always rather do something on his own than follow the advice of those who know better, a charming and troublesome goat, and a generous, sympathetic, old country aunt. The boy is unable to resist bouncing on a feather bed, swinging on a garden gate, or wading barefoot in a small stream, all at wrong times which makes for suspense in the story. And the ever helpful auntie keeps the consequences of wrongdoing from becoming dire, so in the end a good time is had by all!

In the book *Blueberries For Sal* [31] the story is built on a background of seasonal activities for people and bears. A very exciting and satisfying balance is created by parallel activities of a human mother followed by her child Sally, *picking* blueberries for the winter on one side of the hill, while on the other side a bear mother followed by her bear child are *eating* blueberries to get fat for the winter. Each family group is in happy pursuit of free food from nature; each mother is concerned with the safety of her young. After a temporary mix-up of mothers which causes the reader a brief but breathless suspense, each child is delighted to have her own mother back.

Preschool children find a limited amount of suspense not only endurable but thrilling. Knowing this, Louise Woodcock succeeded in writing a well-structured mystery story, *Wiggles*,[32] on a young child's level. At the start of the story Donnie is advised to "find Wiggles to play with you." And neither Donnie nor the reader know who Wiggles is. With each encounter on the farm Donnie's idea of who Wiggles might be changes and the reader's suspense increases. Finally at the very end the mystery is solved by the appearance of a boy in a tree house who is capable of wiggling his ears, a dubious talent from an adult point of view but clearly an asset for a desirable companion for a boy, and a suitable element in a light-hearted story.

On quite a serious level is Lucy Sprague Mitchell's perfectly-plotted story "How Spot Found a Home." [33] It starts out with an urgent need; a poor little thin cat who has "only the street" wants to find a home. But as in many literary works (and in life) she first endures struggle and

[30] Marjory Clark, *Poppy Seed Cakes*, illus. Maud and Miska Petersham (Garden City, N.Y., Doubleday & Co., Inc., 1929).

[31] Robert McCloskey, *Blueberries for Sal* (New York, The Viking Press, Inc., 1948).

[32] Louise Woodcock, *Wiggles*, illus. Eloise Wilkin (Golden Book, Simon & Schuster, Inc., 1953).

[33] Lucy Sprague Mitchell, "How Spot Found a Home," *Here and Now Story Book* (New York, E. P. Dutton & Co., Inc., 1921), pp. 150–155.

defeat. With thoroughly cat-like senses, persistence, and agility, Spot is able to enter and escape from one house that has a scowling, threatening cook, and from another with a spitting possessive cat, in her search of a warm welcoming home. Still hopeful, Spot tries again and in the third house she receives warmth, nourishment, and welcome from two children. This makes the child listeners feel that they themselves save Spot from deprivation and thus help her to live happily.

The Language in Children's Books

Let us focus now on the language of children's literature. No matter what the theme, is not the essential vitality of a literary work conveyed through the artistic language? Literary language is no mere statement of physically accurate fact, no grammatical perfection alone, no artificiality that may pass for style. Literary language springs from an author's original thinking and genuine feeling; it is language in which the words are fresh and important, the meaning clear and interesting. Through the language the reader is able to share in the author's special discoveries, ideas, and loves; he is able to partake of the author's senses and spirit and style.

> There was a little Island in the ocean
> Around it the winds blew
> And the birds flew
> And the tides rose and fell on the shore.[34]

So reads the first page of the dramatic poetic prose story of rhythm in nature, of the changes and contrasts and depths, and of the strength that comes from being

> . . . . a part of the world
> and a world of its own
> all surrounded by the
> bright blue sea.

Although Weisgard's beautiful illustrations here are in perfect keeping with the feeling and style of the story, the story does live on its own merit through language.

Charlotte Zolotow, a particularly perceptive author of many beautifully-written children's books, is an artist with words and phrases that intrigue and delight the reader.

> This is a story about a whole family of Indians,
> a mother Indian, a father Indian, a brother Indian,

[34] Golden MacDonald (pseudonym for Margaret Wise Brown), *The Little Island*, illus. Leonard Weisgard (Garden City, N.Y., Doubleday & Co., Inc., 1946).

a sister Indian, and a very little one named
Indian Indian.[35]

With the greatest economy of words and thus all the greater effect, the author tells of the little boy's undying devotion to a beautiful white horse whom he meets in "the meadow that sparkled with white daisies in the sun." He discovers by himself that the horse is not "a trick of the eye," and he waters and feeds him and comes through darkness and strange noises of night to cover the sick horse with a blanket.

> "You were wise, Indian Indian," his father
> told him, "to test with your own senses what
> I had said."

The children listen attentively to this simple warm story and want to find out what "a trick of the eye" is, and they like to repeat to each other "you are wise, Indian Indian . . ."

Certainly the richness of the English language is felt and made use of by all good writers, and many children's books will arouse five-year-olds' curiosity about big words whose meaning will be remembered because of artful treatment. This is true of Duvoisin's *Veronica* [36] where the word *conspicuous*, as well as the words *famous* and *demolish*, are well dramatized to be remembered, all done as an integral part of an amusing story.

In *A Gaggle of Geese* [37] which is actually a true, serious book by a gifted writer, the author writes of the marvels and effectiveness of the current and past English language. It is a fascinating story of words designating *groups* of animals, fish, and birds: flocks and herds and schools and swarms. You say "flights of swallows" and "tribes of goats" just as correctly as you refer to a "husk of jackrabbits" and "a smack of jellyfish." Such a book would indeed expose children, who are eager language appreciators, to the richness and the unique flavor of the English language.

Literature Meets the Emotional Needs of Children

There is a common saying or at least a common understanding that a good book can be your best friend. This also applies to children's literature and to children, particularly if you regard a friend as one who answers your needs. Such an idea requires elaboration, for children

---

[35] Charlotte Zolotow, *Indian Indian*, illus. Leonard Weisgard (New York, Little Golden Book, Simon & Schuster, Inc., 1952).

[36] Roger Duvoisin, *Veronica* (New York, Alfred A. Knopf, Inc., 1961).

[37] Eve Merriam, *A Gaggle of Geese*, illus. Paul Galdone (New York, Alfred A. Knopf, Inc., 1960).

have many needs. It also requires discrimination, for books are innumerable and we may become submerged in the sea of subjects and in the number of needs books may rightly answer.

Concern with family membership and members. That works of literature can serve children's emotional and intellectual needs should be of great comfort to a kindergarten teacher who is always on call to help an individual child or even the whole class. One of the first interests and sometime concerns of preschool children has to do with their own families. Present a four or five-year-old with a grouping of any objects or show him some animals together, and it is likely that he will ask you or tell you which is the mother, the father, the sister or brother. Children love enumeration of family members in a story and this is another reason for the appeal of *Indian Indian,* (see p. 142) where the four members of his family are important to the little boy. McCloskey's *Make Way for Ducklings* (see p. 132) deals with finding a home, raising a family, and feeding and protecting the children by a careful mother and a daring father. In another animal book the very *number* of family members is fascinating and involves the reader completely! And the numbers change in this family of ten,[38] adding and multiplying prolifically (as can happen with mice). "Three plus two equals five" is not a mathematical equation, but it is a thrill when twins arrive.

Mother is of course most important to the majority of young children and she appears in a large number of stories, as the reader may already have noted. There are some books however, that deal specifically with Mother. *Where Are the Mothers* [39] is a simple picture book of mothers' activities when the children are in school, while *The Night When Mother Was Away* [40] tells sensitively of the loneliness without mother and of the gratifying relationship with father. In still another book, a Russian folk tale,[41] Mother is the subject of profound and universal idealization; in this story a child's contention "my mother is the most beautiful woman in the world" reveals a homely peasant woman with beauty of love.

A picture story of *The Daddy Days* [42] is likely to bring on children's own discussion of what happens on daddy days in their homes. A

[38] Charlotte Steiner, *Ten In a Family* (New York, Alfred A. Knopf, Inc., 1960).

[39] Dorothy Marino, *Where Are the Mothers?*, illus. by the author (Philadelphia, J. B. Lippincott Co., 1959).

[40] Charlotte Zolotow, *The Night When Mother Was Away*, illus. Raisie Lonette (New York, Lothrop, Lee & Shepard Co., Inc., 1959).

[41] Becky Reyher, *My Mother is the Most Beautiful Woman in the World,* illus. Ruth Gannett (New York, Lothrop, Lee & Shepard Co., Inc., 1945).

[42] Norma Simon, *The Daddy Days*, illus. Abner Graboff (New York, Abelard-Schuman, Ltd., 1958).

real contribution to young children's meager knowledge about fathers' work is Helen Puner's *Daddies and What They Do All Day*.[43] This picture book reflects our democratic society and gives the same status to daddies cleaning our streets as to daddies curing our ills, to those giving us elevator rides as to those giving us entertainment.

Relationship with Grandfather can also have much meaning, as shown in a book by Helen Buckley.[44]

Family status and new arrivals. The expectation or arrival of a new family member and the subsequent new family status for the child is of deep interest to young children and can be a cause for unspoken concern. The kindergarten teacher might then find *A Tiny Baby For You* [45] an answer to her quest for a helpful book on the subject. This slim and simple book, with photographs that have profound charm in their reality, is large in its total meaning yet not confusing with details. Nor does it belabor the subject as some books do. This book instead helps the child experience brotherhood or sisterhood. *The New Pet*,[46] which turns out to be a new baby, is another interesting story on the subject.

The kindergarten teacher may sometimes discern that understanding and accepting adoption is a manifest need not only of the adopted child himself but of those who know him. A very satisfactory book that may help meet this need is *The Chosen Baby*.[47] The teacher would need to use judgment in deciding whether a book on such a special subject should be read to the whole class or to an interested few, and whether it should be read in its entirety.

Relationship with pets. Not as special as a chosen adopted human member of a family, and of more universal interest to children, is the chosen pet living as a member of the family. The almost classic saga of Lynd Ward, *The Biggest Bear*,[48] tells of a boy's acquisition of a small bear cub and the care and support the boy has to give this unusually demanding pet. The inevitable rapid growth of any pet from babyhood to adulthood is a dramatic process and it is especially dramatic and near tragic in the case of *The Biggest Bear*. This is a wonderful story with an unusual, authentic country-and-woods background, and it shows the strength of devotion and responsibility a child can have for his pet.

[43] Helen Walker Puner, *Daddies and What They Do All Day*, illus. Roger Duvoisin (New York, Lothrop, Lee & Shepard Co., Inc., 1946).

[44] Helen Buckley, *Grandfather and I*, illus. Paul Galdone (New York, Lothrop, Lee & Shepard Co., Inc., 1959).

[45] Nancy Langstaff, *A Tiny Baby For You*, photography Suzanne Szasz (New York, Harcourt, Brace & World, Inc., 1955).

[46] Marjory Flack, *The New Pet* (Garden City, N.Y., Doubleday & Co., Inc., 1943).

[47] Valentina P. Wasson, *The Chosen Baby*, illus. Hildegarde Woodward (Philadelphia, J. B. Lippincott Co., 1950).

[48] Lynd Ward, *The Biggest Bear* (Boston, Houghton Mifflin Co., 1952).

Another story of devotion to a pet is *Mr. Turtle's Mystery*.[49] Far from a big bear in the woods, this pet is but a small birthday-present turtle which David keeps in a little tank in the room. David feels a most tender attachment for him and when Mr. Turtle disappears there is deep disappointment, which any child can feel over losing a pet. What a relief when Mr. Turtle at long last reappears. What tenderness in the reunion.

The fact that pets and people living in the same family have different lives is told amusingly in *Night Cat*.[50] Not only are the sleepy people unaware of the nocturnal adventures of their pet, but they mistakenly assume that the cat slept home all night.

Having a pet often makes little children feel protective and even big. Being small, or being the smallest one in the family, can be a disconcerting matter to preschoolers and sometimes requires reassurance.

Problem of being little. Some writers treat the theme of smallness with understanding and humor while others may moralize and weaken the effect as well as the literary merit. In *The Very Little Girl*,[51] Phyllis Krasilovsky presents the physical proportions of littleness and how it changes; the very little girl seems bigger when compared to the "very very very little baby brother."

A little older and longer book on the trials of being little is *Rosa-Too-Little*.[52] Five and six-year-olds would be especially interested in Rosa's struggle and determination to be big enough to take her own books out of the library. In *The Smallest Boy in the Class*[53] the author shows how bigness proves to be important not in physical size but in bigness of heart.

Special interest in growing. It is very likely too among fast-growing five-year-olds that a special interest in growing itself will come up. *The Growing Story*[54] would stimulate further interest. The observations as well as the illustrations of the relative rate of growth among vegetables, animals, and children will cause amusement, reflection, and probably inspection of one's own growth. The book conveys to all children the fact that no matter how imperceptibly it may proceed, they are all growing.

Difficulty of waiting. The Growing Story deals sympathetically as

[49] Betty Miles, *Mr. Turtle's Mystery*, illus. Jacqueline Tomes (New York, Alfred A. Knopf, Inc., 1961).

[50] Irma S. Black, *Night Cat*, illus. Paul Galdone (New York, Holiday House, 1957).

[51] Phyllis Krasilovsky, *The Very Little Girl*, illus. Ninon (Garden City, N.Y., Doubleday & Co., Inc., 1953).

[52] Sue Felt, *Rosa-Too-Little*, illus. by author (Garden City, N.Y., Doubleday & Co., Inc., 1950).

[53] Jerrold Beim, *The Smallest Boy in the Class*, illus. Meg Wohlberg (New York, William Morrow & Co., Inc., 1949).

[54] Ruth Krauss, *The Growing Story*, illus. Phyllis Rowand (New York, Harper & Row, Publishers, 1947).

well with the difficulty of waiting common to all young children. There is also an appealing story about waiting and about having to hurry, *Wait for William*,[55] in which the youngest child in the family has trouble keeping up with bigger brothers and sisters. This is also an excellent family story. A beautifully written and illustrated story of a Japanese little girl living in the United States who is waiting and longing for a rainy day to use her beautiful new blue umbrella and red boots strikes a responsive chord in any preschool (or older!) child.[56]

Having disputes. Having disagreements and arguments and seeking arbitration is an experience with which five-year-olds are quite familiar; and they may get considerable understanding of their own feelings by reading about some one else's problems, particularly when problem situations are presented with the humor of Will and Nicholas.[57] In a very impressive and serious way the Beims [58] show children that there are disagreements and quarrels among friends; this is a direct and lively story that has been popular with preschoolers and young school-age children for over fifteen years.

A child's need for privacy. Among the many books by Beatrice Schenk de Regniers depicting poetically the inner world of childhood, one deals charmingly with children's subtle need for privacy [59] and the many ways in daily life that the children try to find it.

Coping with fear. Being frightened, admitting fear, and overcoming it is another part of the inner world of childhood which is treated with artistic insight by good children's writers whose stories help lighten some burdens and confusions that come from fear. In her remarkably brave way of coming straight to the point of a difficult subject, Miss Brown begins her story of the *Little Frightened Tiger*.[60]

> Once there was a little tiger
> who was absolutely scared to death.

And she reveals how differently the little tiger feels when he finds out that all animals have fears.

Learning about death. With her usual directness and great artistry Miss Brown approaches even the subject of death,[61] speaking of the

[55] Marjory Flack, *Wait for William*, illus. by author and Richard Hulberg (Boston, Houghton Mifflin Co., 1935).

[56] Taro Yashima, *Umbrella* (New York, The Viking Press, Inc., 1958).

[57] Will and Nicholas, *Finders Keepers* (New York, Harcourt, Brace & World, Inc., 1952).

[58] Lorraine and Jerrold Beim, *Two Is a Team*, illus. Ernest Crichlow (New York, Harcourt, Brace & World, Inc., 1945).

[59] Beatrice Schenk de Regniers, *A Little House of Your Own*, illus. Irene Haas (New York, Harcourt, Brace & World, Inc., 1955).

[60] Margaret Wise Brown, *Little Frightened Tiger*, illus. Leonard Weisgard (Garden City, N.Y., Doubleday & Co., Inc., 1953).

[61] Margaret Wise Brown, *The Dead Bird*, illus. Remy Charlip (New York, William R. Scott, Inc., 1958).

dead bird as ". . . cold dead and stone still and no heart beating." Hearing the story and seeing the Charlip quiet pictures showing sadness and contemplation and expressing the mood of mystery and beauty of the story, the young readers relive the experience with the young characters in the book. They find some understanding and relief if they have anxiety or guilt connected with death, which is not uncommon.

Experiencing illness. The experience of sickness, operations, hospitalization, or modern medication are matters of daily knowledge to modern children who sometimes discuss the subjects among themselves with brutal frankness. Children's books on the subject are often scientifically objective or photographically detailed, offering more than the child needs or cares to know; they are often falsely comforting, attempting to evade unpleasantness, and evasions, whether offered by parents, teachers or authors are not helpful to young children. But an artistically entertaining and reasonably realistic story on the subject is very well taken by kindergartners and no doubt is helpful. The ever popular *Madeline* [62] is such a book. Waking in the night, summoning help, riding in an ambulance, staying in the hospital, getting flowers, receiving visitors and presents, and no less important, showing off her scars, are all part of exciting living for Madeline and vicariously, for children listening to the story. Dealing humorously with all the childhood sicknesses and with colds and accidents as well is *Dr. Squash, the Doll Doctor.*[63] The book has the following dedication: "For Gwendolyn Thomas in her fifth year who pulled Doctor Squash out of thin air." This author had indeed great talent for using children's thoughts and fantasies as guides for treating serious themes most appropriately for children. Everybody of course gets cured in this marvelous story, including the clown who gets mumps, measles, chicken pox, and whooping cough all at once. Doctor Squash makes everybody "fit as a fiddle and right as rain."

This section in the chapter on children's literature, dealing with children's inner emotional needs and their reflection in literature, may well be extended, and the reader is invited to do so with regard to his particular experiences and taste. There is much to choose from, and one can almost always find a story that is just right.

Literature Meets Intellectual Needs

Let us now focus our attention on children's more outward, more clearly intellectual learning needs, though needs are not of course so arbitrarily divided in children's living and expression. And the children's literature that answers various needs cannot be precisely divided either.

[62] Ludwig Bemelmans, *Madeline* (New York, Simon & Schuster, Inc., 1939).
[63] Margaret Wise Brown, *Doctor Squash, the Doll Doctor,* illus. J. P. Miller (New York, Little Golden Book, Simon & Schuster, Inc., 1952).

It is only for the purpose of gaining more understanding that we are emphasizing one aspect of literature at a time. In looking even briefly at books with predominantly intellectual emphasis we see again such an abundance of material available in the English language that those books discussed here represent just a fraction of the good books.

Books which interpret the environment of men and machines. Children are constantly seeking knowledge and they are tremendously interested in their environment, in stories of nature, in wonders of science, and in great work done by men and machines. And the teacher can select from many old standbys as well as new lists books that satisfy this interest. In *Mike Mulligan and His Steam Shovel* [64] Virginia Burton shows a real dependent relationship between Mike the workman, and Mary Ann his hardworking steam shovel. This book always wins admiration from four to six-year-olds. Similar in literary and pictorial treatment and informational content is another Burton book, *Katy and The Big Snow.*[65]

Many of Mrs. Mitchell's stories in both "Here and Now" anthologies deal with the power and the beauty of various operations in natural and man-structured conditions. "The Little Drop of Water That Always Wanted a Change," [66] "The Workmen Build the House," [67] and "How the Engine Learned the Knowing Song" [68] are some of the inviting titles. In all the stories Mrs. Mitchell gives accurate, strikingly organized information of the subject in simple and creative language. She is particularly successful in interpreting to young children the relation between nature, men, machines, and civilized living. Her story in verse, "The Trees of the Forest" [69] is a beautiful example of such interpretation. There is also a classic children's story, *Pell's New Suit,*[70] that tells in charming folk-tale style of the relationship between man's needs, nature, various products, and different kinds of work.

Irma Black's brief story "What is Work," [71] tells about Tommy who discovers the nature of work through everyday adventure, and in the end philosophizes: "Work means to clean up, work means to cook; Sue's kind of work is to look at a book. The postman is better at bringing a letter. Daddy sells meat for people to eat. The coalman slides coal down into a

[64] Virginia Lee Burton, *Mike Mulligan and His Steam Shovel* (Boston, Houghton Mifflin Co., 1939).

[65] Virginia Lee Burton, *Katy and the Big Snow* (Boston, Houghton Mifflin Co., 1943).

[66] Lucy Sprague Mitchell, *Another Here and Now* (New York, E. P. Dutton & Co., 1937), p. 253.

[67] *Ibid.,* p. 193.

[68] Lucy Sprague Mitchell, *Here and Now Book* (New York, E. P. Dutton & Co., 1929), p. 131.

[69] Lucy Sprague Mitchell, *Ibid.,* pp. 165–170.

[70] Elsa Beskow, *Pell's New Suit* (New York, Harper & Row, Publishers, 1929).

[71] Irma S. Black, "What is Work?," in *Believe and Make-Believe,* Lucy Sprague Mitchell, ed. (New York, E. P. Dutton & Co., Inc., 1956), pp. 187–191.

hole. Even old Bob [the dog] has his own job. People do everything under the sun. I work, too—I think it's fun."

Everybody knows how fascinating transportation is to preschool children and how they enjoy picture books and straight accounts of boats and buses, trains and planes; how they get carried away by travels on land and sea, in air and outer space, attuned to special sounds and super speeds as only late twentieth-century children can be. There are many books on jets and rockets [72] and imminent trips to the moon.[73]

But in the midst of the expert scientific loud travel books comes a gentle, quiet, personal, and very touching book [74] about a child's first ride in a city subway. With literary description and very moving photographs it tells of the intricacies, surprises, special motions, sounds, and the intensely interesting information gathered by a little boy on a subway ride in New York City.

Outstanding in their literary quality as well as in their inspiring knowledge are the many nature books by Alvin Tresselt, such as *White Snow, Bright Snow*.[75] This writer's inspired prose conveys his dedication to nature in a way that is contagious! Mr. Tresselt describes the seasons and gives the rhythms and reasons behind all the action and drama, the color and form in Nature, whether it is a tiny snow flake, a glowing sunrise, or the well-tried travels of the birds.

Leone Adelson is another outstanding writer of nature books for children. Her style has imagination, humor, and definite appeal to young children. Particularly suitable for kindergarten are *All Ready For Winter* [76] and *All Ready For Summer*.[77]

But the world does not consist of specific phenomena in nature alone, and Miriam Schlein [78] explores various concepts in an intriguing, scientific, and personal way for children in books about shapes, weight, and time.

[72] Herbert S. Zim, *Rockets and Jets* (New York, Harcourt, Brace & World, Inc., 1945).

[73] William Nephew and Michael Chester, *Moon Trip, True Adventures In Space*, illus. Jerry Robinson (New York, G. P. Putnam's Sons, 1959). Both books are for slightly older children and would need to be adapted somewhat for kindergartners, but they could still be used to answer many of their questions.

[74] Barbara Brenner, *Barto Takes the Subway*, illustrated with photographs by Sy Katzoff (New York, Alfred A. Knopf, Inc., 1961).

[75] Alvin Tresselt, *White Snow, Bright Snow*, illus. Roger Duvoisin (New York, Lothrop, Lee & Shepard Co., Inc., 1947).

[76] Leone Adelson, *All Ready For Winter*, illus. Kathleen Elgin (New York, David McKay Co., Inc., 1952).

[77] Leone Adelson, *All Ready for Summer*, illus. Kathleen Elgin (New York, David McKay Co., Inc., 1955).

[78] Miriam Schlein, *Heavy Is a Hippopotamus*, illus. Leonard Kessler (New York, William R. Scott, Inc., 1954); *Shapes*, illus. Sam Berman (New York, William R. Scott, Inc., 1952); *It's About Time*, illus. Sam Berman (New York, William R. Scott, Inc., 1955).

The reader may observe that we are now dealing with science content in children's literature. The books referred to in this section may be categorized as scientific, but only in a broad and not a technical sense. They can also be called children's literature because they are creative and artistic in purpose, quality, and effect. Living in a century of science as we do it is inevitable that science should be of concern to good children's writers.

Science books for children. There are however, definite respectable science books written well for young children. And these books treat specific areas of subjects of science with scholarship and clarity and with the purpose of imparting or extending knowledge. For example *Mickey's Magnet*,[79] an unpaged picture book, gives an essential lesson in magnetism; it relates an experience, conveys a concept, and describes an experiment thoroughly, interestingly, and on a child's level. Equally scientifically Irma Webber shows the position and relationship of different parts of a plant; she does it accurately and even diagrammatically in a little book that is thoroughly interesting to young children.[80]

An outstanding writer of science books for kindergarten and early school-age children is Millicent E. Selsam. Her biological books on plants and animals answer the important specific questions children ask on the subject and in a way that can be absorbed by them.[81]

A very attractive and helpful book answering various questions on nature is *All Around You*.[82] Briefly but graphically the books tells about and pictures the sun, the seasons, the soil and the sea, and what is in the sky; it describes what goes on all around us.

A different kind of simple and true biology book with beautiful pictures is *Frogs Merry*.[83] It tells the story of frogs from dots in jelly eggs to merry active adult creatures in a pond, and of their survival of natural hazards.

And a book by science specialist Julius Schwartz, dealing simply with questions on general science is *It's Fun to Know Why*.[84]

[79] Franklin M. Branley and Eleanor K. Vaughan, *Mickey's Magnet*, illus. Crockett Johnson (New York, Thomas Y. Crowell Co., 1956).

[80] Irma Webber, *Up Above and Down Below* (New York, William R. Scott, Inc., 1943).

[81] Millicent E. Selsam, *Play With Seeds*, illus. Helen Ludwig (New York, William Morrow & Co., Inc., 1957); *Play With Vines*, illus. Fred Scherer (New York, William Morrow & Co., Inc., 1951); *All About Eggs and How They Change Into Animals*, illus. Helen Ludwig (New York, William R. Scott, Inc., 1952); *All Kinds of Babies*, illus. Helen Ludwig (New York, William R. Scott, Inc., 1955).

[82] Jeanne Bendick, *All Around You*, illus. by author (New York, Whittlesey House, McGraw-Hill Book Co., Inc., 1951).

[83] Juliet Kepes, *Frogs Merry*, illus. by author (New York, Pantheon Books, Inc., 1961).

[84] Julius Schwartz, *It's Fun To Know Why*, illus. Edwin Herron (New York, Whittlesey House, McGraw-Hill Book Co., Inc., 1952).

A still different aspect of science is treated by May Garelick.[85] In a lighthearted and rhythmic style Miss Garelick not only offers interesting observation of what some animals do when it rains, but she asks some unanswerable questions, such as the one in the title, to ponder and speculate on.

New science books are being published quite rapidly now and the teacher might consult a librarian or look at reviews of children's books once in a while to learn about books that would serve the needs of her particular class or her own special interest!

Quality of Humor in Children's Literature

Although humor is a real element in human life everywhere and greatly regarded in literature, it nevertheless remains something elusive; here you have it and now you don't. Humor differs with countries and people and in books it changes with the readers' moods. The criteria for humor varies with the reader's age too. Because humor is sought and enjoyed by children as much as by adults, it is universally regarded as an important element of good children's books along with aesthetic and literary values. And because humor is an art form (folk art, pictorial art, humor of music and humor of poetry), we cannot dwell heavily on its precise meaning or substance lest we become too objective in our analysis and thus turn dry and cold in our approach—a sure way to strike a blow at the heart of any art and to prove devastating to humor.

Humor in children's books is lightness and amusement with various degrees of laughter. It is the element of surprise and delight in many of the books we already discussed for other reasons but will refer to again this time.

There is great humor in *Caps For Sale* (see p. 139) perhaps because monkeys with their human weaknesses never fail to amuse human children who assume to be at least a little superior. The monkey character is in part responsible for the huge success of *Curious George* [86] with all children. But the main reason children love *Curious George* and laugh at his antics is because they appreciate his inadvert mischief and think his predicaments, though a little worrisome at times, are funny.

Duvoisin's *Veronica* (see p. 143) is unmistakably funny because the hippo heroine is also in a predicament by being preposterously out of place among people and cars. Somehow preschool children who are still learning about where things belong find obvious misplacements hilari-

[85] May Garelick, *Where Does the Butterfly Go When It Rains?*; illus. Leonard Weisgard (New York, William R. Scott, Inc., 1961).

[86] H. A. Rey, *Curious George* (Boston, Houghton Mifflin Co., 1941).

ously funny. Thus author-illustrator Phyllis Rowand also has a humorous misplacement story dealing with a big dog moving in with a family of average size in an apartment,[87] and happily, remaining.

Out of place and therefore funny behavior is described by Krauss in *Backward Day* [88] where a boy does everything backward one day. In a rather contrived way his family goes along with him, but he has enough discomfort to decide that "backward day is done," and to behave accordingly.

Munari's *Jimmy Has Lost His Cap* (see p. 133) seems thoroughly amusing to children because Jimmy's cap turns out to be on his own head, but neither Jimmy nor the reader know it until the end because of the format of the book and the illustrations.

Good illustrations invariably need to carry the humor as it appears in the text in children's books; that is why author-illustrators such as Gag, Duvoisin, and Rey reach artistic success in conveying humor. One of Duvoisin's most popular books is the very funny *Petunia* [89] who is a really big silly goose. Her head swells with false pride to such proportions that it becomes too big to fit on the page of the book! When children laugh at Petunia they seem to enjoy their own superiority to such obvious foolishness. "*I* know better than that" they seem to imply.

Preposterously funny deeds in children's books are not peculiar to animals. In *The Man Who Didn't Wash His Dishes* [90] it is a grown-up whose ideas and actions are way out of kilter when he uses up all the dishes and eats out of flower pots, ash trays, and such. The reader need not worry that children will take over the man's notion of housekeeping, for the author brings an effective and good resolution to the man's problem.

Another humorous book with a wrong-doing adult who gets into predicaments is *Hurry Hurry* [91] in which a conscientious but misguided Miss Mugs hurries herself silly and falls in a manhole. Not heeding a warning that something worse might happen she continues to hurry and gets stuck in spilled glue. Like the man with the dirty dishes Miss Mugs gets reformed in the end (only she does it with the help of a child).

Not infrequently humorous books do have a moral, or they may at least succeed in having the reader question certain undesirable behavior. However there is never any deliberate moralizing in a succssful humor-

[87] Phyllis Rowand, *George* (Boston, Little, Brown and Co., 1956).

[88] Ruth Krauss, *Backward Day*, illus. Marc Simont (New York, Harper & Row, Publishers, 1950).

[89] Roger Duvoisin, *Petunia* (New York, Alfred A. Knopf, Inc., 1950).

[90] Phyllis Krasilovsky, *The Man Who Didn't Wash His Dishes*, illus. Barbara Cooney (Garden City, N.Y., Doubleday & Co., Inc., 1950).

[91] Edith Thatcher Hurd, *Hurry, Hurry*, illus. Clement Hurd (New York, Harper & Row, Publishers, 1960).

ous book. *Harry, the Dirty Dog* [92] is a very funny book in more than name only. Harry's actions in evading washing and find ways of getting dirty are completely understandable to young children. But dirty Harry appreciates the benefits of becoming a clean dog, although there is a bit of a suggestion that he may not stay that way very long.

As anyone familiar with children knows, they find sure cause for laughter in physical mishaps and in slapstick situations, as do many grown-ups. Falling down, getting squashed, and spilling over are the funniest things to happen (to someone else). Accounts of furious fighting are screamingly funny, and inflicting damage in the process makes the situation all the funnier. In *Finders Keepers* (see p. 147) two witless dogs are perpetually quarrelling and getting tricked and appear very amusing! In the end they do arrive at an agreement. Unrestrained physical combat seems especially funny in verse form and there are many examples of it in Mother Goose and in other folk rhymes. *Two Cats* [93] for example could not possibly be as funny in straight prose:

Two Cats

> There once were two cats of Kilkenny,
> Each thought there was one cat too many,
> So they fought and they fit,
> And they scratched and they bit,
> Till, excepting their nails
> And the tips of their tails,
> Instead of two cats, there weren't any.

Could the reader ever translate the above into prose?

Even the subject of sickness can be set to humor and Bemelmans does in *Madeline* (see p. 148); the children invariably smile when at the end the little girls who have never had an operation cry, "Boo-hoo! We want our appendix out, too!"

Names can be terribly funny, like "Doctor Squash"; some children laugh just hearing this name. Could it be that some children feel they have a bone to pick with doctors and enjoy the implication of derision in the silly name? "Mrs. Piggle Wiggle" [94] is a name that affects one like a tickle.

Wanda Gag's *The Funny Thing* [95] also carries out the promise of

[92] Gene Zion, *Harry, the Dirty Dog*, illus. Margaret Bloy Graham (New York, Harper & Row, Publishers, 1958).

[93] *Counting Rhymes*, illus. Corinne Malvern (New York, Little Golden Book, Simon and Schuster, 1947).

[94] Betty MacDonald, *Mrs. Piggle Wiggle*, illus. Hilary Knight (Philadelphia, J. B. Lippincott Co., 1957).

[95] Wanda Gag, *The Funny Thing* (New York, Coward-McCann, Inc., 1929).

humor in telling about "an aminal" who boasts of his appetite for dolls and "jumjills."

In many books words alone strike a humorous note, as in *Gaggle of Geese* (see p. 143) or in many humorous verses which we will discuss presently. The teacher can save such special books to savor humor together with the children, and let the experience lighten the mood and brighten their perception of the fascinating English language.

POETRY AVAILABLE TO CHILDREN

Poetry is also prominent in great literature for children. There are ancient lines of poetry in lullabies for infants, in action rhymes for babies, in the timeless verses of old Mother Goose, and in the linguistic frolics of modern humorists. There is musical, imaginative poetry, both old and new, intriguing, uniquely revealing glimpses of childhood by authors of the past and present, and some succinct and sensory descriptive poems in the contemporary "here and now" vein.

As with stories, poems too must be suitable for the children who are to hear them. Poetry has too much to offer as pure pleasure to be wasted by inappropriate selection. There are several criteria which affect the choice of poems for the very young.

Briefness of Form Suits the Child's Attention Span

As a literary form poetry is particularly appealing to young children provided the subject matter is within their range of comprehension. Many poems are short and direct, so that for young children with characteristic single-mindedness and short attention span, a poem can be just the right exercise in listening. Even a poem of only four lines can be perfectly complete and perfectly attuned to the young child's experience. Here is a four line poem to start a day with:

> I wake in the morning early
> And always, the very first thing,
> I poke out my head and I sit up in bed
> And I sing and I sing and I sing.[96]

Here is one to describe the rain:

> The rain is raining all around,
> It falls on field and tree,

[96] Rose Fyleman, "Singing Time," *The Golden Picture Book of Poems,* Ilse Hayes Govoni and Dorothy Hall Smith, eds., illus. Grace Dalles Clarke (New York, Simon and Schuster, Inc., 1955).

It rains on the umbrellas here,
And on the ships at sea.[97]

or to tell what befell on a winter night:

The snow fell softly all the night.
It made a blanket soft and white.
It covered houses, flowers and ground,
But did not make a single sound.[98]

Going a bit beyond four lines, what five-year-old can resist this tidbit?

Little

I am the sister of him
And he is my brother
He is too little for us
To talk to each other.

So every morning, I show him
My doll and my book:
But every morning,
He still is too little to look.[99]

Or this one, of which one could read only the first or first and second stanzas to start with!

The Squirrel

Whiskey, friskey
Hippity hop,
Up he goes.
To the tree top!

Whirly, twirly
Round and round
Down he scampers
To the ground.

Furly, curly
What a tail!
Tall as a feather
Broad as a sail!

Where's his supper
In the shell,
Snappity, crackity,
Out it fell.[100]

[97] Robert Louis Stevenson, in *Ibid.*
[98] Alice Wilkins, "Snow," in *Time for Poetry*, May Hill Arbuthnot, illus. Arthur Paul (Chicago, Scott, Foresman & Co., 1952).
[99] Dorothy Aldis, in *Read Aloud Poems*, compiled by Marjorie Burns (Chicago, Rand McNally & Co., 1957).
[100] Author unknown, in *Poems for the Children's Hour*, compiled by Josephine Bouton (New York, The Platt & Munk Co., Inc., 1945).

Almost any of the many editions of Mother Goose is also a good source for a short poem that may tell a story, such as the following:

Little Bird

Once I saw a little bird
Come hop, hop, hop;
So I cried, "Little bird,
Will you stop, stop, stop!"
I was going to the window
To say, "How do you do?"
But he shook his little tail,
And away he flew.[101]

or please with a chanting rhythm;

Polly, put the kettle on,
Polly, put the kettle on,
Polly, put the kettle on,
And let's have tea.[102]

The kindergarten teacher can gather her own collection of short poems for reading and rereading and keep them handy by typing each favorite on a 3 x 5 card. Such cards can then be classified and kept in an attractive card file on the desk, always ready for that unexpected extra minute when a poem is just the thing. Short poems heard again and again encourage memorizing and whet the appetite for more and longer selections.

Poetic Imagery Must Be Within the Range of Children's Imaginative Power

The language of poetry has vivid imagery to which children, being imaginative themselves, respond strongly. The teacher must be sure however, that the imagery in the poems she reads is comprehensible to preschool children. Word pictures must go back to something known or experienced in a child's life so that his imagination can make the necessary leaps from there. When Alice Wilkins, in the poem "Snow" (see p. 156) refers to snow as "a blanket, soft and white," children can understand that, since blankets actually have meaning to them in sensory terms. And in this poem about storms,

On stormy days
When the wind is high
Tall trees are brooms
Sweeping the sky.[103]

[101] Toni Frissell, *Mother Goose* (New York, Harper & Row, Publishers, 1948).
[102] Toni Frissell, *Ibid.*
[103] Dorothy Aldis, *Hello Day,* illus. Susan Ilson (New York, G. P. Putnam's Sons, 1959).

the children can follow the fresh imagery of trees as sweeping brooms because they know well how brooms function and they are thoroughly familiar with trees, which in their eyes seem to touch the sky. The easiest images for young children to conjure are images that have roots in the physical experiences known with one's eyes, nose, ears, hands, or feet.

Every word of this poem whispers, is imagery, and yet is all on a child's level:

> Whispers
> > tickle through your ear
> > telling things you like to hear.
>
> Whispers
> > are soft as skin
> > letting little words curl in
>
> Whispers
> > come so they can blow
> > secrets others never know.[104]

An unforgettable, amusing image is ". . . a feather is a letter from a bird," that appears in an enchanting book called *Something Special*.[105] And some children have even had the kind of experience that makes Carl Sandburg's "Fog"[106] clearly visible in their mind's eye:

> The fog comes
> On little cat feet.
> It sits looking
> Over harbor and city
> On silent haunches
> And then moves on.

Poetry is an Expression of Children's Feelings and Fantasies

There are many poets who express feelings, fantasies, and reflections which children recognize as their own but which they usually cannot articulate. Dorothy Baruch is one such author whose poems speak pointedly of the thoughts and wishes of children. In her collection *I Would Like To Be a Pony and Other Wishes*,[107] she gives reasons for wanting to be something, and whether fanciful or humorous, the reasons

[104] Myra Cohn Livingston, *Whispers and Other Poems*, illus. Jacqueline Chwast (New York, Harcourt, Brace & World, Inc., 1955).

[105] Beatrice S. de Regniers, *Something Special*, illus. Irene Haas (New York, Harcourt, Brace & World, Inc., 1958).

[106] Carl Sandburg, "Fog," in *Chicago Poems* (New York, Holt, Rinehart & Winston, Inc., 1944).

[107] Dorothy Baruch, *I Would Like To Be a Pony and Other Wishes*, illus. Mary Chalmers (New York, Harper & Row, Publishers, 1959).

are profoundly childlike; the child's reason for "I'd Like To Be a Whale" is to swallow his mother so he could keep her home that night.

Another successful children's poet, Dorothy Aldis, expresses children's moods and the meaning of daily experiences in a clear and realistic manner, as in the following: [108]

> Everybody says
> I look just like my mother
> Everybody says
> I'm the image of Aunt Bee.
> Everybody says
> My nose is like my father's
> But I want to look like me!

A. A. Milne, who is read as much now as when his poems first appeared in the twenties, tells of the unique puzzling position in being halfway down the stairs, which isn't at the bottom, but half way up isn't up, "It isn't really anywhere!" [109] And he tells of the tiresomeness and even dullness of answering adults' perpetual, polite questions in the poem "Politeness" in the same book. Milne describes the busyness of being a muffin man, a postman, a bear, and then an elephant with one dizzying "round about" motion after another, in the poem "Busy." [110] And he conveys the sense of inordinate pride in achieving six-year-oldness:

> But now I am Six, I'm as clever as clever,
> So I think I'll be six now for ever and ever.[111]

Most of Milne's poems in *When We Were Very Young* and *Now We Are Six* could be quoted in full or in part to show how well he expresses a child's way of thinking, but some of them can be appreciated more by adults than by children and one must be selective.

The Strength and Power of Rhythm in Children's Poems

Perhaps the most immediate appeal of poetry to all young children is the physical appeal of rhythm. Children respond to rhythm and balance naturally with movement of body, or with a clap, a step, a shout, or a song. Just as they enjoy the balance of a see-saw and the bounce on a board, so they wait for the repeat of any refrain. Rhythmic poetry is therefore a natural form of expression to young children. Perhaps the

[108] Dorothy Aldis, *op. cit.*
[109] A. A. Milne, "Half Way Down," in *When We Were Very Young*, illus. E. H. Shepard (New York, E. P. Dutton & Co., Inc., 1954).
[110] A. A. Milne, "Busy," in *Now We Are Six*, illus. E. H. Shepard (New York, E. P. Dutton & Co., Inc., 1954).
[111] A. A. Milne, "The End," in *Ibid.*

strong rhythmic quality of the Mother Goose rhymes is one reason for the survival of these verses in spite of the fact that the content of many is strange to modern children. "Jack be nimble, Jack be quick/ Jack jump over the candle-stick!" has powerful stimulus to keep time and to execute a jump. The same holds for "One for the money/ two for the show/ three to get ready and/ four to go!" Children will say it, breathe it, and move to it without any thought of the meaning of each phrase. The pattern of numbers and of counting occurs often in *Mother Goose* and other folk rhymes and is quite prevalent in children's poetry. A particularly beautiful children's story poem with a strong rhythm and counting pattern is the familiar *Over In the Meadow.*[112]

> Over in the meadow,
> In the sand, in the sun,
> Lived an old mother turtle
> And her little turtle one.

Each animal has a different and appropriate function and an increasing number of young, all living "over in the meadow," although different versions of this folk poem have different animals. It has an enchanting lilt and is highly conducive to memorizing.

In Milne's poem which expresses perfectly a child's rhythmic and spirited motion,

> Christopher Robin goes
> Hoppity, hoppity,
> Hoppity, hoppity, hop.
> Whenever I tell him
> Politely to stop it, he
> Says he can't possibly stop.[113]

the sound, the accent on the word, the length of syllable all contribute to the quality of the rhythm.

The same is true of these lines of Eleanor Farjeon:

> Mrs. Peck Pigeon
> Is picking for bread,
> Bob-bob-bob
> Goes her little round head.
> Step-step-step
> Go her little red feet.[114]

[112] John Langstaff, *Over In the Meadow*, illus. Feodor Rojankovsky (New York, Harcourt, Brace & World, Inc., 1957).

[113] A. A. Milne, "Hoppity," in *When We Were Very Young*, illus. E. H. Shepard (New York, E. P. Dutton & Co., Inc., 1954).

[114] Eleanor Farjeon, "Mrs. Peck Pigeon," in *Over the Garden Wall* (Philadelphia, Frederick Stokes Co., 1933).

Also appealing is the rhythmic quality of the precise action words in Evelyn Beyer's poem "Jump or Jiggle" [115] describing the styles of locomotion in different animals which jump, hump, wiggle, jiggle, ending with "lions stalk, but—I walk."

The Liveliness of Humor in Children's Poetry

Humor abounds in children's poetry. There are innumerable humorous verses in collections of folk rhymes, in *Mother Goose*, and in the verses of Edward Lear who is a specialist in humorous poetry. There are ripples and trickles of humor in much of children's poetry in general because rhyme and humor seem to go especially well together whatever the subject. There are many thoroughly amusing alphabet books in rhyme; among the older ones are Wanda Gag's *A B C Bunny* [116] and several alphabet verses by Edward Lear. [117] Although limericks are generally too subtle for preschoolers five-year-olds do appreciate the humor, the rhymes, and the ridiculous situation of Lear's

> There was an Old Man with a beard
> Who said, "It is just as I feared!—
> Two Owls and a Hen, four Larks and a Wren
> Have all built their nests in my beard." [118]

A gay collection of humorous poetry is *Tirra Lirra*,[119] a volume that first appeared in 1902. It has poems with humorous ideas; in "Talents Differ," a robin boasts of "doing the thing that you cannot do," and a child finally answers in kind. "The Difference" tells what happens when one nose is not enough and the contrary when one nose is plenty. Many of the poems are amusing plays on words and tongue twisters much appreciated by kindergartners:

> Once there was an elephant,
> Who tried to use the telephant—
> No! No! I mean the elephone
> Who tried to use the telephone.

Mary Ann Hoberman has definite humor in the name of her imaginary character "The King of Umpalazo," who is a preposterous kind of a king

[115] Evelyn Beyer, "Jump or Jiggle," in Barbara Peck Geisner and Antoinette Sutter, *Very Young Verses*, illus. Mildred Bronson (Boston, Houghton Mifflin Co., 1945).

[116] Wanda Gag, *A B C Bunny* (New York, Coward-McCann, Inc., 1933).

[117] Edward Lear, *The Complete Nonsense Book* (New York, Dodd, Mead & Co., 1946).

[118] Edward Lear, *Ibid.*

[119] Laura Richards, *Tirra Lirra*, illus. Marguerite Davis (Boston, Little, Brown and Co., 1955).

in appearance and eating habits, consuming "cracker meal and lemon peel", and is "a funny old honey" with nothing royal about him! [120] Appealing and enjoyable as humorous poetry can be, a teacher must use it sparingly to leaven the spirits and loosen limbs with a feeling of fun. For greatest enjoyment it is best not to overdo it.

Poetry as Language Learning

Along with this rapid growth on all levels the preschool child makes notable strides in language development. Huck and Young (see p. 129) point out that the greatest increase in vocabulary occurs between the ages of two and six years. Such readiness for lingual expansion on the part of children should prompt the kindergarten teacher to offer the best in the fascinating English language. Children can increase their vocabulary with words of distinctive meaning, become familiar with poetic imagery, be attuned to the pleasures of rhythm, experience the joy of rhyme, and develop an ear for the richness of sound. Five-year-olds can get to know how only eight different words arranged in four lines can present an impressive panorama and give an exciting feeling about the far and the familiar:

> Over the mountains
> Over the plains
> Over the rivers
> Here come the trains.[121]

And they can feel the sound of "one misty, moisty morning" (*Mother Goose*) on their lips and appreciate such descriptive words as "cuddle-down, hide-away house in the grass." [122] What fun to learn such interesting, stimulating words as encountered in poetry!

PRACTICAL CONSIDERATIONS IN PROVIDING LITERATURE FOR KINDERGARTEN

In this chapter on literature we surveyed the literary qualities of children's books and the appropriate content and use of good stories and poems to serve the emotional and intellectual needs of children. We made reference to a large number of specific literary works. The teacher of

[120] Mary Ann Hoberman, "The King of Umpalazo," in *Hello and Good-by*, illus. Norman Hoberman (Boston, Little, Brown & Co., 1959).

[121] James Tippett, "Trains," in *I Go A-Traveling*, illus. Elizabeth T. Wolcott (New York, Harper & Row, Publishers, 1929).

[122] Lucy Sprague Mitchell, "The House of the Mouse," in *Another Here and Now Book* (New York, E. P. Dutton & Co., Inc., 1937).

course cannot get to know everything recommended. She may therefore have a practical question now as to which ones of the books to use, as well as where and how to obtain them.

Keeping a Variety of Books

Keeping a variety of books and stories is important not only for the development of children's and teachers' taste but to meet the various needs and the changing interests of five-year-olds. There must be some picture books on the shelves for the children to reach and hold and look through in a personal, leisurely way, books which the teacher periodically inspects, replaces, and changes. There must be picture books and content books both on the open shelves for children and on the teacher's private shelves, books used for specific needs and to answer questions pertaining to environment, community, seasons, family, or any subject of current concern to the class. Although preschool children's stories should not be too long because the children's attention span and sitting endurance is short, the teacher must be prepared for the children's development and future readiness for longer stories. Such a longer story may be *Blueberries for Sal* (see p. 141), in which the plot develops to such an extent that the children want to listen and find out how it will be resolved. Another is *Poppy Seed Cakes,* (see p. 141), which has chapters with separate episodes, and children who have sustained interest in the book will remember the previous chapters or request the subsequent ones. As they acquire more literary experience the children become interested in following the adventures of a hero in different situations. They can appreciate a longer story with fuller character development and complexity of relationships and events. A good example of a longer book with chapters is Claudia Lewis' *Straps the Cat,*[123] which is 142 pages long and is written in narrative style.

To insure variety in the kindergarten library, some anthologies of stories and poems are indispensable. *Believe and Make-Believe* [124] for example has a variety of subjects and styles, with fifty-three separate titles representing twenty-five authors. Some stories answer directly the urgent questions about the physical world; some are humorous treatments of familiar situations; the fantasy stories are close to children's own feelings and fancies. The characters in these stories are varied; boys, girls, cats, mice, monkeys, freight cars, freighters, television, rain, water, and wind. One poem, "Rain," by Betty Miles, is an elemental expression of commun-

[123] Claudia Lewis, *Straps the Cat,* illus. Cornelis Ruhtenberg (New York, William R. Scott, Inc., 1957).

[124] *Believe and Make-Believe,* Lucy Sprague Mitchell and Irma S. Black, eds., illus. Ayala Gordon (New York, E. P. Dutton & Co., Inc., 1956).

ion and union with the rain, something that young children sense intensely.

In an anthology the teacher can select a story or poem to reflect the time of year or weather, to express the meaning of special holidays, or to reveal notable traits of particular animals. And any good anthology will of course have stories for fun and laughter.

Several good collections for the kindergarten are Rhoda Bacmeister's *Stories to Begin On*,[125] The Child Study Association's *Read-to-Me Storybooks*,[126] Sidone Gruenberg's *Favorite Stories, Old and New*,[127] Margaret Wise Brown's *The Fish With the Deep Sea Smile*.[128] One or two versions of *Mother Goose* would be useful to have. The Tenggren version (Little, Brown, 1940) has attractive lettering and good printing: the whimsical stylized pictures have a tasteful quality of oldness and tradition, while the version by de Angeli [129] is more modern in design and the distinctive illustrations in it are full page and small, some in color and some in black and white. But each teacher may have her own favorite edition of this curious rich folk anthology with the fanciful yet universally familiar titles of Mother Goose.

Among the many poetry collections is May Hill Arbuthnot's *Time For Poetry*.[130] This is a remarkably varied and fitting anthology for young children and has an inspiring and guiding introduction for teachers.

When the teacher has a fairly satisfactory variety on her bookshelves she still needs to evaluate her collection periodically and make additions and changes in her library as this seems necessary.

Sources

Where should the teacher go to look for, to borrow, to buy, or to in some way obtain books?

To get a general idea of what books are being published for younger children she may write to publishers for the latest free descriptive catalogues. Better still she may read reviews of children's books in newspapers, magazines or professional periodicals. She may also obtain free or for a nominal fee specially selected and annotated lists from various educational organizations of recommended books. The teacher must

[125] Rhoda Bacmeister, *Stories To Begin On* (New York, E. P. Dutton & Co., Inc., 1940).

[126] Child Study Association of America (compiled by), *Read-to-Me Story Book* (New York, Thomas Y. Crowell Company, 1951).

[127] Sidonie M. Gruenberg, *Favorite Stories, Old and New* (Garden City, N.Y., Doubleday & Company, Inc., 1945).

[128] Margaret Wise Brown, *The Fish With The Deep Sea Smile* (William R. Scott, Inc., 1959).

[129] Marguerite de Angeli, *Book of Nursery and Mother Goose Rhymes* (Garden City, N.Y., Doubleday & Co., Inc., 1954).

[130] May Hill Arbuthnot, *Time For Poetry*, illus. Arthur Paul (Chicago, Scott, Foresman & Co., 1952).

make as judicious a use of her book budget as she can and supplement the necessary supply with library borrowing. The pressure to change library books at stated intervals may even prove to be a special advantage. If the library facilities are inadequate and the teacher would like to have certain books that are important but unobtainable with her limited funds, she may ask her librarian to borrow books from a larger collection or she may borrow books herself from other teachers in school. She may also appeal to the parents of the group to raise money or perhaps collect a Christmas Gift Fund for the class to buy books with, providing the parents understand how much books are appreciated, used, and needed by the children. This may serve as a welcome way of eliminating the worry on the part of some parents of purchasing a Christmas gift for the teacher, all of which would of course depend on how the teacher feels both about books and about gifts.

One teacher felt so keenly about having a sufficient library in her class, so concerned about cultivating children's love of books, and so interested in promoting parents' concern with children's books that she evolved a unique, practical project: on a child's birthday, celebrated in school very simply and without gifts, the child presented to the class an inscribed copy of a book which he and his parents selected and purchased from a list of known favorites. Besides giving everybody pleasure in acquiring a new book, this gave the birthday child and his parents an interesting experience in selecting a book and offering a birthday gift rather than receiving one, which a five or a six-year-old can usually appreciate. Furthermore there is special satisfaction in having one's name written in a book, to be acknowledged by present classmates and future acquaintances or siblings. To carry out such a project the teacher has to appreciate books well enough to consult with and advise parents, communicating her enthusiasm to them. She also has to be flexible in order to see when some child may rightly not want to give a book away or when some parent may not care to spend money to enrich the kindergarten. But when such a project is largely successful—in a class of eighteen to twenty-five children, and double that when there are two sessions with most children having birthdays during the term—a sizable library of good books can really be built up over the years. The teacher and the class could then have a special joy in getting a book when it just comes out or is recently reviewed.

Care of Books

Having selected and collected a fairly good kindergarten library, the teacher and children can by no means take for granted the continued good function of such a library; they cannot remain free of responsibility as far as their books are concerned. Good care of books begins with the teacher's own respect and interest in books, and these are reflected in the way in which she picks books up, handles them, puts them in place, and also in her consistently calling children's attention to the protection of books. To facilitate care there must be a definite place for books so they will not be left on the hot radiator, dropped into an obscure dusty corner, or be lost in some miscellaneous pile. Although wide slanting shelves for holding and displaying books are best, even clean, painted, proper-sized orange crates with a cleared table and chairs nearby can be quite servicable if attended to by teacher and children together. The proper way of turning one page of a book at a time, and even the use of a book mark, can be learned and practiced by children with the teacher's repeated demonstration.

Picking up and putting books away in the right place is a habit that a teacher should strive to cultivate in children and herself, but she must do it out of respect for books and not with the righteousness of a compulsive housekeeper. And out of respect for property the teacher should keep, with the children, a record of borrowed books and dates for returning. Appreciating the books and recognizing their usefulness and material worth, the teacher needs to help children detect damages and share in some simple repairs with transparent or binding tape. Such physical care will not only protect and prolong the life of the books, but will further children's appreciation of books.

HOW AND WHEN TO READ TO CHILDREN

It is easy to depend so much on the charm of children's books that one may ignore the very important art of reading a story to children. Often the way in which a story is read, as well as the time during the program when it is read, can make the difference between a thoroughly satisfying experience and a routine one.

Know the Book and Think of Your Listeners

Just knowing the title of a book is not enough preparation for reading it. One Kitten Too Many [131] for example proves to have little to do with cats or children's interest in cats. Instead, it involves the children's feelings about family status and requires the sensitivity of the teacher's inner and outer ear when reading it.

You need to have read a book at least once to yourself before try-

[131] Bianca Bradbury, *One Kitten Too Many*, illus. Marie Nichols (Boston, Houghton Mifflin Co., 1952).

ing it on others out loud. It is important to be sensitive to the total implications of a story in such a way that your phrasing, pacing, and pauses as
you read aloud will point to the particular meaning, the narrative flow,
and the rhythmic pattern of the words. The matter of what to emphasize
is especially pertinent in books of humor, where with the wrong emphasis
or no emphasis at all the humor of a story can elude the children completely. Suspense, excitement, tenderness, anger, surprise, dismay—all
these are carried in the reader's voice and heightened by the tempo with
which the phrases or single words, sometimes, are offered to the children.

Do Not Be Shy

How, the reader may ask, can the average teacher exercise such
fine points of elocution and drama? The answer lies in being an honest
amateur actor and even a ham. Try to overcome your inhibitions about
using voice and gestures freely. Do not be afraid to chant, hiss, or bray
when the dialogue calls for this, and do not be embarassed about devising
necessary sounds or using a foreign phrase in the right place. Children
love their stories read with dramatic emphasis, and if you do overdo it
some child will surely curb your exaggerations with a "You look silly
when you make a face!" If you have never tried reading a story with the
full range of expression and rhythm the story calls for, start now and learn
to love reading to the children as much as they will love listening.

May They Interrupt?

What about interruptions in reading? Let us recognize that the
teacher herself often intrudes on the story's flow of words with a brief
aside, an explanation, or an illustration that makes the story clearer to
follow. In doing so she heightens the satisfaction in the story, for she uses
the interruption to enhance, not destroy, the unity of the tale. Often by
doing this she avoids confusions and interrupting questions on the part of
the children. However, children will interrupt with comments or questions in any case, and there is no formula for what to do. As with the
teacher's comments, enhancement of the story and pleasure in it is the
first consideration. And interruptions from the children are not necessarily
disrupting influences at all. The teacher's decision to curb the children
depends more on the situation than on anything else. Experienced children may not be frustrated at all about withholding comments and waiting for a discussion when storytime is over. But more often a spontaneous
reaction from a child needs to be uttered for its importance to the child,
and one has to absorb it and save the story too. Teachers themselves have
different degrees of tolerance for interruptions. But if one realizes that one

is reading to children for *their* sakes then one can better evaluate whether interruptions are truly important to the children (even if it means not finishing the story, itself an interesting lesson, although *not* a punishment), or whether a gentle reminder that it would be better to let the story proceed is in order.

Kindergartners will adjust to reasonable regulations about interruptions if they have experienced the teacher's genuine interest in literature and her communication with them. They feel these by the sensitivity with which she reads to them, by the way she tries to embrace the group with her eyes, by the way she looks at each child at some point as she reads or shows pictures, and by her special comments pertinent to one child or to the group, and inspired by the story.

Time for a Story

Settling on a good time to read to children cannot be done by formula either. Some teachers may plan a definite time for reading every day and prepare the children for it; others may read sometimes by plan and sometimes when the opportunity presents itself. At no time should one begin a story for which there is not enough time to reach the end, unless of course it is to read a chapter in a continuing tale. When there is a free minute or two when waiting to go home, or during the dull quiet of resting time, a teacher can read a short poem or two. Lovely words reaching children's ears for a mere minute can be remembered for hours or days.

TEACHERS' OWN KNOWLEDGE OF, AND FEELING FOR, BOOKS

As the kindergarten teacher becomes responsible for exposure of children to literature, as she acquires discrimination in selection from the available abundance, and as she becomes sensitive to children's responses to literary qualities and forms, she will be acquiring her own significant knowledge of the field of children's literature. Such knowledge will give her maturity in judgment of books and may heighten her taste.

Continued intellectual involvement with books together with the understanding of children will contribute to the depth of the teacher's feeling for books. A teacher who has acquired a feeling for books will know how to read or tell a story to children effectively. Appreciating the material, she will give it intelligent interpretation, convey her own enthusiasm, and not be inhibited in the proper use of voice and illustrative gestures to give some color and feeling to her presentation.

Bibliography

Adelson, Leone, *All Ready for Summer,* illus. Kathleen Elgin (New York, David McKay Co., Inc., 1955).

——, *All Ready for Winter,* illus. Kathleen Elgin (New York, David McKay Co., Inc., 1952).

Aldis, Dorothy, *Hello Day,* illus. Susan Ilson (New York, G. P. Putnam's Sons, 1959).

——, *Read Aloud Poems,* compiled by Marjorie Burns (Skokie, Ill., Rand McNally & Co., 1957).

Bannerman, Helen, *Little Black Sambo,* illus. Gustaf Tenggren (New York, Golden Press, 1948).

Baruch, Dorothy, *I Would Like To Be a Pony and Other Wishes,* illus. Mary Chalmers (New York, Harper & Row, Publishers, 1959).

Beim, Jerrold, *The Smallest Boy in the Class,* illus. Meg Wohlberg (New York, William Morrow & Co., Inc., 1949).

Beim, L. and J., *Two is a Team,* illus. Ernest Crichlow (New York, Harcourt, Brace & World, Inc., 1945).

Bemelmans, Ludwig, *Madeline* (New York, Simon and Schuster, Inc., 1939).

Bendick, Jeanne, *All Around You,* illus. by author (New York, McGraw-Hill Book Co., Inc., 1951).

Beskow, Elsa, *Pell's New Suit* (New York, Harper & Row, Publishers, 1929).

Beyer, Evelyn, "Jump or Jiggle," in Barbara Peck Geisner and Antoinette Sutter, *Very Young Verses,* illus. Mildred Bronson (Boston, Houghton Mifflin Company, 1945).

Black, Irma S., *Night Cat,* illus. Paul Galdone (New York, Holiday House, 1957).

——, "What is Work?", in *Believe and Make-Believe,* Lucy Sprague Mitchell, ed. (New York, E. P. Dutton & Co., Inc., 1956).

Bouton, Josephine, *Poems for the Children's Hour* (New York, The Platt & Munk Co., Inc., 1945).

Bradbury, Bianca, *One Kitten Too Many,* illus. Marie Nichols (Boston, Houghton Mifflin Company, 1952).

Branley, Franklin M., and Vaughan, Eleanor K., *Mickey's Magnet,* illus. Crockett Johnson (New York, Thomas Y. Crowell Company, 1956).

Brenner, Barbara, *Barto Takes the Subway,* illus. with photographs by Sy Katzoff (New York, Alfred A. Knopf, Inc., 1961).

Brown, Margaret Wise, *Doctor Squash, the Doll Doctor,* illus. J. P. Miller (New York, Little Golden Book, Simon & Schuster, Inc., 1952).

———, *Little Frightened Tiger,* illus. Leonard Weisgard (Garden City, N.Y., Doubleday & Company, Inc., 1953).

———, *The Dead Bird,* illus. Remy Charlip (New York, William R. Scott, Inc., 1958).

———, *The Noisy Book,* illus. Leonard Weisgard (New York, Harper & Row, Publishers, 1939).

———, *The Runaway Bunny,* illus. Clement Hurd (New York, Harper & Row, Publishers, 1942).

———, *Wait Till the Moon is Full,* illus. Garth Williams (New York, Harper & Row, Publishers, 1948).

———, *Willie's Adventures,* illus. Crockett Johnson (New York, William R. Scott, Inc., 1954).

Buckley, Helen, *Grandfather and I,* illus. Paul Galdone (New York, Lothrop, Lee & Shepard Co., Inc., 1959).

Burton, Virginia Lee, *Katy and the Big Snow* (Boston, Houghton Mifflin Company, 1943).

———, *Mike Mulligan and His Steam Shovel* (Boston, Houghton Mifflin Company, 1939).

Clark, Marjory, *Poppy Seed Cakes,* illus. Maud and Miska Petersham (Garden City, N.Y., Doubleday & Company, Inc., 1929).

Davis, Alice, *Timothy Turtle,* illus. Guy Brown Wiser (New York, Harcourt, Brace & World, Inc., 1940).

de Angeli, Marguerite, *Book of Nursery and Mother Goose Rhymes* (Garden City, N.Y., Doubleday & Company, Inc., 1954).

de Regniers, Beatrice S., *A Little House of Your Own,* illus. Irene Haas (New York, Harcourt, Brace & World, Inc., 1955).

———, *Something Special,* illus. Irene Haas (New York, Harcourt, Brace & World, Inc., 1958).

———, *The Giant Story,* illus. Maurice Sendak (New York, Harper & Row, Publishers, 1953).

Duvoisin, Roger, *Petunia* (New York, Alfred A. Knopf, Inc., 1950).

———, *Veronica* (New York, Alfred A. Knopf, Inc., 1961).

Evans, Eva K., *Araminta,* illus. Erick Berry (New York, G. P. Putnam's Sons, 1935).

———, Jerome Anthony, illus. Erick Berry (New York, G. P. Putnam's Sons, 1936).

Farjeon, Eleanor, "Mrs. Peck Pigeon," in *Over the Garden Wall* (Philadelphia, Frederick Stokes Co., 1933).

Felt, Sue, *Rosa-Too-Little,* illus. by author (Garden City, N.Y., Doubleday & Company, Inc., 1950).

Flack, Marjory, *The New Pet* (Garden City, N.Y., Doubleday & Company, Inc., 1943).

———, *Wait for William,* illus. by author and Richard Hulberg (Boston, Houghton Mifflin Company, 1935).

Frissell, Toni, *Mother Goose* (New York, Harper & Row, Publishers, 1948).

Fyleman, Rose, "Singing Time," in *The Golden Picture Book of Poems*, select. Ilse Hayes Govoni and Dorothy Hall Smith, illus. Grace Dalles Clarke (New York, Simon & Schuster, Inc., 1955).

Gag, Wanda, *A B C Bunny* (New York, Coward-McCann, Inc., 1933).

———, *Millions of Cats* (New York, Coward-McCann, Inc., 1928).

———, *Nothing at All* (New York, Coward-McCann, Inc., 1941).

———, *The Funny Thing* (New York, Coward-McCann, Inc., 1929).

Garelick, May, *Where Does the Butterfly Go When It Rains?*, illus. Leonard Weisgard (New York, William R. Scott, Inc., 1961).

Hoberman, Mary Ann, "The King of Umpalazo," in *Hello and Good-bye*, illus. Norman Hoberman (Boston, Little, Brown and Company, 1959).

Hurd, Edith Thatcher, *Hurry, Hurry*, illus. Clement Hurd (New York, Harper & Row, Publishers, 1960).

Kepes, Juliet, *Frogs Merry*, illus. by author (New York, Pantheon Books, Inc., 1961).

Krasilovsky, Phyllis, *The Man Who Didn't Wash His Dishes*, illus. Barbara Cooney (Garden City, N.Y., Doubleday & Company, Inc., 1950).

———, *The Very Little Girl*, illus. Ninon (Garden City N.Y., Doubleday & Company, Inc., 1953).

Krauss, Ruth, *Backward Day*, illus. Marc Simont (New York, Harper & Row, Publishers, 1950).

———, *The Carrot Seed*, illus. Crockett Johnson (New York, Harper & Row, Publishers, 1945).

———, *The Growing Story*, illus. Phyllis Rowand (New York, Harper & Row, Publishers, 1947).

Langstaff, John, *Over in the Meadow*, illus. Feodor Rojankovsky (New York, Harcourt, Brace & World, Inc., 1957).

Langstaff, Nancy, *A Tiny Baby for You*, photography by Suzanne Szasz (New York, Harcourt, Brace & World, Inc., 1955).

Leaf, Munro, *Ferdinand the Bull*, illus. Robert Lawson (New York, The Viking Press, 1936).

Lear, Edward, *The Complete Nonsense Book* (New York, Dodd, Mead, & Co., 1946).

Lewis, Claudia, *Straps the Cat*, illus. Cornelis Ruhtenberg (New York, William R. Scott, Inc., 1957).

Lionni, Leo, *Little Blue and Little Yellow* (New York, Ivan Obolensky, Inc., 1959).

Livingston, Myra Cohn, *Whispers and Other Poems*, illus. Jacqueline Chwast (New York, Harcourt, Brace & World, Inc., 1955).

MacDonald, Betty, *Mrs. Piggle Wiggle*, illus. Hilary Knight (Philadelphia, J. B. Lippincott Co., 1957).

MacDonald, Golden (pseudonym for Margaret Wise Brown), *The Little Island*, illus. Leonard Weisgard (Garden City, N.Y., Doubleday & Company, Inc., 1946).

Malvern, Corinne, *Counting Rhymes* (New York, Little Golden Book, Simon & Schuster, Inc., 1947).

Marino, Dorothy, *Where are the Mothers?*, illus. by the author (Philadelphia, J. B. Lippincott Co., 1959).

Markum, Patricia Mahoney, *First Book of Coal Mining*, illus. Mildred Walter (New York, Frank Watts, Inc., 1959).

McCloskey, Robert, *Blueberries for Sal* (New York, The Viking Press, 1948).

——, *Make Way for Ducklings* (New York, The Viking Press, 1941).

Merriam, Eve, *A Gaggle of Geese*, illus. Paul Galdone (New York, Alfred A. Knopf, Inc., 1960).

Miles, Betty, *A House for Everyone*, illus. Jo Lowery (New York, Alfred A. Knopf, Inc., 1958).

——, *Mr. Turtle's Mystery*, illus. Jacqueline Tomes (New York, Alfred A. Knopf, Inc., 1961).

Milne, A. A., "Busy," in *Now We Are Six*, illus. E. H. Shepard (New York, E. P. Dutton & Co., Inc., 1954).

——, "Half Way Down," in *When We Were Very Young*, illus. E. H. Shepard (New York, E. P. Dutton & Co., Inc., 1954).

——, "Hoppity," in *When We Were Very Young* (New York, E. P. Dutton & Co., Inc., 1954).

——, "The End," in *Now We Are Six*, illus. E. H. Shepard (New York, E. P. Dutton & Co., Inc., 1954).

Minarik, Else H., *Little Bear*, illus. Maurice Sendak (New York, Harper & Row, Publishers, 1957).

Mitchell, Lucy Sprague, *Another Here and Now*, illus. Rosalie Slocum (New York, E. P. Dutton & Co., Inc., 1937).

——, *Here and Now Story Book*, illus. H. W. Van Loon (New York, E. P. Dutton & Co., Inc., 1921).

Mother Goose, illus. Gustaf Tenggren (Boston, Little, Brown and Company, 1940).

Munari, Bruno, *Jimmy Has Lost His Cap*, and *The Birthday Present* (New York, The World Publishing Co., 1959).

Nephew, William, and Chester, Michael, "Moon Trip," in *True Adventures in Space*, illus. Jerry Robinson (New York, G. P. Putnam's Sons, 1959).

Puner, Helen Walker, *Daddies and What They Do All Day*, illus. Roger Duvoisin (New York, Lothrop, Lee & Shepard Co., 1956).

Rands, Ann and Paul, *I Know a Lot of Things* (New York, Harcourt, Brace & World, Inc., 1956).

Rey, H. A., *Curious George* (Boston, Houghton Mifflin Company, 1941).

Reyher, Becky, *My Mother is the Most Beautiful Woman in the World*, illus. Ruth Gannett (New York, Lothrop, Lee & Shepard Co., 1945).

Richards, Laura, *Tirra Lirra*, illus. Marguerite Davis (Boston, Little, Brown and Company, 1955).

Rowand, Phyllis, *George* (Boston, Little, Brown and Company, 1956).

Sandburg, Carl, "Fog," in *Chicago Poems* (New York, Holt, Rinehart & Winston, Inc., 1916).

Schlein, Miriam, *It's About Time*, illus. Sam Berman (New York, William R. Scott, Inc., 1955).

————, *Heavy is a Hippopotamus,* illus. Leonard Kessler (New York, William R. Scott, Inc., 1954).

————, *Shapes,* illus. Sam Berman (New York, William R. Scott, Inc., 1952).

Schwartz, Julius, *It's Fun to Know Why,* illus. Edwin Herron (New York, McGraw-Hill Book Co., Inc., 1952).

Selsam, Millicent E., *All About Eggs and How They Change into Animals,* illus. Helen Ludwig (New York, William R. Scott, Inc., 1952).

————, *All Kinds of Babies,* illus. Helen Ludwig (New York, William R. Scott, Inc., 1953).

————, *Play with Seeds,* illus. Helen Ludwig (New York, William Morrow & Co., Inc., 1957).

————, *Play with Vines,* illus. Fred Scherer (New York, William Morrow & Co., Inc., 1957).

Seuss, Dr., *Horton Hatches an Egg* (New York, Vanguard Press, Inc., 1940).

Simon, Norma, *The Daddy Days,* illus. Abner Graboff (New York, Abelard-Schuman Limited, 1958).

Slobodkina, Esphyr, *Caps For Sale* (New York, William R. Scott, Inc., 1947).

Steiner, Charlotte, *Ten In a Family* (New York, Alfred A. Knopf, Inc., 1960).

The Tall Book of Nursery Tales, illus. Feodor Rojankowsky (New York, Harper & Row, Publishers, 1944).

Tippett, James, "Trains," in *I Go A-Traveling,* illus. Elizabeth T. Wolcott (New York, Harper & Row, Publishers, 1929).

Tresselt, Alvin, *Hi, Mr. Robin!,* illus. Roger Duvoisin (New York, Lothrop, Lee & Shepard Co., Inc., 1950).

————, *Wake Up Farm,* illus. Roger Duvoisin (New York, Lothrop, Lee & Shepard Co., Inc., 1954).

————, *Wake Up City,* illus. Roger Duvoisin (New York, Lothrop, Lee & Shepard Co., Inc., 1954).

————, *White Snow, Bright Snow,* illus. Roger Duvoisin (New York, Lothrop, Lee & Shepard Co., Inc., 1947).

Ward, Lynd, *The Biggest Bear* (Boston, Houghton Mifflin Company, 1952).

Wasson, Valentina P., *The Chosen Baby,* illus. Hildegarde Woodward (Philadelphia, J. B. Lippincott Co., 1950).

Webber, Irma, *Up Above and Down Below* (New York, William R. Scott, Inc., 1950).

Wilkins, Alice, "Snow," in May Hill Arbuthnot, *Time for Poetry,* illus. Arthur Paul (Chicago, Scott, Foresman & Company, 1952).

Will and Nicholas, *Finders Keepers* (New York, Harcourt, Brace & World, Inc., 1952).

Williams, Garth, *The Rabbits' Wedding* (New York, Harper & Row, Publishers, 1958).

Woodcock, Louise, *Wiggles,* illus. Eloise Wilkin (New York, Simon and Schuster, Inc., 1953).

Yashima, Taro, *Umbrella* (New York, The Viking Press, 1958).

Zim, Herbert S., *Rockets and Jets* (New York, Harcourt, Brace & World, Inc., 1945).

Zion, Gene, *Harry, the Dirty Dog,* illus. Margaret B. Graham (New York, Harper & Row, Publishers, 1958).

Zolotow, Charlotte, *Indian Indian,* illus. Leonard Weisgard (New York, Little Golden Book, Simon and Schuster, Inc., 1952).

————, *The Night When Mother Was Away,* illus. Reisie Lonette (New York, Lothrop, Lee & Shepard Co., Inc., 1959).

Collection of stories:

Association for Childhood Education, *Told Under the Blue Umbrella* (New York, The Macmillan Company, 1947).

Bachmeister, Rhoda, *Stories to Begin On* (New York, E. P. Dutton & Co., Inc., 1940).

Child Study Association of America, *Read Me More Stories* (New York, Thomas Y. Crowell Company, 1951).

Mitchell, Lucy Sprague, *Here And Now Story Book* (New York, E. P. Dutton & Co., Inc., 1948).

————, and Black, Irma S., *Believe And Make-Believe* (New York, E. P. Dutton & Co., Inc., 1956).

————, and others, Another *Here And Now Story Book* (New York, E. P. Dutton & Co., Inc., 1937).

Books of poetry:

Aldis, Dorothy, *Hello Day* (New York, G. P. Putnam's Sons, 1959).

Association for Childhood Education, *Sung Under the Silver Umbrella* (New York, The Macmillan Company, 1936).

Baruch, Dorothy, *I Would Like To Be A Pony and Other Wishes* (New York, Harper and Row, Publishers, 1959).

de Regniers, Beatrice, *Something Special* (New York, Harcourt, Brace & World, Inc., 1958).

Field, Rachael, *Taxis and Toadstools* (Garden City, N.Y., Doubleday & Company, Inc., 1926).

Geismer, Barbara, *Very Young Verses* (Boston, Houghton Mifflin Company, 1945).

Livingston, Myra Cohn, *Whispers and Other Poems* (New York, Harcourt, Brace & World, Inc., 1958).

————, *Wide Awake* (New York, Harcourt, Brace & World, Inc., 1959).

Love, Katherine, *Pocketful of Rhymes* (New York, Thomas Y. Crowell Company, 1946).

Poems To Read To The Very Young, select. Josette Frank (New York, Random House, Inc., 1961).

Time For Poetry, May Hill Arbuthnot, ed. (Chicago, Scott, Foresman & Company, 1952).

Tippet, James, *I Go A-Traveling* (New York, Harper & Row, Publishers, 1929).

————, *I Live In A City* (New York, Harper & Row, Publishers, 1927).

————, *I Spend The Summer* (New York, Harper & Row, Publishers, 1930).

Books on children's literature:

Adams, Bess Porter, *About Books and Children* (New York, Holt, Rinehart & Winston, Inc., 1953).

Arbuthnot, May Hill, *Children And Books* (Chicago, Scott, Foresman & Company, 1947).

Huck, Charlotte S., and Young, Doris A., *Children's Literature in the Elementary School* (New York, Holt, Rinehart & Winston, Inc., 1961).

III

the children communicate
feelings and ideas through
arts and skills

9

Scope and Variety of Language Expression

THE HUMAN URGE FOR EXPRESSION THROUGH SYMBOLS

In the last three chapters we discussed the several ways in which teachers can plan for *intake* experiences, that is, for exposure to various types and kinds of intellectual and emotional stimulation. Scientific information, trips, pictures, and books are all intake, all experiences from which one absorbs new material and ideas. We have also discussed the way in which children handle their impressions of the world through play, a process that we might call *outgo* experience. What they have learned is reproduced in a new form, the better to comprehend it. We should like to develop further the relationship between intake and outgo and then explore other kinds of outgo, or expressive, experience. As we use the term, outgo embraces all forms of communication, both verbal and nonverbal.

The most obvious means by which thought and feeling are expressed is language or verbal communication. Less widely used but effective in ways that speech is not is nonverbal communication, including painting, sculpture, music, and dance. All of these forms have one thing in common: they are symbolic ways of handling experience. They capture the essence, or meaning, of the real thing and state this meaning so that it is comprehensible first to the expressor and then to others. Perhaps an example on an adult level will clarify this. A college student listens to lectures in class and reads books on a particular topic. This is intake. Then he is asked to write a paper on the topic. He struggles with the assignment, trying to get its meaning clear. He may start in utter confusion or with only vague impressions, but finds that as he tries to put his understanding into words he realizes better what the topic is all about. How often the thought in such a paper seems clear and obvious only after it is finished! The struggle involved in clarifying and stating the meaning to oneself of what one has been exposed to is a learning process and therefore a necessary step in furthering growth. This is the outgo to which we are referring. One reaches new and deeper levels of understanding with continued intake and outgo experiences, provided of course that these are in accordance with one's capacity for comprehension and expression.

SYMBOLS ARE USED TO EXPRESS EXPERIENCE

Susanne Langer,[1] Harvard philosopher, has advanced the theory that man is born with an urgent, physiological need to express the *meaning* of his experience in symbolic form, a need no other living creature has and one which underpins man's capacity for thought. Man does not need to carry around with him the object or scene that concerns him in order to communicate its meaning to others. He uses words or pictures, three dimensional representation, music or gesture. These are all symbols which stand for an object, idea, or feeling, and serve to recreate the experience as he knew it. Let us take the first of these symbols, words, and illustrate our meaning better by making a comparison between our use of symbols and the way in which an animal uses them.

One can teach an animal to understand that a word, or perhaps an object, stands for something else. Thus, when one says "bath" to a dog he scurries under the nearest bed, and one can guess that he has learned to associate the word bath with the experience of being washed with soap and water. Similarly, holding up a leash for him to see will cause him to run eagerly to the front door. Again he has associated a sign of some kind with an actual experience. Babies do this too. When a mother holds a bottle in front of a baby of several months he reacts with excitement and pleasure at the prospect of eating. He has come to associate the bottle with the satisfying of hunger. One might say that the word *bath* and the objects *leash* and *bottle* are all symbols for an actual experience. But these symbols are used to indicate the occurrence of a particular ex-

[1] Susanne K. Langer, *Philosophy in a New Key* (Cambridge, Harvard University Press, 1942).

perience. They are not used for communication beyond their value as a sign pointing to something.

The animal will never be able to use the word *bath* to discuss its meaning conceptually. He cannot compare bathing practices in different cultures, describe the kind of bathing he does enjoy, or add any comments on how he would like the procedure conducted. Neither does the bottle have meaning for a baby beyond its immediate application to a specific, associated experience. But the baby, because he is human, will learn to speak, which means he will be able to use the *word bottle*, instead of the object itself, to express his anticipation and desire. Moreover, as his experience broadens the word bottle itself will conjure up different meanings,—a memory of weaning, coca cola, a whiskey advertisement, or a perfume dispenser. He will be able to conceive of *bottle* as something breakable, something manufactured, a utensil, or an art object. Even though the baby, like the animal, uses symbols first as signs, he will in time be able to say "Let's go bye-bye" without pointing to the street or bringing his hat and coat to his mother.

Language thus becomes a means for expressing cumulative experience—impressions, feelings, facts, and concepts. Obviously, as we have indicated elsewhere, the more experience a child has the more he will have to express. Language however, has its limitations.

We have all had the experience of feeling emotions that cannot be put into words. And we have all had the experience of finding that nonverbal symbols express our moods and feelings exactly; for example a particular color in a particular dress that is just right for some moods and not for others; a particular piece of music that releases us for gaiety or introspection that we could not otherwise quite capture; a stretching of ones arms and lift of the head, a look, a smile, a gesture that reveals exactly the meaning we wish to convey. Is not a smile the essence of one kind of feeling? Is not musical expression the essence of human emotion without being one person's specific experience? And is not a painting or a piece of sculpture the essence of what it represents rather than the real object itself?

SYMBOLIZATION IS A STEP IN THE LEARNING PROCESS

The urge to express thought and feeling, and the power to do so, are uniquely human, and are essential aspects of growth and development. The animal, in using symbols as signs for specific things or acts, remains locked within the confines of concrete, limited comprehension. But humans can abstract the essence of an experience and give it symbolic form. With symbols they can generalize from their experience, analyze and synthesize, and share the fruits of their thinking with others.

Man is involved in a constant search for meaning. At first meaning is drawn only from the concrete and the immediate, as is true in early childhood. But little by little the young human being begins to deal with the abstract, with ideas and concepts, and his symbolization becomes increasingly complex. Little by little the young human being grows more subtle in his feeling, and simple crying and laughing are not enough to express shades of feeling. It is necessary to express, verbally and nonverbally, both the intellectual and emotional effect of experience if one is to find meaning in life. Expression seen this way is highly personal and represents the uniqueness of experience as each individual recreates it in an effort to understand it.

CHILDREN'S USE OF SYMBOLS REFLECTS LIMITED EXPERIENCE

Children have a limited conceptual range and tend to be highly motivated by their own emotional involvement in what they experience. Consequently what they express may be a mere fragment of what the adult sees, a small part of the whole, or a distorted perception of what is actually there. The results of children's expressions therefore cannot be evaluated by adult standards. Children can only express meaning that is comprehensible to them in the light of their limited understanding and personal emphasis.

Thus the little child who says, "My mommy is the lady with the green pocketbook and the big smile," or the one who draws his teacher with enormous earrings, or the five-year-old who sings, "Thoughts in my head are moving" to describe his dreams, are all attempting to understand the meaning of their experience. What is the essence of *mommy*, of *teacher?* What does *dream* mean?

Werner Wolff,[2] the psychologist, characterizes the differences in child and adult expression as follows:

Generally speaking, the following art criteria differ basically in adult and child. The adult is guided by impressions—the child by his expressions; the adult by imitation—the child by symbolization; the adult by selection—the child by a search for relationships; the adult by intellectual principles—the child by emotional principles; the adult by objective standards—the child by subjective standards. Hence, as is the case with the other manifestations of the child, there is no bridge between the art of the adult and that of the child since both have their own criteria and their own values.

[2] Werner Wolff, *The Personality of the Preschool Child* (New York, Grune and Stratton, Inc., 1946), p. 262.

SYMBOLIZATION IS NECESSARY FOR THOUGHT AND GROWTH

Children must have the opportunity to use verbal and nonverbal forms of expression or they will not grow intellectually or in depth of feeling. This is why the arts and skills involved in communication of thought and feeling are so important in any educational program. They are neither time-fillers nor busy work. And this refers both to the verbal outgo, language arts, and the nonverbal outgo, creative media and play.

Allowed freedom to express present meaning, and exposed to further experience, children will continue the search for deeper and more extended meaning. Opportunities for them to absorb and opportunities for them to express self-selected meaning must be made available. Their particular output must be respected for its value to the individual child on his own terms. To expect a child to see what an adult sees or to feel as an adult feels is to deprive him of the right to mature fully with the strength of his particular capacities. The expression of thought and feeling should be allowed him freely within the bounds of productivity. It must not be tied in with a need to meet adult approval or satisfy adult concepts of content or form.

TALKING IS SPONTANEOUS AND SOCIAL

Five-year-olds are great talkers. Their vocabulary and experience are sufficient to carry on all normal social amenities (and sometimes animosities), to make pertinent (and sometimes impertinent) inquiries, to answer reasonable questions, and to understand important commands. They use speech to greet the teacher, to speak with friends, to select materials, to change activities. They make use of language when making complaints, whispering secrets, responding to a joke, and when singing a song.

Fives love working in groups and that involves constant talking: discussion of what they are building or dramatizing, determining areas of responsibility, and stating agreement and disagreement with the common scheme. When seated around the snack table or working in small groups with art media, they can carry on fascinating conversations sharing personal news, making observations of social happenings, and listening and contributing to the ideas of others. Spontaneously, enjoyably, kindergartners frequently just chat with each other in class, providing of course, that talking is not a forbidden activity!

In all these one can discern the child's quality of thought, powers of communication, and the array of feelings that accompany these. But the five-year-old still requires a great deal of practice to increase his facility and sublety of expression. Kindergarten is a good place for this practice.

Let us listen in on a number of actual conversations of five-year-olds and see the variety of scope and purpose in their use of language.

CHILDREN USE LANGUAGE TO QUESTION AND EXPRESS IDEAS

This is a casual conversation of two youngsters looking at pictures in *The Little Cowboy*.[3]

Richard: "Why are the trees little?"
Robert: "Maybe they are far away. That's why they look little."
Richard: "And maybe they are little because they are not real: sometimes things are *not* real in a story. Just like in *Curious George* [4] he didn't really do all those things."

In another situation of a group response to a story, *Caps For Sale*,[5] the children want to know why people were not buying caps that day.

"Maybe they didn't like any of those colors he had."
"Maybe they didn't have that much money."
"Maybe 50 cents was too much money for the caps."
"Maybe people already had a cap they bought before."

Touching on profound subjects which they have picked up here and there, and exchanging views, children try to distinguish between fantasy and faith on the one hand and factual reality on the other.

Ronnie: "I saw Santa Claus yesterday at Bloomingdale's."
Joan: "There is no such thing as Santa Claus. Your mother and daddy buy you presents. Santa Claus is make-believe."
Ronnie (convinced of it himself, or maybe successfully persuaded): "I *know* it. But this was a *real* one."

". . . . it's a witch."
"There is no such thing as a witch!"

Now listen to this conversation touching on history, death, and resurrection. It is the day after the Lincoln's Birthday Holiday. Several children are working with clay at the table. They are using their hands and talking calmly.

[3] Margaret Wise Brown, *The Little Cowboy* (New York, William R. Scott, Inc., 1947).
[4] H. A. Rey, *Curious George* (Boston, Houghton Mifflin Co., 1941).
[5] Esphyr Slobodkina, *Caps For Sale* (New York, William R. Scott, Inc., 1947).

". . . . Lincoln died."

"He was shot—by a soldier."

"But you can have a birthday (she meant a birthday celebration) after you are dead."

"My father died." (this wasn't true, so another child corrected).

"Not really."

"God doesn't die ever."

"Oh, yes, He died once, and came to life again."

"Jesus was nailed on a cross and he looked horrible with blood coming out."

Children love talking and speculating about the ultimate: the *tallest* building, the *oldest* animal, the *farthest* star. "Is it as big as the sky?" children often ask, sometimes meaning the Universe and not just the immediately visible sky.

". . . well, a giant is stronger than anybody in the world. Than anybody!" (no refutation possible here).

". . . *infinity*. Infinity years—that's how old the sun is." (The friend to whom this is addressed is impressed, but thinking for himself too, he answers): "There is no such thing as 'infinity *years*'. It's just infinity." These children are unmistakably showing exercise of intellect and imagination.

LANGUAGE IS ONE WAY OF EXPRESSING FEELING

Listening, a teacher can hear children expressing the physical intensity of feeling with words. Helen is examining a box of beautiful seashells with a friend, handling, fingering, looking, touching, and even listening. She takes a choice one and confides to her friend, "Ooh, I like it so much I could break it up." Then slowly she puts it down as the two friends exchange understanding glances.

Coming into the classroom from outside, Dale immediately sizes up the tense situation of her friend Brent who is sprawled on the floor in a steaming tantrum, with the teacher nearby, guarding and guiding. Dale looks over the scene without asking questions of either Brent or the teacher, then leans over Brent and says simply and understandingly, "I know how you feel. I feel this way myself sometimes." The teacher is moved by the depth of personal attention and sympathy on the part of a child not quite five, and by her ability to put it into words.

Feelings About Relationships

There is amazing strength and candor in the spontaneous speech of children. Seeing her friend Becky walk up the stairs to the classroom holding another girl by the hand, Helen looks hurt yet faces Becky: "I thought you were my friend." "Yes," Becky answers without any embarrassment or guilt, "but I don't want to *play* with you now." Certainly a truthful friend if not a true one. Friendship is very important to talk about.

> "Are you my friend, Peter?" asks Jimmy.
> "No," Peter answers without any note of unfriendliness in his voice.
> "Why? You were my friend yesterday."
> "But today I don't like you."

For Peter friendship is something you really feel, not something you get talked into or profess for the sake of politeness.

Feelings About Family

In the following scene spontaneous casual conversation takes place between three girls, four-and-a-half years of age, and their teacher while they are busy getting their outer clothing off.

Marcia: "You know, my baby brother went outside for the first time yesterday."
Teacher: "He did!"
Marcia: "Yes, for the *first time*."
Teacher: "What's your baby brother's name—I forgot."
Marcia: "Andrew. Andrew David Lyman."
Debby: "What's my baby brother's name—did you remember?"
Teacher: "Let's see—Norman? Bobby? Richard?" Debby and the others enjoy the suspense and grin. Then Debby starts giving sound hints.
Debby: "It's Da . . Da. ."
Teacher: "David?"
Debby: "Yes!" (happily).
Marcia: "And my baby brother's middle name is David!"
Debby: "Guess what my brother's middle name is? It begins with Je . . Je . ."
The teacher fails to guess, and, noticing the third child, Kathy, watching and listening eagerly without being able to contribute, as she is an only child, the teacher speaks to *her*.
Teacher: "I know *your* middle name is Anne!"
Kathy, strengthened by the attention, takes the opportunity to say something on the subject of names and words: "What do you call that . . . when you wear all that (indicating with gestures what might be a veil)—and you get a name, but its not getting married. What you call that? Sansuration?"
The teacher is at first perplexed, but realizing Kathy's difficulty with k's and f's, and knowing the religious background, she guesses, "Confirmation?"
Kathy: "Yes! Yes!"

In those few minutes of spontaneous conversation the little girls revealed to the teacher their preoccupation with family matters, fascination with names of family members, and struggle to acquire new and difficult words that have to do with family experiences.

Stevie, also concerned with clarifying family relationships, showed interest in family position and status as well. As he got into the school bus one morning the teacher-chaperone started a conversation.

Teacher: "Was that your grandma waving good-bye to you?"
Stevie: "Yes! My *mother* is still in the hospital and guess what, she had a baby and the baby is not big enough to come home yet."
Teacher: "That's good news, Stevie! Is the baby a boy or a girl?"
Stevie: "It's a boy, it's a *brother*. I wanted a sister; next time we'll have a sister. But this one is a brother and I'll be a big brother to the baby—just like my brother is a big brother to me."
Teacher: "So your family is bigger now."
Stevie: "We have . . *five* in the family now: my father, my mother, my big brother Jim, and me, and my name is Stevie, and my baby brother Edward Dennis!"
Teacher: (opening the door for the next child on the bus, Marjie), "Yes, that is good news, Stevie."
Stevie: (in a semi-whisper) "*You* tell it to Marjie." When Marjie was seated, he whispered to the teacher again, "Remember, *you* tell her."
Teacher: "Stevie has a new baby brother. He hasn't come home yet."
Stevie: "And his name is Edward Dennis."

Stevie repeated the pattern with each of the four children who came on the bus after Marjie, asking the teacher to make the general announcement, then himself saying the proper name, adding that he is a big brother now and hoping that next time it will be a sister. "But now it's a *brother* and whatever comes *has to stay*." The children were interested and each responded by saying something about his or her baby being bigger already.

In their conversations touching on family experiences children often ascribe to the father the ultimate in power and prestige. This is clearly seen in the following conversation which is typical of preschool children.

The entire kindergarten class of about twenty-five children was settling down on the floor after some vigorous work. This was a period for a restful time with story or conversation. The teacher held the open book on her lap and listened:

"My mother had a birthday. She is thirty years old now."

"My mother is thirty-*one!*"

"Well, my daddy is thirty-five." The teacher smiled, feeling quite sure of what would come next.

"And my daddy is a hundred!" a little boy said with conviction in his voice and a sense of the ultimate. The little boy was not conveying chronological or statistical facts about his father; rather he was expressing the enormity of his father's importance to him.

Fives can be so free in their comments about their families that we must add a brief caution here. In their spontaneous conversations children often reveal information which the bystander, in this case the teacher, may find embarassingly intimate. In such cases tact and discretion constitute the wisest response to childish innocence.

Feelings About the Body

Often in their spontaneous conversation children express feelings about the body and fascination with various parts of the body.

Annie, four-and-a-half, was absent from school for a week. When she came home on her first day back her mother asked, "Did you have a good time in school?"

Annie: "Oh, yes, everybody was glad to see me—and I had a talk with my teacher."
Mother: "You did? What did you talk about?"
Annie: "About Aunt Aggie's kidney." The mother felt somewhat shocked and even embarrassed to have her child reveal to a stranger intimate items in the family medical history, but understanding the child's interest, she did not censor. "See," Annie elaborated, "I told her about the pains . . . Mommy, when is Aunt Aggie going to have her operation? I want to tell my teacher *when* she is going to."

So Aunt Aggie's kidney is a fascinating and serious subject. Feelings about the body and bodily condition is often reflected in children's humor and response to humor. The following dialogue is typical of both nursery school and kindergarten children:

Jamie: "Where is Marjie?"
Teacher: "She has the chicken pox and couldn't come to school."
Stevie: "I had the chicken pox last year."
Jamie: "You had the chicken pox! Then you are a chicken!"
Stevie (earnestly): "Oh, no. I am a boy. Once you are a boy, you stay a boy."

(Next Day)

Judy: "Where is Marjie?"
Teacher: "She has the chicken pox, but she'll be back in a few days."
Stevie: "If you have the chicken pox, then you are a chicken! Isn't it funny? *And,* if you have the rooster pox, you are a rooster!"

VERBALLY EXPRESSED HUMOR

A play on words can be very funny to four, five, and six-year olds, and makes for good joking. "If it's a dandelion, it must be a *lion*—ooh, I am afraid of it!" "You said this tree is a *sycamore*. If it's sick, you should call the doctor!" It is surprising how often children will catch the sound and meaning of part of a word for a joke. But a joke on one's self, even a word joke, is very hard to take: "I am not a chicken, I am a boy," Stevie protested with characteristic earnestness.

Children often laugh uproariously as they tell jokes of simple mishaps and mistakes and misplacings, or of some preposterous physical happenings; ". . . and there was somebody on the roof, and he slipped and fell and *smashed to pieces*." This is just the punch line to cause an outburst of laughter. Or, ". . . and she couldn't eat her nice lunch because she didn't have any fork, and she didn't have any knife, and she didn't have any spoon, so she took a great big broom from the kitchen, and she *swept* her lunch from the plate!" That joke was so good it had to be repeated.

But unlike adult jokes which are mostly heard and then passed on, children's jokes are told ad lib; they are completely spontaneous and original, and it seems that spontaneity is part of the humor since it surprises and amuses the teller as well as the listeners.

Somewhat like grown-ups, kindergarten children love to tell "dirty jokes." What is more, there seems to be no distinct sex difference among children in the enjoyment of such jokes, as might be true of older people. A "dirty joke" consists of an exaggerated and rather sly tale, told with lascivious expression, about parts of the body or functions of the body, the point or purpose of the tale being to shock or at least surprise the hearer and to enjoy a good laugh together with one's comrades who appreciate a good dirty joke when they hear one! Thus the subject is any part of the body conventionally concealed by clothing, sometimes extending to conventionally concealed clothing itself, such as underwear. The functions are all gastrointestinal and told with sound effects. But the manner of telling, when the general conversation gets a bit dull perhaps, and the laughter with the implied delight in the social subversiveness of the joke, is analogous to adult dirty jokes.

WHEN DOES A TEACHER STEP IN?

The reader may have noted in all the preceding spontaneous conversations that the teacher did not try to clarify or question beliefs or exaggerations which were of an emotional and personal nature. If she had interfered she might have spoiled the spontaneity and there would not have been true conversation then. There are times indeed when a teacher ought to speak only when spoken to. At other times however, a teacher may need to enter a conversation to help resolve an argument or clarify confusion, as in the following instance, where the teacher clearly overheard the subject of discussion among a small group of four-year-olds. It was tonsils.

"Tonsils are in the mouth, where the tongue sticks," one of them explained, indicating with a finger poking past the tongue.

"No, it's in the throat; and tonsils give you a sore throat, my mommy says."

"But how do you get the tonsils out?" the first child asked. The teacher was listening as a third child, Rickey, gave a serious and graphic explanation.

"I know! The doctor cuts off the head!" Rickey demonstrated a drastic incision with a finger under the chin while several more children gathered around him and listened without any questioning. "Then he takes the tonsils *out* (again agile finger demonstration) and puts the head back on again." None of the other children could think of a better explanation of a tonsilectomy, and although the teacher's authority was not consulted she nevertheless took advantage of the children's intense attention and explained convincingly: "When my brother had his tonsils out the doctor used a special instrument which he put in the open mouth. Then he quickly snipped the tonsils off—just the tonsils, nothing else."

Had the teacher not stepped in some of the children might have been influenced by Rickey's explanation when getting ready for their own tonsilectomies.

The teacher's responsibility in children's spontaneous use of language is therefore to maintain a relaxed free atmosphere and keep a steady ear open for the feelings, meanings, and misconceptions in what children say. She will then learn about the children's interests, their thoughts, their level of understanding and areas of misunderstanding. And what the teacher thus learns from the children she can put to use in planning a program for their language learning and development.

TEACHER-GUIDED DISCUSSION

Since children in the kindergarten are great talkers and frequently engage in spontaneous discussion, the teacher can use this capacity as a valuable tool in a more structured educational framework. After a few weeks or a few months, when the teacher has a fair acquaintance with the children, she can utilize short periods of discussion for maintaining or establishing rapport with the class, advancing language development, providing intellectual stimulation, and establishing a situation from which group feeling may evolve. A further important value of discussion is that it can serve as a guide to program planning and program evaluation with children.

Let us examine an actual class discussion and see what purpose it serves. There were twenty children present one day, most them past five years of age, some almost five. Each of them had just finished some group or individual work and had taken a place in the circle on the floor in response to the teacher's call for storytime. There was the evidence of comfort and ease in their physical movement and personal give-and-take that comes by the middle of the year after experience in working together. There was a feeling of familiarity and freedom as they talked. And there was a positive and receptive expression on their faces as they looked up at the teacher, who was seated on a low chair and was just slightly above them. The teacher felt her position; she was aware of the children's attention to her and her own attention to the children was undivided. There was a sympathetic smile on her face, a perceptive look, and genuine regard for the children. Although they had come to the circle for a story and the teacher's intention was to read a new book as she had promised, both the children and the teacher knew that if something important should come up they would defer reading and have a discussion, for this had often happened and usually proved to be very satisfying.

The story this time was *Veronica* by Roger Duvoisin.[6] It had immediate appeal because of humorous illustrations of an adventurous hippopotamus. As the children listened they sympathized with the heroine, at first in her wish to be noticed and later in her effort to pursue life and gain liberty. At a crucial time in the story, when Veronica the hippo is about to be locked up in jail, the children had become so concerned and so ready to help out and to take part in the story, that the teacher, although she had control of the class and could make the children wait to have a discussion till she finished the story, left the book and had an orderly discussion in which the children expressed their feelings and ideas one at a time as she called their names.

"They shouldn't put Veronica in jail. They were mean," said one child, protesting the injustice.

"Why did they decide to put her in jail?" the teacher asked the children, calling their attention to some facts of the story now.

"She *stole* the vegetables" (saying the apparently new word carefully).

"And she parked the wrong way!"

"Yes, she parked *herself* because she was like a car."

"She was a hippocar!" one boy contributed enthusiastically, repeating a word he had actually invented listening to the earlier part of the story. Here the children stated some knowledge of violating the law, especially the traffic law, and continued with their expression of interest in Veronica's jailing.

[6] Roger Duvoisin, *Veronica* (New York, Alfred A. Knopf, Inc., 1961).

"Veronica's too big to fit in the jail."

"She's too wide to get through the door."

"The policemen can't make her—the hippo can step on their toes!" (laughter from some children). "She'll *squash* them!" (more laughter, with a note of raucousness). The teacher, sensing the slight departure from self-control in the group, brought her influence to bear and led the children back to the subject of discussion: the mechanics of jailing and the devices of jail-breaking. She said:

"But in the story Veronica is made to go through this jail door. Do you have an idea what happens next?" There were lots of ideas judging by the eager hands, expressive faces, and bright eyes. It takes words however, to truly articulate ideas and test their meaning to others, and so the teacher encouraged them to speak.

"She is strong, she can knock the door off with her nose."

"A hippo's nose can't knock—it can rub though, hard."

"*I* know: she can push the jail walls with her body, and that's heavy. She's a heavy hippo!" The teacher noticed the child's satisfaction with the last phrase and repeated it aloud:

"Yes, she's a heavy hippo."

The children's interest was still keen both in speaking and in listening as several of them offered solutions having to do with size, strength, and conquest of enclosed space. Then a little girl said rather timidly:

"Maybe her family, her mother and father and everybody, will find Veronica and *they* would help her get out of jail." And just as the teacher was thinking that the fifteen-minute discussion had provided enough expression and stimulation to be important (and to tire everybody), a child spoke up: "Read us the story! Let's hear it!" Everybody was pleased with the happy ending—Veronica's humane, not merely mechanical, rescue. The children were ready to stretch limbs, move about, and digest the discussion.

In examining the discussion we see that it was a genuine one; it involved a group of children giving verbal consideration to one subject of mutual interest and gaining something from it. As far as the teacher was concerned it served an educational purpose in many ways. It expressed the children's feelings, directly for those who spoke and vicariously for those who listened, feelings of sympathy for a fellow creature in a predicament, feelings of resentment towards punitive laws. It provided a medium for the expression and sharing of ideas about the solving of a mechanical problem having to do with forcing, fitting, breaking, and with laws and violations. It gave the teacher useful knowledge for evaluating the children's language and thought. She noted the inventiveness of the child who said "hippocar"; she remembered the interest in using new words on the part of another; she was impressed by the children's ability to think beyond the immediate physical scope to solve an urgent problem.

Since this discussion just happened in the midst of reading, it will be interesting to examine another, deliberately planned one.

THE TEACHER HAS CERTAIN EXPECTATIONS IN PLANNING A DISCUSSION

By early spring, when she was planning her program for the rest of the year, Miss Santino became increasingly aware that of all the educational materials they had had in the class, of all the interesting items they had constructed, nothing held the children's attention as much as the various animals they had had in class from time to time. Nothing aroused so much feeling and curiosity and provoked so much comment as did the animals. Some project therefore of a zoological or biological nature seemed right and worthwhile. At the same time she learned at a staff meeting that an incubator for hatching chicks was available from an educational supply company. Although the teacher had doubts that the children would understand unseen embryonic development she thought they would respond to the results and sustain an interest for important learning. She herself planned to learn a great deal from it.

After she had obtained the incubator and fertile eggs and found some excellent pictures of the development of a chicken from an egg, she decided to discuss the project with the children. From this discussion she hoped to find out the extent of the children's interest, the level of their comprehension, and therefore the value of undertaking the project at all. She believed that the discussion would give the children an introduction to a biological beginning, for they would observe and handle the concrete items, see pictures, and talk about it. She believed that the discussion would also stimulate the children to further observation and thought. She realized while thinking about it how little she knew herself and she was nervous about having to answer children's questions. However, she reminded herself that this was to be a learning discussion, not a teaching lecture. And she told the gathering children, "We have something special to talk about today." All the children slid into a circle formation on the floor. They immediately noticed the eggs in the two bowls.

"We have eggs at home!" "Where did you get these eggs?" "Are we going to eat them?"

"I have different kinds of eggs here," the teacher replied. "These come from the store and these Mrs. Gregory brought from a farm!"

"The farm eggs are brown," said one child. The teacher realized at once that the child was concluding that all eggs coming directly from a farm are brown and store eggs are white. How was she to correct that?

"Well," said the teacher, "some chickens lay brown-shelled eggs and some lay white-shelled eggs. But only the color of the shell is different; the inside is the same. Here, you can see for yourselves."

The teacher let one child break a white egg into a bowl and one a brown egg. The children noticed the hardness of the shell, the "yellow part," the "wiggle" of the white; the teacher could tell by their comments that the error was corrected, and she put aside the bowls with eggs for the time being.

"Let me tell you about these eggs from the farm. They are special because a baby chick can grow from them," the teacher said. Some children smiled pleasantly, perhaps thinking of a soft baby chick; others stared in puzzlement. One child asked, "How?" The teacher realized that her information was too remote and the children had nothing to say or to think on the subject. She brought the five unbroken eggs and said:

"See these eggs."

"Let me see."

"Let me feel one."

So the teacher let each child hold an egg in his hands, look at it, turn it, feel its weight, and rub its surface, always being careful and even mysteriously quiet while beholding the egg. When the eggs were safely placed back in the bowl, there were many comments.

"It's heavy. Maybe there is a baby chick in it already." Other children wanted to respond to this and the teacher held off her comment.

"But how could the baby chick *fit* inside an egg?"

"And how would it get air?"

"It couldn't see anything . . . !"

"Then how would it find food?" The teacher was listening to all this expression of faith, skepticism, practicality.

"Yes," she answered, holding an egg in her own hand, "it is quite heavy. It has that white part for the baby chicken's body to grow from, and the yellow part is the baby chick's food while it is growing inside. But there is no baby chick in the egg yet."

"But when will the baby chick grow?"

"To make a baby chick start growing inside this egg, we will have to do something to the egg."

"What?" the children asked eagerly, all the eyes, big, eager, and hungry for knowledge.

"First, it has to be kept very warm—warmer than your body. Then it has to be turned over once in a while. When that's done day after day after day a baby chick will grow and peck its way out." The expression on the children's faces clearly said: "What wondrous things can happen," but pragmatic thinking was expressed by others, so that there was an exchange of both.

"Can we do *that* . . . ?"

"On some farms," the teacher explained, "the mother hen sits on the eggs most of the time for twenty-one days and keeps the eggs warm that way and she turns them with her body and feet."

"Birds sit on their eggs in the nest," contributed one child. There was a relevant exchange of information about the phenomena of birds hatching eggs. The teacher used the word *hatch* repeatedly. Then the teacher added:

"But we can keep the eggs properly warm without a hen. We can do it in this incubator with a little electric bulb; and the eggs can hatch in *it* after twenty-one days, just as with the mother hen." The incubator was very interesting to the children. They seemed to understand the control and efficacy of electric heat and the operations of providing moisture and turning so the egg would get warmed on all sides.

The teacher at this time thought that the discussion, though unfinished, should terminate before the children got restless, but a little girl made an important request: "I want to hold the egg again." Other children did too, so the teacher brought the eggs back. The little girl looked at the egg, then put it up to her ear. "I could *hear* the chicken a little bit," she confided to the child next to her. Immediately the other children put the eggs to their ears and they too "heard" the chick. Not wanting to intrude on their imagination, yet remembering that she was offering the children accurate knowledge, the teacher said:

"There is no chicken there yet," and she let the child break open the egg to see a familiar raw egg. "But there is a beginning of a chick in *this* egg and in the other egg we broke." The teacher placed both bowls in the center on the floor and pointing to the fertile spot said, "This little spot means the egg is fertile; a baby chick can grow from it."

"If you keep it warm and everything," came an appropriate qualification from a child.

"Can we eat the broken egg in the bowl?" With that practical comment the teacher terminated the half hour discussion, deferring to another time the showing of embryological pictures and the construction of a calendar for marking the passing days.

This was a vital discussion and it took a good deal of emotional and intellectual energy. Most valuable for the teacher was the realization that it is difficult for young five-year-olds to comprehend the abstract, the potential, the future, but that they have very intense concern with the immediate, the egg in the hand. They perceived all the attributes of the egg they were holding and readily endowed it with life. She realized from the discussion that more direct experience with egg hatching, more time to make individual observations, and more group discussions were needed by the children to learn some of the numerous biological concepts and practical knowledge involved in the hatching of eggs.

TECHNIQUES IN HANDLING DISCUSSIONS

From the two examples given we can point to several useful techniques for handling discussions. On the physical side, the children should be able to see and hear each other well, stretch their limbs, or move a bit. Sitting on the floor is sometimes less confining for them than a circle of chairs. Children known to have difficulty concentrating are best seated near the teacher. Putting together at the far end of the circle those children who are most likely to become restless is to ignore reality. At all times a teacher is conscious of the individual children, looking at each and referring to individuals by name as part of the conversational mood. Since young children tire easily from relative physical inactivity, which happens during discussion, a discussion period should not last too long. From ten minutes to about twenty minutes, depending on the particular children and the time of the year, may be considered a suitable duration. After the children mature more and the discussion skills are better developed, the discussion periods can be a little longer. The rules of taking turns, of raising hands when the group is large, of listening until a person has finished speaking and keeping to the subject of the discussion, are introduced one or two at a time at the beginning and are learned by practice and patient reminders from the teacher and children throughout the year. Some really courageous teachers have been known to help kindergartners carry on a discussion without any hand-raising. The fives of whom we speak learned to listen for cues and await their turn with much more sensitivity to each other than we usually assume such young children to have.

"What do you think of Jamsie's idea, Nina?" "Why did Martin think that, Judy?" "Did that ever happen to you, Lila?" "And then . . . and then . . ." Sometimes discussions are started by helping children remember what they experienced with their senses. "What did you hear?" "What did you smell?" "What did you see?" Or they can be started by summing up the high points of an experience and encouraging the children to discuss its meaning in other connections, developing relationships with other areas of knowledge or pinning down what else they now need to know.

Unless it occurs spontaneously a discussion should have a specific purpose, such as the planning of a program, the introduction of a project, orientation for a trip, summation and clarification of experience, or further probing. Sometimes the discussion follows a topic that came up during a story, a question raised by a child, or an experience shared by all. The nature of the teacher's questions and her handling of the discussion will reflect her purpose.

The chief responsibility of the teacher, after making sure that the subject of discussion is interesting to the children and is one to which they themselves have something to contribute, is for her to lead children through thought processes by her challenging questions. She does not always tell the answers herself! Sometimes she throws the children's own questions back at them in Socratic fashion, if she thinks they are capable of working out the answer. Obviously she does not expect children to know facts which they have never learned. But relating facts to each other to form new understanding is something they can do with teacher's help. Letting the children answer each other's questions and comments encourages exchange of ideas and genuine communication.

Since success of a discussion depends so much on the value the teacher places on its use in the curriculum and on the children's interest and capacity for expression, no formula can be offered that is suitable for every discussion. It helps to remember however, that young children easily go off into tangents. One unimportant comment can trigger a long sequence of personally interesting, but actually diverting episodes or comments, and drawing children back to the discussion at hand has to take feelings as well as logic into account. Furthermore children do not always listen as enthusiastically as they talk and teachers must keep the flow as interesting as possible to all. Children talk best and most effectively when they can discuss what they have seen, felt, heard, tasted, or smelled.

Whether it is for remembering together, straightening out misconceptions, thinking one's way to new questions, planning an experience, or just socializing, a teacher must know her purposes. Children need to use language in different ways and discussions are a means of group communication that is a very necessary aspect of our group-centered learning.

LANGUAGE FOR PERSONAL EXPRESSION IN YOUNG CHILDREN

In language used for personal meaning, which we want to consider next, a great deal of power, strength, and beauty can be expressed with the 2,600 words five-year-olds are supposed to have—providing that their freedom is encouraged and their originality recognized. Of course correctness of speech and vocabulary are important for simple and direct communication, but making up a story to which the whole class listens, dictating a poem which the teacher writes down word for word, and contributing an idea to a group narration which is then read aloud, bring into focus for the child the effectiveness and versatility of language which is used deliberately and colorfully for expression of feelings and ideas. Such language efforts on the part of children often have elements and aspects of true literature. Once again we urge the reader to become acquainted with Lucy Sprague Mitchell's *Here and Now Story Book* [7] and *Another Here and Now* [8] in which there are original, profound, and exciting discussions of children's language and literary powers at specific ages.

Not infrequently children's compositions are extremely brief by adult standards; they may be no more than a few sentences, yet in them a child can tell a complete story, an original idea, or an important thought. The following dictation is a good example of such a brief composition. It consists of only thirty-eight words and was dictated by the child as a news item in response to the teacher's request: "Does anyone have some news for the school newspaper?" This took a few minutes of the teacher's time.

Judy Brings the Moon to School

"One day this winter early in the
morning, when I was coming to school,
the moon was up above the bus, and
it followed me from home all the way
to school. It followed the other
children, too."

What a simple but perfect account, an unforgettable word picture, perhaps more deeply communicated through a child's words than through any other graphic medium. When it was read to the class several children were inspired to dictate their stories.

In this class the teacher's aim was to allow each child in her class of four-and-a-half to six-year-olds to have something of his own written down approximately once a week. During this time the teacher worked with about four interested children, or those who wished to claim their turn, one child dictating at a time. They worked either in an alcove of the classroom or in an adjoining room that was free. During this time the rest of the class was helped or supervised by a student-teacher or two high school girls who received school credit for this work. Sometimes the student-teacher took the dictation. This was at a boarding school with a farm, which explains the following subject:

[7] Lucy Sprague Mitchell, *Here and Now Story Book* (New York, E. P. Dutton & Co., Inc., 1929).

[8] Lucy Sprague Mitchell, *Another Here and Now* (New York, E. P. Dutton & Co., Inc., 1937).

Tim and Nellie

Tim is a black horse and Nellie is white.
They are both so nice.
Tim and Nellie work so hard,
They help Manumit * a lot.
Yesterday they got new shoes,
And then went back to their stables.
In the morning they go plowing the garden.
In the afternoon they work again
Plowing in a field by the dump.
Then John and Oscar put the seeds in.

In the night Tim and Nellie go to pasture.
And they sleep, and they lie down on the grass.

The six-year-old author was focusing on practical details and values in this here-and-now story, yet he conveyed much feeling and love for horses in the flow of his story, in the pauses, and in the completeness of the cycle from the morning until night, when Tim and Nellie "lie down on the grass." And the privileged teacher was the recipient of this.

An intensely poetic description by five-year-old Peter is quoted by Mrs. Mitchell. The dictation was a result of a class trip to a nearby bakery where they had seen a baker decorating a wedding cake.[9]

Here it is in part:

It was in Sutter's Bakery.
I saw decorations on it.
The wedding cake looked like a flight of stairs.
It was white.

They were flower decorations that were made of icing,
and they were white as snow.
The icing looked white and sort of wet like white mud—
like white icing.

The wedding cake looked very white with snow,
Just
very,
very,
WHITE.

Not mere information, but emotion as well seems to have been caught and expressed by Peter, and so fluently! But children's writing is not always fluent. Sometimes the labor and the mental struggle show, as it does in this composition by Robert, aged five.

* Manumit was the name of the school.
[9] Lucy Sprague Mitchell, *Here and Now Story Book* (New York, E. P. Dutton & Co., Inc., 1929), p. 143.

Little Bird

Little bird, little bird!
Aren't you beautiful when you fly;
When you fly in a family row,
Don't you hurt your little toe.
You fly in the air
Just like a cadet in an airplane.

Twit, twit goes the bird every day,
(if you see the same bird.)
Little bird, chirping, chirping every day.
Some people go on a bird walk to look at you
With their binoculars;
You can see them,
But they can't see you!

You fly to protect yourself, when people come.

Yet both the labor and the result were thoroughly enjoyable, especially to Robert himself. How well Robert stayed with his subject as stated in the title and the first line. Although he became intrigued by rhyming he gave it up to get across his observations about that little bird whom he addressed so sympathetically and poetically.

The following story by Dora, a six-year-old kindergartner in a Child Care Center, has elements of suspense and intrigue, plot and humor. Dora dictated the story one day during rest hour. The teacher later made a readable copy; she enjoyed reading it to the group and saved it to show to other teachers.

Once there was a little girl named Susie Pusie. She was a very small girl, much smaller than our Susie. Susie Pusie had a little dog named Tobie. Tobie liked to run and play tricks on Susie.

One day Tobie felt very hungry. He jumped up on the window and into the house. Tobie wanted some milk and he knew it was in the refrigerator.

A man was standing in the kitchen. Tobie asked him for some milk in a very soft voice. Tobie didn't use his loud bark because the man was a stranger and Tobie was a little bit afraid of him.

The man understood what Tobie wanted and gave him the milk. Tobie lapped up the milk quickly until he didn't feel hungry any more. Then he walked up to the man and rubbed his nose against the man's pants.

"You are a nice dog," said the man. "I'll help you fool Susie Pusie." He took a red dress and a pair of green shoes and put them on Tobie. Then he tied a pretty yellow bonnet on Tobie's head and Tobie looked just like a little girl.

Tobie went outside and walked over to Susie Pusie. Susie said, "Oh, what a nice girl! Will you be my friend and play with me?" Tobie said, "Yes, I will," in a very soft voice, "if you let me play with your doll."

"Yes," said Susie, "here it is." Tobie took the doll and rocked it in his arms. While he was rocking the doll his skirt began to fall—it fell right down to the ground.

Susie Pusie looked at her new friend—she saw a long tail, a furry body and two furry paws. "You are not a little girl. You are Tobie, my dog. You played a trick on me."

"Yes," said Tobie, and he ran away laughing.

There is obviously tremendous variety not only in the subjects children use in freely expressive writing, but also in style, in talent, in effort. And as is true of adults, a good story or poem is not always followed by another good one. This can be seen in the following episode, which suggests that the teacher must be considerate and open-minded in her expectations.

In this class the teacher started the children off by saying to them, "This is a story I made up," and read slowly from a manuscript,[10] one sentence to a page.

Kitty Can

> Kitty can walk
> Kitty can stalk
> And run
> And race
> Hold her tail like a sail
> And stare into your face.
> Kitty can stretch her back
> And hump;
> Twirl her whiskers
> And do a high jump;
> Wash her face
> And brush her fur
> Partly close her eyes and purr,
> Kitty cannot talk like you,
> But she hears you, and says, "Mew."
> Come, Kitty-kitty. Quick!
> Here is food you like to lick:
> Fish to chew
> And milk to lap
> Then curl up
> And have a nap.
> Wake up! It's a sunny day!
> Kitty dashes out to play,
> She climbs a tree,

[10] Marguerita Rudolph, "Children's Reactions to a Teacher's Story", in *Children, Here and Now*, Bank Street College Publication 2 (New York, Bank Street College, 69 Bank St., 1954), pp. 18–20.

She bats a ball.
She watches
Shadows on the wall.
Kitty can be very friendly
With a child
Or a man,
Kitty can.

The reading naturally did not make an equal impression on all the children; some were especially interested in the idea of a teacher making up a story and questioned the lack of illustrations; others responded with acting out the kittenish play, but Walter became inspired. "Read the book again!" he begged. But when the teacher barely got through with the third line he interrupted, saying, "Now I want to tell you a poem about Jonathan." He dictated carefully but unhesitatingly:

Jonathan likes to walk
Jonathan likes to stalk
But he *mostly* likes to talk!

Walter was thrilled with his perfect poem about his two-year-old brother! And before the glow of creation left him he took a deep breath and said, "Now I want to tell you a poem about the whole wide world. Did you write that down?" He leaned his elbow on the table and held his head in his hand. The poem apparently was not created as easily as the one about Jonathan, but finally it came as the teacher waited patiently without prodding.

A world can't fall
And it can be cold.
But we aren't cold
Because we have clothes.

Well, the abstract world proved to be bigger than Walter could manage, and he came down to earth and people and warm clothes! But still he was not through, and had "another poem" to offer, this time not about the world or the sublime, but just a ridiculous rhyme (since the rhymes had amused him in "Kitty Can.") But alas, he could muster only two lines:

A table can break,
But it can't be raked!

Although the lines amused him thoroughly the expressive urge, not being an inexhaustible fountain, was clearly diminished and squeezing at it produced only small slow drops in comparison with the rushing, sparkling original flow.

The teacher of course must be encouraging and receptive to all effort, and appreciative of any suggestion of creativity. She must realize that practice over a period of time will not only bring further inspiration, but freedom of expression and assurance with words. Children who have had experience in telling stories and in dictating have greater fluency and discipline in creative writing. Just read this well structured poem of Alicia's—"I Want To Be a Grown-up."

As part of a six-year-old birthday celebration Alicia's mother read her A. A. Milne's "The End," [11] which follows:

When I was One
I had just begun.

When I was Two,
I was nearly new.

When I was Three,
I was hardly Me.

When I was Four,
I was not much more.

When I was Five,
I was just alive.

But now I am Six, I'm as clever as clever,
So I think I'll be six now for ever and ever.

Alicia's reply to Milne's highly sophisticated poem was an inspired "No, I don't want to stay six all the time! And I want to make up a poem about it." Then followed the uninterrupted dictation.

I Want To Be A Grown-up

When I was one—
I slept in a crib.

When I was two—
I did the same thing.

When I was three—
I slept in a bed
And could do some things.

When I was four—
I could do some more
And wished I were five.

When I was five—
I wished I were six.

When I am six—
I wish I were a grown-up.

[11] A. A. Milne, "The End," in *Now We Are Six* (New York, E. P. Dutton & Co., Inc., 1961), p. 102.

> And when I'm seven—
> I'll think I *am* a grown-up.

Alicia had had considerable experience in using language without inhibition at home and at school. Although she had taken over Milne's theme and style in this poem, her feeling and thinking are completely her own, originally and aptly expressed.

The above selections have been included not only to arouse the reader's admiration for individual compositions but to present the power and variety in children's language. To add to the variety here is one more, a confused and complicated "Life of Peter" by five-year-old Helga.

There once was a little boy whose name was Peter. His father bought him toys. He didn't play with them. His father got mad and gave him a punishment when he was sleeping. His father didn't buy him any toys for his birthday. Peter learned that he should play with all the toys his father bought him.

Peter went out one night when his mother and father weren't looking. He fell in a hole, and he heard some voices. They brought a rope to take Peter out.

They gave him to a Giant. The Giant brought him home to his mother. His mother and father punished him very badly.

They bought a brand new baby. Peter got married and they gave it to Peter.

Peter's mommy and daddy gave him milk before he got married. Peter played with toys when he was a little boy.

Before Peter got married he bought a tunnel for himself and he bought some cars for it.

Peter got married. Her name was the same name as Peter's mommy.

Peter was a doctor, and that's the way he made money to buy clothes. Every day he made money to buy little babies and all sorts of things.

One day he went out to buy Chiclet gum. He ate all of it and didn't give any to his wife.

Now Peter had gotten a beautiful pocketbook for his wife. He usually treated his wife nice. Peter ran out of the house to buy a new baby. It was a girl. After it grew up it went out in the night time, and her father went out to see what was happening. She climbed up a ladder and she hid under her covers.

After she got married she bought a child.

End
She played games with it. It was a good little baby.

Well, our hero Peter certainly lives in a big, busy world of buying power, where punishments are as real and inevitable as growing up, getting married, and acquiring babies (the same way one acquires everything, by buying them). But whatever the interpretation, the significance to the individual child dictating the story cannot be denied. The story contains feelings about family and punishment, and a concern to relate bits of knowledge about childhood and adulthood; you get milk and toys and punishment when a child, and money and babies when you grow up. To complete the story there is an effort to make all end well. Helga's was a distinctly individual story, which puzzled the teacher more than it pleased her, and which she did not share with the class.

By now the reader may have an urgent practical question: how can a kindergarten teacher fit such experiences into her curriculum? Language, when expressly composed, has to be written down, and the teacher has to do the writing. The teacher who values the strength and power of children's language will manage to provide for them an occasional opportunity for dictated writing. Although only part of a class may respond and participate at any one time, such activity helps create a climate for freedom of expression which is important for all children. An excellent guide to such experiences is the book about older children, *They All Want to Write,*[12] which has the point of view with which we are concerned.

GROUP WRITING

In the kindergarten personal writing need not always be individual. Many teachers find group dictations and stories meaningful for the whole group, whether small or large, and deeply satisfying for those who contribute. In this class the teacher had included in her program from the beginning an occasional period for writing down a story, usually through her own initiative but sometimes at the children's request. These stories were read to the children and sometimes sent to parents. The subjects were usually current happenings. Here is an example.

Caterpillar

Bella brought a caterpillar to our classroom. He had a long winter nap and now he woke up and stretched and stretched himself from the long nap.
First we named him Furry, then Fuzzy, then Early Bird, then Fuzzy Wuzzy. Fuzzy Wuzzy Brown is his name now.

We built him a cage from blocks. We got him some green leaves and he ate them: he left some nibbles on the leaves.

When you touch him he curls up like a ball.

When he goes to sleep, he rolls up like a snake.

When he walks he creeps.

Paddy put Fuzzy Brown on his hand, and said, "He tickles me. He likes me."

[12] Burrows, Alvina Treut, and others, *They All Want to Write,* rev. ed. (Englewood Cliffs, N.J., Prentice-Hall, Inc., 1952).

A brief, casual telling, yet with a literary dimension: a vivid, sensory picture with charming details ("he left some nibbles on the leaves") and with a communication of personal delight from several children.

In this youngest class of five to seven-year-olds in a private school in the country, the teacher focused her curriculum that season on the farm activities in which the children had participated. Approximately once in two weeks the teacher was asked to contribute some small item to the *School News*. Rather than write something herself quickly the teacher took this opportunity to help the children write news. Usually when the teacher asked the children for news several of them spoke up and most of them showed considerable curiosity in listening. "Let's hear it then, while I write it down," the teacher would say. The children quickly learned the two reasonable rules: only one person at a time could dictate, and dictating needs to be slower than ordinary speech. Following the dictation the teacher read the "news" to the entire group, sometimes making additions or corrections, as indicated by some child. The story was read again later from the pages of the *School News*, at the children's request. Here are the stories.

We Saw a Bonfire

First Mr. Schmidt cut down with a saw some big branches and twigs from all the apple trees. He did it to make the apple trees grow better. There were piles and piles of wood. So we helped Mr. Schmidt get all those branches and sticks in one pile and make a big enormous fire. Mr. Schmidt put kerosine on the fire, throwing it from a pint can. It was a very cold freezing day and the fire was warm. There was a rattle snake in the fire—alive. But it was really a piece of wood curly around. Then for helping to rake the grounds Mr. Schmidt finally gave some kids a ride. We had to ask him and ask him, first, though. A ride on the farm truck is our favorite treat!

What honest and fine reporting, clear description, and communication of personal pleasure in the bonfire and the truck ride that was shared by the children and the teacher. This was no language "lesson," and the teacher only asked "Why?" at the end of the first sentence to make sure the child knew the correct reason for such drastic operations. However, the teacher refrained from supplying the proper word, *pruning*, during the composition in order not to spoil the freedom and the style of the children's language. She did tell them later about pruning, using the correct term.

The Cows

Our cows came into the garden. The farmer didn't want them in the garden. The cows ate beans, some onions and rhubarb and some beets. The farmer didn't want them to do it. The cows ate strawberries, too, and some ripe ones.

And the cows ate a good Praying Mantis. The farmer asked us to chase the cows out of the garden. We chased them with a stick.

It's fun chasing cows!

Tommy got kicked in the heels—almost. And Michael in the rear. You get slapped by the tail, too.

One cow, Bosco, ran so fast she got her tail wrapped around the milk bag and some milk squeezed out! (Everybody laughed at that—the teacher and all the children together!)

The prompting from the teacher in "The Cows" story consisted of a question after the second sentence: "Tell why he didn't." "The Cows" was an excitingly-told story ("you get slapped by the tail") and it presented a thoroughly amusing picture of a cow being milked by her own tail!

Both stories are coherent, realistic, and imaginative reports. They reveal to the teacher not only the level of children's language, the quality of interest and children's learning and pleasures, but also the precious element of shared humor!

Different from the above in style are two group compositions in the form of a thank-you letter. Following an exciting experience with animals supplied by outsiders, the children responded to the teacher's suggestion to dictate a letter.

Letter #1

Dear Mrs. Shapiro: Thank you for inviting us over to see the rabbit. We were very pleased that we saw it.

Thank you for the lemonade. Thank you for the cookies.

Thank you for bringing the rabbit there.

We learned that when a cat runs after a rabbit the rabbit gets afraid. We learned that when a rabbit gets chased by a cat he always wins because he jumps—he can jump high up and a cat can't run and jump at the same time. We didn't like the cat so much because he was chasing the rabbit.

We learned that a black rabbit has black eyes. He has a pink nose. We learned that a rabbit squeaks when it's scared.

When you get a rabbit you pet him down to his tail.

A wild rabbit lives in a hole. The rabbit we saw lived in a cage.

> Love from all the kindergarten
> children and the teacher.

Letter #2

Dear Mrs. Rudolph: Thank you for bringing the guinea pig here. We liked it very much.

We learned that a guinea pig hides when there's paper and she sees it. We learned that she eats very slowly. She likes carrots and lettuce. We liked the way she cut the carrot in half: she ate around the carrot. We learned that she likes to finish one thing at a time before she starts another thing. We liked the guinea pig very much.

We saw that guinea pigs have pink noses. The guinea pig has no tail. She is white. When you hold her up she squeaks. We learned that she has red eyes and that guinea pigs can have black and red ears. We didn't know she had sharp claws. When you let us feel the claws they tickled us. We like the way she squeaks very much. We learned that she could sometimes be taken out of the cage and petted—but not too much. When Guinea walks her hind legs go up. We loved the way she got into the box and jumped out again.

When Billy told his mother about the guinea pig he said, "A guinea pig came to school!" and she didn't believe him. She thought Guinea walked to school.

We are happy that you wanted to bring Guinea to see us.

Love from the kindergarten.

We see in both letters that in spite of certain formalities appropriate in a letter, which the teacher and the children respected, and the teacher's guiding comments, such as "say what you learned about the rabbit," the letters represent creative composition by a group of twenty-two children. They represent the children's own thinking and observation and some original use of language. The letters show the children's ability to give an accurate sensory and live picture in words: "a cat can't run and jump at the same time." In the letters the children were able to report impressions honestly ("We didn't like the cat so much because he was chasing the rabbit") and to convey their keenness of observation, omitting no detail of the animal's anatomy or movement. They conveyed unmistakably their love of contact with the animal guest as well as their amusement: "We loved the way she got into the box and got out again."

Thus a letter, aside from practice in courtesy, is practice in being articulate in one's appreciation. And a brief news report provides opportunity to cultivate a story style. Hearing one's own words read back gives a unique pleasure that kindergartners, and all of us, enjoy.

THE TEACHER'S ROLE IN STIMULATING CREATIVITY IN LANGUAGE

How much responsibility does the kindergarten teacher have for the cultivation of children's language? How does she exert her influence when she is not listening or taking some part in the conversation, or patiently taking down children's dictation? The influence on the group of her understanding, acceptance, and of her own language, is subtle. It is specific and direct in relation to the actual piece of writing. Let us examine the more general influences first.

Children in the kindergarten, in spite of all their spontaneity and self-expression, look up to their teacher, listen to her, emulate her, and are apt to copy her speech. The teacher's own language therefore,—not only her words and meanings but her manner of speech and even mannerisms —influence the children greatly. What then should be the language of the kindergarten teacher?

(a) *Simplicity and clarity.* Above all the teacher's language must be simple and comprehensible, with no cliches and tricky phrases. One teacher always said to her kindergartners whenever she thought they were wasting time, "You are letting your golden moments go by." The phrase, in spite of its nice sound and perhaps intriguing meaning when first heard, had dubious influence on the children who did not really understand it. Another teacher constantly referred to "the poor starving children in other countries" whenever she thought a lesson in thrift was indicated. What do five-year-olds know of that!

Still another teacher practiced a solemn ritual each time she escorted the children through the corridor to the music room. After calling the group to attention she gave them this instruction: "Take the key and lock your lips." Occasionally a brave one would refuse to do any locking and claim to have lost the key, but the rest of the children locked their lips tightly and walked through the corridor in ghostly silence. What this teacher needed to do was to communicate to the children in comprehensible terms, and with confidence in the children's faith in her leadership, that it was necessary to walk in an orderly way and to talk quietly when passing through the corridor.

(b) *Naturalness of manner.* The adult teacher speaks normally and naturally to children even though they are immature. So many people seem to think it is necessary to change the voice by adding a pinch of saccharin or taking on a condescending tongue-in-cheek tone. Undoubtedly adults who speak naturally to other adults and in a completely different way to children, think they are thus talking at a child's level and can be better understood. Unhappily this condescending, overly sweet attitude and voice is often practiced on children's radio and television programs by established authorities, thus perpetuating a stereotyped notion that one cannot speak sincerely and simply to young children, but must use extra and artificial endearments to communicate with them. But this is not actually so. To be of good influence a teacher's own communication with children must be honest, natural, and we might add, courteous. Courtesy implies that vocabulary and concepts be understood by the listener. It does not imply condescension or amusement at the other person's expense because he happens to have lived for a shorter period of time. It is also an act of courtesy for a kindergarten teacher to remember that if she is average in height she may always be towering above and speaking down, in a physical sense; thus she might find a way to be more nearly face-to-face with the children so that she might speak to them directly and personally. Sometimes she sits on low chairs and sometimes she stoops when conversing with a particularly small child. It is much more meaningful for children when a teacher makes it possible for them to talk to her face-to-face rather than face-to-legs.

(c) *Good structural quality and imagination.* Does the kindergarten teacher have poor articulation, rapidity, or loudness or harshness of voice? If so she is handicapped in providing a good model for the children. Understanding the flaws in the mechanics of her own speech the teacher can work to overcome them, perhaps with some professional help.

A suggestion we would make for increasing creativity in language by the teacher herself is some practice of creative use of language in whichever way would be suitable to her: relating a true episode, making up words for a song, or collecting news stories. The effort will definitely be rewarding even if inadequate in a literary sense, for it will involve judging appropriateness of subject, thinking of right words, trying to discover and add something funny, anticipating a reaction of pure delight, and then having the experience of reading her own story to the children and revising her opinion of it. All this will increase the teacher's perception and appreciation of plots and patterns, of ideas and originality in children's creative writing. There is a highly enlightening and inspiring book, *Writing for Young Children* [13] by Claudia Lewis in which the author shares her extensive experiences with children's language and techniques of writing for children.

Creative writing may seem a frightening undertaking to the average teacher, for it is so difficult to sit down alone and struggle with words until a story is finished! Perhaps *telling* a story will seem easier and not so demanding: the teacher may work over an idea in her head, think about an outline of a plot or general pattern, and then fill in, develop, and enliven the story in the process of telling it, encouraged by the children's responses. Often this serves as a stimulation to the children to follow suit. The easily successful kind of story for young children is the strictly autobiographical. "When I was a child your size I had . . ." Or, "On my way to school this morning, I saw . . ." The story could be quite ordinary in plot and characters and undistinctive in language, yet it can command attention, arouse response, and create strong rapport between teller and audience. The directness of this first person relating seems to have dramatic quality and unmistakable appeal to children.

Another seldom used storytelling technique for the kindergarten teacher is the interpretation to children of selected news stories that

[13] Claudia Lewis, *Writing for Young Children* (New York, Simon and Schuster, Inc., 1954).

might appeal to them, such as the two already referred to on page 123 of chapter 7.

Relationships of men to animals do make interesting and often exciting stories, but other suitable subjects can easily be found in daily newspapers too. The subject of construction—buildings, bridges, big boats —is often reported in the papers. News of farm crops can be very interesting too. Then there are frequent reports of heroic, scientific, or humorous experiences of important or even ordinary people which can be read to the children with but slight editing of language. Such authentic current stories stimulate interest in news and present a ready-made source for communication in which adult and child can participate equally well.

TECHNIQUES IN STIMULATING CREATIVE LANGUAGE

In developing any skills or talents in young children the teacher must first become acquainted with the children themselves. In the case of creative language the teacher needs time to learn about the levels of language development and facility in her group, the emotional and aesthetic responses, and the intellectual concerns and particular enthusiasms of the various children. She will then be able to pick up and use appropriately what comes from the children themselves.

Listening, a teacher will note that five-year-olds are still young enough to use spontaneous rhythmic chants and refrains. In the housekeeping corner a little girl may accompany her tender attention to a doll baby with repeated sing-song words which the teacher may jot down and then recall to the child later, and the child might then want to enlarge such a fragment of a lullaby into a fuller composition; with the child's interest the teacher or the child could recite it to the class. Or a group of children may use effective, repeated chants or refrains as part of dramatic play. The teacher could present the children's own rhythmic refrain as a beginning or an idea for a story or a play. Five-year-olds, being talkative and sociable, will not infrequently be heard saying: "Guess what happened!" or "You know what!" in a tone of newsy promise. They may then proceed with a lively accounting, engaging the attention of several children. The teacher may write down only the opening phrase and the highlights of such an account and then use these later as a spontaneous start for creative writing. Every nursery school and kindergarten teacher hears some original expression, apt descriptions, and delightful poetic phrases which she loves sharing with her friends. Such phrases, fragments, and fun words written down by the teacher and brought to the attention of children as creative language, can serve as a start for creative writing.

The teacher can initiate creative writing by focusing the children's attention on sensory language. For example, one teacher said to her group of fives, "Somebody told me that something was 'easy as pie!' Do you think pie is something easy?" Several comments about pie were offered, none indicating its "easiness." Then the teacher asked: "What do you think is easy?" And many thoughtful original expressions and concepts of *easy* were offered by the children (easy as breathing, smiling at a friend, jumping, eating ice cream). The teacher wrote down the brief lines and the result was an "Easy Poem" that was continually edited by the children. A similar group literary expression might be achieved with: "What do you know that is little?" or "Have you seen the dark?" The brief responses from children can be truly poetic, and expressed in original words.

The teacher can also use as literary material an exciting event, such as fire engines speeding and clanging by, an injured or dead bird which the children found and examined, perhaps the capture and the caging of a beetle, or a local snow storm that made daddies stay home. Suggesting an account of such an event will stimulate children to practice real narration and description.

Writing a letter or a report in connection with an interesting trip is also a good technique in practical composition that can at times become creative.

There will be many times when attempts at creative writing produce a great deal of repetition, dullness, or straying away from a set subject. Such failures or inadequacies need not be at all discouraging to the teacher, for better results may certainly come at another time under different conditions or with a different mood. Besides, this may be the time when editing, which is not too strict, is in order. Repetitions, unless they are poetic or patterned, should be eliminated ("you said that already"), dull or bare phrases amplified ("tell me, Johnny, *why* Peter went home"); straying can be redirected with, "*That* will be another story, now you are telling about the airplane pilot."

Reading children's compositions back to them gives them real satisfaction and pride and stimulus for further composition. The fact that the teacher finds the children's creative writing worthy of reading to the group as she does regular books is often an incentive to further effort. If a teacher has mimeographing facilities she may compile a "book" of selected group and individual pieces from the class to send to all the parents and thus further encourage practice by showing respect and giving status to the children's creative writing.

What is particularly cherished by preschoolers after their interest in creative writing has been established, is to have a scrap book in which a child will secure his own poems and stories, attach individual decorations, and often add fitting original illustrations. Such a book of collected

*creating in color
and form
contributes
to the inner
contentment
of every child*

a cuddly toy gives moments of pleasure

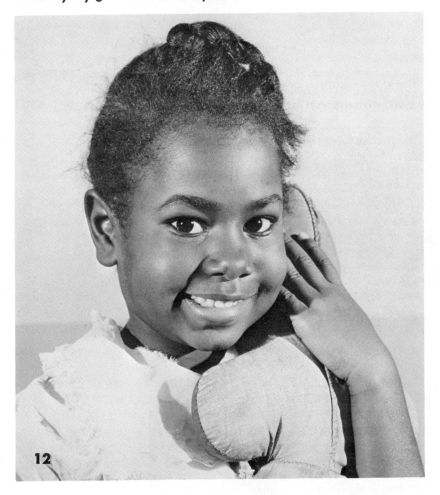

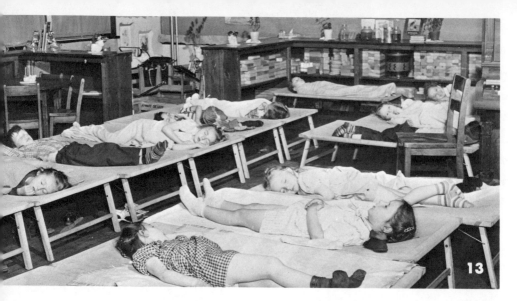

rest is a response to physical need

the towel may tangle, and the cup may slip, but
you don't give up on a job

the inside and outside of a building have different dimensions

books attract,
absorb, inspire

a vessel must be readied, its destination carefully
considered, its course steered and watched

domesticity in our time is practiced by boys as well
as girls

material a child or teacher will suggest. In this case clay is used as a substantial and effective base from which the child reaches out. One child, shaping a small amount of clay, calls it a mountain, then reaches for a twig and plants a tree. He sticks on a dab of cotton with glue and beholds snow on the tree. Another child scoops and extends her clay form until it is a lake for the fish she has created from a scatter of little shells.

Thus accessory materials made available to children at the appropriate time can add an extra dimension of enrichment to clay work.

Protection and Care of Clay Products

Although the greatest value in clay as in other art work is in the meaning to the child and the process of discovery while at work, some products, such as the above, are also important and the teacher has the responsibility of saving and protecting them. The teacher must set aside one clear shelf on which to keep clay during drying or before it is taken home. (When a child himself saves clay in his cubby or locker it is very apt to get broken.) Some area in the room should also be provided to display clay work, with the display changed often enough so that all children have a fair chance to see their work on view.

The child's name must be inscribed on his work with a nail or stick before the clay dries, and the clay piece should then be placed on a paper to dry slowly so it will not crack. When the clay product dries the children usually love to paint it. Here the teacher needs to explain or demonstrate to the children how fragile a clay figure can be and how to handle it securely, in this way preventing some disappointments from broken pieces. After a clay product is painted it may be further enhanced by a coat of clear shellac which gives it gloss and a finished look. This must be done with a brush which is used only for shellac and later cleaned with denatured alcohol. A simpler way to get the same effect is to put the clay piece in a bowl and pour liquid floor wax over it; lift the product with tongs, place it on paper to dry, and reuse the surplus wax. All such operations are fascinating to children, who quickly learn to respect the time, the place, and the supervision required for the procedure of beautifying their art work before taking it home.

PLASTICINE AND SALT DOUGH

Plasticine is a pliable, easy to store, and relatively inexpensive artificial material that provides a useful medium for manipulative and experimental work. It has the practical advantage of not sticking to surfaces or clothing and does not require extensive cleanup. It can therefore be used when there is limited time or limited supervision. To keep plasticine in good soft condition, a small amount of vaseline may be added. It should be kept covered in a warm place.

Children enjoy pounding hunks of plasticine with a mallet or fist to make it more pliable, or they knead and press it between their hands. When it is sufficiently smooth they roll and shape and structure it to suit their fancy. Some teachers find plasticine so convenient that they do not use clay. This is an unfortunate limitation, for clay, being a natural medium, has stronger sensory appeal and challenge. But plasticine does provide a useful and diverting supplementary art material.

Another pliable material which children love is salt dough. This is a mixture of 1 part salt to 3 parts flour (1 teaspoon of alum can be added to a cup of flour as a hardener) mixed with approximately one part of water, kneaded until it is of firm and smooth consistency. Children are fascinated by preparing this material and using their hands. Food coloring or poster paint may be added to the water to give the dough color. The virtue of this material is that when properly kneaded to a consistency of baker's dough it is very smooth and does not stick to the hands, and children can quickly make various shapes and objects with it. The products can be left to harden and then be painted.

Interestingly, since the material is dough it naturally suggests cooking and food, and children often use it as dramatic play material, such as "cookies" which are put in the "oven" and "meat" which is sliced and "served" on plates. Children love using various utensils and dishes with play dough, all of which has more utilitarian and imitative value than the more freely expressive value of an art medium, but which is just as important in children's lives.

SOME CHILDREN WORRY ABOUT GETTING DIRTY

Sometimes we see an individual child hesitant, perhaps even fearful, about using spilly paint or sticky, clingy clay, messy finger paint, or even squashable plasticine and dough. To the child there is good reason behind such hesitancy and the teacher must respect this feeling rather than be disappointed that the child is not producing as everybody else is. Often such a child benefits from simple reassurance. He may be concerned about getting paint on his clothing, in which case an adequate smock and reminder (or demonstration) that school paint is washable will serve to allay his concern. If dirty hands bother a child and keep him from using clay, show casually how it comes off or provide sticks, such as tongue depressors, with which to poke and cut and smooth clay so that this particular child can prepare himself for freely using his bare hands. Let such a hesitant, fearful child have a chance to see how children wash finger paint from their hands. He may well have been over-taught at home to stay clean. Sufficient time, a relaxed atmosphere, and no urging usually bring about a change in such a child in a few months. When that happens it not only makes the child happy with the new freedom and new activity, but brings a real thrill to the patiently waiting teacher. "Jimmy painted for the first time today! Isn't it wonderful!" This is a common exclamation of a teacher's satisfaction.

WHAT TO DO WITH CHILDREN'S ART WORK

Although up to now we have been concerned mainly with the value to the children of using art media, we need for both practical and educational reasons to be concerned also with the care and clearance of products.

Children often work quickly and are apt to produce innumerable paintings, drawings, and other creations in a short time. The teacher is then faced with the problem of saving, displaying, and sending home, as well as judiciously discarding, the variety of products of the entire class, which may include as many as fifty children in two sessions. The teacher needs to be sensitive to the children's feelings about their work, practical about storage, and tactful about sending work home or discarding it.

In placing value on children's art work the teacher makes it a point first of all to notice each child's work and protect it. Paintings need to state the child's name and be dried carefully either on portable clothes racks, on the tops of unused tables, on clothes line fastened with pins, or on guarded floor space. Without provision for drying, paintings can very easily be ruined. When dry, paintings need to be stored. It is good to have some shelves for storing art work. Some teachers solve the problem by designating a special place on the wall for each child, hanging each child's paintings one over the other in that one place. After a week the teacher has a chance to see what the child did; she may then pick some for display, send some home, and if there are many similar ones, do some discarding, unless the child wants to take them all home. Some teachers keep a hard cover scrapbook or ring notebook made from large sheets of oak-tag for each child's drawings and paintings.

Displaying Pictures

Matting and framing pictures add to their beauty, but even without that the display of his work by the teacher gives the child a wonderful satisfaction about his own handiwork and thus about himself. A teacher must not keep any one child's work up too long because the display area is necessarily limited. She must take the trouble to display at some time each child's best or most important work. Changing displays weekly allows a teacher to do this, and even to include the work of the relatively unexpressive child, who although undramatic, also needs the support of being noticed. This is something to remember, for the natural tendency is to hang the showiest, the most advanced, and the most interesting work. Perhaps an uninteresting picture will not be given a prominent spot, but it should be up. It helps the appearance of a room to balance the children's pictures with some attention to the effect of one upon the other as they hang in proximity on the wall.

FAMILY REACTION TO CHILD'S ART

Taking art products home often satisfies the kindergarten child's practical sense of having something to show for his day in school, and it usually pleases parents and other relatives. A child will often be eager to take as many things home as he can. Here the teacher will benefit from some knowledge about how the child's art work is treated at home. If on the whole the parents accept the child's work kindly, personally, and with genuine appreciation, the kindergartner has a good experience taking his art work home. But if the parents have only perfunctory words ("Those are nice pictures, honey—run along and wash your hands now.") then it may be better for the teacher not to send many pictures home with that child. Or an older sibling at home may jeer at important works of the five-year-old ("That's *baby* stuff you do in kindergarten. Look at that scribble-scrabble!") In that case the teacher may need to build up the child with extra confidence to take home along with the pictures. Some parents may be critical of the child's art because they do not understand it, especially when he attempts representational work. "This is a girl jumping rope? Where is the *girl?*" they might ask. In this case the parents would benefit from a teacher's brief explanation about children's art. Perhaps the teacher might send home explanatory notes to all parents about five-year-olds' art work, or plan a parents' meeting on the topic. Then there would be more of a likelihood that the child will at least not be discouraged, even if he does not receive appreciation of his art products and art work.

Of course every teacher hates discarding large accumulations of work, yet for the sake of expediency and orderliness, discarding as well as selecting is not disastrous and is necessary. A child himself can see that if he has a number of similar pictures only one or two need to be saved. Every teacher finds out how prolific children can be and how capable they are of making more and more beautiful creative products. Usually these products are not meant to be permanent.

HOW ARTISTIC HERSELF MUST THE KINDERGARTEN TEACHER BE?

Will a kindergarten teacher have a more successful art program if she has had some personal experience and some skill with painting or clay modeling? Will she have greater understanding of the children's expression and development, and deeper sensitivity to the problems and pleasures of the media if she herself has struggled with them? Emma Sheehy, in *Fives and Sixes Go To School*[9] tells about a most creative teacher who is not an artist herself in any specific medium, yet is able to create a classroom environment which encourages freedom of expression and invites artistic activity. For the kindergarten teacher this is really a more valuable asset than the ability to create at a high level herself. But if a teacher is an artist herself, her special skills and knowledge should make her art program, as well as her entire curriculum, that much richer, provided her standards are realistic for young children. In any case it is the teacher's attitude of encouragement, her faith in the validity of a child's expression, her offering of variety and suitability in materials, and her organization of working areas and boundaries, that enable the children to get the most out of creative media.

Bibliography

Alschuler, Rose H. and Hattwick, La Berta W., *Painting and Personality: A Study of Young Children* (Chicago, University of Chicago Press, 1947).

Biber, Barbara, *Children's Drawings,* Bank Street College Publication (New York, Bank Street College, 69 Bank St.).

[9] Emma Sheehy, *Fives and Sixes Go To School* (New York, Holt, Rinehart & Winston, Inc., 1954).

Bland, Jane Cooper, *Art of the Young Child,* Museum of Modern Art (Garden City, N.Y., dist. by Doubleday & Co., Inc., 1957).

Erdt, Margaret, *Teaching Art in the Elementary School* (New York, Holt, Rinehart & Winston, Inc., 1960).

Gaitskell, Charles and Margaret, *Art Education in the Kindergarten* (Peoria, Ill., Chas. A. Bennet Co., Inc., 1952).

Grozinger, Wolfgang, *Scribbling, Drawing and Painting: The Early Forms of the Child's Pictorial Creativeness* (New York, Frederick A. Praeger, Inc., 1955).

Hartley, Ruth E., Frank, Lawrence K., and Goldenson, Robert M., *Understanding Children's Play* (New York, Columbia University Press, 1952).

Kellogg, Rhoda, *The How of Successful Finger Painting* (San Francisco, Fearon Publishers, Inc., 1958).

Lowenfeld, Victor, *Creative and Mental Growth* (New York, The Macmillan Company, 1957).

———, *Your Child and His Art* (New York, The Macmillan Company, 1955).

McIlvain, Dorothy, *Art in the Primary Grades* (New York, G. P. Putnam's Sons, 1961).

Mendelowitz, Daniel, *Children Are Artists* (Berkeley, Calif., University of California Press, 1954).

Schaeffer-Simmern, Henry, *The Unfolding of Artistic Activity; Its Basis, Processes and Implications* (Berkeley, Calif., University of California Press, 1954).

Sheehy, Emma, *Fives and Sixes Go to School* (New York, Holt, Rinehart & Winston, Inc., 1954).

Tomlinson, R. R., *Children as Artists* (London and Baltimore, King Penguin Books, 1944).

Film:

"The Purple Turtle," 13½-minute color film from The National Kindergarten Assoc. Produced by ACI Productions for Association Films Inc., 1108 Jackson St., Dallas 2, Texas.

II

Music and Rhythm in School Life

When we consider the physical powers and creative imagination of five-year-olds, their ready response to rhythm, their advanced coordination as compared to nursery school threes and fours, their agility and grace in movement, their fascination with sound (in spite of intolerant adult ears), it is obvious that music should play a vital and influential role in the active kindergarten curriculum. We need only to hear children's spontaneous chants and melodic taunts, listen to the strong rhythms and precise rhymes that go with ritual games, and observe the delightful playfulness and inventive pantomime in original dancing to recognize that children are inherently musical.

This natural love and delight in rhythm, sound, and movement, leads easily into a kindergarten program of personal expression with voice and body, satisfying experience with a variety of instruments, and new acquaintance with different musical forms. There are available to teachers many excellent books dealing with appropriate musical programs and materials for four to six-year-olds, which any conscientious teacher should consult and use. (See bibliography at end of chapter.) Underlying the specific activities and materials however, must be a philosophy of music and dance education. As in so many other phases of children's learning in the kindergarten, the teacher looks to the spontaneous, individual expression among the children as the starting point for expansion and enrichment of experience. She encourages the children's own creative powers with rhythm, sound, and movement, yet continues to increase their existing store of knowledge from her own wider experience with musical possibilities.

WITH SONG AND DANCE

To help answer the question of just how one protects and encourages the spontaneous and creative at the same time that one also feeds known ideas and material to children, let us analyze the several aspects of a good musical experience for young children, in an effort to know how to incorporate each phase into the total rhythms program.

In a broad sense we are dealing with the expression and enjoyment of both movement and sound, and earlier comments about children's responses pertain here too. We have pointed to the highly physical character of young children's behavior and learning again and again, as well as to the fact that they themselves must see and touch and must smell and taste in order to crystallize and deepen understanding. This active quality, so intrinsic to their conceptual learning, applies especially to their dance and music experiences. The space surrounding a child is conquered and understood by the movement of his own body into it, not by diagrams and charts. *Under* is defined through the sensation of a humped back as one crawls beneath the low roof of a table or bed; *over* is the victorious stretching of a long and crooked limb above an obstacle in one's way; *up* is the sweep of one's neck muscles under a tilted chin as one stares at the top step of the slide; *down* is a sudden deflating drop into space. Older people, and that includes young adults, take their spatial learning for granted. Older people, and young adults too, are no longer so needful of using bodily energy to explore and enjoy the possibilities of movement for its own sake. The tastes and aptitudes of the adult include a variety of other developed areas as yet unknown to the young. But a growing child feels himself in his body, enjoys victories through the successful use of his body, and locates himself in the world through moving in all directions and in all kinds of ways.

MOVEMENT IS LOVED FOR ITS OWN SAKE

Movement is as natural to children as breathing itself. Here, for example, is a boy running after a windblown paper. He is stretching, reaching out, running, stopping, starting, falling. A little girl is enjoying the flapping of the wind on the teacher's scarf; she is given the scarf and runs with it against the wind, delighting in the muscular sensation resulting from the rising and the swelling of the "sail" in her hand; she

raises her hand, expands her chest, and finds amusement by elevating herself on her toes. A group of children in the spring of the year goes rolling down a grassy hill. There is such boldness as they abandon themselves to the thrilling and dizzying rolling. The shyest and most inhibited children cannot resist the tumbly, bouncy bodily contact with the earth. They do it over and over again. It is exhausting, yet exhilarating. The hats roll off, the jackets slide away, the shoes slip off. The children adore the disheveled roughness and the freedom from restrictive movements. "I didn't know where my head was, but I found it," says a child as he rises after rolling down the hill.

"I am a wheel." "I am a ball—watch how fast I go!" "I am a submarine—going way down." "I am a statue."

It is easy to see that such vigorous activities can later be refined, controlled, or intensified by the teacher with rhythmic, musical direction of pattern. But the children's inherent joy in spontaneous movement must first be there.

FROM MOTION TO SONG

Edna Buttolph, a music educator of wide experience, tells us,[1]

The natural sequence with children of nursery and primary years is from motion to song, rather than from song to motion. Full free use of the body not only relaxes the children, but makes them ready and eager for singing time. Yet too often in special music periods, children are gathered in small chairs in a circle, and the very first procedure is the singing of songs. The children's urge to move, almost invariably strong, is criticized by the eager specialist, convinced she has something beautiful to give. She may become annoyed when the children do not give her their immediate and quiet attention, and she creates for herself some totally unnecessary problems.

The observation is a wise one, and successful rhythms periods frequently begin with a formalization by the teacher of the movement and rhythm that have already been started by the children; the spontaneous and high-pitched marching of paraders becomes orderly and controlled when the musical accompaniment of drum or piano is added by the empathic adult. The slightly wild galloping of cowboys who have just dismantled their block ranch, and the dizzying spinning and twirling of experimenters in space, fall into patterned reliability when the teacher introduces a musical accompaniment that stabilizes an almost out-of-control activity into a solid experience of group unity. And the teacher can terminate it all by the magic of the music whenever she decides to

[1] Edna G. Buttolph, *Music for the Classroom Teacher*, Bank Street College Publication (New York, Bank Street College, 69 Bank Street, 1958).

do so. Or rhythms may begin with a teacher's intuitive response to the children's unexpressed need for physical activity. Because she knows the children have been absorbed and quiet for a long stretch before the actual music time, she opens the period with jumping or running or stamping.

DISCOVERING THE POSSIBILITIES WITHIN ONESELF

Whether at the beginning, the middle, or the end of a rhythms period, the teacher is sensitive to the spontaneous, unplanned movements that children indulge in all the time. In addition to picking these up and helping to give them pattern and control, there are ways of deliberately fostering ingenuity and imagination in body movement. To do this a teacher might think for a moment of the body in space, using her own body as an illustration. Actually trying the suggestions that follow makes them clearer! The space that surrounds each of us offers several levels and planes for body functioning. Let us start with the lowest plane of all, the floor beneath us, and put the body into its flattest position—flat on the back, arms and legs at sides. What can you do in the prescribed space occupied by your body and yet remain on that plane? You can rock from side to side, you can lift one or both legs upward, one or both arms upward, behind you, across your chest. You can lift your head, or lift everything that can be lifted at once. Suppose you remained in the same prescribed space on the floor but turned over on your stomach and chest? What could you do then? Rocking from side to side has a different sensation from this kinesthetic view; lifting limbs and head is also a different experience from the earlier prone position. Can you do anything else without removing yourself from that spot on the floor?

The next plane to consider brings you into a sitting position. With knees drawn up, you can spin around like a top. If you set your legs down, you can sway from side to side, bend forward and back, rest on your arms extended behind you or do whatever else you can think up. Getting onto your knees, new possibilities open up again. Rooted to one spot, on your knees, what can you do? Your whole torso can bend backwards as one straight rod, with the knees as pivot, or you can fold into a seat on your upturned heels and bounce gently. Now stand up, but remain in one spot on the floor. What can your body do as it stands in space? Notice that we have not yet moved out into space with the more familiar walking, running, skipping activities. Those will come. What we are concentrating on first is the exploration of less obvious kinds of movement within the muscular structure of the body as it relates to a prescribed section in space. Thus, initially, we use no more space than the inches we actually occupy on the floor, although we may begin from a variety of initial postures, such as lying down, sitting on knees or buttocks, or standing. Try offering five-year-olds the opportunity to explore body movement in this way and you will learn that there are possibilities for movement you never could have dreamed up yourself. Help each child not only to an awareness of the possibilities within himself, but let him look at other children's different movements to imitate and build on. In that way each individual expands his vocabulary of motion while at the same time feeling pride in what he himself has discovered. This technique may be used on other planes of course, but one need not go through the gamut—from the floor, upward, and then on to movement across the room—in any one rhythms period. Over time, one explores movement away from the one spot and across the floor. This may be on one's stomach, on one's back, on one's bottom, on one's knees, on the soles of the feet when squatting low, on the feet when bending over, or on the soles, the heels, and the toes when standing upright and moving out into space. Tempo can be added to these, and variation in pitch. Sometimes we move fast, sometimes slowly, sometimes alternately fast and slow. Sometimes the teacher's accompaniment is staccato, sometimes smooth and evenly paced. Sometimes it is quiet (for walking on tiptoe) sometimes loud and crashing (for stamping). One not only goes forward and backward into space on different planes, one goes up and down, leaving the floor in little jumps that spring from the ankles or in prances that lift the knees high. In time one moves forward and up into space with leaps, skips, and jumps that take one up and out.

Much of the exploratory movement grows out of an individual child's own sense of rhythm and timing. Standing by with a drum, a gong, or any other percussion instrument, the teacher hears the child's beat and sounds it on the instrument. Sensitive to his tempo, she dramatizes but does not control it.

When a teacher understands how varied are the possibilities for body movement and realizes that children take pleasure in the discovery and use of kinesthetic sensation for their own sakes, she has the basis for encouraging creativity and freedom. Every rhythms period should have one portion devoted to movement for the pure fun of moving. Without becoming a dancer herself, any teacher can become sensitive to the possible planes on which a body can function in space, and then adapt her program to the actual amount of physical space available and to the number of children who will use the space at one given time.

Personality Differences are Revealed Through Body Movement

Not all children are quite ready however, to reveal themselves without inhibition, and therefore no one should be forced to participate in rhythms who does not want to.

There are children whose normal urge to movement has been repressed, children who have been told to sit nicely, to be quiet, to stop running, to stop jumping, in short, to stop being children. Such children may need a longer time, perhaps several months, to recapture the freedom and imagination that is their birthright. To such children one may offer ideas to get them started. Shake your hands floppily, roll your head loosely, and wiggle up and down. Jump up in one spot and stretch your arms and head up as high as they will go. Stamp your feet in alternating patterns of fast and slow, loud and soft, even when sitting, just to let the children know that to move with abandon is right and good.

In an inspiring booklet, *The Magic of Music*,[2] the teacher-author describes graphically the effect of rhythms on particular children:

Careful observation of children in music can give valuable understanding of their personalities. Watchfulness for the roles they play, the freedom or restraint with which they move, can help a teacher know her children. It was revealing to see, for example, that Susan avoided the more vigorous activities of music. When we connected this with her conversation about how hearts beat loudly when tired we realized that her avoidance was based on anxiety.

George was an aggressive, poorly coordinated boy, who tried hard to be as skilled as the other boys in the group. He came into his own in music. In music only could he move with abandon, marking out the rhythms incisively and accurately with his head and feet, swaying happily.

I have watched a withdrawn, self-absorbed little girl blossom into a respected member of the group in music, and seen the respect carry over into group play of other kinds. Music gave Jean "ideas" and even though she was one of the few children who could not skip or perform other feats requiring muscular coordination she was happy to keep moving and often performed alone, the group her audience, her face becoming alive with happiness, an unusual picture.

OUT INTO SPACE

In addition to the exploratory experiences which a teacher guides but allows the children to develop in their own way, there are the common childhood movements that children adore. There is *walking:* fast, faster, *very fast;* slow, slower, heavy and droopy; walking with long steps, tiny steps, ordinary steps; walking on toes, on heels; walking to a song one sings, to a drum, to a piano or victrola accompaniment; walking alternating with running and then ending perhaps with a jump! *Marching* and *stamping* are variations of walking that allow for different emphases of the arms, the torso, and the head. *Skipping* is a new skill for most five-year-olds, and perhaps not yet accomplished by all of them. They love to

[2] Naomi Freilicoff, *The Magic of Music* (New York State Assn. for Nursery Education, New York City Chapter, May, 1953).

skip, alone or with a partner, in little jumpy skips, or high leapy skips. Many settle for hopping. *Running,* free and yet within limits, is a much loved experience but is possible indoors only if the room is large enough. Then small groups can run in a circle, all going the same way of course. Or one at a time each child can run catty-corner across the cleared space in the middle, the teacher maintaining a rhythm in the timing of each child's entry into the arena. Galloping is learned before skipping, although an occasional child gets his legs mixed up and cannot seem to get the beat and the emphasis quite right. But gallop they do, singly, in pairs (one behind the other and holding hands), or in a threesome (one in front, arms stretched back to the two behind). In time children learn to recognize the music that lends itself best to skipping, to galloping, to running, or to marching. They enjoy hearing a familiar accompaniment to such activities, but it is important too to test and strengthen their rhythmic sensibilities by offering them new marches, gallops, and skips from time to time.

DRAMATIZATION

Movement for its own sake and the enjoyment of rhythmic variation and intensity are only part of the possibilities open to children. With their keen eye and imitative powers, fives take pleasure also in reproducing the movement of animals and machines. Fives waddle like ducks on their haunches and heels, wiggle like fish on their bellies, leap like kangaroos, frogs and rabbits, stretch their heads cautiously up and around like turtles, and inch along on hands and flat feet like the inchworm himself. With a salute to their industrial environment they are equally happy to zoom like airplanes with wide wingspread, swing their hammers up and down, chug along like a train, or bend their backs to become unloading trucks. Some of these dramatizations come from experience outside of school, some result from trips and stories that introduce new ideas, and some are responses to songs that lend themselves well to acting out. Hardly a songbook for children exists that does not have a number of musical dramatizations in it. One portion of the rhythms period could easily include a few of these and still leave room for other activities. While the teacher may or may not suggest a theme, its development should be the children's own. Her major role would be in making it possible for the children to see firsthand the many animals and machines that they will model themselves on so successfully.

Instrumental accompaniment to such dance-dramatization is not always necessary. Consider the following poem [3] which a teacher can read to children in carefully considered cadence, with properly-timed pauses:

[3] Mary B. Miller, "Cat," in *Sung Under the Silver Umbrella* (New York, The Macmillan Co., 1958).

CAT

The black cat yawns,
Opens her jaws,
Stretches her legs,
And shows her claws.

Then she gets up
And stands on four
Long stiff legs
And yawns some more.

She shows her sharp teeth,
She stretches her lip,
Her slice of a tongue
Turns up at the tip.

Lifting herself
On her delicate toes,
She arches her back
As high as it goes.

She lets herself down
With particular care,
And pads away
With her tail in the air.

MAKING THE MOST OF SOUND

Children are as interested in sound as in movement and they frequently take cues from the environment to reproduce and develop. In one class we see each child eager for a turn at the noisy, vibrating electric sander at the work bench, enjoying particularly the noise production which they might imitate quite accurately. When using sand paper on rough wood, children discern the raspy rubbing sound as much as the rubbing motion and the change in surface. The rhythmic sharp sound of the saw contributes to the immense popularity of woodworking; the heavy flat whack of a hammer absorbs the children and invites repetition regardless of results. The crashing sound that can be made with pot lids, the clatter with tin cans, the varied tapping with finger and fingernails on different surfaces, the whirring of egg beaters, the popping of balloons, all produce a rich variety of sounds which children enjoy differentiating.

Appreciating and allowing such play with sounds by bringing in appropriate materials leads naturally to play instruments such as shakers (boxes or cans filled with pebbles or dry beans, covered securely); drums (large cylindrical cans, boxes or pails covered tightly with rubber or leather); tambourines (paper plates with attached shaky bottle tops);

sanding blocks (two hand size blocks of wood covered with rough grade sand paper); a zylophone made by a series of glasses filled with water on different levels so a musical scale is produced; and various other instruments the teacher may know about or invent with the children. These instruments are fun and valuable to make in the class and to keep in the room for the children's inspection, possession, and sound experimentation. However, the teacher must not overlook the fact that the homemade instruments are seldom of high musical quality; they are more in the nature of play things and provide only a limited musical experience, and they alone cannot satisfy the musical appetite of children.

REAL INSTRUMENTS

The musical value of good and expensive instruments will not be lost on kindergarten children. A good drum expertly constructed, that responds to palm and fingers, an attractive well-made tambourine that vibrates with the least turn and jangles gorgeously when shaken, beautiful South American gourds and maracas, metal triangles that have a range from a gentle "ing" to a clear strong "cling," zylophones with good musical tone and cymbals that vibrate when clashed, are all necessary adjuncts to a musical program. Very good drums and zylophones and tambourines may prove to be relatively expensive. In that case purchasing one of each would still enable the children to become acquainted with the nature of the instrument, with its musical range and possibilities, and with the feel of using it. Another common and inexpensive instrument suitable for young children is the bell. There happens to be a good variety of bells each with special form and sound and beauty. There are dainty table bells, tiny jingle bells that can be attached and worn on wrists and ankles, beautifully decorated Indian bells, clay bells from Mexico, old sleigh bells that are lovely to hear, and big crude cowbells. The reader must be familiar with many others from particular lands, regions, and peoples. In many kindergartens the children successfully handle the autoharp and relish the chords its strings produce. But whatever instruments the teacher collects and keeps it is important that she make them available for the children to use and enjoy individually, before and along with participation in a controlled group rhythm band in a formal music period.

THE RHYTHM BAND

The formal organization of a band must wait on the readiness of the children to work as a group, to have some awareness of the role of a leader in starting and stopping the group, and enough familiarity with how each instrument is handled to free the children for joint effort in making music. For this reason instruments must be freely available to the children for experimentation and guidance in the weeks before the band is formed. They must learn, not be told, that the triangle can sound clearly only when hanging freely from its string, the cymbals resound when clashed in an upward movement rather than flatly against each other, and the drums boom differently when struck by the palm or a padded stick. And they must learn that the vibration of each can be stopped with the touch of one's hands.

Exploring the possibilities of rhythmic beat also precedes the rhythm band. The teacher organizes clapping to names, to drum beats, to known songs, and to deliberately changing rhythms at the piano or on a drum. She adapts the familiar walking and stamping to two-quarter, three-quarter, and four-quarter time in order to heighten the sensitivity to beat which will later make more likely the satisfaction of a shared band rendition. When the children are first given the instruments formally, as a group, they can start with the familiar clapping patterns but then quickly move on to known songs that lend themselves well to the rhythm band, from the simple "Three Blind Mice" to "What Shall We Do with the Drunken Sailor?". As in other experiences of shared group activity, some guidelines are helpful. The instruments stay on lap or floor until the teacher gives the signal. When the music ends, no further playing by individuals goes on; instruments may be exchanged, but in an orderly fashion.

After some experience in playing selections straight through the children often reach a level of sophistication with the instruments that allows for more complexity. Songs with a chorus can be played by two different groups within the band, the verse part by triangle, bells, rhythm sticks, and the chorus by drums, cymbals and tambourines, for example. Fives who are familiar with instruments and have had good opportunities for musical experience, are often intrigued with the possibilities of arranging a piece of music, with or without words, for their rhythm band. In a very simple way they can grasp the concept of organization, and do very well with it.

LISTENING TO "GROWN-UP" MUSIC

To further children's acquaintance with musical instruments the teacher might invite a musical parent, relative, or friend to visit and perform for them in class. The personal quality and directness of such an informal concert are meaningful and impressive to children and such an occasion provides genuine musical stimulation. Whether the instrument is a piping piccolo, a breathing bassoon, a strumming guitar, or a sighing cello, the kindergarten audience will have an unusual experience. Neither teacher nor artist need worry about performing special children's music, although many of the great composers from Bach to Bartok did indeed write especially for children. Any short piece or short portion of a larger composition that has a clearly defined rhythm and definite melodic line and that does not introduce too many musical ideas in too brief a time, will be suitable for children. The music, the person playing, and the instrument itself, will all arouse the curiosity and interest of five-year-olds and hold the attention of most of them.

The live concert is not as readily available as a concert of recorded music, and the teacher can enhance the children's familiarity with instrumental music by using well-chosen records. Good marches and old-fashioned dances are always favorites, and lullabies can be soothing and appealing. Composers like Haydn, Mozart, Schumann, and Schubert, later Saint-Saens and Moussorgsky, and still later such moderns as Prokofieff, Britten, Stravinsky, Persichetti, Křenek, and others have turned their fancy and their talent to writing brief, rhythmic, dramatic presentations that appeal to adults and children alike. Interestingly enough, in music written from the fourteenth to the eighteenth century there are also many lovely pieces, brief and rhythmically clear, that are readily enjoyed by our twentieth century five-year-olds.

Teachers must acquaint themselves with the recorded offerings available, some of them organized by recording companies in categories of age and grade for best usefulness. But much good music crosses age lines, and in the end it is the teacher's own pleasure in music that will stimulate her to share this enjoyment with children.

An important category of music which is used liberally in kindergartens is folk music. There are many fine collections (see bibliography) of American and world folk songs. The special qualities of directness and earthiness, of free humor, the musical use of the absurd, and sometimes the appealing numerical pattern, make folk songs very popular with children. A professional or amateur folksinger might come to sing and play folk songs with the children. Children and teacher can pick up songs from the many good recordings available, and if the teacher plays any accompanying instrument and dares to sing she can share with the children any number of choice folk songs from her own repertoire.

TIME TO SING

It is a pity that we Americans did not continue the custom of our many forebears of singing at work, while walking, and at play. An Israeli visitor to American kindergartens commented on this lack of singing as she described an Israeli kindergarten, "We sing all the time, as we put away, as we clean tables, as we go to the playground. Why do you dole songs out so sparingly?"

Perhaps the main reason we Americans do not sing enough lies in our school practice of isolating children who could not carry a tune, thus setting up standards for singing that few teachers feel they themselves can meet. In truth, group singing can carry all the voices, and the satisfaction of lifting one's voice in song is one we should encourage in children and give them opportunities to enjoy. Not all fives can carry a tune—but then they do not care too much as yet because their sensory discrimination is still gross and unrefined. More important is the fact that the ear and the voice are both capable of learning but need continued experiences in discrimination to do so. In other words singing improves with practice! The teacher herself certainly contributes more to musical pleasure if she can sing, but if she is not talented vocally she can still free the children to do so by her own lack of inhibition and her introduction of suitable song material.

WHAT MAKES A SONG A GOOD SONG FOR FIVES?

Perhaps the best way to provide properly for the children whose tastes we wish to nurture is to choose songs we think will appeal to our classes out of collections that have the approval of musical authorities. There are some things however, that all teachers can understand. One is the fact that to musicians no one style or period of music is in and of itself the best one. Just as in the selection of books, the classics are hardly the whole story. Musicians say there is good and bad classical music, good and bad contemporary music, good and bad jazz, good and bad popular music, and so on. We are therefore not limited to one style or type of music for our five-year-olds. But five-year-olds themselves have limitations which we must heed. Their attention span is short, they love repetition, they enjoy dramatic quality, they can feel either bold or tender (but actually do feel bold more often than tender), they enjoy the familiar but have a sense of humor about the odd and incongruous, and their voice range is not too great and tends to be higher than adults but not as high as some children's song books seem to imply. Therefore in seeking a song for fives out of a collection gathered by musicians who have chosen songs for musical quality, let us bear in mind the following.

A song for fives can be as short as a poem of one verse if each line expresses a different thought or a separate part of a thought, thus making the little piece really quite complex. Such a song might be "Tirra-Lirra," [4] "Winter Good-bye," [5] or "Down by the Station." [6]

A song for fives can be much longer when a basic chorus is repeated regularly and the story line is developed by a simple change in the main verse. In such songs the repetition carries the children along and the changes are easy to apply. This is not the same as learning a song of many verses, each quite different from the ones before. Examples of such songs would be "There's a Little Wheel A-Turning" [7] or "Skip to My Lou." [8] Fives adore the dramatic, and a song with a surprise ending, like

> Jack is quiet
> Down in his box
> Until somebody opens the lid! [9]

or a song about a process they can understand, such as this one, which begins,

> Once there were some children in the kitchen,
> in the kitchen
> Washing, washing apples with their cooking aprons on.
> Once there were some children at the table,
> at the table
> Eating, eating apples with their cooking aprons off! [10]

They also love songs with definite, repetitive rhythms of special character, such as a swinging song, a rocking song, a marching song, or songs that capture a mood of snow, or rain, the spirit of a holiday, the ticking of a clock, or the sounds of machines and animals.

Fives love to sing, and they should sing not only at the prescribed singing time but while walking in and out of their classroom if it seems right (not as rigid routine), as they work at cleaning up, as some experience reminds teacher or children of an appropriate song, and wherever it is natural and right to express the joy of living in a song.

This means of course that teachers must build up a repertoire of

[4] Archibald T. Davison and Thomas W. Surette, *140 Folk Songs For Grades I, II, III* (New York, Concord Series, G. Schirmer Music Co., Inc., 1952).

[5] L. P. McCarteney, *Songs For Nursery School* (Cincinnati, Willis Music Company).

[6] Satis Coleman and Alice G. Thorn, *Singing Time* (New York, The John Day Co., Inc., 1931).

[7] Beatrice Landeck, *Songs to Grow On* (New York, William Morrow & Co., Inc., 1950).

[8] Ruth C. Seeger, *American Folk Songs* (Garden City, N.Y. Doubleday & Company, Inc.), p. 166.

[9] "Jack in the Box," from *Another Singing Time* (New York, The John Day Co., Inc., 1937), p. 1.

[10] "Baking Apples," in Satis Coleman and Alice G. Thorn, *op. cit.*

suitable songs, which they can do by studying some of the many excellent collections available (they are in public libraries too). The main task is to overcome that common feeling of "I can't sing," or "My two years of piano lessons are not for showing off." Freedom from inhibition may be even more important than technical skill in a kindergarten teacher. If you cannot play the piano get a friend to go through some song books with you and take the trouble to learn a song or two by heart at each session. The same thing can be accomplished by listening to records. As you start to introduce the songs to the children, you will be repeating them again and again and building a repertoire at the same time. You will find yourself enjoying the pleasure of the music just as much as the children.

TEACHING SONGS TO CHILDREN

When you feel you do know a song well and you are at ease in singing, sing it through for the children so they can get the whole sense of it in one sweep. Sing it through a second time and the third time start to teach it. Sing a line and have them repeat it, sing the next line and have them repeat that, and so on until the end. Sing the song through again slowly, and let the children follow along as best they can. Then, and only then, should you make an official try at the song together. Let it go after that, but on another day introduce it again by singing it through as a reminder, and then have the children sing with you. Sometimes children learn a song best by hearing it without the piano accompaniment, which may drown out the words for them. In that case know the song well enough so that you know the tune and do not need to look at the words. You need not sing like an opera star in order to carry a tune. Just about everybody can sing "America" in tune because of the endless repetitions of that song during school years, and yet many people claim they cannot carry a tune. If you are slow at it, try a little more practice with a piano accompaniment or listen to someone else's voice to guide you. No matter how difficult, do not give up without a fight even if you really think you cannot possibly sing. The richness of a kindergarten program is considerably enhanced by lots of good, lusty singing.

MAKING UP THE RHYTHMS PERIOD

Rhythms time in the kindergarten can be planned or spontaneous, but should certainly occur with regularity, if possible, several times a week. The period can last from ten minutes to thirty, but in the course of the passing weeks and months all aspects of the sound and movement experiences we have been describing should be included. A teacher can choose and make up a balanced rhythms period from among the following:

1. Movement

    a. Free, exploratory movement within one or several planes or in new directions in space (sidewards, backwards while moving away from one spot) including individual experimentation, building in time to a simple dance.

    b. Movements suggested by the teacher to free inhibited children and give ideas to those afraid to try their own as yet.

    c. Dramatizations, to song, poems, percussion, piano, or victrola accompaniment, of imitatable animals, machines, workers, etc.

    d. Rhythmic responses to clearly defined musical patterns: marches, skips, gallops.

2. Sound

    a. Singing some familiar songs, learning a new song, making up a song, or making up a new verse to an old one.

    b. Use of instruments.

    c. Listening to live or recorded music.

3. Rhythm and Pitch Games

    a. Rhythm

        clapping:
        children and teacher
        child as leader
        group against group
        variation in beats (teacher or child led)
        guessing clapped out songs that are known

        stamping:
        similar to clapping, but using heels, when seated, varying with hands beating on chair, wall, floor, and of course stamping around room to different tempi and degrees of loudness or softness.

    b. Pitch

        scale songs, using parts of the octave or the whole, and going up and down, for example,
        "As-I-climbed-up-the-ap-ple-tree
        (c d e   f g a b   c)

        "All-the-ap-ples-fell-down-on-me."
        (c b a g   f   e d   c)

(This one is easily accompanied by gestures, stretching up as high as one can reach on the way up, and slowly lowering arms and body on the way down.)

echo songs, such as "Echo I can hear you
(hear you, hear you)" or

"Who has the penny?"
I have the penny . ."

games of imitating familiar sounds: horns, whistles, cows, ducks.

identifying higher and lower pitch on the piano.

4. Organized group singing games simple enough for five-year-olds, such as "Muffin Man," "Looby Loo."

CONTROLLING FOR FREEDOM

An important consideration for the teacher who wants to offer maximum freedom of expression and yet keep inexperienced fives from losing all sense of proportion and going out of control, is to establish clearly stated and clearly understood signals by which she can bring the group back to the piano, back to their seats, or just get them to stop and listen by sheer force of conditioned response. Early in the semester therefore, the teacher acquaints her group with her signals: a particular phrase on the piano that means "Come back to the piano," a special gong for quick silence and attention, a chord at the piano, or perhaps a special clapping rhythm that means "go sit down at your seats." Such signals are individual and it does not really matter precisely what they are, although an attractive sound is preferable to a harsh one. The important thing is that a teacher shall not have to shout above the noise of excited five-year-olds to get their attention. Therefore, after introducing her signals early in the year, time must be spent helping the children learn to respond to them automatically. Games similar to musical chairs and musical spots can teach the children that when the music stops, the movement stops. As the children complete an activity on the floor, the signal for returning to the piano or their seats can be given as often as needed to get everybody to respond. Such conditioning is important if young children are to be allowed to be free, because the better judgment and perspective of an adult may suddenly be needed to help fives out of a potentially unsafe situation (if they are running in different directions in a small space and are headed for collisions), or to halt contagious behavior before the children find themselves exhausted.

Another important consideration is the balance of active and quiet activities that help children to catch their breath and relax as necessary. This means concern for what *they* can do comfortably. They cannot come back breathless from mad galloping and start immediately to sing. It would be better for them to flop onto the floor "like a burst balloon" and lie there several seconds before coming for the singing. A teacher must be sensitive to what *quiet* means. Singing a lullaby is not necessarily a quiet activity since one must use one's breath, although a lullaby itself is quiet in contrast to a gallop. Change of pace, change of mood, and change of muscular involvement all go into the consideration of a balanced rhythms period.

THE TEACHER'S ROLE

If the teacher recognizes that through the rhythms experience she is encouraging exploration with movement and sound, introducing new material in these areas to the children, allowing for individual and group functioning, and protecting children from both self-consciousness and precocity while giving them full opportunity to enjoy the elements of music and dance, then she can be satisfied that she has opened the possibility for lifelong learning in these fields for these children. But any teacher owes it to the children and to herself to explore the pleasures of motion and song for her own enjoyment. Her enthusiasm and interest are needed for the building of a repertoire of songs and instrumental selections, for the willingness to explore and learn, as well as to share these age-old satisfactions with a new generation of youngsters.

Bibliography

Song and rhythm books for children:
Boni, Margaret, *Fireside Book of Folk Songs* (New York, Simon and Schuster, Inc., 1947).
Bradford and Woodruff, *Keep Singing, Keep Humming* (New York, William R. Scott, Inc.).
Buttolph, Edna, *Music Is Motion* (Cincinnati, Willis Music Company, 1951).

Coleman, Satis N., and Thorn, Alice G., *Singing Time* (New York, John Day Co. Inc., 1931).

——, *Another Singing Time* (New York, John Day Co. Inc., 1937).

Davison, Archibald T., and Surette, Thomas, *140 Folk Songs for Grades 1, 2, 3,* and *Kindergarten Folk Songs* (New York, G. Schirmer Music Company, The Concord Series 9, 3, and 7, 1952).

Diller and Quaille, *Rote Pieces for Rhythm Bands* (New York, G. Schirmer Music Company, 1930).

Hughes, Dorothy, *Rhythms, Games and Dances* (New York, The American Book Company, 1942).

Hunt, Evelyn, *Music Time* (New York, The Viking Press, 1947).

Huntington, Harriet, *Tune Up* (Garden City, N.Y., Doubleday & Company, Inc., 1942).

Landeck, Beatrice, *Songs to Grow On,* and *More Songs to Grow On* (New York, William Morrow & Co., Inc.).

McCarteney, L. P., *Songs for the Nursery School* (Cincinnati, Willis Music Company).

Norton, June, *Sing and Be Happy* (New York, The John Day Company, Inc., 1957).

Seeger, Ruth, *American Folk Songs for Children* (Garden City, N.Y., Doubleday & Company, Inc.).

Books and pamphlets for teacher reading:

Andrews, Gladys, *Creative Rhythms for Children* (Englewood Cliffs, N.J., Prentice-Hall, Inc., 1954).

Buttolph, Edna, *Music for the Classroom Teacher,* Bank Street College Publication (New York, Bank Street College, 69 Bank St., 1958).

Cleveland Association for Nursery Education, *Cane Review,* biannual publication containing songs, stories, and games (2084 Cornell Rd., Cleveland 6, Ohio).

Driver, Ann, *Music and Movement* (New York, Oxford University Press, Inc., 1936).

Eisenberg and Krasno, *Guide to Children's Records* (New York, Crown Publishers, Inc.).

Jones, Betty J., *What is Music for Young Children?* (Chicago, National Association for Nursery Education, 155 East Ohio St., 1958).

Krone, Beatrice, *Music in the New School* (Chicago, Neil Kjos Music Company, 1941).

Mursel, James L., *Music and the Classroom Teacher* (Morristown, N.J., Silver Burdett Company).

Sheehy, Emma, *There's Music in Children* (New York, Holt, Rinehart & Winston, Inc., 1952).

Musical instruments, records, and song books are available from the following companies. Catalogues will be sent on request.

Child Craft Equipment Company, 155 E. 23rd St., N.Y.

Curriculum Materials Center, 5128 Venice Blvd., Los Angeles 19, Calif.

Folkways Records Children's Catalogue, 121 W. 47th St., N.Y. 36, N.Y.

12

The Many Purposes of Blockbuilding and Woodwork

How can a set of wooden blocks that children simply play with have an important place in a kindergarten curriculum? And why should scraps of wood and dangerous materials be considered suitable curriculum materials? These two questions, though not articulated, are often in the minds of many teachers. In fact the usually noisy and often exciting block play is quite distracting to some teachers, while to others the clutter and noise that accompany woodwork simply seem obstacles to orderliness. Yet both blocks and woodworking are among the approved curriculum materials for kindergarten and first grade in bulletins issued by state departments of education and local school boards. Why then do so many kindergartens have meager supplies of blocks and no work bench at all? Perhaps the answer lies in the difference in the type of activities indulged in by boys and girls. These particular materials are usually thought of as boys' play materials rather than girls'. Is it possible that kindergarten teachers, all women, do not have an affinity for materials they have never themselves employed?

Blocks and wood are so essential to a good program for young children that we will analyze their functions in detail. However, although blockbuilding and woodwork depend on the same basic material, they are quite different in meaning and use, and we shall discuss them separately from here on. Let us begin with the blocks.

251

WHAT ARE BLOCKS?

When we speak of building blocks for the kindergarten class we mean the large set of standard unit blocks made of hardwood and distributed by educational equipment companies. These blocks were originally designed by Caroline Pratt half a century ago when she started the City and Country School in New York City and developed her own educational materials.[1] Lucy Sprague Mitchell tells us [2] that Miss Pratt never bothered to put her name to her design, so that now blocks sometimes bear the name of the manufacturer or distributor, or are simply referred to as floor or unit blocks. By definition, a unit block is twice as wide as it is thick, and twice as long as it is wide; all other blocks are either multiples or divisions of the unit or related to it in width, thickness, or length. In most sets a unit block measures 1⅜ x 2¾ x 5½.[3]

When first introduced, these blocks were an instant success with children; teachers too, particularly creative ones, were quick to recognize their potential.

In addition to these solid indoor blocks there are also available from educational equipment companies large hollow blocks of uniform related sizes. Since these blocks are larger (5½ x 5½ x 11; 5½ x 11 x 11; 5½ x 11 x 22) and require more space for building and storing than the smaller unit blocks, they are particularly suitable for outdoor use. Being large they lend themselves to quick construction which immediately stimulates dramatic play. And being relatively heavy, these blocks provide considerable physical exercise and practice in coordination to the children who lift, carry, place, and replace the blocks as they use them. Although both kinds of blocks—the simple outdoor hollow blocks and the more advanced indoor unit blocks—are important building materials for kindergartners, each kind of block serves a different purpose. We shall reserve detailed discussion on the outdoor blocks for the chapter on outdoor play and confine ourselves here to the indoor unit blocks.

WHAT STUDIES OF BLOCKBUILDING REVEAL

Harriet Johnson made such a basic and thorough study of blockbuilding in the nineteen twenties that we are still learning from her

[1] Caroline Pratt, *I Learn From Children,—An Adventure In Progressive Education* (New York, Simon and Schuster, Inc., 1948).

[2] Lucy Sprague Mitchell, Introduction to *The Art of Block Building*, by Harriet M. Johnson, Bank Street College Publication (New York, Bank Street College, 69 Bank Street).

[3] New York State Department of Education, *Equipment for Children in the Kindergarten* (Albany, 1960).

unique observations and insights.[4] She noted that children go through developmental stages in handling this material, in the construction process itself, in understanding of building principles, in freedom of artistic expression, and in skill of elaboration. She pointed out further that "The really dramatic quality about these young builders is not their mastery of techniques, but their attitude toward the material. It is essentially that of the artist. Even when they do representative building it is the essence, not the bald form, that they make alive."

After studying hundreds of records of blockbuilding by preschool children almost thirty years later, Hartley and Frank [5] observed the value of blocks for emotional release and for personality development in young children. Making strong block buildings of their own design and with their own bodily effort gives children a feeling of strength and security. Seeing how high they can build and balance a precarious structure gives children a satisfying sense of adventure, excitement, and risk which they can enjoy with safety, as when a shaky structure is stabilized and a collapsed building built up again. The authors point out that blockbuilding can serve the aggressive child by calling on his initiative and energy, and can help the shy child by allowing him individual uncompetitive activity which brings him solid results with little effort. For both kinds of children blocks bring the opportunity for recognition and even pride. For the inexperienced, blocks allow solitary and gradual participation and afford a natural contact with a neighboring builder. For children who are experienced with the medium, blockbuilding is an opportunity for advanced cooperative planning and working.

Esther Starks, in her careful and well-illustrated account of blockbuilding,[6] describes the many practical educational uses of blocks in all areas of learning in the kindergarten. Blockbuilding is helpful in improving physical coordination, in learning mathematical relationships, and in gaining concepts of space, as well as in grasping geographic concepts. With blocks, children can work out ideas on city planning or building design, and can coordinate other materials in valid relationships with the blocks. Children's block buildings can express their down-to-earth quality and their keen observation of actual experiences: two boys build a bridge "over the Ohio River" and a girl builds a "refrigerator house" for cooling milk on a farm.

[4] Harriet M. Johnson, *The Art of Block Building*, Bank Street College Publication (New York, Bank Street College, 69 Bank Street), p. 35.

[5] Ruth E. Hartley, Lawrence K. Frank, and Robert M. Goldenson, "In the Block Corner," Chpt. 4, *Understanding Children's Play*, 9th ed. (New York, Columbia University Press, 1959).

[6] Esther B. Starks, *Blockbuilding* (Washington, Department of Kindergarten-Primary Education, National Education Association).

THE APPEAL OF BLOCKBUILDING TO CHILDREN

Although the attention and respect given to blockbuilding by teachers varies, there is no doubt of the special popularity of this medium with children themselves. Hartley and Frank [7] record in their study that children choose blocks more often than paint, clay, or other materials generally made available in the classrooms, and that only dramatic play approaches blocks in general popularity. It is easy to be convinced of this if one enters a classroom populated with four and five, or five and six-year-olds, for whom blocks, floor space, and ample time have been provided.

In the first classroom Joey, not yet five, hurriedly peels the sweater sleeves off his arms and stuffs the garment, inside out, into his cubby without looking at it. With a deft skip and a slide he lands in front of the richly stocked block shelves, clanks down several piles of blocks, and possessively slaps the smooth surfaces of the top ones. Joey's gestures and facial movements all bear an expression of appetite for those blocks. The teacher is obliged to make a restraining comment. "You may not need any more blocks, Joey; start your building first, then you'll see," she says, the way a mother restrains a child who is helping himself to a favorite food. Joey's teacher is just in time with her restraint, for several children surround him with accusations of greed. When they appeal with their need for heavy blocks for the bottom of a garage and long ones for a new road, and "a lot of blocks" for a wall, Joey understands them well and responds.

In the second classroom the teacher is asking for a show of hands on available activities for the session. When blocks are mentioned hands are not merely lifted from the elbow, but raised vigorously from the shoulder, sometimes one hand holding up the other for firm support and palm of the raised hand shaking with the demand to be noticed. Not quite sure their demonstration *will* be noticed some children follow the hand routine with an irrepressible "me!" "me!" The minute they are free the potential builders make a rush for the small block corner in the large crowded room. All of them are fleetfooted, arm-swinging, quick-grabbing boys. "I got them first," claims one, guarding three large curves from other eager hands. Dispute among the six is reconciled with little help from the teacher, for the children are so anxious to get their hands on the blocks and begin building that they are ready to make concessions. These energetic, bright five-year-olds know what is in store for them, even with a limited supply of blocks and the need to share before they have enough

[7] Hartley, Frank, and Goldenson, *op. cit.*

for themselves. One can tell that they know by the way they survey the blocks, select the place and measure the space, speculate on height, and however crudely, lay out the plan. One can tell by the vigorous gestures, the satisfying physical exertion, the delight with the rhythm and the sound of blockbuilding which attracts the nonbuilders, that this activity rates!

BLOCKS HELP CLARIFY CHILDREN'S UNDERSTANDING OF THE WORLD

Blocks can offer a variety of learning opportunities for children. Let us first look at this unique medium to consider its significance in furthering intellectual growth among young children. To see how blocks provide an outlet for, and stimulate inquiry into, solid knowledge and information, we can do no better than to examine the early records of a full week's block play described by Jessie Stanton in the long out-of-print *Before Books.*[8] The section we are quoting is from the chapter *Block Building, Third Week in January.* The time is the nineteen-twenties; the place, downtown New York City. The episodes of blockbuilding followed a number of trips in the immediate environment.

The most complete block scheme of the year resulted from the trip to Staten Island. The whole group took part in it, and the constructions were played in with much zest and interest.

On Monday, after a discussion of our trip, Meta said she wanted to build the Statue of Liberty. I asked her where she would put it and she said "in the bay." Albert said he would make Governors Island. Sonia said she would make Battery Park and the Staten Island Ferry House "at the bottom of New York." I asked the children in what part of the room the bay should be and they pointed correctly to the southern end. Then I asked what lay to the east of New York, and when they said the East River, I drew two chalk lines on the floor, repeating this on the West to make the Hudson.

As soon as the rivers were outlined, Florence said she would make the Sixth Avenue elevated in New York, and Fred that he would make his apartment house on Sixteenth Street. Edna decided to build the Lackawanna Railroad in New Jersey. Sonia wanted to make Staten Island, so I asked her where it should be and at her direction drew a chalk line to represent it in the extreme end of the room.

Both Albert and Meta used blocks laid flat to represent the small islands they were making. Both felt the form of the islands enough to make them circular, not square in shape. Meta began Bedloes Island on the same side of the bay as Governors Island, but she corrected this after I had suggested that she look at the map. She built the pedestal and placed a doll on top of it. The doll stood

[8] Caroline Pratt and Jessie Stanton, *Before Books* (Adelphi Company, 1926).

erect with one arm in air, the hand being covered by a small clay jar which suggested a light. This fell down repeatedly and finally she took a Statue of Liberty drawn by Richard, and thumb-tacked this to two blocks, so it would stand erect.

Opposite her, across the bay, Albert worked absorbedly on Governors Island, building two lighthouses, and a round pile of blocks suggesting a fort.

Sonia made the Aquarium in Battery Park, with five small enclosures for fish. In one she placed Albert's clay walrus, in another Richard's duck. Then she ran for the peg lock fences (made by the children for the farm play in November and December) and made a little enclosure to represent the park, with one lone tree and a little grass in it. Below this she built the ferry house. She made a narrow entrance which led to the ticket office, a small square enclosure with a small window through which tickets could be purchased. She put two dolls inside at a table, and made strips of tiny red and blue tickets, "red for grownups and blue for children." Beyond this she made a ticket box and seated a doll beside it to watch it. Next she made the ferry slip and the ferry.

Florence, meanwhile, was working on the Sixth Avenue elevated. This ran South in the center of Manhattan Island and curved over to the East just as the real "El" does. One signal was placed at the curve, arranged just as we had seen the signal on our trip, and another was placed just in front of the Battery Park Station. Elaborate stairs led down to the ground level.

Fred made a large six story apartment house, "my apartment house on Sixteenth Street." His interest was well sustained. Celia made the *Leviathan,* using triangular blocks to form a pointed bow. It was not so large as the liners built by the boys last week, but in shape it was quite accurate.

Edna started the Lackawanna Railroad in New Jersey. The space to work in was limited and she did not progress far with it.

On returning from their naps, the children flew to work again. Faith and Celia built a church at the northern end of Manhattan. They seated the dolls in rows before the doll minister in the pulpit. Meanwhile, Sonia had run her ferry to Staten Island and had been bitterly disappointed to find "no houses there." Meta immediately said she would build a house there. Albert and Richard built a freight yard we had seen there on our trip.

Fred now finished his apartment and went to the shelf for dolls. He was disgusted when he found they were all in use and most of them at church. I suggested that as a church could not feed and lodge people, the dolls might live in Fred's house and merely attend services in the church.

The children welcomed this proposal and it was put into effect, except that Fred tried to take the people out of church at once, and Celia remonstrated violently saying, "We are right in the middle." He let the service come to a close and then took eight of our new toy farmers out and arranged them on a block, two by two, saying to me as he pushed them down toward the lower end of New York, "You know those long crowds that come out of church, Miss Stanton." Sonia was ready to weep because no one had come to see the

Aquarium, so Fred said all his family were coming. He arranged the dolls in front of the enclosures and let them stand there for some minutes, gazing at the specimens. Faith, walking by, said to Sonia that she didn't think her turtle could be seen at all, as it was back of the big bowl containing the goldfish.

Next, Fred took the dolls to the ferry house. He arranged them in a long single line and let each one stop at the ticket window. Then Sonia tore off a ticket and handed it through the window. Fred made the doll drop it into the ticket box and then go into the waiting room. Finally when all the dolls had dropped their tickets in, the two children marched them on to the ferry. There they had to be left until morning as the time had now come to go out in the yard.

Celia and Faith, meanwhile, had made automobiles out of blocks for the other worshippers, who were leaving church. Each doll sat in state in what appeared to be a small wooden chair. These were placed one behind the other in a straight line, twelve of them in a row, looking for all the world like a traffic jam in a very busy street. I said to the children that it looked just like a crowded street except for one thing. Faith said, "We need a policeman," and they placed a doll with raised arm in front of the cars.

On Tuesday the children objected to going out in the yard, they were so eager to get to work at their block scheme. Richard worked on Brooklyn Bridge again. He had built very crudely on Monday.

Celia and Faith flew to their church, turned around the automobiles that had been carrying the people away, and brought them back to attend a service. Albert became interested and brought some of his men from Governors Island. Celia and Faith started fooling, so I stopped the church play and asked them to look at New York and see what else the city needed. Celia said, "The Wool-worth Tower," at once, and Faith said, "The Metropolitan." Each knew the correct location of these buildings. Celia built the Woolworth near Battery Park. I told Faith that Fred's house was at Sixteenth Street and she counted up to Twenty-third Street, making a line on the floor for each street. Then she built the tower. It fell twice, so I suggested that she try an entirely different way of making it. She builds very roughly, as a general thing, but this time she settled down to concentrated work and evolved an entirely new method of placing the blocks which was strong and satisfactory. She made a pointed top which was much admired.

Fred and Sonia ran at once to the ferry boat, on which Fred's dolls had been waiting since the day before, and pushed it down the bay past the Statue of Liberty, past Governors Island into its Staten Island dock. Fred ran for his red lantern and gave this to Sonia to set on the end of the pier, to represent the light we had seen on the trip. He took his dolls off the boat and let them look at the freight trains, but Sonia soon called "Twelve o'clock now, the ferry's going," so Fred rushed his dolls on board for the return trip. Sonia made a clock of blocks as soon as she reached the New York pier, so that she would know when to run the ferry. Fred then took his dolls to the elevated station and asked where to buy tickets. Florence said she would make a ticket office and tickets which she did. Then the dolls were put on the train. Meta told me at this juncture that she did not want to play with her house on Staten Island, so I suggested that she help Florence as the latter needed a station at Fourteenth Street for Fred's family, who were on their way to Sixteenth Street.

Albert took his men on a visit to the Statue of Liberty, but complained that it was not safe, as Meta had not put any railing around the edge of her island.

Edna continued her Lackawanna tracks and made a freight yard. She said she would bring food and coal for the people.

While struggling with the removal of his leggings on Wednesday, Fred said, "I can't wait a minute, I want to work all the time." He added a chimney to his house making long tails of "smoke" out of paper and thumb-tacking them to the block representing this. He took his dolls on excursions over the city again, adding great zest to the boat and train play.

Celia and Florence made blue "uniforms" out of paper for the ticket sellers on the elevated. Meta took over the running of trains, and was thrilled with this new interest.

Sonia decided to build the school on Twelfth Street, so Richard, who was not building, ran her ferry for her. She cautioned him particularly about changing the pilot from one pilot house to the other at the end of each trip.

Fred complained that his family were starving as there were no stores at which to buy food, so Albert built a store on Seventeenth Street.

On Thursday, only Albert, Fred and Sonia retained their interest in building. Albert built a dredger in the bay, and Fred did the same, after some play with his house. Marie, who had been absent for ten days, joined Sonia in the construction of a motion picture theatre, which was very completely worked out, with a stage on which Sonia's own pictures were shown, an orchestra of dolls "playing music," and rows of seats, on which all the available dolls were placed.

On Friday, owing to wet weather, our usual trip had to be postponed. The children, having laid out Twelfth Street and the adjacent streets and avenues, built the school, the hospital across the street, the jail on Tenth Street and Greenwich Avenue. Marie built this all alone, accurately reproducing the counters and cashier's desk. Dolls served as sales people and customers. Faith and Florence were drawn into this play, making pies, cakes and jelly-rolls out of clay. Ovens were made in which to bake these.

The reader may think that the children in Miss Stanton's class are intellectual geniuses and the program of trips and blockbuilding guidance too ambitious for kindergarten. Yet, in reality, average five to six-year olds are this curious about their environment and ready to learn all kinds of concrete details, including directions and names of places if they go and see *for themselves*. Average children dramatize their experiences while blockbuilding if they have usable content that lends itself to dramatization. (See the chapter on trips). The Stanton records show quite clearly that blockbuilding that develops around themes that have intellectual implications (i.e. their fulfillment depends on inquiry and retention of information) leads to *reasoning* (in what part of the room should the bay be?), *problem solving* (how do you build the stairs down from the station?), *generalization* (traffic needs a policeman), *thinking in terms of relationships* (where do you place the Statue of Liberty in relation to Governors Island?) and *concept-formation* (geographical layout of a city). But there must be content to use, a good part of which must be content shared by all the children. It is this background of common experience which the teacher may consciously have to provide; for it is this which lays the basis for intricate and stimulating play.

MATHEMATICAL CONCEPTS GAINED FROM BLOCKBUILDING

There is a distinctly mathematical activity in the handling of building blocks which may also be considered intellectual learning. Children have experience with quantity when they ask for "Many *more*—for this big building," or complain of "not nearly *enough* for me and Jerry and Jane," or resort to hoarding a particular kind of block. Since kindergartners have an individual and personal awareness of numbers from their actual experience (fingers, toes, T. V. channels, address and telephone number), using blocks for different kinds of construction enables them to test and put into practice quantitative concepts of numbers.

When making "a double track," or "a two-lane road," a young child makes the general concept of *two* concrete. He gains a clear notion of four sides when he constructs a rectangular enclosure, although he does not know the word *rectangular* and may not know the abstraction of *four*. Here is an interesting illustration from a classroom record.

Mike, not yet five, is putting away blocks with his teacher. The teacher hands him a pile, saying "here is a pile of three for you." Mike puts them away on a shelf where they go three high. She hands him two more piles of three, without saying anything, but with a rhythmic gesture corresponding to Mike's own. Then Mike says, "I want to get my own pile of *three*, and you put away the long ones." He proceeds, stacking up a dozen piles of three, without any error, then calls to the teacher seriously, "I need two more, I need two more—there is only *one* in this pile."

To achieve measurable, correct height, Mike is spontaneously practicing subtraction *and* addition, even though this is not the isolated process it will become in the grades.

It is easy to see that with all the variations in dimension, style, and function of blockbuilding, the opportunities and demands for mathematical considerations, brief and elementary as they may be, are incalculable!

The related *shapes* of the blocks constitute another mathematical aspect that interests young children. "Look," says Bernice, rolling a small and a large cylinder block simultaneously, "these are the same, only this one is bigger." And Warren, running out of single unit blocks for his barn, picks up a couple of triangles and turns them around in his hands experimentally, trying, perhaps, to see if they would do in place of the rectangular piece he needs. Then a light of discovery shines on his countenance as he beholds a definitely four-sided block of the right size born from the fusion of two triangles placed next to each other. This magic of two triangular pieces combining to produce a rectangular one is so fascinating that Warren abandons the completion of his barn and keeps working on his discovery for the rest of the session. Nor does he forget about it the next day.

As can be expected, when a teacher herself uses the correct names for the block shapes the children, with experience, also use correct names to express learned concepts of shapes, as we can see in the following scene.

Joan and Susie are painting on adjacent easels. Joan says: "I made a *triangle*. Now I am going to blue the triangle." Indeed she has painted a triangular shape pretty much in the center of the paper, and carefully fills it in with blue paint. Susie glances, nodding approvingly, apparently understanding Joan's experience of triangular shaping. When the triangle is completed to Joan's satisfaction, she says, talking both to herself and to Susie, "Now I'll cover the triangle with a square." And she does this surprisingly accurately. Although Joan usually did purely artistic work when painting, the deliberation, calculation, and even precision of this particular experience in painting showed her interest in geometric concepts gained from blockbuilding, as she had used the terms *triangle* and *square* freely.

BLOCKBUILDING CAN HAVE IMPORTANT MEANING TO AN INDIVIDUAL CHILD

We can best see the meaning of blocks to a particular child by looking in on the experiences of Billy, a wiry little five-year-old who loves to be big.

Billy loves blocks so much that it is hard for him to get enough of them. He often reserves building partners and accessories as well as special shelves of blocks. He takes out large piles of the heavy long kind, and hopping and skipping and stepping around them he lays out what looks like a base. Then he labors using the largest blocks as well as the various units of them, erecting a structure on the base. He then develops and shares ideas pertaining to technique or purpose. "I need *two* doubles here to *hold* the floor." "No, it won't work. I tried it." "But it's not going to be a house now. It's going to be a skyscraper." With such an ambition for a superstructure in size and importance, Billy has a great deal to do to keep the towering structure from leaning dangerously. He is intent on reaching the desired height. The higher the building the more tiptoeing and the more care in placing the blocks properly. Soon the building becomes beyond reach of his stretching body and hands, and after a moment of thoughtful looking around Billy uses a chair to achieve the needed elevation. This determined, self-directed, strenuous work, and the fast growth in the height of the building, is now relieved by a physical slow-down, by an inventiveness in design and a happy regard for decoration and beauty. He makes one story of the "skyscraper" with triangular blocks, producing a mosaic effect. He then inserts slender, rising cylinders in an area otherwise flat and low. Painstakingly he places small colored cubes in such a way that it makes the building look lively, lighted, and altogether charming. There is a roof on the building now and a final traditional topping with a chimney. Billy's eyes and teeth flash in a smile of pleasure. He actually rubs his hands gleefully and clasps them with self-satisfaction. Ah, but there is a gleam of further creativeness in his eyes. He hops from the chair, dashes over to the shelf with small wooden animals and plucks a little red rooster. He wants to place him on the "tippy top." But he cannot reach from the chair and prefers not to entrust this delightful ultimate and personal task to the teacher. And so he pleads with her for relaxation of the rule against standing on tables. Winning that and standing on the table, Billy raises himself to sufficient height, gingerly places the rooster in just the right spot, then jumps off the table with a whoop and a whirl and an expression of satisfaction in his surveyal of the entire work.

Would Billy take down such a laboriously and proudly completed structure when it is clean-up time? "Not just yet," he pleads, and reasonable allowance is given. However, the reality of the situation demands that blocks be put back on shelves for use by the afternoon session. Billy's need to show his strength and bigness comes into play again. "Look, I can carry more than five." "Watch out, watch out, I am steering this tug to the dock," he says, as on his hands and knees he pushes a heavy pile of blocks into place.

It is easy to see that to Billy the blocks meant full bodily activity, with both general and precise coordination, resulting in a relaxation of tension; it meant organizing, arranging, measuring, and counting; it meant striving for bigness, persevering with an idea, exercising control and patience; at one point compromising, at another point agreeing with adults (dismantling a building), and practicing orderliness in putting blocks away.

But could blockbuilding mean something else to another child? Let us follow Paul. As soon as the children get into their activities of the main part of the morning, Paul keeps an eye on the pile of blocks which he and several others keep enlarging by bringing armsful from the shelves (a little distance away from the area for building). Soon he begins assorting the general pile and takes for his own use a stack of quads. "I don't need these," he says, pushing aside shorter ones. Another boy is helping Paul, bringing the requested kind and amount of blocks. Soon two smooth even parallel walls rise five blocks high. The blocks are placed not on the flat broad side, but on the high narrow side so that the wall looks smoother and rises more quickly. Paul is delighted about the height. "Ooh! Let's build to the ceiling!" Without hesitation he proceeds to build a roof using the same kind of blocks, without realizing that the unstable walls only *look* strong. As the building inevitably collapses, the boys dodge, hurting their hands. Both seem to enjoy watching and studying the wreckage. Paul immediately starts building up the same walls again with the same method and effect, the same observation and satisfaction, and apparently the same expectation of results. Sure enough, the building collapses and Paul is again delighted with the sight of the wreckage. The teacher comes over, expressing her concern for safety and the need to *avoid* making collapsible buildings; she tries to demonstrate the greater stability of placing the same blocks broad side down—but such a building neither gives the effect nor reflects the intention that Paul has in mind. Paul, however, listens amiably, unprotesting. When the teacher leaves, the two boys engage in quite a serious argument about the method of constructing their tunnel-like building. Paul is very clear and determined about the thin, smooth high walls, such as he built before, but his friend wishes to comply with the teacher's suggestion. The teacher does not arbitrate and Paul's fellow worker leaves, apparently without any hard feelings on the part of either child. Paul resumes his building alone now, but at the halfway mark asks an interested onlooker to help him. He asks the child to bring over the same size blocks (quads) and help extend the same building. Now the building is twice the size it was before, with a roof covering the entire building and an impressively long deep inside. Paul is thrilled. He calls jubilantly to the teacher (remember that the building was made against her advice), "See, it *worked!*"

The teacher smilingly acknowledges Paul's success. Other children come to admire the building and of course cannot resist getting inside. When one child climbs into the building and accidentally bumps the wall, the whole structure crashes. Paul complains to the teacher, "Stevie did it!" However, nobody is really unhappy about the destruction. And Paul is ready to build it up again! This time (and maybe just as well) the work period is coming to a close and the teacher reminds "five more minutes before clean-up." Paul, together with the others, is at last responsive to the teacher's suggestion. But in the process he gets an idea. He piles a few blocks on top of one long block, as if it were a carrier. After pushing it briefly towards the block shelf Paul gives a jerky pull to the bottom block and watches the load of blocks fall off. He promptly gathers them and stacks them up in a definite pattern on the long block, and again jerks out the bottom one, watching the load fall off and disperse. He would repeat the operation but the teacher calls his attention to the practical task at hand and Paul now propels the load forward while moving quickly on his knees toward the shelf.

BLOCKBUILDING PROMOTES SOCIAL RELATIONSHIPS AND COOPERATION

As the children experience satisfaction from individual expression and discovery of the uses of blocks, and as they develop some skills, they also gain interest in building with others in larger group projects. We have indicated earlier how very important children are to each other in the kindergarten. Blocks offer an unusually fine vehicle for sharing interests and ideas. A good illustration of this can be found in the following account.

During a typical day in the kindergarten, Johnny, Eddie, Jill and Dennis were building together with the blocks. Their joint efforts eventually produced a complicated structure including a tall building, several low ones and a network of roads. Johnny and Eddie built the tall one together. Jill worked on a low one nearby and Dennis made a garage and highway. Before long, Dennis' road had passed Jill's building and had reached the skyscraper. Eddie left the tall building and started adding to the road with curved blocks, his most recent enthusiasm in highway engineering. Jill became preoccupied with putting little wooden "people" in the building, adding animals for good measure when the supply of people ran out. Johnny continued to make the skyscraper higher, finally needing a chair to reach the top. "It'll touch the ceiling!" he announced to the room in general. During all of this activity, there was much talking among the four children, Johnny dominated, with many commands. Dennis tended to do as Johnny ordered, Jill quietly went about populating the structure, apparently paying no heed to Johnny's directions and Eddie countered with suggestions of his own.[9]

In another situation there is a more complicated involvement of many children in a larger group.

Entering a large kindergarten class of thirty-seven children towards the end of the work period, one observes that the most conspicuous part

[9] Elizabeth A. Vernon, "Moving Into Group Life," *Good Living for Young Children* (New York State Council for Children, 1960), p. 15.

of all the productivity and activity is the blockbuilding. It occupies a substantial portion of the room, using three sections within the area. One sees that a great amount of energy seems to be exerted as the six children involved move back and forth, lifting, holding, and carrying quantities of blocks. One feels an urgency in the tempo and the sound of the builders. It is as if a sign is hung saying: Children At Work—Respectful Attention Requested.

And indeed, not only are the children building but they are also organizing, giving commands, arguing, deterring intruders, claiming credit for success, and disclaiming guilt for mishaps! When it is time to put the blocks away there is further organization, distribution of labor, matter-of-fact cooperation, and joint effort not only on the part of the six builders but several others (especially girls, it seems) who are happy to give a hand in such splendid noisy work as clearing space and filling shelves. There is a distinct feeling of satisfaction that means, "Mission accomplished by *us!*"

Equal Opportunity Is Important

Many of the records in this chapter indicate that boys and girls are equally interested in blocks, although perhaps in different ways. The teacher must make sure that the opportunities are equal for all children. It is not uncommon to see the blockbuilding space in the classroom dominated by boys. It is true that the hardness, toughness, and aggressive possibilities of blocks do appeal especially to boys and challenge their energies; the teacher readily sees the meaning of blocks to the boys and may unthinkingly let it be a boys' activity. Thus the block area may become established as the boys' domain; the boys feel and act possessive about the blocks and unhesitatingly exclude the girls. Some girls, seeing that there is little chance for them in the area, do not even bother fighting for a chance. Other girls counter such discrimination by rushing into a free block corner "before the boys get there" and then enjoy building with their own kind of social involvement. Teachers must make it a point to provide the opportunity for the girls when this occurs, and to even go further in encouraging an expansion of their interests to draw them into mutual play with the boys when this seems possible.

THE PHYSICAL ACTIVITY INVOLVED IN BLOCKBUILDING BRINGS SATISFACTION

When children think about and discuss plans for projects, or conceive ideas about the special structure and function of a building, it is urgent for them to use their bodies and muscles immediately to execute the plan. They cannot hold plans and ideas in their heads too long; they must get to work and make the abstract ideas or theoretical notions concrete. *Action* is one of the essential characteristics of five-year-olds, and it is therefore worth giving attention to the purely physical aspects of block-building at this point. When a child spends a full period of forty-five to seventy-five minutes in blockbuilding he has a good deal of physical exercise, bending and straightening, lifting and carrying, carefully placing and replacing heavy blocks, and using special coordination of eye and limb muscles in the process.

First, before the actual building there is the need to remove the blocks from the shelves. Whether this is done by taking blocks one by one, in twos, in stacks of fives, or in piles reaching from hand to chin—depending on the child's style or plan of the building—he becomes immediately physically involved. This preparatory process is itself often enjoyed by the children for the sheer muscular satisfaction, and some children will take blocks off the shelves even if they have no plan to build with them. In fact, *reaching* for blocks seems by itself to be a thoroughly accepted and challenging kind of task. In one particular classroom there was a tall cabinet, rather than open low shelves, where the blocks were kept. The two highest shelves required standing on a chair to reach, but this in no way deterred the children. Other sturdy chairs nearby were also incorporated into the block equipment.

As the boys removed blocks from the high shelves with swinging, energetic rhythm, they gloried in the physical activity. Stretching, lifting, holding, dropping—they loaded up the chairs as if they were wagons. When one chair was fully loaded one boy called importantly, "Someone come help me!" "Okay," replied a co-worker, "I will!" and together the two pushed the loaded chair carefully to the middle of the area, really exerting strength. Then, workmanlike, they dumped the load, supplying material for construction, and went back for another load. This loading up and transporting with one's own muscular power, getting the load to a destination, and releasing all that weight with proper workmanlike racket, seems very satisfying to little children.

They also enjoy accumulating piles, stacks, or even mounds of blocks preparatory to building. This purely physical operation is quite exciting and sometimes serves as a stimulation to building ideas. Usually the teacher needs to guard against the possibility that the possessive piling of blocks in mere preparation for building does not go on for too long. Some children may need a little push at this point.

At putting-away time children naturally turn from self-structured, purposeful activity with blocks to a freer, noisier, more aggressive, and more physical kind of activity. They knock blocks down, push and scoop them together with hands, feet, and whole body, stack them, slide piles into "port," and load up "barges." The children manage to do a great deal of physical exercise—twirling on their own seats on the floor, sliding on stomachs, spreading arms and contracting legs while in practically prone or in sitting positions on the floor. (They do put blocks away also!) They experiment with methods of conveying blocks to the shelf, gaining practice in particular kinds of muscular coordination before finally accomplishing what they set out to do.

Looked at this way, the physical activity of ample blockbuilding sessions may be seen as a supplement to otherwise inadequate opportunities for exercise in programs limited by time, space, and consistently poor weather.

TEACHER ORGANIZATION OF BLOCKS FOR USE IN THE CLASSROOM

We see that the extent and nature of block play and the value that the individual child or the group derives from blockbuilding depend on the teacher's continued, active interest in blocks as an important medium. What, then, should the teacher do?

Importance of Sufficient Blocks, Adequate Work Space, and Shelves

The teacher should request from the management of the school (whether that be a public school principal or a committee of parents) a sufficient quantity of blocks for her class,—approximately 700 to 1,000 unit blocks composed of 17 to 25 different shapes, or as close to it as is practically possible. She needs to designate a large enough area for building activity so that limitations and frustrations will not inhibit the children's development in the use of blocks. She must see to it that enough shelves of proper depth are available to keep the blocks in an orderly arrangement. Seeing blocks properly placed by type, children can better appreciate the distinct shapes and can enjoy putting blocks back into their proper places. When the teacher respects the blocks as a medium she will discourage children from stepping on them while building on the floor, dumping them from shelves, or marring the wood. She will encourage the children to remove stains and scratches with sandpaper, and in general will keep the blocks clean and the block shelves dusted periodically.

Necessity for Safe Handling

Together with the children the teacher will need to institute rational safety rules, for an impulsive, strong five-year-old with a block in his hand and anger in his soul may have too powerful and effective a weapon at his command. Thus, using blocks as building and playing material *only* might be one logical safety rule. Sometimes demolition seems as attractive to young children as construction, but demolition of another child's building can be disastrous in more ways than one. Also, demolition of a block building with children nearby can cause pain and injury. Here again a logical rule concerning efficient and safe dismantling of buildings could be instituted and observed by the children. However, for the occasional child to whom the deliberate crashing of his own building may have some urgent significance, *understanding*, rather than punishment for breaking a rule, is the better road to eventual control. It is important to remember that although rules are a necessary security, applying them rigidly without occasional exception can be unfair and even retard learning. In one classroom, for example, to avoid dangerous crashing a rule was made that buildings be erected no higher than a child could reach by standing. But then the smallest child in the class designed a tall building that required standing on a chair in order to reach the top and test a theory of balance. Realizing the importance of that particular building, the teacher and the other children cooperated in guarding both the building and themselves on that occasion.

Accessories Are Needed to Enliven and Beautify Buildings

Excellent as blocks are as building material, children soon find blocks alone insufficient and may by themselves seek supplementary objects. Because children are creative, building to them is not only definite, mechanical structuring; rather, it calls for elaboration, decoration, and items that symbolize action. We saw in Miss Stanton's records how children constantly used figures of people, transportation toys, and clay objects as properties in their block play.

The basic accessories for block play in a kindergarten are: transportation toys, such as cars, trains, planes or whatever else is familiar or interesting to children in this age of transport; simple, even abstract figures of people and of animals, wild and domestic (these can be wooden, rubber or plastic); and a few boxes of colored cubes which children use so charmingly for decorative and symbolic functions. It is desirable to have enough accessories for the size of the group using the block area. In addition, each teacher can purchase or otherwise provide blockbuilding accessories of different kinds. One teacher kept on the block shelves a few pails of selected beach stones which the children used for roof decorations, chimneys, cars, and for farm products in connection with block play. Another teacher advised the children to keep the sticks which they had collected on a trip to use as block accessories. Cut to approximately even size and stacked in a low box, the sticks looked like cords of firewood and were favorites with the children when they needed cargo at the dock or wood in a lumber yard. Still another teacher collected a few dozen empty thread spools from the parents, painted them and placed them in a box marked "for block building." The important thing to remember with homemade accessories is that they must be safe, sturdy, have uniform design, and be in sufficient quantity to be useful in a class.

EFFECTIVE GROUP PLAY CALLS FOR TEACHER GUIDANCE

Good, rich, and interesting group play with blocks just does not happen by itself. It takes real nurturing, at two levels, by a perceptive teacher. At one level is the *broadening* of children's horizons, the introduction of content, and the supplying of raw material which, if suitable, the children will seize eagerly. At the second level is the help in *human relationships* involved in group thinking and planning. Kindergarten children are quite dependent on teachers for this type of guidance.

Adele Franklin observes that with the teacher's planning of relevant neighborhood trips on the basis of children's interest, meaningful group building usually follows. That this is so is beautifully illustrated in the Stanton records. These children painstakingly reproduced details of the life of the society around them with such realism that we, of a later generation, can feel quite nostalgic reading them. But they could not have done this if their teacher had not given them the opportunity to see for themselves the comprehensible aspects of life beyond the street they lived on. From this they dramatized what could be expressed dramatically. Following their keen personal observations, how creative their mutual work and play with blocks became! Clearly, this type of play, as suitable today as forty years ago, will flounder if not fed by continuing information and redirection into new areas of comprehension. The teacher's interest and efforts on the children's behalf are not only supportive, as when she *allows* blockbuilding, but she must *continuously nurture* this activity through trips, books, and accessories if the maintenance and development of good group blockbuilding is to proceed in increasing intricacy.

But on rereading Miss Stanton's records we also see dynamic relationships and absorbing social dramatization constantly being created with the use of blocks. In such play the children learn forcefully how a contribution from each group member has different worth in the integrated whole scheme, and how interdependent the children are in the fulfillment of their ideas. All this occurs with the teacher's full awareness and carefully gauged intercession. When Fred's apartment house was completed and ready for occupancy he was eager to have people move right in. But Faith and Celia had meanwhile built a church, installed a minister in the pulpit, and shepherded all the people to the service. So the people were "right in the middle" of a sermon when Fred wanted them, and the teacher helped Fred understand the use of both the apartment house and the church by the same people; this required concession and cooperation, and led, subsequently, to more meaningful play among all the builders involved. Or, observe the social involvement and dependence when Sonia builds the aquarium, using animals and fences made by other children, a ticket office with a doll attendant, and separate tickets for grown-ups and children. Miss Stanton reports that then "Sonia was ready to weep because no one had come to see the Aquarium, so Fred said all his family were coming." After that the two children work together and with the aid of dolls they make full and proper use of the ticket office, tickets, and entrance into the aquarium to enjoy the sight! The right question, an appropriate suggestion—and the children can go on.

Judgment Must Be Used in Directing Block Play

Sometimes it is difficult for a teacher to decide when to let the children carry out their own ideas and when to use her influence by direct intervention. Perhaps we can understand the problem better by looking in on several more teachers.

During a work period in Miss Howard's kindergarten a conspicuous building is being erected with the large, hollow, outdoor blocks in a central part of the room. The children are piling the blocks energetically and practically instantaneously they put up a house some four feet high. Miss Howard notices that although the children improve the building somewhat as they go along, the play, mostly social in this hastily put up and crude structure, tends towards a repetitious going in and out of the building, with undertones of giddiness developing fast. Miss Howard says, in the spirit of offering something better than what they are doing, "Let's put these blocks away now, so you can have time to use the others today, too." Agreeably, the children put away the large blocks and proceed to make completely different use of the clear space in front of the shelves. Building with the smaller, more adaptable unit blocks, they are confronted with new challenges—*what* to make, *which way*, *how* things could fit and to what *use* the building could be put. The children are now thinking—of design, of structure, of function.

Although actually redirecting the children's building, Miss Howard, who knows her group and has a good relation with the children, succeeds in stimulating their imagination and strengthening their interest in building. Knowing her children, Miss Howard is able to recognize when they are at a dead end and need direction towards a more fruitful activity.

In Miss Cameron's kindergarten class, however, a group of four (and later seven) children are quite involved rebuilding and operating "a farm" saved from a previous day. Care of the distinctly domestic animals and their placement and replacement in the barn and pasture seems to be the chief concern. Then one child finds an elephant (a large rubber animal, bigger in size than the farm animals) in their midst, "and an elephant doesn't belong!" So with a view to protecting the farm animals the children not only drive the intruding "wild" elephant out but try to "shoot him," actually striking him with block "guns." The teacher does not see this as violence, but is rather appreciative of the children's regard for the farm animals and their ability to distinguish domestic animals from wild ones. Not all of them were able to do this in a discussion a few days back. She therefore says nothing.

On another day the same teacher notices the children building docks and boats and arguing. She knows that all the children in class have either been on or seen different boats, and she feels that they could have an intelligent discussion. She asks the children what the boats hold and which way each one is going. When she sees that the children are not sure, yet eager to know, she produces a boat book.[10] The children leave the blockbuilding for a moment and pore over the pictures in the boat book, examining minutely the details of the various boats in the pictures and promptly applying the knowledge by correcting the structures or shape or dimension of their boats.

What makes the teachers decide at one time to step in with suggestions and help to the blockbuilding children, and at other times not to interfere? There are several reasons for both actions.

When the children's building consists mostly of repetitious stereotyped play, the teacher, with knowledge of the children's interests, can suggest a new idea, offer different accessory materials, add stimulating information on the type of building, or ask the children questions on the nature and purpose of the building. Any of these may liberate the children from a stilted position. A proper length of string, for instance, can make a vague reference to cables and change the block play to active dramatic building as the securing and supporting of the cable is engineered. Or a piece of earth-brown or grass-green paper may give direction and stimulation to an overdue plane landing.

Sometimes a building project, though stemming from a good initial idea, can come to a standstill because the children do not have the necessary information to develop the play. By supplying the information

[10] Marjory Flack, *Boats on the River*, illus. Jay Hyde Barnum (New York, The Viking Press, 1946).

the teacher is helpful to the planning and later to the executing in detail of the children's ideas.

When, perhaps as a result of fatigue, tension or even bad weather, the children's behavior becomes silly and uncontrolled, the teacher's help becomes urgent. She will need to redirect the children's attention and perhaps change the responsibilities of particular children.

Violation of safety is another reason for a teacher's prompt intervention in blockbuilding. A wobbly structure, for instance, may not be noticed by children close to it; unless it is made secure it can literally crash on their heads.

Interference with other children's rights may be a good reason for a teacher to take decisions relating to block building into her own hands, or to help the children to make a fair disposition of a social problem.

Still another reason for a teacher's active help is a child's inability to get started or to get finished. Her help may be physical (getting particular kinds of blocks or suggesting a good place), or it may consist of verbal encouragement ("I think *you* are a good builder, too!"), or it may be moral support only by a sympathetic glance or an approving smile.

A teacher should not interfere when the children are working well themselves on a problem they encounter in blockbuilding. Neither should she interfere when children need time to correct their own mistakes. Knowing the children in her class, the teacher may be able to see that a relatively simple building is as much as the children can do at this point in their experience, and that leaving them alone is necessary for their development.

Thus, a decision as to when to give and when to withhold help in blockbuilding is not a simple one. Each situation requires subtle understanding and sensitive action on the part of the teacher. When giving help she must not give too much so that the children can carry out *their* ideas and build on their own level. When not interfering the teacher must not neglect and ignore the builders. Perhaps her concern for both the lively children and the lively art of blockbuilding can help her in making a wise decision.

WOODWORK BELONGS IN THE KINDERGARTEN

In spite of the general recognition by educators that woodworking is a valuable activity for preschool and young school children, there is not much literature on the subject and standard textbooks give only perfunctory accounts of the place of woodworking in a kindergarten curriculum. Yet when a preschool child comes with his mother to nursery school or kindergarten for the first visit before school, the woodworking bench in the classroom invariably makes the strongest impression on him.

"Look, mom!" a child exclaims, touching the rough bench tentatively, and when nails and a hammer are offered in response to his curiosity his face lights up with excitement and pride. His satisfaction is unmistakable both to the teacher and mother. Many a supervisor or teacher who has observed children's woodworking speaks of their insatiable desire for this activity. The most frequent comment one hears is: "They can't get enough of it," and "they" means all children of both sexes. We read in *Nursery-Kindergarten Education* [11] that "Some boys and girls would spend most of the kindergarten day at the work benches if they were allowed to, for this type of activity offers satisfying rewards, both tangible and intangible."

However, there is much confusion on the part of teachers as to the importance of this activity or how to develop it.

What Is Woodworking?

Is woodworking primarily a "work" activity, completely apart from intellectual interests, something a boy would do with his father in his spare time, and only a "frill" subject in school? Does facility at woodworking preordain a child to become a good worker in the manual, menial sense, without quality as a scholar? Or is woodworking to be regarded as an "artistic" activity along with blockbuilding, painting, drawing? Children do derive sensory pleasure from handling wood and they construct not only representative utilitarian objects such as airplanes, trucks, tables, and doll beds, but create abstract and fanciful structures, using wood with accessory materials.

Perhaps there is a scientific aspect to woodworking? In this activity children do learn elementary mechanics of fitting, fastening, connecting, and cutting; they learn physical properties of different materials —roughness, softness, sharpness; they learn about the grain of wood and the source of sawdust.

But some children like woodworking for the purely physical exercise. Such children would just as soon pound in as many nails as they can get, as long as they can use the hammer. Or they move the arm back and forth with a saw until they are exhausted from sheer physical exercise.

Perhaps woodworking is most important for providing preschoolers with a rare opportunity for blowing off steam? What could be a better way of getting rid of some aggression than whacking soundly with a heavy hammer and cutting into lumber with a noisy saw, and then, relieved and relaxed, returning to quieter activities?

[11] Jerome E. Leavitt, ed., *Nursery-Kindergarten Education* (New York, McGraw-Hill Book Co., Inc., 1958), p. 182.

As with everything else there are tremendous individual differences in children's interest and approach to woodworking. Some child may find great fascination in just using sand paper to smooth and smooth a piece of wood, while another may be determined to make a truck on wheels that move or a big barge with a smokestack to use with block buildings. Some five-year-old may find the sawing of endless short lengths off a long board completely satisfying, while another child wants to figure out how to make a table with four legs that require measuring, marking, sawing, sanding, nailing, and perhaps gluing and painting. All these children will require various amounts of help from the teacher, but all need an equal degree of recognition.

Woodwork Has Strong Appeal to Children

Children are fascinated with the transformations that take place in woodworking. One long piece of wood can, with effort and the use of a tool, become four short ones. Two separate pieces can be fused into one completely whole piece with the use of a particular tool and definite technique. An ordinary box, four unattached wheels, simple washers, and nails of a certain length can, through systematic steps with only a hammer as a tool, be transformed into a "real wagon." When the wagon is further refined by being sanded, brightly painted, and then given a handle of string attached at the front with a staple, a cup hook, or a metal eye, it becomes a treasured wagon—treasured because the child himself produced all the transformations.

As with other media, children need to master this one on their own terms in the early stages; the aids given must be technically accurate but geared to allowing a child to accomplish his own ends, if these are practical. In the following instance the teacher did not understand this at all.

Miss Smith's kindergarten had excellent woodworking equipment and supplies, and in accordance with administrative advice Miss Smith had a woodworking project for her class as part of the year's plan. For this, each child was given a chance (and help from the teacher) to make a small bench. This bench was well designed (but not by the children or the teacher), required simple construction, and was generally quite satisfactory. Every child in the class made this prescribed bench of uniform dimensions, which required some hammering, a little measurement, and final painting. The children took home the finished products; each of them had carried out an assignment. In reality, however, the project failed to give the children more than a taste of the woodworking experience and no chance to use their own ideas or practice woodworking on their own level.

Teachers can and should be helpful, but obviously they need to know something about wood and tools themselves. While a rare woman does have a feeling for the craft, this is not typical among American women. As a result, this highly satisfying experience for young children (and older ones too!) goes by the board for want of training among the women and a paucity of men among the teachers of the young. The techniques are not at all difficult and do not call for extraordinary strength. If there is no one who can teach an aspiring kindergarten teacher we suggest a look at some older children's books dealing with the subject, among them Jerome Leavitt's *The True Book on Tools for Building* [12] and Jeanne Taylor's *Child's Book of Carpentry*. [13]

THE MATERIALS AND METHODS FOR WOODWORKING IN THE KINDERGARTEN

Woodworking requires its own unique materials. Principally these are a work bench with simple but good hand tools; a sufficient quantity and variety of suitable wood; nails, sand paper, and such accessories as string, spools, wire, or scraps of cloth and leather in proper containers. It also requires a clear introduction of the activity to the children and careful guidance and supervision of the special techniques to insure physical safety as well as beneficial outcomes. We will take up the various points separately.

Work Bench

This simple, sturdy, stable object is the first item to be obtained. It seems to signify the purpose and the character of woodworking—nothing to fool around with. It has something basic to offer. It may be an expensive and good commercial work bench with easily adjustable vise, roomy drawer and an ample shelf or two—a work bench made to last through many years of hard use. It may also be a homemade one (made with the help or at least advice of an experienced carpenter or skillful handyman). It may be a more crude one, made of a discarded door or even a heavy packing box, but properly reinforced and having correct dimensions (see Appendix), with a well-attached clamp and conveniently placed shelves or drawers for supplies. Or it may even be a temporarily installed but durable pair of workmen's saw horses with a heavy board

[12] Jerome E. Leavitt, *The True Book on Tools for Building* (Chicago, Children's Press, Inc., 1955).

[13] Jeanne Taylor, *Child's Book of Carpentry* (New York, Greenberg Publishers, 1948).

secured so there will be no tipping. Any one of these offers a specific, strong, and safe place for woodworking.

The location of the work bench must naturally be such that two to four children around or in front of it have room to move their hands and arms safely without touching anyone else. It is best to place the bench where other children will not be passing too often and where the necessary woodworking noise is not a serious disturbance to others. If there is a nearby separate shoproom or workroom, even in the basement, where a few children with an adult can work undisturbed, that can be an advantage.

Wood

In this age of plastics and alloys we are almost unaware of the properties of wood—its density, its graining, the fact that it is cut in widths of different thicknesses (*e.g.* 6 inches wide by ¾ inches thick) and is more or less splintery, according to origin and type. Only when we buy furniture do we become aware of the quality of wood, and then with different criteria than we use for children. Children need raw wood, unfinished and unpainted, and of a density that will challenge them but not defeat them when they saw or hammer. It is good to have to exert effort in conquering wood, but it must be conquerable to five-year-old hands. Plywood, for example, is unsuitable because it is too hard; fir is unsuitable because it is too splintery; soft pine is about right.

Obtaining and keeping the wood itself for kindergarten use presents special chores and problems to the teacher, but these are worth the effort. There are many ways of getting wood. At any lumber yard in the neighborhood or community a quantity of several sizes of white pine can be bought. White pine is particularly soft and smooth to work with both for hammering and sawing. Balsa, poplar, and basswood are also good soft woods, but not as suitable for sawing as hammering. If the right kinds of scraps are available free, so much the better. Often lumber yards will give away scraps up to 12 inches long. Make sure the thickness is suitable, however. There may also be a furniture factory or repair shop in your locality which has useful, discarded pieces of wood. Here it is important not to take pieces of such hard woods as oak, maple, or birch which are very difficult for children to penetrate with nail or saw, although interesting small pieces may be used for gluing in connection with woodworking. Some teachers procure wooden boxes (fruit and liquor boxes with solid ends, as well as small packing boxes) and remove usable boards free of nails and splinters. Each teacher may need to find her own source of wood in the vicinity of her school or home and may perhaps secure the cooperation of other teachers or parents (even friends and family, as some teachers do) in getting wood for her kindergarten class. Once in the classroom, the wood must be placed in a receptacle—a sturdy carton perhaps, a wide barrel, or an empty oil drum. The receptacle must not only be sufficient to hold the wood, but should enable the children to see the pieces in it to pull a desired piece out.

TOOLS AND WHERE TO KEEP THEM

Woodworking tools constitute a most interesting item to children, although these tools may at first put teachers to fright.

For the sake of both the children and the teacher only the basic essential tools should be made available to kindergartners. These would include four to six hammers of different weights and kind: perhaps two or three flat-head, 10 or 13-ounce hammers which are most secure for preschool beginners, a couple of hammers with claws for pulling out or redirecting nails, and a full size heavy adult hammer. One number 8, 12-inch sharp crosscut saw for straight cutting is necessary, although some tall children can use 14 or even 16-inch ones. There can be two saws if there is provision for two children to saw at the same time. A rasp is a good safe tool for children to handle and use for smoothing a rough or splintered edge against the grain, and for such shaping of the wood as rounding a corner. This tool also has an interesting name (no doubt a new word to the children), representing the raspy sound it makes. Later in the year when the children are more experienced and responsible with tools, a 10-inch smoothing plane and a hand drill may be added to the supply of tools. The plane not only makes an amazing change in the surface edge running with the grain, but produces delightful curly shavings. As for the drill, the holes in the wood produced by different size bits are endlessly intriguing to make and to use.

A one-foot rule and either a fat regular pencil or a flat carpenter pencil will be necessary for measuring and marking wood. In addition, pliers are handy to have and to know about, as are large scissors for cutting string or wire or sand paper. Still another tool is a brace and bit which does the work of the drill in a more complex fashion. This should be introduced late in the year when kindergartners operate it with eagerness and delight. Although screwdrivers are often found among kindergarten woodworking tools and used with screws or for prying or splitting, a screwdriver is really not as safe in the hands of inexperienced five-year-olds as is assumed. It may therefore not be wise to have this tool available to children, especially at the beginning.

The other indispensable material to be obtained from the hardware store along with tools is a supply of different size nails; there must be the broad headed ones, 1 to 1½ inches long, for the crude and easy hammering, steel nails with sharp points that go in easily and do not split wood, ranging from 1 to 2 inches, nails of different lengths and thicknesses to fit the wood and the purpose—in short, enough variety of nails for the child to exercise selection, discrimination, and judgment. Necessary too is sandpaper of different grades of roughness.

Having selected, obtained, and paid for the best kind of tools, a teacher must turn her mind to the care of them, for if not cared for they can become worthless in a few days and the whole woodworking area can turn into mess and ruin. The saw left lying on ledges is dangerous for the child and harmful to the saw; hammers may soon be missing and lost if not regularly replaced; nails become very easily scattered; and sandpaper can turn up inside pockets, books, and wastebasket if proper places for it are not provided. On the other hand, nothing is more attractive and inviting than tools that are cared for and are in their proper place, and once order is rationally instituted it is reasonably easy to maintain. A special place on a wall, or a tool board, is therefore a must. On such a board an outline of each tool can be made and appropriate hooks, nails, or holding gadgets put in; then children and teacher can easily get in the habit of putting tools where they belong and consequently have no trouble finding them. A drawer or two and some shelves in or near the bench are also important for tools and materials. Sandpaper blocks with handles can be kept in a drawer or in a marked box on a shelf. Saws should be professionally sharpened once or twice a year, oiled and wrapped in newspaper when put away for the summer, then cleaned off in the fall. If a hammer or saw handle becomes loose or damaged it must be removed and repaired or replaced, for broken tools create low standards and low morale, and of course they are not safe.

Although mixed up and scattered nails can be the worst looking mess of all, keeping nails in assorted plastic jars, tin cans, or wooden bins is really fun. Just to look at a whole series of separate, uniform suitable containers, each holding a particular kind of nail, is a real pleasure to children, adding interest to the challenge of finding just the right size nail that will not come through unwanted and will not split the wood. A fascinating way of picking up nails from the floor is, of course, with a magnet, which should also be kept in a prescribed place and put back after use.

Accessories

The kind of extra materials a kindergarten class will have at the work bench depends not only on what is available but also on the imagination and sophistication of the class members, including the teacher. These could include:

(a) *metal gadgets*—cup hooks, metal eyes, and staples (for coupling), wire on a spool or roll (for fastening or decorating), paper clips, thumb tacks, small tin cans for expected and unexpected uses, and the tiny, silvery coasters that normally go into chair legs but which make wonderful headlights on trains.

(b) *string*—a ball of twine and string of several different thicknesses. It has innumerable uses.

(c) *rubber*—rubberbands and pieces of rubber which can be cut from an old inner tube or discarded galoshes (children will surely find interesting uses for these).

(d) *wood*—spools of different sizes, small wheels of different sizes which can be bought from educational equipment companies, doweling of different thickness, cheese boxes, cigar boxes, tongue depressors (all useful to inventive, constructive children).

(e) *leather*—scraps from a shoe repair shop or pieces of discarded leather belts or shoe tongues make good hinges and handles when needed.

(f) *cloth*—needed sometimes for sails on a boat or upholstery for furniture.

To use the various accessories other tools and materials will be needed besides the scissors already available on the tool board. These include glue, a big needle and thick thread kept in a well-labeled box on a shelf or in a pocket on the board, and a sturdy wastebasket with dustpan and brush—all marked "woodworking" and kept in a specially designated place. A box of labels may also be useful to keep in a special drawer.

Introducing Children to Woodworking

Obtaining the work bench, tools, wood, and accessories, putting everything in place, and establishing the time of day for the activity does not necessarily mean that woodworking can then start right off, as the children usually think it must. There must first be some introduction, usually a few weeks after the school year commences. When the teacher and children have achieved a reasonably good rapport and an understanding of each other, when general routines, safety rules, and the need for taking turns have been established, introduction to the woodworking activity and all its fascinating sidelines is in order.

The inexperienced teacher may feel worried about putting real tools into the hands of some of the energetic children, or she may feel all thumbs herself in this activity and hold off woodworking until she tries out this work without the children watching her—a very sensible precaution. When she does tackle the job the teacher may have the entire class or half of the class at a time for an initial session of explanation, discussion, inspection, and testing of the equipment. It will not suffice for her to say, "This is a nice strong bench." Instead, the children, one or two at a time, will need to knock on it or try to lift it to determine the strength or weight of the bench. And it will not be enough merely to admonish, "This saw is very sharp and dangerous, so don't fool with it." It would be more effective to allow children to feel with their fingers the flat side of the teeth, inspect the thin sharp points, feel with their own hands the hardness of wood, see and hear the teeth of the saw cut into the wood. The teacher must give a graphic and instructive demonstration of the movements of the arm in sawing—gripping the handle firmly, one pushes *down* with emphasis and comes *up* easily. The teacher should also explain the definite rules for safety—where to keep each hand, how far away from the saw other children must be, and how the saw is taken off, put down, or put away.

The weight and function of the hammer can be demonstrated and tested by some children to dramatize for others its crashing power on an empty carton or perhaps on a tin can or rock. Then the tentative blow followed by the resounding, firm whack on the nail can be demonstrated and the hammer's place on the tool board pointed out. The other tools can also be touched, inspected by each interested child, called by the right name and tried out, or at least demonstrated to the children. To emphasize correct techniques the children can be allowed to take turns using the tools right then and there. Just a demonstration will do to convince them of the necessity of putting the tools where they belong and of keeping materials and nails in proper containers. Orderliness is really fascinating to children, as long as the teacher cares about orderliness without being rigid. Since the chief difficulty will be the assignment of turns (probably no more than three children at a time can use the work bench), a decision will have to be made as to how long the turn should last—whether it should be twenty minutes, half an hour, one hour, or as long as interest and energy last. It is a good idea to prepare a calendar with an alphabetic list of the children so that at each woodworking session the children know who the workers are.

Supervision for Safety and Satisfaction

Even with an interesting and effective introduction to woodworking, and the children *saying* they know the rules and can handle tools, the teacher must always realize that with their strong impulses, curiosities, and energies, kindergartners must be supervised and guided while acquiring skills and controls for satisfying woodworking activity. Although four to six-year-olds normally respect the need for caution with a tool and will refrain from abusing it, lack of such respect is not uncommon. Children of this age do not really appreciate the cutting power of a saw that is too close to a friend's gesticulating hand. They may make sudden friendly but unsafe movements toward him with a tool or may make a quick grab of a sharp object which is perfectly safe to pick up slowly. An erupting argument with tools in hand may be potentially dangerous and children's attention would need to be promptly called: "If you have to argue, put down the tools. That's a rule, remember." Without intimidation or nagging, safety must be articulated by the teacher on all appropriate occasions to assure that the rules are understood by the children.

When, after several sessions, the teacher feels secure about the children handling themselves and the tools safely at the work bench, she may find that it is not necessary to give them close attention and that merely keeping an eye on them (one of the many eyes a kindergarten teacher is mysteriously equipped with) provides sufficient supervision. The children remain free, of course, to ask for help or advice. Woodworking safely and independently will give them added opportunity to develop responsibility. There actually do exist properly equipped woodworking areas in classrooms which children use with no more supervision and with as much responsibility as is required with heavy blocks, spilly paints, or messy clay. Children need good direction to reach this point.

Good supervision in woodworking not only guards the children's safety but allows them interesting individual experiences, discoveries of their own powers, strengthening of techniques, and much exciting learning. But it gives a great deal to the teacher as well. It can reveal to her children's traits which she never suspected: dainty little girls enjoying a turn with the rough work; a boy who is usually hopping from one thing to another staying attentively put with a sawing task until completion; children asking searching questions about wood and simple mechanics during active physical involvement. She also learns something of the nature of children's difficulty in planning in this activity. Though older children are encouraged to have a plan before starting working, a kindergarten child may not know at all what he wants to do or to make until he looks and touches and tries something first. Often he makes a decision only after responding to the materials actually available or to the activity of another child. He may also get a brand new idea while already working on something and insist on changing his project from his original idea. It is therefore important to allow children to evolve their own plans rather than give them a ready-made plan and a set design for a product or insist that they have a blueprint before they start.

Practical Relation of Woodworking to Other Activities

Woodworking is not only popular as a separate activity with individual children but it also serves in a practical way to further other classroom pursuits. Children may make flat cars, barges, traffic signs, and other imaginatively conceived and easily constructed objects to use in block play. In one class several children together made a large cage, using doweling for vertical bars, in which the wild animal figures were kept on a shelf next to the blocks. In another, a little girl collected the wood shavings which resulted from planing, took them to the housekeeping corner and filled a pot with "spaghetti." Similarly, sawdust was collected for use as "cereal." In one class, where paint brushes were often lost or missing, a boy who was especially fond of drilling thought up a secure device for keeping brushes from straying and for allowing them to be easily counted. This consisted of a narrow wooden shelf with as many small holes drilled into it as there were supposed to be brushes. This device was attached to the wall near the painting activity, which not only eased checking on brushes during clean-up but also stimulated interest in painting.

When air holes are needed in a closed jar to keep a captured bug alive, the jar lid can be taken to the work bench and with nail and hammer holes can be easily punctured. Should a cutting board be needed in cooking, one might find just the right piece of wood to make one at the workbench. If pails are needed for collecting things or for the sand box, milk cartons or empty cans can have holes punched into their sides, and can have string or wire handles. If nails are loose in the roof of the playhouse outdoors (apt to be discovered by a child), the teacher may take a claw hammer from its place and either pull them out or hammer them in as an emergency measure.

"The packing box has splinters—look!" a child calls. The teacher answers him:

"What do you think can be done about it?" The child thinks a minute.

"I know! Get sandpaper from the work bench drawer and rub it smooth!" No sooner said than done.

Another time children are arguing as to who is taller, until one remembers the use of a ruler in woodworking. That same ruler is now used to measure the height of the children against the wall, and with the teacher's help the argument is rationally resolved. Such practical uses of the woodworking equipment, accessibility of the work bench, and familiarity with different tools on the part of children and teacher will lead to freer and more meaningful activity and unexpected learning.

THE VALUE OF WOODWORKING PRODUCTS

Not all the children's products are worth keeping or even preserving with paint. To fives, the pleasure of the process is quite often as significant as the pleasure in the product.

When a child does make something he or the teacher feels should be preserved or decorated, it should be possible for a child to use paint and beautify his product as he sees fit. Watercolor paints are sufficient to begin with in painting wood, but the color fades and rubs off onto hands. "Fixing" the color with shellac is somewhat messy for kindergartners, so that inevitably the time comes when "real" paint seems the best thing to use.

It is necessary to set up a place for this supplementary activity of painting wood products. What will be needed is old newspaper on which to work and oil paint in a secure container with special brush and turpentine. If poster paints are used instead, then after drying shellac should be applied with a brush of its own. Shellac brushes must be cleaned in denatured alcohol. Since the importance of painting wood products depends on the children and kind of work they are doing, the teacher will supervise and guide this activity accordingly. Sometimes restriction may be necessary, as when a child is so fascinated with painting wooden surfaces that he would use up half of the available wood if not stopped. In one such case the teacher told Lenny, "You can paint wood only after you make something with it and it *needs* to be painted," whereupon he very quickly and crudely constructed an airplane and logically and justifiably demanded a right to paint it. When the teacher realized that it was painting and not woodworking that mattered to Lenny, she gave him a big old crate to paint.

Real paint brushes must be cleaned in turpentine, and obviously the activities of painting and cleaning require careful adult supervision. Fives can be quite responsible and the possibility of spilling should not be a deterrent to trying materials. But fives are not grown-up and it is unfair to expect more skill from them than they have. They will be cautious and respectful of paint, shellac, and turpentine. But an adult must be close at hand, especially if more than one child is working with these materials.

Woodworking does indeed satisfy many needs of young children. For some it may be an enjoyable physical exercise, for others a chance to observe carefully how a thoroughly visible nail disappears into the depth of wood and is no longer visible. To other children, woodworking can be satisfying for the aggressive type of activity it provides, such as

music time means movement and rhythm, sound and tune and beat

27

28

working and planning with all the precision they can muster, children enjoy constructing, inventing, achieving

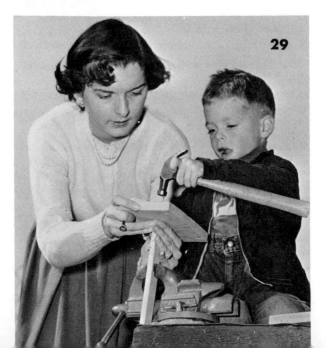

29

hitting, splitting, and cutting. "Want to see me hit it real hard?" can often be heard at the work bench.

But perhaps the phrase heard most frequently from children in connection with woodworking is "it's real." "These are real tools, not baby things." "This is a real work bench, like my daddy has, with a drawer." "No, I can't talk to you now, I am busy. This is real work I am doing." To be even briefly involved in real work and to be using grown-up tools is immensely satisfying to small children; it makes grown-upness seem attainable.

Bibliography

Antin, Clara, *Blocks in the Curriculum* (New York, Early Childhood Education Council of New York, 32 Washington Place, Rm. 23).

Franklin, Adele, *Blocks, A Tool of Learning*, Bank Street College Publication (New York, Bank Street College, 69 Bank St.).

Hartley, Ruth E., Frank, Lawrence K., and Goldenson, Robert M., *Understanding Children's Play* (New York, Columbia University Press, 1959).

Johnson, Harriet M., *The Art of Block Building*, Bank Street College Publication (New York, Bank Street College, 69 Bank Street).

Leavitt, Jerome E., *The True Book on Tools for Building* (Chicago, Children's Press, Inc., 1955).

Moffitt, Mary W., *Woodworking for Children* (New York, Early Childhood Education Council of New York, 32 Washington Place, Rm. 23).

New York State Education Dept., *Equipment for Children in Kindergarten* (Albany, 1960).

———, *Let's Make It* (Albany, Bureau of Elementary Curriculum Development, 1958).

Nursery-Kindergarten Education, Jerome E. Leavitt, ed. (New York, McGraw-Hill Book Co., Inc., 1958).

Pratt, Caroline, *I Learn From Children—An Adventure in Progressive Education* (New York, Simon and Schuster, Inc., 1948).

———, and Stanton, Jessie, *Before Books* (Adelphi Company, 1926).

Starks, Esther B., *Blockbuilding* (Washington, National Education Association, Dept. of Kindergarten-Primary Education).

Taylor, Jeanne, *Child's Book of Carpentry* (New York, Greenberg Publishers, 1948).

13

Problems and Pleasures
of Outdoor Play

Before discussing the various purposes and the many pleasures of outdoor play for kindergartners, we need to disavow some of the common negativisms which teachers have about the outdoor play period. Here are some of the common misconceptions:

1. Playing outdoors is of secondary importance and is generally of incidental value in the total program. As one teacher expressed it when asked how often her kindergarten class used the well-equipped, accessible playground, "The children used it every day at the beginning of the school year because they weren't able to do more settled work; but now there isn't *time* to go out, except once in a while."

Yet common sense as well as a medical point of view tells us that however successful the "settled work" in the classroom may be, a day in the life of young children must include the outdoors for their general health and learning. Children need the fresh air, the physical exercise, the change of pace, and the reorientation in space just as much as they need the productivity of indoor activity. They welcome the general stimulation and the different kinds of play that are possible outdoors. In addition, the children's individual powers of observation of their environment and especially of nature are often sharpened by going outside.

2. Children should play outdoors only in the *right* kind of weather—not when it is cold, not when it is hot, and certainly not when it's about to

rain, nor when the wind is blowing. Thus, on a snow-bright sunny morning Mrs. Fiddler looks out of the window onto her well-equipped, accessible playground and says, making a shivering, shrugging motion, "It's bitter out, children. Let's stay in."

But shortly after Mrs. Morrison, also a kindergarten teacher, opens her door onto the same playground. She sniffs the still, frosty air, observes the sparkling snow, and says invitingly to the children as she grabs her own jacket and scarf, "We are going out!" Mrs. Morrison feels the vigor with which the children run through the yard on the soft snow, enjoys seeing the glow on their faces, and loves hearing the joy in their voices as they shout freely after the period of relative quiet and confinement of classroom work.

Apparently some teachers are better able themselves to withstand variety in climate than others. To maintain reasonably objective criteria, therefore, it is wise to consult the school nurse or local pediatrician for standards in such basic conditions as lowest and highest degrees of temperature bearable, velocity of wind, and the wisdom of play in direct sun during different seasons.

Even if it is too cold to stay out more than twenty minutes, there is still an advantage to the children in the physical release and stimulation of interest which they derive from outdoor play. Sober, stay-on-a-spot adults seem to forget that being active outdoors in the cold weather keeps one warm. Interesting exercises, a variety of races or such activities as hopping and skipping, tiptoeing and stretching, can all be resorted to if the time is too brief for pulling out equipment.

On the other hand, when it is very hot outdoors brief periods in the shade of trees or shelters, the use of sun hats, and water activities timed for the least oppressive periods of the day, can play a reasonable part in weathering and adjusting to conditions of climate.

But worse than the prejudice towards more than moderate heat or cold is that towards wetness, mud, and snow. In one suburban school it was not uncommon to see children arrive at school dressed in raincoats, rain hoods, boots, carrying umbrellas, and bearing a note for the teacher saying that the child should not go out. Too often no distinction is made between a cold downpour, a gentle warm drizzle, or a soft gray mist. The latter two can be very much (and harmlessly) enjoyed by children who are adequately protected against the rain.

Teachers often avoid going out if there are visible puddles, even if the children have rubbers and can put them on themselves. If they do go out the children are strictly admonished to "stay away from the puddles!" This usually happens in the spring of the year when the air is warm and the shallow puddles could be safely inspected with sticks and certainly could be swept or bailed away by the children. The children themselves, of course, are drawn to these natural phenomena, and if they are not taught how to enjoy them with practical consideration to their health they will defy adults and mishandle the situation whenever they can.

3. Teachers often have the notion that supervision can relax when children are outdoors. Not infrequently two kindergarten teachers sharing a yard decide that the two classes can be together outdoors with one teacher only, while the other can use the time as opportunity for a break or for clerical work. Or, if out together, the time seems a good one to catch up on local gossip and personal news. On the surface this seems reasonable. Is it sound?

Safety controls the ratio of adults to children, and a really large group needs more than one adult. A teacher of preschool children must always keep her eyes open for possible or imminent danger requiring her quick wits and action. For example, a foolhardy child may be dashing to the top of a high-climbing apparatus, while another may become panicky when he is not sure how to get down. A mishap may occur when heavy equipment is shoved or shifted, or boisterous play may turn to a quarrel and cause tempers to rise and hands to reach for sticks, stones, or sand scattered on the ground. Children's safety requires no less than full supervision in the playground!

Secondly, children often need help with an outdoor project or problem which may be just as important to them as one in the classroom. A good illustration of this can be found in Muriel Ward's book.[1] She describes a typical playground incident in which Jackie, pulling a wagon quite easily, takes no notice of a rock on the road and is stumped by his inability to proceed as before. Although persistent, Jackie is unable to understand the problem or the solution. "Shall we let him go on like a nonswimmer floundering in the water?" Miss Ward asks, and in answer tells how an observant teacher leads Jackie toward perceiving the obstacle. He thereby achieves a solution to the problem and success in his pursuit.

If the teacher is present and attentive during the outdoor period she can find many things to enjoy and observe about the children and she can contribute to many kinds of learning. She might see some shy, solitary child who is less inhibited in physical movement outdoors than indoors, prove also to be freer in responses to children, as in moments of chumminess with a whispering partner inside a packing box. The teacher may take part in children's collecting and playing with leaves and seeds in season and she may meet their intellectual curiosity about *what, where*

[1] Muriel Ward, *Young Minds Need Something to Grow On* (New York, Harper & Row, Publishers, 1957), pp. 18–19.

and *how much* in nature. Or she may take the initiative and bring things to their attention. She may observe some children's special bodily skills and courage, and others' fears and hesitancies. The teacher will appreciate also the practical necessity for the children to learn to take turns with certain pieces of equipment and to consider the rights and safety of others under outdoor conditions, which are quite different from those indoors.

It is important to remember that outdoor play for kindergartners is not the time of release for children and relief for the teacher that it is for older children when they have their recess time in the playground. Kindergarten teachers should make a legitimate allotment of time for outdoor play rather than relegate it to a time left over from class, and they should use the time constructively.

PHYSICAL EXERCISE IS AN IMPORTANT "FIRST"

As we pointed out in Chapter 2 when describing the nature and needs of the kindergartner, five-year-olds must have a chance to exercise their growing muscles, especially the large ones, and to use their abundant energy. They must have the opportunity for continued practice to develop coordination and mastery of a variety of activities and skills, because the confidence and satisfaction that follow mastery of one's own body give a child a feeling of total well-being and adequacy as a person. Such opportunity for physical exercise can best be provided during outdoor play, with suitable equipment.

The openness of sky and air, and the proximity of the outside world, often have a releasing effect. It is difficult to hold children down when they go out, so eager are they to run and race, to push the heaviest packing case, to reach the highest rung, to balance breathlessly on narrow boards, to hold on tight with straining muscles to a rough, tough rope. Even common playground activities that are hardly noticed by adults provide needed physical exercise. Let us watch a five-year-old on a slide. He *runs* up to it, *climbs* the straight ladder (changing his visual perspective of ground below and around him), *adjusts* his balance, and changes his breathing and vision from the new height; he *lets go* of his whole body, experiencing motion and speed, and comes to a *stop* with a hop. Then he follows the same steps of running, climbing, sliding, and stopping (perhaps with some improvement) again and again. To be convinced of the exercise which this apparently simple operation provides, you, adult reader, try it! But if this seems too childish or too tiring try walking a straight line across a yard, one foot directly in front of the other with arms extended, and then backwards the same distance. If we consider the many other activities in which kindergartners generally engage in a playground we can see what a wealth of opportunity for physical exercise there can be during outdoor play, and how essential it is for children.

Another important contribution of outdoor play is acquaintance with nature and the elements.

THE ROLE OF THE ELEMENTS IN OUTDOOR ACTIVITIES

As we pointed out earlier, children four to six-years-old are often quite protected by adults with admonitions to cover up against the wind, dress warmly so as not to feel the cold, and definitely to avoid slush or snow. Yet wind, cold, slush, or snow may offer stimulating and valuable possibilities for perfectly healthy physical play and good sensory experience and learning. Protection is needed, but the elements are not simply enemies to be avoided and fought.

With cap or kerchief over the ears and jackets zipped, even wind, if not too strong, can be well endured and put to exciting use. Children can make sails by running with a piece of cloth held high, flying kites, testing the force of the wind by moving with and against it, and observing its direction through various kinds of evidence. Even on a raw, damp day with gray skies and drippy atmosphere children can, if properly dressed, have an enjoyable, comfortable time in the vigorous exercise of hauling, carrying, and constructing, or in tossing a bright ball or marching to the rhythm of a drum.

Rain, which is often synonymous with bad weather in the eyes of adults, can contribute much to children's enjoyment of the outdoors. Immediately after a rain there is apt to be much to do. There is the work (always fun) of wiping slides or bailing the lower part of them, the splashy sweeping of the paved part, and the wiping of rungs and flat surfaces. This is all good activity, bringing immediate satisfying results. If children are allowed they will discover and explore mud patches, scooping and digging and feeling; they will collect worms to watch, gather stray stones to sink, and find floating objects on fresh shallow puddles.

And snow holds so much fresh and strange appeal to children. It has such rich possibilities for physical activities and true poetic experience that it should provide a limitless challenge to a kindergarten teacher. There is warming-up exercise in shoveling or breaking up hard snow and in packing snow for snow sculpture and snow architecture. There is fun in bashing snow balls against a solid wall, and there are also other enjoyable snow-throwing games in which five-year-olds can engage safely. The teacher, whatever her chronological age, must be youthful and must appreciate the children's kind of adventure for at least part of the time.

But if she regards such play as entirely childish and beneath her to enjoy, and if she merely puts up with it or limits it drastically, the play will have less freedom, energy, spirit, and initiative and some children may refrain from the activity altogether.

Of course we are assuming that any conscientious teacher always checks the children's efficiency in buttoning top buttons, fastening hats, putting on gloves, and zipping boots. It goes without saying that full enjoyment of the outdoors depends on appropriate attire.

GOING OUTDOORS CAN LEAD TO THE UNEXPECTED

This group of twenty children is going on a walking trip to a neighboring wooded area, taking with them containers for possible findings after an unusual autumn storm. Almost immediately they come upon something truly impressive. A huge limb of a maple is sprawled on the hill. With all its leafy branches it looks like a full tree.

"It's a tree lying down! A whole *tree*."

Then the children and the teachers notice the broken bark and the raw white wood showing. The broken tree is so long and wide in circumference that the whole group clusters around it and several children straddle it. It is so huge and heavy that no child can budge it alone, although many of them try.

"Shall we move it to our playground?" the teacher challenges.

"Yes, yes, yes!" comes the response from the children, but the joint strenuous effort of pulling the tree by the scratchy branches brings frustrating results. Something else has to be devised. This is not only a problem of strength and endurance but an engineering and mechanical problem for the teacher and the children. They all concentrate, are all concerned with figuring out a method of pulling the tree, and finally lasso it with a stout rope (a piece of clothes line). With a team of four two-footed "horses" working in 10-minute shifts, the tree is actually pulled into the playground. What brute strength is needed for such a job!

"And we could do it!" the children say emphatically as they talk about it to friends in other classes and to parents at home.

THE ATTRACTION OF CITY SIGHTS

This wire-fenced kindergarten playground is facing a city street. The children here do not see many trees but they do have exciting moments noticing and playing out city scenes and modern city services. Telephone men straddling smooth poles, ascending above the street, and perching dangerously while performing with wires; pipe and cable men crawling into manholes and disappearing below the street; tough, broad-shouldered truck drivers wielding huge steering wheels and manipulating screechy brakes—all these attract and hold the children's attention and stimulate interest in what is going on here and now.

In a booklet published by the New York City Board of Education [2] the authors reveal the astonishing wealth of elementary science and social studies material in city streets. Although the information in this booklet consists of studies conducted in New York City, the approach to looking and learning and the extent of opportunities would be similar in any city. Within the area of a city block or the space surrounding the school building, or even just the paved school yard, children can determine topography (flatness, depression or rise in surface), they can investigate the surface (cement, stones, or soil), and the kindergarten teacher can help children see the effects of heat, frost, and moisture on various structures. In their city school yard children can observe plants persevering and peeking through cracks and crannies and small pockets of soil. They may also get acquainted with such outdoor animals as ants in a bit of earth, worms after rain, ladybugs on shrubs or fences, or perhaps spiders in a quiet corner. All such uncelebrated creatures in their wild state can prove to be as interesting and exciting as expensive specimens in a zoo, tamed captives in a pet shop, or caged guests in a classroom.

Playing in a school yard almost any time of the year, children can also get acquainted with birds. There are the hardy English sparrows and starlings, the perky pigeons, and often the bright and noisy jays. Occasionally one can catch a glimpse of migrating wild fowl in flying formation passing through the sky.

WHAT IS PLAYGROUND EQUIPMENT?

In order to have satisfying outdoor play the teacher must assess the children's energies and interests, and with whatever means are at her disposal she must rearrange, add to, or replace the available equipment from time to time. Besides the standard stationary objects it is desirable that there be a variety of movable items that can be adapted to the children's own ideas.

What Does Standard Stationary Equipment Mean for Children?

A very common piece of playground equipment is the slide. Slides are appealing for the experience of momentary exhilaration at the top, the brief fun of swift descent, and the easy use of the whole body. Slid-

---

[2] *Operation New York* (Curriculum Research Report, New York City Board of Education, 1960).

ing is often shared fun when a group uses it for a dramatized trip, with rhythmic controlled movements and planned destinations leading to or combining with other activities and sometimes with other equipment. No healthy, lively five-year-old adheres indefinitely to the necessary safety rules (feet first, no pushing) without becoming bored and resorting to some variation. He may use different ways of reaching the top, may experiment with legs or arms to change the course, may invent difficulties and obstacles, or may add adventure by mere disobedience to a rule. Given a chance and some materials and encouragement, children will often extend the ordinary slide by adding an extra climbing structure to get to it, or will expand its function by placing a stack of tin cans at the foot. They laugh uproariously at the clatter and the scattering of the cans as they come down.

In one class, adventurous five-year-olds added excitement to their use of the slide by letting a ball roll off the top, bounce, and continue rolling in an unpredictable direction. Each child would follow a ball on the slide. After a while a wheel was let loose from the top of a slide and with proper precaution to bystanders, a small stone. Then the children observed the relative speed and sound of the large ball, the small wheel, the small stone and a boy of average size going down the steep incline of a slide! Thus the involvement of the body with its muscles and its senses naturally leads to still further activity and experimentation.

See-saws and the making of see-saws with boards and saw-horses of different heights enable children to enjoy another dimension of space, experience a sense of balance, of weight, and of gravity. Watch Phillip and the part played by the fulcrum of the see-saw in creating balance. He is a restless child who gives up easily in anything that seems demanding, and according to his mother and his teacher, does not concentrate well. Here he is eager to use the see-saw alone. With caution in his approach, arms extended, head inclined, feet moving gingerly, and almost breathless concentration on his face, Phillip walks up the grounded side of the see-saw with measured sliding steps until he reaches the precise middle, when the uplifted side is about to go down from the weight of his deliberate tread. Then, catching his breath, he runs down the rest of the slide.

Kenny looked tiny compared to many husky five-year-old boys and girls, and had a difficult time straining and pushing in order to make himself heavy enough to go down on a see-saw when any other child sat on the other end. "I can't make it go," he complained. The only time he enjoyed a see-saw ride was when there would be a pack of children on either end. Kenny wanted to do something about this frustrating situation, so he worked on the see-saw alone and made a weighing scale out of it by placing large blocks on one end, then another block and various objects on the other. He thus had an interesting experience controlling weights and balances, illustrating the various purposes to which a piece of equipment can be put when a child is using his head as well as his muscles.

The standard jungle gym used in many kindergartens is far from being strictly a climbing apparatus to imaginative four to six-year-olds. It is exhilarating to reach the highest point, to learn to stand without holding on, to survey the scene below, to get around the entire circumference, and to climb down, a process which is always surprisingly slower than climbing up. But once children learn to manage it with ease and it ceases to be a challenge, other materials should be made available to keep their interest in the jungle gym.

Tommy looks like an ant when he drags a 12-foot walking board to the jungle gym. He attaches this board to the middle rung.

"Why are you using the *walking* board where children are *climbing?*" the student teacher asks Tommy.

"So I can walk into the jungle gym."

"But you can climb on it without attaching the board."

"It's too easy that way. Don't you know?" Tommy walks laboriously up the board, then climbs on higher and slides out of the jungle gym on the board instead of climbing down or using the sliding pole.

The space, stability, and structure of the jungle gym can be used by children for various important purposes, allowing for a variety of physical activity. Four and five-year-olds appreciate their own strength and enjoy lifting and pulling objects. Thus, a child-directed (though probably teacher-guided) game involving hoisting full pails by ropes onto a high shelf placed on the level parallel bars can hold the attention of many children and lead to constructive dramatic play. Filling pails with rocks or pebbles or mud or sticks and discovering the weight differences in materials calls for adjustment in coordination as children haul and pull and hold heavy objects safely.

Children like to make their own special private places right in the midst of public activity, and a jungle gym is apt to be used as a ship, a house, a lodge, or a submarine with the addition of a few boards, perhaps a blanket, and a ladder entrance. A few children are apt to take possession of it as if they were moving into a special house, a special world. Such a small group can be quite determined about excluding or even fighting off other interested users of the jungle gym. The teacher might be inclined to say to the few children in the group that the jungle gym is meant for all the children, that it cannot be monopolized by a few, and that in school we always share. But must we *always?* Can fair concessions not be made in order to allow individualized small group activity, to support children's departure from the usual, the conforming, and to nurture some independence without really depriving others? This is an important question. Perhaps a teacher could instead say that the small group may use the jungle gym for a while and then give it up to others. This is especially possible if the teacher has enough other equipment in the yard for climbing, construction, and interesting and vigorous play.

The Swing

The most common playground equipment of all for a kindergarten is a set of swings. Swings are, of course, familiar and delightful to many children. They afford satisfaction from rhythmic motion in space and perhaps a certain exhilaration from pumping and being pushed to a daring height.

However, the standard swings set in a row are often a hazard to young children who have no judgment about the speed-space-motion dynamics, and run up to the back of the swing the instant another child is propelled in the air. They often do not hurry to escape the swing on its forceful return. The extra burden this places on the nerves of a conscientious teacher is not always worth the passing pleasure of such swinging.

What about the modern playground equipment that is appearing in playgrounds throughout the land? According to a recent magazine article,[3] "The new gear, some of it as colorful as modern art, is as different from the old-fashioned slide, see saw and teeth-busting swing as Telstar is from a Conestoga wagon." Besides spectacular steel constructions in the shape suggesting rockets and submarines, the article has a picture of an architectural-sculptural tree-trunk forest in a Kansas City, Missouri playground. The sections of tree trunks are embedded in concrete under sand and children climb and stand and move around on them for enjoyable physical and dramatic play.

OUTDOOR EQUIPMENT WITH CREATIVE, IMAGINATIVE, AND MECHANICAL FUNCTIONS

Although we do not wholly accept the stationary, hazardous metal swings, we know that the sustained rhythm and the pleasure of motion in swinging have a strong appeal to young children. Therefore, if possible the teacher should provide for some safe swinging activity. The ideal equipment for swinging, as well as for many other activities, is a wide-limbed tree.

This older nursery school class had such a tree in their yard—a large maple with rich foliage most of the year and straight and bare

[3] Playgrounds Take a Space-Age Spin, *Life* (March 15, 1963).

branches in winter season. When a rope was flung across a strong limb away from the trunk and an inner tube from an automobile tire attached securely to it the children rushed for it. One at a time they explored every possibility, style, and technique of swinging. Thus, swinging while suspended from a limb of a tree the children became interested in the structure and strength and dimensions of the tree.

Later a rope ladder was attached to a stout branch of the maple and the children were thrilled to climb up to and onto a high branch, to have the feel of getting into the tree, and to touch and grasp the leafy limbs. They liked holding on tightly to the rough ropes, using the wooden smooth rungs on the rope ladder for a trapeze swing. Gentle, petite, soft-spoken Lucy was just as insistent about her rightful turn at the rough, challenging climbing, swinging, and jumping as was the aggressive, agile, and able climber, Tim. When one child was climbing many others were watching and sensing the adventure of it!

There were other gifts from the bountiful maple. In late spring and fall the children collected immeasurable quantities of the winged maple seed pods from the ground, and noticed the large clusters of them hanging on the tree. They learned to split the pods with fingernails and uncover the seeds. And one time after a rain the teacher pulled on a branch, causing a surprising shower. Then the children became very excited about "making rain" and together with the teacher, figured out a way of shaking a branch with a broomstick and thus producing a shower. Some children would stand as near as possible and quickly "get out of the rain." All the children became interested in the source of the shower and intrigued with the leaves' capacity to hold the rain.

What Is Good for Climbing?

Since climbing seems so important and interesting to all young children while they are growing in limbs and stature, a kindergarten teacher must not overlook obtaining equipment for this purpose other than the jungle gym described earlier, and particularly if there is no jungle gym in the playground. Lucky are the children who have a tree they can climb into, as the one just described which was utilized in this way with the aid of a rope ladder.

Also interesting and challenging for climbing up and down and for straddling is a large log, or better still, several logs.

In addition to this natural equipment, or if such cannot be found in the yard or neighborhood, some ladders should be obtained. It is good to have the ladders in two or three heights to accommodate different children and different areas of reaching, and to have wooden and aluminum ones illustrating different qualities and weights of materials. Watch the workmanlike body motions and expressions in carrying the ladders and in placing them in a stable position against walls or fences. Observe too the dramatic play that results from the use of even as few as half a dozen ladders in the yard.

A secure fence that is safe for climbing offers not only physical challenge to boys and girls but can lead to different kinds of dramatic play.

If there is a storage house or a playhouse in the yard it is a good idea to have a permanently attached ladder from the ground to the roof. A strong flat roof with a railing is wonderful to climb onto and interesting to climb down from.

Often sedate grown-ups, being instinctively protective towards small mobile children, feel horrified at seeing children in what appears to be a dangerous position—perching or moving on narrow rungs. And often adults will caution and admonish youngsters quite automatically. But normally developed five-year-olds do have the strength, agility, intelligence, and what is especially important, the reasonable caution to do such climbing. Those children who are at first fearful and inhibited become so fascinated seeing other children climb easily that they persevere until they accomplish the feat! Children gain control and confidence in this exhilarating activity much quicker than adults. And rarely does a child attempt what is physically beyond his powers.

Equipment Which Invites Travel

Since transportation is an outstanding aspect of our life, young children make important use of actual items of transportation or of props that symbolize transportation for dramatic play. Durable wagons that have loading and passenger capacity are put to ingenious use and can involve several children and different kinds of equipment and materials. Although good wagons can be bought from manufacturers and hardware stores, wagons that are made by fathers or mechanically talented adolescent relatives are equally interesting to children!

A few tricycles in good condition are valuable in the yard for trips, races, stunts, and sometimes for "harnessing" to a wagon. If there is sufficient space a scooter can be delightful for practicing balance, propulsion, and self-direction. But the best transportation item for children of kindergarten age is the wheelbarrow. It gives the child an appreciation of weight and balance, power of muscle push, basic power of the wheel, and the general handiness and earthiness of this ancient tool.

Transportation on water is equally appealing and dramatic to children. If a real old rowboat can be put in a kindergarten play yard its constant occupancy can be practically guaranteed. Of course, such an item should be safe from splinters or nails and have a coat of bright paint; a turning steering wheel securely attached would add to the boat's function. And the children would make of it a tug, a rescue ship, an ocean liner, or even a rowboat, especially if oars are provided. In lieu of a real boat, any sturdy safe stationary box in which some seating spaces can be devised will also be put to speedy adventurous transport on deep and wild waters. In one community a parent in a cooperative kindergarten contributed from his place of business two excellent long deep wooden boxes. These were painted bright colors and they proved to be most popular for both land and water journeys.

While children enjoy the manageable, testable transportation items, they are also concerned with less concrete and less understandable means of transportation, such as speedy jets, air ships for celestial navigation, and capsules for orbiting through space. But here simple props, including boxes, small board, perhaps colored chalk for marking the "instrument panel," and helmets will suffice. The rest of the construction, operation, and success is provided by the children's imagination as they talk about and play at the most advanced kind of transportation at the moment.

Equipment With Which to Create Motion

A ball, which is perhaps *the* universal action toy, is a must for the kindergarten playground. Although a strong bright good rubber ball of a size fit for grasping with both hands would be very useful for preschoolers, balls that are different in size, color, texture, weight, and composition can also provide exciting exercise. With a ball, children can cause the motions of rolling, twirling, spinning, throwing, and falling in various directions, and catching and bouncing at various speeds. Games with balls can be traditional, individual, or group, and certainly highly experimental. Lightweight bicycle wheels or hoops are good for rolling or running with, and give the children experience in guiding motion. Blown up inner tubes and old automobile tires are also useful for this purpose, although teachers will need to judge the safety of heavy rolling tires and caution the children accordingly. In this connection spinning tops provide play that goes beyond mere diversion and becomes an investigation of speed, motion, and visual impression, and which can take place both outdoors and indoors.

Other Attractive Equipment for Outdoors

A sandbox with equipment for sifting, straining, shaping, pressing patterns on damp surface, measuring, and counting is a must for kindergarten children. The utensils for the sandbox are often better found in kitchen cupboard discards than in a toy store, since the first are generally sturdier, of better size, and more interesting and usable.

We must not overlook that ordinary wooden box which can be picked up free from liquor stores, groceries, and fruit markets. A set of such boxes, sanded and painted, can be a very welcome addition to the large packing boxes that are already in the play yard, and certainly desirable if there are none of the latter. If enough of these boxes are obtained the children stack and build with them. They are good to jump from, and when arranged in a row with space between each, are fun for a stepping-over-space game. If holes are made at the end of the boxes or hooks screwed in, ropes, leather or wire can be used for coupling the boxes and making freight cars. A single box can be fitted with soft lining to become a nest.

Another ordinary item interesting to children is a bag. Bags made of paper, plastic, canvas, burlap, or other kinds of cloth can be used not only as practical containers, but for different kinds of play and investigation outdoors.

HANDLING MISHAPS

In addition to being aware of the many possible activities involving the standard playground equipment the teacher needs also to be aware of possible abuses of equipment. Children and equipment need respect. Occasionally there are mishaps in the playground and the teacher must be prepared to handle these calmly. In this connection we advise a conveniently located first aid kit. It should contain tweezers or sterile needle to remove splinters, a nonstinging antiseptic solution, sterile cotton to clean a superficial cut or bruise, band-aids for satisfying display as well a hygienic protection, and whatever else may be advised by the school nurse, pediatrician, or principal.

Although an occasional kindergartner may resist any emergency medications from a teacher, most children actually enjoy it and are pleased by the personal attention and special emergency devices. In one situation a teacher obtained an ice cube for a bump on the head and the injured child was so intrigued in handling the ice beyond its therapeutic use, and was so envied by the others, that there was a veritable epidemic of bumped heads for a few days!

That children actually enjoy the drama of a disaster more than they fear its consequences is well shown by that classic child heroine Madeline, (see p. 148) whose appendectomy was the envy of her class. However, while children generally will not attempt to do what they cannot do comfortably, and therefore safely, they do not always use good judgment and may not be sufficiently aware of the surrounding environment to recognize inherent danger in the task they undertake. Teachers must be watchful of potentially dangerous equipment, such as high pieces, pieces with hinges for catching fingers, and heavy pieces that can hurt small toes. Without hovering anxiously over children, adults can foresee the consequences of poorly balanced boards or crowded climbing apparatus tumbling and dropping by children without concern for what is below, and other common precursors of mishaps. Children can be taught to be reasonably cautious and considerate without impeding their sense of freedom seriously.

Upkeep of the Yard

What exactly is involved in the upkeep of a play yard? Any yard or playground can get messy from the elements overnight and can confront the children on their arrival with slippery, slushy snow, splashy puddles, stray objects blow in and on which the children can trip, or even broken bottles thrown in from the street. The yard can get messy from activities and be full of spilled sand, strewn papers, and forgotten containers. Clearing a yard right when this needs to be done is appealing and very interesting to kindergartners. Sweeping the paved part or raking the grass and dirt part, pushing water towards the drain, shoveling snow, and even collecting trash should be initiated by the teacher as a valid school activity demanding a workmanlike attitude. The activity will arouse interest in the proper tools and utensils, provide stimulating large-muscle activity, and give an understanding of various practical problems. It would therefore be very important to have one of each kind of working tool and a place to keep them. This does not mean that the teacher and children must take entire responsibility for cleaning the playground. But it does mean that the teacher must recognize the usefulness and interest of such work to children, and give them the opportunity and encouragement to do it.

If outdoor equipment needs to be stored, ways of stacking, fitting and using space, carrying, rolling, wheeling or dumping objects can challenge average, active five-year-olds.

When a child says, "We put everything away—see!" he says it with pride. Children also like being inspectors and detectors of damaged equipment. "This block has a crack, see, teacher? It can give you a splinter!"

"Thank you, Jimmy, let's put it aside to be fixed."

"Hey, there is a big nail in the red barrel. Tell the teacher we need a hammer to pull it out."

"I saw broken glass in the playhouse. That's dangerous."

Those are typical four, five, and six-year-olds' comments, and the teacher can sense in them clues of children's readiness for responsibility as well as a practical recognition of reality.

BRINGING THE OUTDOORS IN

Once in a while one meets a kindergarten class which has no outdoor period in its program. The reasons may be lack of a play yard close by, reluctance of teachers to curtail important indoor activities, lack of playground equipment to make the outdoors interesting to children, or insufficient help for the teacher to get the class ready to go out. In that case, while efforts are being made to make at least occasional outdoor play possible the teacher might also try to obtain some appropriate facilities indoors. The classroom, with its different space, furnishing, accoustics, and materials, will automatically preclude certain rough outdoor play. But if the room is large enough there can be a permanently-placed piece of climbing apparatus. Here is a kindergarten with a wide climbing structure with enough space left to use during a music period or for dancing, with a large area for table work and blockbuilding, and a cozy library corner. The children use the climber all the time for active play, for dramatic games, for doing "tricks." The teacher reports that the climber does not interfere with the children's interest in or attention to all other activities.

Some classrooms have rope-ladders hung unobtrusively in the room, some a fireman's pole for sliding down from a balcony. Some have suitable areas for bouncing a large ball. Some teachers make it a point once in a while to bring in some equipment for physical exercise if the children had to miss vigorous outdoor play because of inclement weather. Such equipment may consist only of some boards and a packing box or a few of the strong wooden boxes which can be arranged to allow sliding, jumping, bouncing, balanced walking, or other "tricks." Because all such equipment is unstructured, requiring no instruction or rigid organization, the children will use it freely with their own initiative and ingenuity, developing confidence as well as various muscular skills and coordination. This can be very important for a child's overall achievement for the year.

The more we watch children the more we see that whether indoors or out, they need to stretch their growing muscles and feel their budding strength.

Bibliography

Criteria for Selecting Play Equipment, and *The Use of Large Muscle Play Equipment,* free pamphlets from Community Playthings, Dept. 2, Rifton, New York.

Franklin, Adele, *Home Play and Play Equipment* (Washington, U.S. Dept. of Health, Education and Welfare, Children's Bureau).

Hawkins, Reginald, *Easy-To-Make Outdoor Play Equipment* (New York, The Macmillan Company, 1957).

New York City Board of Education, *Operation New York,* Curriculum Research Report (Brooklyn, New York, 1960).

Ward, Muriel, *Young Minds Need Something to Grow On* (New York, Harper & Row, Publishers, 1957).

Catalogues can be obtained from the following equipment companies:
Community Playthings, Rifton, New York.
Creative Playthings, Princeton, New Jersey.
Educational Equipment Company, 69 W. 23rd St., N.Y.
The State Education Dept. of your particular state, located in the capital, will also have a recommended list of outdoor equipment suitable for early childhood education.

IV

*organizing the classroom
to facilitate learning
and growth*

14

The Meaning of Discipline

There has been considerable discussion in the last decade about "permissiveness" and "old-fashioned discipline," "healthy freedom" and the importance of saying "no" to children. All these popular phrases reflect confusion as well as concern. The confusion becomes understandable if we bring some historical perspective to bear on the situation.

"STRICT" AS OPPOSED TO "PERMISSIVE"

An examination of the pamphlets on baby care issued by the United States government over the last fifty years reveals a persistent trend towards increased freedom for children, despite the ups and downs in feeding and toileting routines. Europeans looking in on our families are often shocked by the absence of manners and the intrusion into adult conversation by children "who should know better." Yet many other traditionally reared adults from foreign shores will remark, "Children are so much closer to parents in the United States than in our country; they are not afraid of parents." Both views have truth in them and both are part of changing mores. It is worth examining the development of these changes.

For centuries authoritarian relationships among people were accepted without question in many cultures and countries, and relationships within the home reflected the practices of society at large. Democratic America challenged all kinds of long-standing customs and attitudes in human relationships: the right of the upper classes only to education and

303

opportunity; the right of the majority religious, ethnic, or racial group to suppress minority rights; the right of men to dominate women solely because of their position; and the right of parents to dominate and control children without regard for the children's feelings. A number of things contributed to the last, such as the concept of respect for the individual, regardless of position in life; the new knowledge that children are not little adults but subject to laws of development consistent with age and maturation; and the greater opportunity with increased leisure time to enjoy children. All these contributed to the breakdown of authoritarianism in the home and the school, while at the same time a search began for ways of functioning in interpersonal relationships that would encompass the rights of all individuals regardless of rank, status, position, or age. This view of human relationships based on greater sensitivity toward the rights of individuals in society, was bound to affect disciplinary practices. Few Americans today can or do consciously accept the authoritarianism of the past.

But new forms of behavior do not always develop logically. Often they come as a reaction *against* the old instead of striking out towards fresh paths. Consequently, many parents and teachers who were against authoritarianism, were not at all clear what they were *for*. Such people gave up any and all control in order to avoid being overcontrolling. It is to them that we owe the present confusion about good disciplinary practices. Too many people assume that permissiveness towards children necessarily means no limits and no controls and that that is the only alternative to very strict control. An interesting observation here is that adults who allow themselves to be dominated by children (ostensibly so they will not themselves dominate the children) are often simply perpetuating their own childhood relationships. Having been dominated by parents and teachers as children they continue to be dominated as adults, only dominated by children this time. In reality, by failing to exercise necessary controls over children they abdicate their responsibility towards them as adults. Such extremists, although in the minority, have done much to shape the popular view that permissiveness means license.

Present knowledge from the fields of psychology and education show that absence of definite limits or controls (which are disciplinary measures) is as harmful to children as we know harsh and severe punishment is. Neither license nor excessive punishment is good teaching. Neither takes into account children's needs, stage of development and readiness for learning, nor is either conducive to building inner discipline that will work when adults are not around (surely an important consideration). And neither builds relationships between adults and children of the kind that will be most profitable to both. By and large, teachers and parents are aware of this and extremists at either end are not in the majority.

A study by Goodwin Watson [1] a few years ago on the effects of permissive versus strict upbringing was somewhat limited in the population studied because Watson actually had difficulty finding enough samples of permissive parents in the middle class community where he sought them. Sears, Maccoby and Levin,[2] in their study of child-rearing practices, also found that parents are very aware of the need to exercise controls.

Perhaps these findings are partly true because "permissive" to the psychologist does not mean the overindulgence and license it means to the lay person. But let us set aside for the moment the argument as to whether permissiveness means license or strictness means harshness, and state the issue as we see it. It is not "to control or not to control." The issue really revolves around the question of which criteria adults can use to help them decide where, when, and how limits on behavior are to be set for children, and where, when, and how children should be allowed the freedom to learn from their own mistakes without adults stopping them.

It should be obvious that our position is clearly affirmative for discipline in the education of young children, in the work of thoughtful teachers, and in the successful functioning of a kindergarten class. But good discipline needs to be defined. We define it broadly as a balanced combination of *love,* by which we mean acceptance and understanding of children; *respect,* by which we mean awareness of individual and group needs; and *order,* by which we mean sufficient supervision, intelligent, and effective control for satisfying group living. But words have a way of remaining words. To expand and develop these ideas, let us look in on several classrooms and see different teachers actually involved in typical disciplinary situations with young children.

WHAT KINDS OF BEHAVIOR CALL FOR DISCIPLINE?

Rebellion in the Ranks

There are twenty children in this private nursery school class, many of whom are a month or two short of five. It is a bright, crisp day and the two teachers feel that the first part of the session, during the early afternoon, should be spent outdoors by *all* the children, including those who have often resisted going outdoors. As the children arrive gradually they are informed: "We are playing outdoors first today." In response they all

[1] Goodwin Watson, *Some Personality Differences in Children Related to Strict or Permissive Parental Discipline,* Journal of Psychology, Vol. 44 (1957), pp. 227–249.

[2] R. R. Sears, Eleanor E. Maccoby, and H. Levin, *Patterns of Child-Rearing* (New York, Harper & Row, Publishers, 1957).

run out eagerly where one teacher is already in charge. The other teacher is inside waiting for the last arrivals. As anticipated, three children who at the moment constitute a special, intimate group within the class conspire to rebel; in addition to these there is Nancy who is a determined nonconformist. She also protests the teachers' definite announcement.

"We want to stay in," says Miriam, the spokesman for the rebels now numbering five.

"I know," the teacher grants, "You like to play in the doll corner; but you can use the play house outdoors. You'll have a good time outside."

"It's too cold out," another child answers.

"No, the weather is fine," the teacher stated.

"But *we* don't like to go out! *Do* we?" offers another child, upholding the solidarity of the group and still questioning the necessity.

"Even so, Janie, today we are *all* going out first and there will be no teacher in the class. You will play indoors later." Plainly, the teacher was not just arbitrarily denying them an immediate pleasure, but neither was she backing down.

"But we don't need any teacher. We'll play by ourselves," explains the spokesman rationally.

"No, a teacher must always be in the room with children in case some one does need help. That's a school rule. Come, I'll hold the door open," the teacher says confidently and with finality, making clear that *she* is in charge. And the rebels come out agreeably, all except Nancy, the determined nonconformist. "No! I already played outdoors this morning at home. So *I* had enough fresh air. My *mother* even said so," Nancy protests, trying to test her legal powers by pitting parental authority against the teacher's.

"Well, it is nice sunshiny weather," the teacher answers placidly enough, "and *all* of us are going out," she adds, firmly, reasserting teacher control for Nancy's benefit.

"I am staying in." Nancy at this point does not want to lose face by giving in and wants to have the last word. "Anyway, other days I stayed in," she says, offering consistency as her last argument.

"Those days we had three teachers (student-teacher), so one was in the room," the teacher explains matter-of-factly. "Come!" she calls, invitingly, "See the jump-off bridge the children built!" The teacher is now interested in appealing to Nancy's curiosity rather than carrying the argument further; she is sure of her position and she is giving Nancy an out.

Outdoors, Nancy is perfectly cheerful and enjoys the bridge, playing on it cooperatively with a group of several children. The other five all enjoy jumping and climbing and hiding in packing boxes. After a while

Miriam, the spokesman for the resistance, says, "We were outside long enough. Can't we come in now?"

"Five more minutes," answers the teacher cheerfully, and in five more minutes other children who had been out forty minutes are also ready to go in. The teacher then goes inside with about half the group (excluding Nancy) and together they attend to necessary routines and to indoor pleasures.

We see here that the teacher has deliberately exercised control of the situation and of the particular children's behavior, which means she used discipline. The control was rational and intelligent and the children felt free to question and test the control until they understood and accepted the whole situation, convinced of the teacher's unmistakable authority. Because of the teacher's firm stand the children were learning that supervision and protection in their behalf are part of a teacher's work. The teacher, for her part, did not moralize; rather, she answered each argument in such a way as to help the children understand the reasons for school rules. (The authoritarian demands obedience because he says so, and does not feel at all impelled to give reasons or tolerate questions.) It is to be hoped that in most instances there is a rational basis for school rules! Discipline clearly based on the well-being and safety of the group helps individuals control their wishes and conform to class regulations with a sense of the larger, social necessity that tempers the frustration of individual denial. While there may indeed be times when absolute unquestioning obedience is in order, as in a fire drill or while crossing the street, generally it is possible to let children in on the reasons for necessary controls. This acts in the long run to give them a basis for judgment when they must make their own decisions.

Despite the expressions of assertiveness and resistance from the children the adult authoritative statements were not offered to imply punishment or bargaining on the part of the teacher, and there was neither unquestioned submission nor lasting resentment on the part of the children. Thus discipline exercised with consideration of the children's needs and with confident control on the part of the teacher resulted in a change in attitude and behavior on the part of the children.

Bad Language and Poor Manners

In another situation discipline may be difficult to maintain because it is hard for a teacher to be calm and collected when dealing with an irritating situation, as in the following case.

When the teacher heard four-and-a-half-year-old Martin burst out with an explosive phrase "Shut up, shut up!" which he flung around indiscriminately at children and teachers, she controlled her own irritation, postponed judgment of the unsocial aspect, and listened calmly for a while. She realized that Martin was experimenting with a freshly learned phrase, experimenting with rebelling, and with repelling people. Hearing his unpleasant "shut up, shut up," the teacher did not forget Martin's otherwise excellent vocabulary and his ability to talk reasonably most times; she therefore did not judge this to be personal rudeness. She was able to speak to Martin objectively and casually, saying in effect that it was tiresome to hear the same phrase over and over again and that it was time for a change. To this Martin responded by talking in a similarly casual manner about a new subject!

The discipline in Martin's case, then, consisted of the teacher's disapproving of and redirecting the child's undesirable behavior, but not without first considering the nature of the child and the nature of the offense. As far as the child was concerned his unsocial behavior was not overlooked by the adult in charge, and when spoken to with quiet conviction and directness (in no way belittling) he was given a chance to change his own behavior. The latter is important, for the attainment of self-discipline is the aim of discipline.

Specific Behavior Related to Total Personality Need

Larry, almost five, has shown special concern about being "a big boy now." He asked the teacher "Guess how old I am going to be on my birthday?" and without waiting for an answer he stated powerfully "ten." When questioned soberly by other children he adjusted this number to eight, but apparently wanted to be a bigger boy still. "I went to New York with my daddy and he let me drive the car. Then pop! we had a flat tire and I got out and changed the flat tire, because I know how." Then he concentrated on making a "big building." He built and built till he was satisfied that the building was bigger than himself, bigger than the teacher, a building bigger than any other children had made that day. But that same day he threw another child's hat over the fence. It was a wild gesture. The other child was upset by Larry's "meanness" and received comfort and help from the teacher. The teacher called to Larry but he eluded her approaches. "I can't hear what you are saying," he said defiantly, holding both hands to his ears. When the teacher picked Larry up bodily to bring him inside for discussion in private, he resisted her control by kicking and then crying. The "big boy" was reduced to a crying, kicking baby, and subsided only in the teacher's arms.

Growing up was far from easy for Larry. He worked so hard at bigness he could not take it any more. He was tired, and so crumbled to littleness and even to a temper tantrum. At that moment the teacher could not possibly have asked him to "act like a big boy" or "stop the nonsense." She simply protected him as well as others, leaving him safely alone till he regained his composure and self-respect. At an appropriate time she tried to direct him to relaxing and releasing activities. And the other children, taking the cue from the teacher, asked sympathetically as well as cautiously, "Is Larry all right now?" They learned that a little boy in trouble will get help and will be "all right."

Larry's opposite performances in the one day were related. We might see relationships elsewhere if we go back and take another look at nonconformist Nancy whom we described earlier as resisting her teacher with such persistence.

Following that same outdoor period Nancy's teacher took special notice of the child and observed what a deeply sociable child she was and what a strong interest she showed in others. Standing by the easel and watching carefully Miriam's mixing of paints, Nancy was thrilled with the result of the colors and the design in Miriam's painting. "Did you see how Miriam made that beautiful purple with red and blue?" she asked other children and the teacher, and soon inadvertently gathered a group of articulate admirers who, far from disturbing the artist, encouraged her to heights of inventiveness. Nancy, herself an able painter, was able to become absorbed in another child's creativity and by her strength of generous feeling, to draw others to the scene. Bearing in mind this generosity and leadership, Nancy's self-assertion can perhaps be seen in better perspective as springing from the same source of positive conviction about her feelings that led her to both a warm appreciation of Miriam's work and to insistence on having her own way in regard to the outdoor play period. The teacher, by holding her ground with equal conviction but broader reason, helped Nancy accept realistic, socially based inhibitions on her will, without questioning her right to hold strong convictions.

DISAGREEMENTS

Among kindergartners, as among any children, arguments may spark up a hot quarrel and this in turn can lead to hurt feelings. Two boys, each just five-years-old, are arguing about the creation of the world.

". . . . God made the whole world, and he made the people and everything *in* the world, every single thing. *God* did it!" Jimmy asserts passionately, addressing Richard. The teacher, who is clearing a table nearby, listens without comment as Jimmy's friend Richard answers with a bold, cold statement: "God didn't make the world." Richard then offers a learned reference to biological origins. Jimmy interrupts him with even greater passion: "God *did* make everything!"

"But how could God make *different* things at the same time?" Richard asks analytically, and adds with finality, "That's silly." Jimmy's voice quavers, his mouth drops, and he flounders with distress. Richard hurts him further by taunting him for his belief. Jimmy's frustration and pain are clearly seen in the bitter tears rolling down his cheeks. At this point the teacher states her position clearly to Richard: "It's all right to talk about your idea of how the world was made. But it's *not* all right to tease Jimmy about *his* idea."

"I didn't do anything to him," Richard defends himself.

"You were *hurting* Jimmy by teasing him. You may disagree with people, but you may not tease. That hurts people's feelings."

The teacher did not attempt to reconcile the difference in beliefs or presume to be on the side of one or another child in the argument, for the children's was a personal discussion. The children needed to express themselves and to hear each other out. But when one child inflicts pain on another, whether psychological or physical, a teacher's sensibility as a mature person and her responsibility as a teacher require her to stop such undesirable behavior and discourage a bad relationship.

In another situation two girls choose the same book from the library shelf. Each claims to be the first to have chosen the book and each pulls on the book and on the other's hand. The teacher sees that no solution to the struggle is imminent, and furthermore that the book, if not the girls, was certainly about to be damaged.

"I'll take that book, please," the teacher commands. "We can't let our books get torn!" Putting the book away the teacher tells the quarreling children that they should decide by *talking* whether one, the other, or both together should look at the desired book. The teacher refrains from any moral pressure such as "Shame on you, girls! Can't you just be friends?" because that does not really tackle the issue at hand. Instead, she appeals to their common sense and the logic called for by the situation itself, and the girls respond. In a few minutes they make their decision, ask the teacher politely for the book, and sit down to look at it together!

Fighting Is an Early Technique

Arguing that leads to physical blows is not uncommon among young children. It comes naturally to them to use physical means to attain ends and they must painfully learn to control hands and feet and use words instead. Loretta Bender,[2a] studying aggression in disturbed children, found that normally developing children, by contrast with the disturbed, went through a stage of *saying* they must not hit before they acted on the

---

[2a]Loretta Bender, *Aggression, Hostility and Anxiety in Children* (Springfield, Ill., Charles C Thomas, Publisher, 1953).

command. Such verbal understanding before the actual performance is typical of young children. By five a good deal of internal assimilation of the words has taken place—in comparison to age three. But the assimilation is not yet perfect and certainly is not the same for all children. More fives than threes express verbal injunctions against hitting. But as a group fives are not yet completely reliable. Individual differences in temperament and experience affect this development of control.

Kindergarten teachers need to know that children may receive very different kinds of training at home in regard to fighting. Some children are taught never to fight under any circumstances, but to come and tell an adult. Others are taught to fight back when hit but not to start a fight themselves. Still others are taught by life, if not directly by an adult, that the way to avoid possible attack is to hit the other fellow first, before he makes a move. Consider the differences in experience that lead to these different views. A favored child whose mother sits on the park bench while he plays nearby, grows accustomed to having his mother step in with guidance, admonition, or protection at the first sign of troubled relations with other children. He not only hears what she says, he watches her in action and he learns from her. He expects the same involvement from his teacher. But what happens to the child of an overburdened, harried mother who sends her toddler outdoors alone or with an older child because she cannot take care of her large family under difficult circumstances and give individual attention to each child? This little one, confronted with the sink-or-swim philosophy of children left early in life to their own devices, learns that he either fights for survival or might just as well stay indoors. Both kinds of children come to the same public school kindergarten. But they feel very differently about this matter of fighting. The teacher is likely to support the home views of some of her children, but the others will find her expressing a point of view that is incomprehensible to them in view of their experience. For the less protected child in particular, the teacher who says "Talk it over" is contradicting the evidence of his own eyes.

When children have difficulty controlling direct physical outbursts of anger and irritation, a kindergarten teacher must first get over the shock of witnessing primitive behavior, which is not to be unexpected at five, and then get into the situation from the point of view of guiding it. First, she must honestly and fairly try to understand the child's subjective appraisal of the situation. Although he may be wrong he does not know this yet; unless the teacher sees the issue from his eyes she has no real approach to him. On the other hand, he might be right but may nevertheless have a poor way of dealing with people. Something impels him to act and the teacher must see things as he sees them in order to understand his problem. Only by sympathetic awareness of what really bothers a child or of what he is trying to do, can she hope to communicate to him an altered perspective or more suitable techniques. Words and fists are after all only different means for handling feeling. Feelings are universal and therefore understandable to teachers, especially to those who are sympathetic to young children's growing pains. Techniques of handling feeling have to be learned, and they are learned from adults. This is the teacher's job—recognizing the validity of a child's feeling (even if she does not like what he feels), she shows him the socially acceptable methods for coping with them.

Appel [3] studied the causes for fighting in low-income and middle-income preschool centers. In the first, children fought mainly over possessions; in the second, over leadership. In the first center the teachers employed "stopping" techniques ("No more fighting!" and "Both of you sit down!"). The number of fights did not decrease. But in the other center the teachers tried to help the children understand their own and other children's motivations. ("You thought he would break your building but he was only reaching for that board which he needs for his building.") The number of incidents decreased as the children themselves came to apply this same kind of probing for causes to the solution of their differences.

Contradictions in Mores

The differences described in attitudes towards aggressive behavior carry over into other areas as well. Often a child defends his refusal to participate or comply with the teacher's request with a determined, "My mother says . . ." School may indeed represent a contradiction of home values and standards, and this is not easy for either the teacher or the child to reconcile. The overprotected child may not see why he should do anything for himself; the child taught too well and too soon to be clean and neat may not be able to enjoy the messy paints and clay; the child taught to fight back may be confused by the teacher who says, "Fighting is not nice." Sometimes children use, "My mother says . . ." as an excuse. But just as often there is genuine confusion that may be at the root of resistance to what a teacher considers reasonable.

Destruction

In almost every group of children there is one child who is destructive for the distorted satisfaction destruction brings to him. He mishandles materials and tools, destroys children's work, smashes clay, and kicks

[3] M. H. Appel, "Aggressive Behavior of Nursery School Children and Adult Procedures in Dealing with Such Behavior," *Journal of Experimental Education*, Vol. II (1942), pp. 185–199.

down block buildings. While all young children take some pleasure in seeing things crash and even in deliberately causing a crash, it is not the usual pattern of healthy children; it occurs sporadically and then as a kind of unexpected outburst. The child who is consistently destructive is a child who must be looked at carefully. His strong and misdirected anger will probably be apparent in his behavior toward people as well as to materials. When children occasionally delight in crashing a building with a kind of guilty joy in this absolute breakdown of the control they have come to accept in their daily lives, one can sympathize with the escape from controls which this represents and can recognize the behavior as a safety valve. It is when destructiveness is continuous, deliberate, and perhaps even tinged with malice that one should feel alarmed. In such a case destructiveness is a symptom of some disturbance and the task of soothing and reeducating a sorely troubled child may be beyond the teacher. She can only hope to give him safe outlets, such as water play, clay, and carefully supervised woodwork, where he can destroy with impunity. At the same time a teacher must continuously make clear to such a child the restrictions on destroying other people's things, which protect him as well as the other children.

The destructiveness described above must be distinguished from the accidental destructiveness that comes with inexperience, and from the misuse of materials for experimental purposes. A child who breaks a vase, snaps off the leaf of a plant while watering it, drops a pile of blocks on someone's toes, or spills paint on someone's picture while filling a jar, may only be showing signs of inadequate attention to normal precautions which have to be learned with experience. Such destructiveness must be taken in stride, and to a certain extent, expected at the beginning of the school year.

In any case destructiveness, like so many other aspects of behavior, may have different causes and different meaning. The *meaning*—exuberant defiance of bonds, malice and hate, inexperience and poor coordination—will determine the nature and extent of the treatment.

SH! BE QUIET

There is another phenomenon common in school discipline that we might profitably examine here. It is quiet. Quiet is still regarded by many educators as a sign of a well-managed and properly disciplined class. "Children should be seen and not heard" lies behind this.

One day an elementary school principal met a group of nursery school children who had come with their teacher to visit the kindergarten which they would attend the next term. He had come out of his office especially to greet them in the school corridor.

"Good morning, boys and girls! How do you like our *nice quiet* school? Now remember, when you are going to come to kindergarten next fall, *you* are going to be nice and quiet, too."

The children were indeed impressed with the principal's words and stood and stared for a moment in silence. But one irrepressible four-year-old broke through the silence: "I am going to be in the second grade." (Safe distance away from the quiet kindergarten, he figured.)

Quiet for the sake of quiet needs to be questioned by those working with young children. A little boy begins to whistle while children are finishing up work and beginning to clear away systematically. It is an awkward tentative sound, yet a sound of fun and some individual assertion coming from a child who has probably learned to whistle only recently. "Who was whistling?" the teacher asks in a tone of unmistakable criticism. The child frowns and hangs his head in shame. Several children's glances are directed at him. "I didn't do it," comes a self-protective remark from one. "We don't whistle in class—you know that." So set was this teacher on keeping her room quiet that she overlooked the pleasure of whistling while you work, as well as the special victory whistling represents to a five-year-old who achieves this enviable accomplishment.

No good teacher would question quiet in relation to something meaningful for all the children. When a teacher requires quiet so that her own or a child's talking, or a story, or music may be heard, understood, and enjoyed, such a request makes sense to the children and they can be expected to exercise vocal control in their behavior. The teacher often need not even state such a requirement, as most kindergarten children readily learn to discipline themselves to some degree in such a situation. The kind of talk and the type of story and music will have something to do with the length of time children can be expected to be quiet or sit still.

In a well-provided kindergarten room we see a pleasant spacious library alcove. With ample light streaming from the window, attractive and accessibly arranged books on shelves, and a cozy round table with chairs and extra side seats, the area looks sociable. It *invites* quiet attention. The children, without any reminding, approach it with natural quiet and pleasant anticipation. Most children take choice books out, look at them, and return them; two children "read" a book together with congenial intimate conversation, which does not bother the others at all and which incurs no disciplinary action from the teacher. One perfectly quiet boy in the library alcove had been busy only a few minutes ago making the ferocious, growling sounds of a bull aboard a "cattle ship," and another had been busy producing shrill jet sounds on his space journey. How useful the power of sound from his own controllable, skillful vocal cords can be to a child! So a teacher of young children needs to be conditioned, or perhaps the word is *disciplined,* to accept children's use of a certain amount of noise and to plan for and respect their quiet when it serves a purpose.

When a kindergarten is not quiet what are the sounds that we hear? Here is Mrs. Gilson's kindergarten with forty-six children. She allows a full hour or more for a free individual work period, while she and her assistant help with materials when needed. During the work period there are many sounds in the room. There is laughter in the doll corner, full conversation at the clay table, some indescribable, human machine noises emanating from the sand box, some experimental scraping sounds coming from the work bench, the sound of humming in many areas, and lively skipping here and there. Mrs. Gilson does not admonish the children to be quiet, for she believes in having the least restrictions on children's spontaneity during the main work period in the session. She announces the time before clean-up by speaking personally to several groups in the room and sending messengers to others. She addresses the group when it is necessary to have attention, as "boys and girls" or "people" and the children do listen. A quiet voice aimed directly at eyes and ears is more effective than loud shouting that goes over children's heads and envelops them in meaningless noise. During clean-up she does not act as a foreman but goes *among* the children, helping, encouraging, or reminding as needed without undue praise or irritable scolding. While some children are still cleaning up, five children who have finished their task organize a lively song and dance game under the leadership of six-year-old Debby. Mrs. Gilson certainly notices it but does not interfere by giving praise, or "shushing," or with the admonition to "save it for the regular music period." Mrs. Gilson realizes that it is a good way for Debby to show her leadership and a good way for the small group to enjoy music without really disturbing the class.

Mrs. Gilson is concerned with quiet, however, at the end of the session. "It seems so chaotic sometimes but it doesn't really hurt the children," she says. "Some of the kindergarten teachers have the getting-dressed-to-go-home time very organized and quiet, but I can't stop these children from talking."

It is true that following an exciting music period with singing, acting, dancing, and impromptu composition, the children are noisy. They are not wild, however, and are quite efficient and independent about dressing. But they speak freely to each other and several children try to speak to Mrs. Gilson at the same time. Mrs. Gilson puts her hands to her ears and shakes her head with mock distress. She does try to hear each one and exchanges pleasantries with many.

Mrs. Gilson's room is not quiet and is even perhaps too noisy for some, but all the sounds are natural and relate to the activities and to important expression for children. This is a distinction we must bear in mind. Activity is inevitably accompanied by noise, and it is not the same kind of noise as uncontrolled, useless expenditure of energy in sound which grows out of boredom, confusion, or simple immaturity. In the one case sounds accompanying production need to be recognized and adjusted to with some grace. In the second instance the children need guidance and help in attaining constructive outlets for their energies. Teacher tolerance must certainly be considered too, and we shall discuss this in greater detail later. For the present it is enough to note that some noise is inevitable in a busy kindergarten. The larger the kindergarten class the higher will be the volume of sound. Certainly there will be times when children will need reminders to lower their voices because there are so many people saying important things at once in one room. But such restrictions are not the same as the sharp injunction that "Silence is golden."

GUIDANCE AS OPPOSED TO DOMINATION

Summing up the point of view implied in the previous pages, let us quote Laura Zirbes [4] on the findings of research in this area of discipline.

It is significant to note that research does not support the irate, antagonistic approach, or countenance harsh, domineering tactics or vindictive concern . . . Whatever the disciplinary medium, the approach needs to be helpful, and friendly, the guidance patient and understanding . . . Room must be left for initiative, choice, and self-direction (on the part of the child). To those who are open-minded toward the new approaches, discipline is no longer a mere matter of regimentation and control. Discipline which does no more, is not good enough.

But we need to clarify such terms as regimentation, control, domination, guidance, strictness, and permissiveness which are used so freely and often with such different interpretations. Let us return briefly to Watson's study, quoted earlier, on the differences in personality related to strict or permissive parental discipline. If the children were loved they were secure children and had good character *regardless of the strictness or permissiveness* of the parents. The real and significant difference between the two groups was in the degree of independence, creativity, and social adeptness, in which the permissively brought up children were definitely more developed. This difference, and not such superficial differences as whether children say please and thank you

[4] Laura Zirbes, "The Contributions of Research Towards Discipline for Freedom," *Childhood Education,* Jan., 1951, p. 228.

when they are still young, is the important pivot around which our understanding of the disciplinary relationship revolves. It should be fairly clear that in the points of view characterized as traditional, as well as in the points of view summed up as modern or progressive, there are variations in practice going from an extreme (harshness in the one, license in the other) through degrees of reasonableness and good sense, that depend pretty much on the individual interpretation of what the point of view means. Under the two broadly different positions, however, no matter how they are practiced, we do discern a basic difference in attitude towards children which accounts for Watson's findings and which proves to be a useful guide to a teacher in determining her own point of view on discipline.

The strict or traditional approach seems to be built on an assumption that children will not know what to do without continuous and careful direction. Whether out of protectiveness and love, or anger and fear, restrictions are set up in all areas of a child's life. He is deliberately made dependent on the wisdom and judgment of the adult, and his freedom to think or act independently is curtailed more by the adults' values of right and wrong than by their awareness of the urges to growth that propel a child to action and thought. Strictness may be kind or unkind. Either way its effect is to limit the possibilities for approved independent action by the child.

The permissive or progressive approach on the other hand, seems to depend more on *watching* carefully but allowing more opportunity for a child to learn many things through his own efforts, even at the risk of making mistakes and often of contradicting such adult values as thrift, cleanliness, manners, and appearance. Limitations are clearly stated and imposed when safety, health, other people's property and feelings, or long-range irreversable consequences are involved. The criteria are rational and based on faith in a child's capacity to learn from mistakes, if the conditions of learning include common sense precautions and adult supervision where necessary. The strict approach probably is more heavily based on fear that children will get into trouble if they are not carefully directed into known, safe, and proper channels; the permissive approach is more trusting of the children's capacity to handle themselves and learn from their own experience, with the condition that the watchful adult will limit potentially dangerous behavior. The less one trusts children (and oneself) the more it seems that control is imposed. Yet inadequate knowledge of children's real limitations may lead people to overtrust them and allow them liberties they are not able to handle. This can also be dangerous. Obviously the more strictly brought up children (but not the ones treated with severity and harshness) are easier for teachers at school. They have been taught to obey adults without question. Yet adults who are secure in themselves and in their own power to control if they have to may find the child who asks questions, even to the point of questioning adults with a confidence that verges on brashness, a delightful challenge. Such a teacher will not hesitate to ask for conformity when necessary, as Nancy's teacher did. But the adult who is insecure about his role feels safest when he holds the reins tightly, since he is afraid he will not be able to take hold again if he once lets go. This complete and dominating control by the adult may be easier in some ways, but life with children is far more stimulating and enriching for the adult and certainly for the children when youngsters can test their powers without fear of reprisal. At the same time they are secure in the knowledge that they will definitely be stopped if their actions go beyond the bounds of safety, health, consideration for others, or lead to irreversible, far-reaching consequences.

The teacher who misinterprets her role out of fear is not uncommon. Let us visit with one teacher who has no intention of letting her class ever get out of hand, and see how familiar she is.

After a highly organized work and clean-up period the children in Mrs. Cuttney's class have the routine heads-down-eyes-closed "rest period" with no whispering allowed. Before switching out the light Mrs. Cuttney practically threatens them: they *must* have a good rest or else they cannot go out to play. As the lights go out she detects some restless movement and hears a whisper, followed by the fall of an object and a child's muffled laughter. Mrs. Cuttney snaps on the light. "All right," she says sharply. "We'll start *all* over again." The class is now silent. She turns the lights off and surveys the room with an "I-dare-you" expression. Some one clears his throat. This arouses another child's curiosity and he peeks stealthily, then raises his head a little, and then a tiny bit more. But he promptly puts his head down again, for the teacher spies him. She calls his name loudly and the sound carries in the still room.

Mrs. Cuttney's aim was to have a perfect rest period, for she believes this is necessary for the children's health, with "no nonsense about it." She considers herself a pretty good disciplinarian although "not perfect," she concedes, and she expects the children to "respect" her orders. The fact that the means by which she is achieving "rest" causes tension among the children and produces for the most part superficial quiet without inner relaxation does not seem to enter Mrs. Cuttney's thinking. She apparently also considers "respect" to mean implied obedience. She fails to notice that the head-on-table position is a strain on some children's neck muscles and is actually uncomfortable and not conducive to relaxing. Nor does she realize that she is probably building unhealthy, negative attitudes towards rest in many children. She is overlooking everything in the name of discipline, in the narrow sense of complete control by the adult.

Such discipline is typical for Mrs. Cuttney; she demonstrates her disciplinary tactics in the next period, which is devoted to getting in line, after the children are dressed, in order to go out into the yard.

It happens to be an ordeal for five-year-olds to stand in a straight, quiet line for very long. In addition, these children are looking forward to letting off steam and so they are restless and pushy and talkative. But Mrs. Cuttney does not seem to be concerned with causes of child behavior. She is concerned with the externally undesirable symptoms, as she sees these disrupting her absolute standard of how children should behave. And she exerts her brand of discipline to squelch the symptom rather than to help the children attain control reasonable for them in a situation which calls for some kind of control.

So Mrs. Cuttney sits down on a chair in front of the long line, throws up her hands petulantly, and says, "I suppose you children just don't *want* to play outdoors. *I* don't mind. I'll just sit here and wait." Some children stare at her, some look confused and embarrassed, some bite their nails, some look at the other children searchingly. One child pipes up, "I am quiet. I want to go out to play." At last the teacher seems satisfied with the attention and dismisses them grudgingly: "You may go out now. In a straight line." At last the children are free to run and climb and slide and talk for the rest of the period, which was reduced by the difficult "rest" and the delayed exit to a mere twelve minutes!

Unquestionably Mrs. Cuttney believes in discipline and is exercising a form of it. But let us consider what her aim is and how she is achieving it. She wants the children to go outdoors in an orderly fashion, surely an aim with which we can agree. Obviously she thinks that orderliness means a perfectly straight line. But does it? Can there not be an orderly exit into the yard without an absolutely straight line? It is difficult for children to see themselves in relation to the entire group, and physically they cannot achieve a view of the line. It is hard for them to wait while the straightening process goes on, which only means they inadvertently break the straightness and have to wait some more. Is it not possible for a teacher to be in full and complete control of a slightly wavy, somewhat unevenly spaced line, if she has the kind of rapport with her group that will cause them to listen attentively to her when she feels it necessary to call for attention? Children attuned to their teacher, can have quite a straggly exit to an outdoor yard and not for a minute be out of control. Of course, having an assistant and sending half the group out first with her would also relieve the congestion which causes restlessness, irritating the teacher who then deprives the children of time for outdoor play. But this is not always possible.

The children in Mrs. Cuttney's class know that the teacher is boss. There is no evidence, however, that they even begin to understand why she is so annoyed with them. The distance between Mrs. Cuttney's standards and five-year-olds is just too great. Mrs. Cuttney is boss but she is not a genuinely respected authority. Children obey her out of fear, but when she is not there they are not likely to maintain order.

FACTORS AFFECTING DISCIPLINE

Young children unquestionably require discipline, and sometimes need to be convinced that controls are inevitable and necessary. The adult in charge of a group must be aware of children's needs in any disciplinary situation, and balance the rights of the individual against the rights of the group. But theoretical understanding is not always a guarantee of good discipline on the part of the teacher. Other factors may play an even more important part. Among these are the personality of the teacher herself and the composition of the group, over which she may have no control. Let us examine the first of these.

Teachers as People

Where do a teacher's ideas on discipline come from? A school superintendent, in discussing the young teachers he hired, made the following rueful remark: "When I interview a candidate she gives me all the correct theories about children that she learned at school. But when I observe her in the classroom she acts towards the children just as her mother did towards her!" This is not far from the truth. Almost everyone, layman or professional, has ideas about how children should behave and how they should be disciplined. These ideas come from the upbringing we ourselves received, which some of us copy slavishly and others of us reject out of hand, sending us to an opposite extreme.

Ideas on discipline differ with class and social status as well. Studies suggest that middle class families expect more inner control of their children earlier, use words as mediators between feeling and approval, and discipline according to standards of behavior that will be useful in society later on. Lower class parents are more likely to be immediately annoyed, punish physically, and expect their children to use physical means of defense when necessary, which they themselves use on children without compunction. Teachers on the whole follow middle class ideas on discipline, which may bring them into conflict with working class children and parents. Many a teacher has stood speechless before a well-intentioned parent who said earnestly, "Hit him, teacher, if he's not good. Hit him. He *must* mind."

Every teacher is a product of her own class and especially of her own family. Ideas about good and bad behavior are learned early and learned emotionally, so that years later a reaction to what a child does may not be an objective reaction at all, but a spontaneous response to what one learned early to approve or disapprove. Let us take as an example learned attitudes about what boys and girls may or may not do. Boys are not supposed to cry, even when little. They should be brave, defend girls, and certainly never hit them. Girls may be tomboys and get away with it, but boys pay a heavy price for gentleness and nonaggressive attitudes. Are teachers guided by these standards, learned in childhood, when they judge the actions of boys and girls? Are teachers likely to be furious when a sturdy little boy hits just as sturdy a little girl in absolutely justifiable anger, because *gentlemen do not hit ladies?* Or can she be impartial regardless of a child's sex?

What is learned early in life becomes part of us and influences our attitudes towards "good" and "bad" behavior in children. For this reason, difficult as it is, teachers must make an effort to understand the sources of their own reactions. Discipline is more than a bag of tricks and should not be governed by such questions as, "Is it better to put children in the corner or outside the door, when they misbehave?"

We are dependent on others; others are dependent on us. In supervising student-teachers one of the authors found that again and again the core of the disciplinary relationship with children lay in the innermost feeling of the fledgling teacher concerning her right to be up in front of the room as the teacher, the authority, the controlling adult, instead of the child in the seat. Teaching for most people begins at just about the time that they are in the process of achieving final emotional independence from their own parents. The more prolonged the struggle for autonomy at home the more difficult it seems for the student to take over a class with conviction that she will be able to handle those now dependent on her. Not yet in complete control of themselves, the outstanding fear of the student-teacher group seems to be the fear of losing control of a class. Discipline is the most popular topic of discussion in seminars and coffee klatches term after term.

Readiness for authority. The beginning, then, of any disciplinary relationship between teacher and children must be an examination of the meaning that being an authority has for the individual teacher. Is this at long last a chance to hold the upper hand? Is this a chance to treat other children the way one would have wanted to be treated oneself? Is there a fear that children will not like you if you say "no" to them, and is it so important to be liked that you will not do anything to jeopardize this? Are you determined to teach children all the "right" things because you believe so strongly that children are little animals and it is your job to civilize them?

These are not idle questions. Under every professional veneer of objectivity, no matter how well polished, is the human being who was once a child and who grew to adulthood with learned convictions about right and wrong. Are these so overpowering that they blot out the fact that young children are only just learning right from wrong and need more help than censure?

Teachers' feelings influence their actions. The following story about Kevin, a generally quiet, serious, and quite tense child, is a story about a teacher as well.

Kevin was apparently the kind of five-year-old who was always pushing his curiosity into strange nooks and crannies with some safety. But one time he went to inspect the teacher's purse while she was not in the room, removed a dollar bill, and left the purse wide open. The teacher soon learned that her money was missing and promptly took the law into her hands. She commanded everyone to attention and demanded that the guilty one give himself up. None of the children, admitted guilt. Policeman-like and with a spirit of wrath and vengeance, the teacher searched methodically each child's pockets, and sure enough, discovered the money in Kevin's. Silent, frightened Kevin was then brought to the front of the class as a bonafide thief. And to make sure that the "lesson" in legality would not escape the kindergartners, the teacher informed them of the consequences of stealing. "You go to jail for it." So righteous did the teacher feel that she unhesitatingly reported to Kevin's mother both the offense and the details of her own police action. The mother acknowledged the news curtly and took the weeping child home. He was inconsolable. That evening he had fever and remained ill for several days.

Was this teacher acting as she did only out of a rational desire to help Kevin learn not to steal?

Before answering, let us look at another incident of stealing in the kindergarten. In this case the teacher reluctantly admitted to her principal that the depletion of scissors in her classroom was the result of the children's helping themselves. "They don't have any scissors at home," she pleaded. "I feel so sorry for them. How can I punish them when they are just little children who love scissors and are too poor to buy them?"

In both these instances the teachers believed that what they were doing was best for the children. Yet both teachers were far too motivated by their own emotions of indignation in one case and pity in the other to recognize clearly what the children's real learning had to be. Both Kevin and the children in the other class were five-year-olds. This meant that their consciences were hardly developed enough to restrain them from following their impulses, even though verbally they might repeat "Stealing is wrong." Because understanding is relatively superficial at this age, such behavior is hardly unusual. Therefore, stealing should never be given the weight at five that is given to behavior of the same type by fully grown men and women. However, no one can develop a conscience and a clear sense of right and wrong unless he is taught; and a child learns best of all when he is taught by someone who respects and understands his problem. Both teachers, therefore, failed in their responsibility to help the children learn. The first teacher, in her fury, gave Kevin a burden of guilt he was far too young to carry, much as the teacher herself had probably once experienced. And the second teacher literally taught her children that it is all right to take what does not belong to you if you want it badly enough. Control must be accompanied by understanding if it is to be meaningful control.

Accepting "unacceptable" behavior. Little children have not been around long enough to have picked up the good manners and accepted graces that we call civilized behavior. There is a simple directness of expression, a quick response to the urgency of feeling, and a tendency to *do* first and *think* later, that can make them seem uncouth and even barbaric at times. The same children are, of course, quite capable of charm, sweetness, tenderness, and even charity to others. Adults who have never worked with young children generally have a way of finding the graces absolutely to be expected and the crudities a bit of a shock and a surprise. Perhaps the second major learning of the kindergarten teacher, after she has worked out her leadership role, is to learn to be shockproof. Anything can happen in a kindergarten and usually does. While most children are usually nicely behaved, the rawness of early physical reactions to life is not too remote. Frustration, anger, envy, rivalry—all human, if not pretty—can cause a child to do quite uncivilized things. Illness, fatigue, insecurity, feelings of rejection can also cause unhappy behavior. The teacher who has finally, and more or less painfully over the years, learned to control her emotions and handle body processes with dispatch and even indifference, may have a long way back to go in her acceptance of what is normal if she is to live comfortably with children who are on their way to civilized living, but backslide once in a while.

Fairness to all and bias towards none. Let us carry the matter of learned standards into another realm. Do we not all find certain kinds of children more attractive than others? Blond ones perhaps, or snub-nosed, or freckle-faced children, or ones with long braids? Bright ones, shy ones, easy-going ones, perky ones? Clean ones, nicely dressed ones, nonsmelly ones, carefully brought up ones?

We have mentioned the acceptance of individuals before but perhaps in discussing discipline it is pertinent to raise the question again. People do have favorites and they do find some children more appealing than others. It is not too hard to forgive a child you like for some transgression you then consider minor, and see the same act as major in a child whom you do not like. Studies show that teachers at the upper levels of school tend to grade girls higher than boys; studies of juvenile law show adolescents punished more severely than much older men for the same crimes; a child with a reputation for being bad is expected by each new teacher to be bad. We cannot condone these things as being human and therefore to be expected. It is an absolutely necessary part of the professional growth of anyone in an interpersonal profession to recognize his particular prejudices, no matter what they are, so that he can give to each child the fairness that child is entitled to when he needs disciplining and guidance. Teachers, no less than other members of the population, may make scapegoats of certain children. Children will often tell their parents that one child is picked on by the teacher and that the children do not know why because *they* accept each other pretty much as they are. We have said before that no one can be expected to love every child. But a teacher must *respect* every child and offer him an equal chance with others to grow. Certainly neither race, religion, ethnic background, socioeconomic class, nor individual idiosyncrasies should be a barrier to full acceptance; this is a right guaranteed to each child by our democratic principle of respect for the individual.

Teachers understand some children more readily than others. Miss Kane was an outstanding teacher who had a way of establishing a group long before anyone else. No one in her class remained on the outskirts. In one way or another all were made to feel welcome and to find a place. But Miss Kane was talking to a fellow teacher one day when five-year-old Ellen Barker edged near, and with great curiosity, obviously listened in on the conversation between the adults. Miss Kane became ruffled. "Go back to work, Ellen," she said. "I want to talk to Miss Duggan in private." Ellen skipped off and was soon in the midst of an active group of youngsters, apparently unbothered by the reprimand. But Miss Kane continued to muse about her. "There is something about that child I can't stand," she said. "She reminds me of the girls at college who were 'in,' and who treated me as if I didn't exist. She doesn't really do anything wrong; it's just that she always knows what's going on, and has a finger in every pie. Somehow, that type doesn't appeal to me."

Miss Kane could not see as any outsider could that her manoeuvering to include all the children reflected her own feelings about being left out, and her feeling for Ellen was certainly affected by her former envy of the girls who were "in."

Discipline is often affected by this kind of identification with a child. More than one teacher takes secret pleasure in acts of aggression that cause another teacher to wince in remembered fear. When people become teachers they do not cease to be the people they always were. They must face their feelings if they are to offer children the guidance children do need.

How much can a teacher take? It is evident that teachers differ considerably from each other, not only in teaching techniques but in personal tolerances for various kinds of behavior. Each teacher must understand her own level of tolerance. How much noise can you take without getting irritable? How do you really feel about messy, sloppy, sticky hands and tables?

What is the point at which sassiness ceases to be cute and becomes obnoxious instead? How many times does it take to say the same thing before you feel ready to explode? How much disorder can you stand while children are at work? How much resistance can you take from children without losing your temper? And perhaps we should ask, too, what are your physical tolerances? Are there times when you get headaches, cramps, or otherwise feel so miserable that you are likely to let the nearest victims feel the impact of your irritability?

There is no reason why you cannot tell children honestly, "You are not doing anything wrong but I can't stand so much noise today." And although you might not say, "I guess I am a bit cross because I stayed up late last night watching a show," you have to face this truth within yourself. It is not fair to give children the feeling that what *they* do is the cause of their teacher's displeasure, when it is really the teacher who is having the problem.

What we are saying in all the above is that teachers are people and are subject to the same range of human feeling as all others. Because they have chosen to work with other human beings they have a responsibility to be as fair and objective as they can be when they apply limits, controls, censure, or whatever is needed to help children grow in social maturity. Teachers may not indulge in personal whims, prejudices, squeamishness, or other forms of personal bias allowed to the average citizen. Precisely because they are teachers and can influence the lives of young children for better or for worse, they must face themselves and at least be *aware* of what it is in the adult-child relationship that they are not able to handle with objectivity. Awareness may not mean an immediate change in attitudes. But awareness will put a teacher on guard and eventually influence her attitudes. Immediately, she will at least question the application of disciplinary measures on the basis of a blind feeling that what she is doing is right; hopefully she will use her intelligence and training to make the wisest and most helpful decision for any child or group of children.

One little episode that occurred in a college teacher-education class bears repeating here. Barbara Atkin, a lively and devoted education student, insisted vociferously in a class discussion on discipline that the thing to do with an infractious child was to put him in a separate room and let him think things over. "Barbara," her teacher asked her, "is this what your mother did to you?" "Yes," Barbara answered righteously. "And did you think things over?" There was a long pause before Barbara meekly answered, "No. I did not."

The Group Affects Discipline

In all fairness, we must point out that the teacher's personal responses are not always the major cause of disciplinary problems. The most mature teacher, the most patient, understanding, and wise person may have a group that has more than its share of individual problems, or she may have a particular set of children who react to each other so poorly that try as she will she cannot unify them as a group. Fritz Redl discusses this fully in the excellent pamphlet, *Discipline for Today's Children and Youth.* Although he refers to older children in the main, the dynamics of group life operate in the kindergarten too. It may happen that in one community the children coming to kindergarten are almost all quite immature, and the size of the group will be too large for children who still require large doses of individual attention. A group may have more than its share of badly treated children who are hostile to adults and perhaps to each other too. Many physically charged, highly active children may make it difficult to plan for anything but the shortest periods of sitting-down activity. On the positive side, regardless of group composition is the fact that kindergartners are predisposed to love school. And the kindergarten teacher, with recognition of the limitations as well as the assets of any particular group, can, by being flexible about curriculum, usually win them over to more mature social behavior. But it is important to recognize that groups come with different backgrounds of experience and that some are more ready than others to share a teacher, to sit still for a story, to take turns with equipment, to handle tools and materials competently. If a teacher has a stereotyped notion of how children should behave, and a standard program of exactly the same stories, songs, trips, and materials for *each* class, she may find herself confronted with discipline problems because she failed to recognize that differences in groups call for differences in such things as time allotments for specific activities and long-range learning, differences in how directions and instructions are offered, and even differences in degree and kind of supervision.

The group as opposed to the individual. One last important aspect of group life is discussed with great insight by Redl, and that is the persistent conflict between the interests of the group and the needs or interests of individuals. It is easy enough to agree that one tries for the satisfaction of all individual needs, and this will take care of the group. But it happens that sometimes an individual interferes too seriously with group life, or, conversely, that a group gangs up against an individual. Occasionally there is a child in a group who has more serious problems than even the best teacher can cope with in a school setting. Redl then suggests his principle of "marginal antisepsis," which he defines as action taken by the teacher to protect the group, *but which is not harmful to the individual,* or action taken for the individual, *which is not harmful to the group.* One kindergarten teacher created a situation of the individual versus the group herself when she went out of her way to ease the entry into school of a recently arrived Japanese little girl. She praised the child lavishly, displayed her work prominently, took every opportunity to mention her virtues to the class, and showed her own affection overtly and unrestrainedly. The class reacted as one to make life as miserable as they could for this child. The harder the teacher tried to win acceptance for her the more intolerable her position became. In despair the teacher called for a conference with the class. From the children themselves she finally got the clues. Befriending the Japanese child in the way she did caused the rest of the class to feel that she did not care as much about them, which was certainly not her intention. Action taken for an individual must at the least not be harmful to the group, and vice-versa. When a child must be isolated from the group teacher and class should not stand as a solid unit against him. No matter how much he deserves isolation he should always feel that he is a member of the group, even though he must conform to group standards to be liked. His *participation* may be curtailed, but not his *membership*. Unless he feels he belongs the chances of helping him are completely eliminated.

Curriculum Affects Discipline

Because groups vary it should be obvious that curriculum which does not meet the needs of a particular group may be the cause for restlessness and quarreling in the kindergarten. Inadequate supplies, materials too hard or too easy to use, reliance on the same program and materials day after day, unawareness of effects of weather, seasons, and illness on children, too many group-controlled activities and not enough opportunities for individual experimentation, standards for achievement that are unrealistic—all these may cause more disciplinary interference than might otherwise be called for. Interesting, stimulating activity leads to greater satisfactions among children and therefore to greater readiness to cooperate and enjoy a good life with each other.

DISCIPLINE IS TEACHING

Of the many definitions for the word discipline, perhaps the most popularly accepted is the interpretation of discipline as punishment. While it is true that there are occasions when punishment (to fit the crime) is in order, it is even truer that the best interpretation of discipline is that of teaching. If we see the child-adult relationship as the child's lifeline to socialization, then the teacher's role as disciplinarian is primarily a role of guidance, support for effort, and clarity of standards for right and wrong. It is easiest to function in this capacity if we recognize that children are born absolutely unaware of the standards which any society upholds and are dependent on adults for learning what these standards are. There is no reason to scold and censure for what they have not learned at all or may not yet have learned thoroughly. Five-year-olds are old enough so that one can reason with them and appeal to their beginning need for group participation and acceptance. But they are still young enough to be struggling with growth of inner controls without which a social being does not develop. They need help in controlling their impulses and they need instruction in suitable techniques for group living. But they need a minimum of censure for the normal mistakes which they are sure to make while they are learning how to behave in a civilized society.

Bibliography

Appel, M. H., "Aggressive Behavior of Nursery School Children and Adult Procedures in Dealing with Such Behavior," *Journal of Experimental Education*, Vol. 11 (1942).

Bender, Loretta, *Aggression, Hostility and Anxiety in Children* (Springfield, Ill., Charles C Thomas, Publisher, 1953).

English, Horace B., *Child Psychology* (New York, Holt, Rinehart & Winston, Inc., 1951).

Sears, R. R. and Eleanor E., and Levin, H., *Patterns of Child Rearing* (New York, Harper & Row, Publishers, 1957).

Sheviakov, G. V., and Redl, Fritz, *Discipline for Today's Children and Youth* (Washington, National Education Association, 1201 16th St., N.W., 1956).

Watson, Goodwin, "Some Personality Differences in Children Related to Strict or Permissive Parental Discipline," *Journal of Psychology*, Vol. 44 (1957).

Zirbes, Laura, "The Contributions of Research Towards Discipline for Freedom," *Childhood Education* (Jan., 1951).

15

Classroom Management

No matter how well-intentioned a teacher may be, the success of her curriculum in the long run will depend heavily on the amount and quality of planning she invests in her task. While the role of the teacher has elsewhere been described as mother substitute, friend, instructor, guide, or evaluator, we prefer in this chapter to see the teacher primarily as an *organizer*—organizer of experiences through which children grow and learn, and organizer of the means by which learning can take place. Paradoxically, the more we believe that children should function with independence and creativity the more organizing and planning has to be done.

The ideal kindergarten will look, after a while, as though the children are running it themselves with the teacher not even obviously in view. But this can only happen when careful provision has been made for the children to get along pretty much on their own, when the stage has been set, so to speak, for the children to work and play productively without excessive dependence on the adult. The authors are guided in their view of classroom organization and management by two underlying assumptions: (a) Children and adults who live together in a limited space for several hours each day must have conditions set up that will make the mechanics of living together as comfortable and smooth as possible without denying individual rights to anyone. (b) Children's needs must be met if all concerned are to enjoy living together and are to gain from the experience. Consequently, not only must special needs

330

of group living be planned for, but age level needs and individual needs as well. In addition, the nature of the curriculum, which concerns itself with intellectual growth, social learning, and emotional and physical satisfactions, calls for special provisions other than those involved in the mechanics of sharing space and supplies.

PLANNING STARTS OUT AS LONG-RANGE

Before school gets under way in the fall a teacher needs to do basic planning and preparation, some of it with the administrator, to underpin the entire year's work. Every child needs a chair to sit on and a spot at a table where he can work. Every child needs a place to leave his clothes and any precious possession he wishes to safeguard. Toilet and water facilities must be available, and if not in the room, as is the case in old buildings, a teacher must know exactly where they are and just how the group will have access to them. Storage space for the quantities of materials to be drawn on during the year, as well as storage space for children's work-in-progress, has to be accounted for. Supplies in sufficient quantity and variety, especially of expendable materials, plans for changing supplies throughout the year, (perhaps by exchange with another teacher, perhaps by new purchases), and specific locations in the open for supplies likely to be in use each day, must all be provided. And of course conditions of health and cleanliness have to be met with proper tools, equipment, and practices. In addition, if the kindergarten is part of a large institution the teacher must know just how her special group is expected to fit into the larger organization of the school; will she share a yard, is there a set time for recess, does a music teacher come at certain times on certain days; are there areas considered out-of-bounds within the building, are there regulations concerning trips and unexpected expenses (as when the goldfish must be replaced or hamster food is used up)? What are the fire-drill regulations, and which entrances and exits may the class use? Not until the overall details for the year are settled can a teacher get closer to her daily program and think about the exciting details.

Even then, before deciding what to do on the first day and thereafter, there is planning. The neighborhood and school grounds must be familiar to the teacher so she can see what possibilities exist for the children's explorations. The time and nature of arrival and departure, snack and lunch, and provisions for rest, must all be known so that they can be guides around which to schedule. Is there a piano and space for rhythms in the classroom or must one use the gymnasium at set times? Is the room to be vacated for another teacher in a split-session school or will the class have complete freedom to use its room in its own way?

Once these basics are determined a teacher is ready to think about her unique role in organizing for the children.

ROOM ARRANGEMENT AND ORGANIZATION

There is no single superior arrangement of a kindergarten room, although suggested arrangements abound. Any arrangement will be determined first by the amount and kind of stationary cabinets and other items, then by the size and shape of the room, by the availability and type of portable equipment, and most important of all, by the program the teacher envisions as meeting the needs of five-year-olds. Since the first few limitations are usually beyond the teacher's power of determination, let us concentrate on the way in which children's needs affect the organization of a room.

Fives are physical; we have been saying this all along. Are there provisions in the room for physical activity? Some kindergartens have climbing apparatus right in the room, some bring outdoor blocks, boards and ladders into the room during inclement weather, and some have space for running, skipping, and leaping. Others, in confined space, must rely on jumping up and down, stamping, stretching, and twisting in place to meet this need.

Fives are social. Are there areas where small groups and larger groups can enjoy companionship? Is there a nook where a child can retreat and be by himself? Room arrangements of chairs and tables and of movable cabinets and screens, set out to provide alcoves or sweeping space, will reflect the recognition of changing needs for sociability or solitude.

Fives love to play, to use materials, to make things. Is there provision for this? Where can they build with wood and blocks? Is the woodwork bench sufficiently remote from the library corner so that the banging of a hammer does not pound into the ears of a child who wants to look at a book? Are the block cabinets arranged so that several children can have access to the shelves at one time, and is the floor space in front of the cabinets sufficient for several children to build at once? Easels must be near light and if possible water; mops and sponges close enough so that children working with wet materials (paint, clay, water, fingerpaint) do not have to drag these supplies clear across the room and over the blockbuilder's feet in order to use them as needed. Odd materials, such as dress-up clothes, need hooks or shelves or even orange-crate closets—but they must have a place.

EACH ROOM IS UNIQUE

Thus, a room arrangement that is to allow for the fulfilling of children's needs requires careful estimation of just what the needs of healthy five-year-olds are. Then, given the conditions available in a particular school a teacher adapts her quarters in the best way possible so that the children's physical needs can most comfortably be met. Sometimes the best use of a room is not discovered with the first try at arrangement. A teacher, especially a beginner, has to be prepared in the first weeks of school to watch the children in action to see if changes are necessary. It is true that children enjoy the security of knowing where everything is, but if a change has to be made a discussion with the class as to what the stumbling blocks and the reasons for the change are will make them feel involved, and will hasten their cooperation.

SETTING UP A ROOM FOR AUTONOMOUS BEHAVIOR

A teacher's attitude towards children and her philosophy of education affects the way in which she conceives the placement and distribution of materials and supplies. If she believes that these are little children who are likely to waste supplies, spill liquids, and harm themselves and others, she will cautiously dispense all items for their use from a carefully locked cabinet, under carefully controlled conditions of supervision. But if her belief is that it is important that children develop competence and efficiency in the handling of materials, and that they need freedom to express and develop feelings and ideas with and through materials, she is more likely to have supplies available in an orderly fashion on open or otherwise accessible shelves. Rules for use—no obvious waste, return what you do not use, no hogging, no misuse of material (clay is not to be stamped underfoot and paint may not be applied to walls or faces)—are certainly in order. But it may cost the loss of some paper, clay, or even a tool before the learning takes full effect. Trusting children, albeit spelling out the rules for respectful use of materials, a teacher helps them to take pride in their competency. In time the children actually help each other learn how to share and use constructively the available materials in the classroom. It is far better to accept the challenge of teaching children how to handle materials and allowing them free access to these for their individual, creative use, than to dispense materials as if doing a child a favor by giving him a piece of drawing paper and a box of crayons. In the long run the teacher eventually frees herself of a good deal of unnecessary supervisory concerns if the children are permitted to grow as a result of good instruction at the beginning. They can then function with competence and skill on their own.

GOOD ORGANIZATION ALLOWS FOR WIDE LATITUDE IN CHOICE OF ACTIVITY

Here is a kindergarten in a modern suburban public school, housed in a separate wing of the building. The room has ample space so the eye can rove from one end to the other of the attractive modern walls, fixtures and surfaces, and gay colors. The whole room shows cleanliness, openness, warmth, and something interesting and inviting to make a visitor (adult or child) want to say "Look at that!" or "What's this?" This is the kindergartners' own place to work, play, and learn in a way suitable for five-year-olds.

Although there are no more than twenty-five children in the class, there seem to be many more. It would be difficult to count them accurately during this main work period, for they are in many places and are performing many different activities. There is a variety of lively sounds in the room—a discussion at a table with construction materials, the sound of a saw and of sandpapering, and mock yelping of a little "dog" reprimanded by its "mistress." All the sounds are definitely audible in a meaningful and not just noisy way.

Mrs. Higher, the teacher of this lively kindergarten, is an older woman with pleasant looks and manner. She seems thoroughly relaxed. Although she is keeping an eye on what goes on in all the areas, she is not intrusive. It is important to recognize that this is close to the spring of the year and Mrs. Higher's knowledge of the children, and their own knowledge of what to do, are such that not much supervision is required. A good deal more help, stricter supervision, and more encouragement was given by Mrs. Higher earlier to prepare the children for the independence and competence they now show.

We will see now how the teacher functions in the specific activities. There is a quiet intermittent conversation around the easels where three children are painting seriously and beautifully. Mrs. Higher is actually not near those children and not watching them. But she has checked earlier on the consistency and sufficiency of paints in the containers, and although the children themselves put their paintings on the drying rack, Mrs. Higher comes over later on to affix the names and dates. When one child tells her about "clouds in the sky" she adds the notation to the picture; this is important to the child and interesting to the teacher.

In the farthest corner of the class there is special liveliness. This area is almost like a little room in itself, with half walls and a door. There is clanking of dishes in that little room, with explosive domestic talk and banging of doors, and dressing up in odd-fitting, gaudy grown-up clothes. These children, too, are getting along without a teacher, except that a modern, medically-conscious member of the "family" rushes over with an urgent request. "Mrs. Higher! We need some pills for the sick daddy! Would you give us some pills!" The teacher recognizes the need for "medication" and she turns to the supply of dry cereal usually used for that purpose. They work!

What appears to be the central activity in the class is an impressive blockbuilding project. The blocks are held up by intricate balance and there is an interior structure into which the children are peering from above and peeking from a small side opening. There are also external supports and fortifications. Earnest consultation among the builders can be heard.

"I don't want the roof to fall down!" one child asserts.

"But people will bump it when the roof sticks out," another explains.

"We have to finish it," insists a third. Hearing this, the teacher offers some construction material for the roof and helps to make a requested sign for the finished building.

Relaxing somewhat from her involvement in the complicated building project, the teacher watches the profound aesthetic absorption of a pensive, poetic little girl, as she slowly turns the pages of a charming book. This expression of concentration and feeling on a child's face is a beautiful sight to any teacher.

In Mrs. Higher's kindergarten class the children are free to choose from a variety of appropriate activities and materials. Some go to the mechanical tools and the muscular action of woodworking; some like the fluid paint and the feel of color as they put it on blank paper; some are ready to be involved in intimate groups as they play out creatively and dramatically various relations; another enjoys solitude with a beautiful book. In this class the child is free to follow his tastes and preferences, to use initiative and independence. True freedom of choice in both materials and companions can be easily destroyed, however, under the guise of organization when the teacher's concern over equitable distribution of space and materials causes her to assign people in "fair" fashion, but without regard to individual needs. It is important to understand that some children may need to spend weeks at the sandbox or to blockbuild instead of paint, and some may need to stay with the same companion for a long time in order to learn how to play at all. Freedom of choice must mean just that, except where waiting for a turn becomes necessary. In this case a child should still have freedom of choice—to wait or to turn to something else. Naturally all freedom of choice is curtailed by reality. There may be only one work bench, for example. But it should not also be curtailed by a strict plan of assigning all children to all activities.

Real freedom of choice for the children is possible in Mrs. Higher's class because Mrs. Higher has set the stage for it. She has seen to it that the tools and materials are in working order, safe and accessible, and the room arrangement such that a variety of activities could be carried on without confusion. She knows that when children are planning some paper construction, for example, they need paper, scissors for cutting, perhaps string for tying, rubber bands and clips for holding things in place, or crayons for marking and decorating. If they are to carry out their purpose with relative efficiency they need to know where such things are, learn to use them, and learn also the importance of putting them back for the next time's use.

When a simple cooking project, such as making jello, is carried out in this class the teacher initiates and supervises an orderly arrangement of bowls, stirring spoons, measuring cups, eating spoons, and a potholder for the pot with boiling water. She plans for time to read directions, needed time for chilling the jello, and the most rewarding or appropriate time for eating. Though perhaps all this planning cannot always be discerned, the resulting orderliness of the activity can be felt and noticed in the atmosphere of the class, and this orderliness will be absorbed and learned by the children. The teacher also sees to it that the activities are maintained on a satisfying and constructive level; neither damage nor interference is tolerated.

ORGANIZATION CAN BE BOTH ORDERLY AND FLEXIBLE

Mrs. Lu is a teacher in the kindergarten of a private school. The class consists of about sixteen five-and-a-half-year-olds in a small room which is first arranged for work, then adapted for lunch, then rearranged for nap, and again set up for informal snacks. Although one does not hear any orders from Mrs. Lu, one is attracted by her knowing, confident, yet particularly gentle manner. The room itself is full of children's mobiles, framed pictures, displays of clay work, and pots, cans, and jars of a variety of germinating, rooting, and budding plants. At lunch time the teacher is seated among the tables with children, attending to some serving. The children also help themselves in a casual and orderly fashion. There is lively table conversation that at once suggests informality, good relations, and a sensible attitude towards eating and food. Each child clears and stacks his plate independently. The children are so relaxed that when a visitor appears and Mrs. Lu suggests that the children introduce themselves to her, each child tells the visitor his or her name without any interruption in the meal. As some of the children were eating their desert, others clearing the tables, and the teacher attending to the finishing touches and general supervision, a father of one of the children came in to take his child home for a special reason. He immediately attracted a great deal of happy attention, especially from his son, and for about fifteen minutes most of the children sat or stood around and talked to the man about baseball, traffic, and birthdays. The man had a good time talking and joking freely with the children. The teacher was aware of the slight delay in the routines, but she was equally aware and respectful of the visit with the father, joining in it herself. She did not rush the man away or nag the children about getting their cots; she simply reminded them and worked with them, and in a few minutes the room was rearranged and quieted for napping.

Thus, it is entirely possible to have a room in which routines are respected by the children and consistently supervised by the teacher, in which flexibility absorbs the unexpected, and extra social pleasures can take place. In spite of the fact that Mrs. Lu happened to lack both supplies and space, thus limiting some activities, her orderly use of what she did have and her strong sense of organization carried over to the children and created a room in which children had adventure as well as stability.

CHILDREN, TOO, PARTICIPATE IN ORGANIZATION

Attending to the many chores connected with group living involves much real work, which kindergarten children can and should share with the adults. Considering the subject of children's work broadly, we might say that there is moral value in a child's acquiring respect and admiration for some kind of work through good early experience. But there is economy too when able energetic five-year-olds attend to tasks with healthy independence and even with some appreciable skills. Work is at the core of the adult world, and children live in a world of adults. They depend on and want to be part of this world. Work means grown-up responsibility; it is something real, as compared to exclusively playful activities or make-believe. It has physical appeal and importance to children. It carries prestige and social satisfaction through recognition gained from other children as well as grown-ups. Work is a challenge to various skills, and entails learning. It can therefore be exciting to fives, who are such avid learners.

But work must come into the school life of young children under proper guidance and in relation to the school environment and young children's needs. What does it consist of? We will begin with what might be thought of as the more mundane areas of responsibility.

Cleaning the Classroom

If there is an invisible porter attending to the *entire* work when the class is not in session, or if most of the children have servants at home to do all the cleaning, the children may hold cleaning in low esteem; the teacher must be aware of this as well as of her own values. However, whatever the children's backgrounds their eager response and interest will be stimulated by the understanding that the classroom is theirs, and that together with the teacher (as well as the porter) they can take some responsibility.

First, there are the tools and equipment that go with cleaning and which are attractive to young children. These include floppy mops, tough brushes, absorbent sponges, stiff brooms, and soft rags, all kept in proper places and in good condition, and replaced when needed. To use a suitable size mop on the classroom floor when spills occur is an acceptable job to any five-year-old. The necessary use of a broom and dustpan and brush makes good sense to the practical-minded kindergartners. If such children's work commands the teacher's respectful attention and is accompanied by the teacher's own readiness to practice such work, the kindergartners can enjoy the physical activity of cleanliness and order and not take it for granted as if it were done by fairies and elves.

Scrubbing

Scrubbing tables with soap and brush or cleanser and cloth and making them shiny is satisfying to any child between the ages of two and six. The splashing of water, the sprinkling of cleanser, the different uses of brush and sponge and cloth are actually fun to children. In fact, they are liable to get carried away with it and the teacher may need to *remind* them that although this may be enjoyable, the purpose is cleaning tables.

Children are generally fascinated by seeing surfaces transformed. Thus, in one class, the most popular job was scrubbing, on hands and knees, a large piece of oilcloth which was kept under the standing easel and was speckled with paint. All the children enjoyed seeing it conspicuously clean as much as they enjoyed the process of scrubbing.

The same class became negligent in the routine care of the bathroom. The result was faucets left running, used paper towels strewn on the floor, and objects left in wash bowls. The teacher called a special meeting and said that she noticed wrong things in the bathroom and

asked who else noticed anything wrong. Several children mentioned noticing things out of place. When asked by the teacher, they also had an
idea of what could be done. The teacher then suggested that one child
have charge of checking the bathroom before the end of the session.
Six volunteers responded at once. The enthusiasm for checking the bathroom, which consisted of cleaning out and scrubbing the wash bowls,
lasted for several weeks with these four-and-a-half to five-year-old children. The floor was indeed spick and span and the sinks actually shining.
They enjoyed the responsibility, the activity, and the results. There was
no scolding or nagging on the part of the teacher, but only relevant attention to an immediate need and of course recognition of whatever positive response came from the children. Scrubbing sinks with scouring
powder and special brushes or mops, polishing mirrors, or even washing
and wiping a window until it is shiny, when it is an accepted or shared
rather than an imposed task, is dignified and even delightful labor, bringing a sense of self-sufficiency.

"Dirty Work"

Attention to the wastebasket, or trash can, may also be considered
just "dirty work" but is something important. If the place where classroom
trash is emptied is reasonably accessible children enjoy, as an occasional
if not a daily job, carrying a heavy trash can, emptying it into a large
can, and clapping the lid. If in the process they should encounter the
"real garbage man" and perhaps even the garbage truck, so much the
better.

"Watch out! This is hard work," the teacher cautioned Danny and
Jimmy, who applied excess energy in lifting of wastebaskets.

"But I can do hard work."

"You have to be careful, so the stuff won't spill," Jimmy spoke
from experience.

"And I can do hard work. I am strong," Danny added, and with
great concentration this strong, muscular five-year-old Danny lifted up
the basket, then pushed it through a hallway, and balanced himself and
the basket as he managed a couple of stairs. Yes, the teacher followed
the "hard workers" in that case. But that much individual attention the
teacher felt was as important as individual attention to children's reading
progress. In that situation the teacher had found out before the end of
the session that the school porter had taken ill, and the children discussed
the porter's work and how much of it they could do. Emptying wastebaskets was considered very important!

In planning for classroom cleaning the teacher needs to check
herself. Is she inclined to be fastidious rather than simply orderly? Does

she feel disgusted when there is "an awful mess" during children's work or play or during clean-up itself? As long as the mess does not endanger safety (wet floors, broken objects, obstructions in necessary passages, in which case the teacher must be alert, prompt, and efficient) the teacher must aim to be casual and must either ask the children for constructive suggestions or offer her own. A teacher's disgust with a mess can discourage an interest in cleaning. The teacher must also check on the standards she has for the children's work. Children's abilities and interests vary not only with individuals but with the home experience. Furthermore, five-year-olds may well become tired and bored, and the teacher will need to provide change and variety and perhaps some attraction. A colorful dustpan, a new brush, a different kind or shape of cloth, a design on the mop handle, or a sign (perhaps made or decorated by a child) can serve to stimulate or maintain a regard for cleaning.

Routines For Putting Things Away

Putting things away should be required and *expected* by a helpful teacher, but not made compulsory in authoritarian fashion. This may sound contradictory, but what it means is that fives, who are still learning, should have expectations set before them. But a teacher does not with any realism expect full acquiescence. Actually, most of the group will be cooperative and willing most of the time, and the picture is not too discouraging. But there is always the one!

It must not be forgotten by the teacher that working materials are put away to maintain the welfare of the entire group, and as such the task is social in implication. It is a meaningful activity which may lag at times or be uneven in tempo and result, but which need not deteriorate into a mechanical act of compliance for which, with effort, kindergarten children can be trained. We must also avoid giving children a common adult notion that work is something we suffer through and therefore get done and over with expediently. There are satisfactions in work well done. And certainly it is not done for the sake of fostering individual virtue or for a child to ingratiate himself with the teacher.

Let us consider separate areas in the work of putting things away. Blocks must not be shoved off the floor to some out-of-the-way spot, as is often the case. They must also not be dumped in a basket, stuffed into some chest or container, or piled and squeezed on shelves haphazardly. Such procedures bring confusion and have no place in good work practices for children. Order and purpose must be observed in putting blocks away on sufficient shelves of proper dimensions, stacked according to shape, distributed with some eye for balance, and in such a way that they are particularly handy to take out for use. All accessory materials need also be put away where they can be attractive and accessible.

Putting away painting materials usually has special appeal. This includes disposal of unusable paint, washing of brushes, scrubbing jars, and cleaning the easel, all of which provides a good deal of sensory satisfaction and often calls for ideas for improvement. Ways of putting things away and ways of keeping materials provide interest and stimulate responsibility. Clay must be kept moist to be usable. Crayons cannot be stored near heat. Boxes or baskets or cans with materials must be sorted and labeled with some original designation as well as the teacher's writing. Receptacles for putting work and play materials away can stimulate work interest. Not only cubbies and closets, but earthenware crocks, tin cannisters, wooden buckets, aluminum pails, plastic containers, string and drawstring bags, cellophane bags, paper bags, and gunny sack bags, all lend interest and are useful.

"When I was a child we had only one kind of bag in our house," one of the authors told a class of children once.

"Was it a paper bag?"

"No. We had *no* paper bags. You'll never guess. So I'll tell you. It was a sleeve bag."

"A *sleeve* bag?"

"Yes, when a linen shirt wears out the sleeves are not yet torn, so you cut the sleeves off the shirt and sew up the end of the cuff, and there you have a strong bag to store things like roasted pumpkin seeds, or hazel nuts, or . . . a picnic lunch maybe."

Interesting and suitable receptacles, planning and organizing *with* the children, and fairness in dividing responsibility are all important in establishing effective and meaningful routines for clean-up and general order.

Chores in Caring for Plants and Animals

Taking care of plants and animals is closely related to the enjoyment and learning which children derive from living and growing things. Children frequently observe unusual conditions and changes while doing these chores, and these should be capitalized upon by the teacher.

Here is a group around a fish tank. It was Peter's turn to feed the fish that whole week. This was the third day and he had already distinguished the different appearance, behavior, and even disposition of each of the three goldfish. "This is Firstie; he's always the first one to take a nibble of the food, and *he* is Snoopie; he snoops around and waits. I don't know what he's waiting for . . ."

"Maybe he's finding out if it smells good, and maybe that would prove . . ."

"Can fishes smell?"

"Of course, you dope . . ." Now the teacher is consulted and the goldfish book is looked at and an encyclopedia referred to. Another child calls Peter's attention to the water level in the tank. Peter then checks with the teacher and replenishes the tank with bottled water of room temperature. He does this slowly as he watches the stirring in the tank, the movements of each fish, and the precise rise in water level.

Betsy was attending to the watering of the potted avocado plant on the windowsill. On close inspection she had noticed a strange leaf on the tall stem. What was it? Well, Freddie had played a trick and attached a green cut-out paper leaf with scotch tape right onto the real stem. Betsy soon discoverd the "fakeness" and the culprit, and since that time she was particularly interested in inspecting the leaves when attending to the watering. This time it was her luck to notice something strange. One leaf was all rolled up into a little tube.

"Did you do that to the leaf, Freddie? Who did it? Why is this leaf rolled up?" On further most careful inspection Betsy discovered a caterpillar in some cozy wrappings turning over as Betsy rudely moved in on him. At this point Betsy's excited high voice rose even more than usual and her normally keen eyes blazed. She pleaded urgently to be the one responsible for the avocado plant for "another few days. Just a few, please!" The teacher decided at this point that fairness in the strict sense had to be abandoned. The avocado plant, conspicuously enriched by its moth guest, had to be in Betsy's possessive charge until, some ten days later, a pale, slight, feeble common moth emerged. To Betsy this common moth, in its magical transformation from a crawly grounded caterpillar to a mobile winged creature, departing and ascending, might well have been an angel. For five-year-olds there is so much novelty and freshness, so many possibilities, that a prescribed chore need have none of the sense of dullness, repetition, or imposition that the work connotes to adults.

It is also true, however, that teachers cannot count on a steady performance of such chores by five-year-olds. Watering plants, taking turns feeding animals, or helping regularly with cleaning a cage, all bring proud and desired responsibility. But alas, five-year-olds are easily diverted to interesting sidelines, or they may forget their chores completely as their interest is captured elsewhere. Though they can work with real care, fives cannot be held down to full responsibility. Teacher reminders are much in order here. Even charts allowing for changing names and jobs cannot do the entire job of reminding kindergartners. Intrigued as the children are by charts and changing tasks, they do forget. Nevertheless, it is worth encouraging responsibility, and making sure that the standards for workmanship relate to age as well as particular interest. It helps when the teacher also takes some share in the children's work and does not confine herself to supervision alone. But overemphasizing the value of work is neither necessary nor helpful. For the five-year-old, work should be neither punishment nor reward. It is a normal and necessary part of living with its own inherent difficulties and pleasures.

ROUTINES OF SELF-CARE

Dressing and Undressing

In the fall of the school year children in most parts of the country come to school without heavy outer clothing, and dressing and undressing does not seem a problem at all. But when seasonal changes bring heavy clothing and perhaps layers of it, the program schedule has to be altered to allow time for sweaters, boots, jackets, hats, scarves, mittens, and possibly raincoats. As in all other phases of development, groups of fives vary somewhat in independent handling of dressing and undressing. In general, poorer children learn this kind of independence earlier than middle-class children, but all are quite capable of dressing and undressing themselves during the kindergarten year. They do need help in the *group* phases of the task: How many and in what order shall they go to the clothing closets? How shall they come to the teacher for last minute touches without overwhelming her? How can the teacher expedite techniques for slipping into ski pants, sweater, and boots for large groups of individuals who are still awkward at this?

The aim in this mundane task is of course efficiency and reasonable speed so that the group can get on to more interesting activities. But for many five-year-olds this simple routine is still a challenge, especially if they have had too protective and domineering a mother. For many others it is a matter of real indifference whether boots or mittens match or whether collars are turned in or out. To still others it is almost traumatic to misplace a boot or mitten or to leave with a hat that is not properly buttoned. These are the personal meanings of dressing and undressing, meanings of competency and independence or helplessness and dependence; fear of adult censure for awkwardness or security with adults no matter what; responsibility for personal possessions or disinterest in possessions. Therefore, while the teacher helps each child find a place for himself in the hustle and bustle of a large-scale operation by establishing suitable regulations to expedite movement and avoid confusion, she also remains aware of the individual meaning which this simple operation can have. For the sake of the mothers' peace of mind the teacher should also make a quick check of the collars, ties on hats, mittens, boots, and scarves to see that each child leaves properly dressed for the weather and wearing home what he came with. If the mothers can be persuaded to label their children's things, much confusion can be avoided. This whole matter of helping individuals help themselves in a group situation of this kind is a suitable topic to discuss at an early parent meeting.

Resting

The rest periods automatically included in every kindergarten program call for fresh appraisal, or they may deteriorate into the hardly restful battle that Mrs. Cuttney had with her children. Just why and how resting came into the kindergarten program to begin with is not known. We believe that it is good and even necessary for children (and adults too) to relax between sessions of hard work. We also believe that it is possible for children to relax completely and thoroughly without necessarily stretching out on rugs or mats, with eyes closed tight. Scheduled rest is often unnecessary and a waste of precious time in a short program. Therefore we do not believe relaxation ought to be legislated into a program and tyrannically enforced.

The key to relaxation in a morning or afternoon kindergarten session lies in the balance of activities as the teacher plans them. Common sense tells us not to have a rhythms period, go on a trip for several blocks, come back to the gym for some exercise, and then run relay races. Ordinarily a program should include a listening time (story or records), a crafts time which offers little exertion, table games, opportunity to look at books and pictures, and, woven throughout, the chance for an individual youngster to withdraw briefly and relax with a game, toy, book, instrument, or just slouch on the floor and watch others. Good programs definitely intersperse quiet activities with active ones. By five most children have outgrown their need for a regular nap, and their bodies are accommodated to a sunrise-to-sunset schedule of wakefulness. Living in a group however, can be a tiring experience, especially at the beginning of the year. The noise, conflicts of views, and continuous exercise of control over impulses certainly can affect one's equilibrium. It may be quite necessary, therefore, for a teacher to plan for times when all noise ceases, times when the intensity of preoccupation and the intrusion of discord come to a brief stop. But this planning need not be the rigid, arbitrary daily rest hour which children hate and teachers find hard to administer. Nor does it necessarily mean sitting or lying in a particular position, such as heads on table or flat on one's back.

Children do need to relax, especially those who by temperament tend to become overintense. And sometimes they need to be taught how to relax and enjoy it. In no case, though, need the resting time become a battle between the "I-know-what's-good-for-you" teacher, and the "You-can't-make-me" child.

Planning for a period of cessation of noise and discord may mean a storytime with everyone sprawled comfortably on the floor, or a record time with the children in similar comfortable positions. One teacher collected a wide assortment of small gadgets, mechanical and magnetic toys, locks and keys, pipe cleaners, erasers and colored pencils, small pencil sharpeners, shoe polish, fingernail polish, and whatever else normally appears first in kitchen catch-all drawers and later in children's pockets. These were kept in several boxes which were constantly refilled with new items as she found them and cleared temporarily of old ones. At rest time the children could take one thing they wanted from these boxes, or a puzzle or book, to their cots. For the forty-five-minute rest in this all-day school the children played quietly for part of the time, stretched out peacefully for part of the time, and heard a story or music for the last part. They got up from rest quite toned down, as was evident from the quiet, relaxed conversation that accompanied the putting away of cots.

But when we see a teacher start her two-hour afternoon session with a one-half-hour resting time ("They come in tired"), we cannot help but wonder about how necessary this is. We have also been in schools where the children are undernourished, share a bed with several siblings at home, and are kept awake at night by adult activity in crowded quarters with no privacy. These children need their rest just as they need a good hot lunch, and provision should be made for these. Well-fed, healthy youngsters who come to kindergarten for two or three hours of play will probably manage quite nicely with the balance of quiet and action planned by the teacher and the individual choice of restful sprawling as they feel the need. Except for special occasions, such as the return from a trip or a high pitch of excitement sustained all through the play, the rest-break need not be more formal than indicated.

Toileting

There is one constant routine in the kindergarten class which needs to be looked at separately because it still has much personal meaning for five-year-olds, and that is the toileting. Fives are generally quite capable of handling their own needs, although many a little boy or girl, lost in the fascination of play, overestimates his holding capacity. "Accidents," while not too common, still do occur, to the intense humiliation and chagrin of the five-year-old, let alone the discomfort of the teacher and fascination of the rest of the class. Newer school buildings usually place the kindergarten room quite close to bathrooms, so that a child may continue his individually determined habits by leaving the group as he will. This is not so all over however, and in many schools the bathrooms are at the end of one or more long corridors and perhaps down a flight of stairs. In this event a teacher is justifiably reluctant to allow a five-year-old complete freedom so far from her watchful eye, and she may be compelled to arrange for the entire group to take a daily trip to the toilets. This exodus has to be planned with concern for time and is obviously a waste of precious time. But conditions in the building may make it necessary. Even within this framework however, it is important for a teacher to understand that toileting may still carry overtones of emotional significance to individual youngsters. Some children are quite inhibited from using public toilets and will suffer tortures rather than do so, teacher or no teacher. Some are more prone than others to tease and peek, to the acute discomfort of others. For some children the disclosure of each other in a partial state of undress is a simulus to sexual curiosity and play. Kindergarten teachers must face realistically the fact that the emphasis on group practices in this regard may have the effect of heightening symptoms of immature behavior, since the experience cannot be casual and of minor matter under the circumstances, as it normally should. It therefore is important to recognize that children's individual differences in need and attitude must be respected and understood, even under the trying circumstances of regimentation.

The first question many a new kindergartner asks his mother is "Where is the bathroom?" It is probably a good idea for the teacher to take her class to the bathroom as an initial school orientation experience, and to point to the difference between an individual, locked room at home and a multicubicled, perhaps different looking receptacle at school. Asking them what the differences are may bring forth surprising observations on the strength and length of the flush, the difference in mechanism of the flush, the special smell of disinfectant, the unique type of faucet at the sink, perhaps the absence of hot water, certainly the fascinating little receptacle for liquid or powdered soap, and the novel way of dispensing towels. Reassurance about the differences can lead readily to discussion of suitable behavior—protecting the privacy of each individual, avoiding the misuse of equipment, not lingering for play when the whole group is waiting. Since this is an independent activity and usually without the teacher's direct supervision, the children's faith in the teacher who shows understanding leads to the comfortable sense of trust little children still must feel in adults so that they will be better able to bring problems in this area to her. It goes without saying that the child who does have an accident will need real comforting and face-saving. Having learned control and the pride in control quite recently, kindergartners have no humor about their mistakes. (They are very ready to laugh in relief at others in distress!)

Teachers must know that a child may develop diarrhea at the start of an illness as well as when under tension; he may wet himself because he is afraid to use the school toilet and cannot hold out, as well as moisten underpants because he cannot bear to leave exciting play. These events are to be expected and indeed still appear in first grade. Readiness on the teacher's part to handle them with sympathetic efficiency protects the child from unnecessary shame and guilt. In the course of a happy and fulfilling school year the children mature and their growth is reflected in this area too.

EMERGENCIES

The best run class is bound to be confronted with the unexpected at one time or another. A nursery school teacher of a private school walked into her classroom one Monday morning together with a group of children who had arrived early, and beheld with horror a broken window and glass strewn all over the otherwise clean and well-prepared room. But in spite of the shock and distress the teacher did not overlook the children and their impression and interest. The teacher felt she should have the children take part in the problem all the way. Physical safety was, of course, the first concern and the teacher indicated the small area in the room and the hall which the children could occupy. That was understandable to them. Second, proper report of the accident and immediate help had to be obtained. "Tell the office," suggested Larry. The teacher sent a note with three children, which resulted in having the secretary and another teacher come in with a large broom. Two of the children served as guards, telling all the arrivals not to go into the "dangerous" place until the adults finished the sweeping. Then the children were assigned to a job of being "inspectors." They examined with closest attention every area for "small, almost invisible specks of glass." Then they realized the room was too cold, and the teacher told them that a man would come in later to fix the broken window.

"But can't we cover up the hole now?" After some discussion and search for a board the hole was covered up with a piece of cardboard. So the problem of physical safety and protection was attended to with sufficient understanding and with security for the children. The teacher had gained cooperation from the children easily enough in a moment of need; they had also shown responsibility and given necessary help. But the episode led to the serious question of cause, which in turn led to the moral issue of wrongdoing which was involved in the broken window.

"How did the window get broken?" several children asked of the teacher right away.

"I am not sure. Have you any idea?" Fantastic answers of jets and bombs and flying saucers came from those four to five-year-olds, showing what children are thinking about. Some thought the break came from a ball.

"Maybe a boy was playing and he didn't *know* the ball was going to hit the window." Consideration of cause brought to mind responsibility and the possibility of someone's guilt.

"Maybe a *bigger* boy did it."

"I didn't do it." This was said very seriously and a hush of consternation settled over the group of children.

"I know you didn't," the teacher said confidently, relieving the hush.

"Maybe a pussycat did!" This child wanted to be funny and succeeded. Everybody laughed and made pawing motions of breaking a window. The laughter and movement served to relieve the children's tension. Then a little girl said, "Whoever did it, should clean up."

"But it's already cleaned up." They were thus back to the concrete solution and the teacher ended it at this point.

SCHEDULING

Units in the Kindergarten

Many curriculum bulletins and syllabi suggest specific themes around which to organize the activities of the children, with attention to their general interests. Thus, one might find a teacher organizing class experiences around the seasons, holidays, or major community events like the circus, and see carefully prepared lessons in language arts, art, music, and mathematical concepts related to the specific theme of the week. In most kindergartens in the North one finds jack-o-lanterns in October, turkey pictures on the wall in November, Christmas trimmings in December, snow in January, valentines in February, daffodil cutouts in March, pictures of rabbits on the windows in April, and flowers in May, with appropriate accompanying activities. We have tried throughout this book to develop an approach to curriculum for kindergarten children that will take them further afield into stimulating intellectual learning than the traditional projects allow. Consequently, we suggest that units and projects should be allowed to grow out of the children's interests and concerns for the most part, and that the introduction of such important aspects of our culture as the traditional holidays, high points of seasonal change, and the circus and zoo should be more casual and take up less time than is usually the case. There is a great comfort to a teacher to plan in advance a number of projects likely to interest little children. But too heavy reliance on projects planned and conceived by adults, introduced into groups that may or may not be ready for them, and so tightly scheduled as to leave little room for the spontaneous, can only lead to less valuable learning in depth than units and projects developed by the teacher as needed to satisfy the curiosity and keen interests of the children. Five-year-olds change interests fairly rapidly; they are interested in everything but do not stay long to study everything in depth. Interest in a single theme, such as firemen, cowboys, a circus, or a farm, cannot usually be sustained for more than a week, although children may return to a theme again and again at different times.

Individual variations in concentration span exist too, and the patience to stay with an activity because the whole group is doing it is not as strong as it will become later. Time blocks must be planned with these developmental characteristics in mind.

The project that is carefully organized ahead of time may be a necessary introduction for children lacking in ideas and experience, but even then it is important that the experiences offered for their enlightenment be of the kind that stimulates further inquiry and exploration. When this is so, units flow out of each other as children are really thinking, and this is the fun of creative curriculum building.

In any case kindergarten children do not always need to be on a unit. The fluid and divergent range of their interests speak against too formal an organization for them. While all the experiences we have described—trips, science, literature, discussion, blocks, woodwork, art, and music—are necessary for their growth, these do not need to be so limited by specific themes as to discourage exploration and discovery by the children themselves into totally unexpected areas. Introducing children to the traditions of our culture is after all only one part of their education, much of which they get outside of school. At school we should be concerned with the stretching of minds and enrichment of intellectual experience. Kindergarten teachers can feel quite comfortable about pursuing the leads gleaned from the children or suggested by the environment, without worrying about how carefully organized these are into neatly laid out, continuous units.

Building up Experience over Time

The rapidly changing attention of kindergartners and the brevity of the kindergarten day does mean that one has to plan for a *cumulative* effect from repeated, brief experiences, incorporating repetition of certain kinds into the schedule. Music is one of these, and since time does not allow for music every day, even if that were desirable, then an experience once or twice a week will add up at the end of the year to a repertoire of songs and competency with instruments. But the once or twice a week must be scheduled. Stories, on the other hand, give a child a basis for appreciating books, an important part of his preparation for reading, and story or poem time should be included every day, however short the time. Science need not be deliberately scheduled on a regular basis but it must be intrinsic to the program through the availability and restocking of materials and through the constant awareness of the challenges to scientific exploration that lie in the immediate world. We have shown this often in the records in this book.

The Daily Schedule

Scheduling, thus, is best done broadly, allowing sizeable periods of time each day for a work period, a five to twenty-minute story time, at least half an hour for outdoor time, snack, and toileting time, and ample time for dressing and undressing, which is not yet a speedy operation for most children at age five. Discussion time must be included but might be part of the snack period, an opener for the day, or scheduled twice a week once the framework of basically unchangeable activity is set. The daily program often is built on activities of the day before, and unexpected interruptions (the new litter of hamsters, or a sudden snowstorm) must be built into the curriculum too. Compared with the formal programming of the upper grades the kindergarten program may seem too amorphous for a person who must know ahead of time what each hour will bring. But such people are not counting on the children. With plenty of materials and well-utilized space, children will offer many clues for a teacher to pursue. She must be on her toes and ready to be a resource person and guide. She must prepare materials and know the song she will teach. But while she knows in broad terms how her day with the kindergartners will go, one of the pleasures in working with young children is the excitement of exploring new paths opened by any new group of children. This is what keeps the teacher herself a learner and gives teaching its spark and zest.

Planning the Work Period

During a work period or free play, as it is called in some places, children may enjoy one or several activities. The organization of this basic aspect of the kindergarten program must allow for time to make up one's mind, time to get involved, perhaps time to change one's mind and try something else, and time to put away materials and products. Usually this period lasts from forty-five minutes to an hour and a half, depending on the maturity of the children, and therefore must be scheduled so that latitude of ten or fifteen minutes will not be affected by prescribed yard time, going home time, or anything else that is unchangeable.

In many kindergartens it is the first experience of the day, with children entering and immediately picking up their activities and friends with zest. In other situations scheduled activities like assembly, music, and outdoor yard allotment mean postponing this period until later in the morning. At the beginning one can start with the shorter work period (forty-five minutes) and watch to see how it is going; then the time can be extended to what seems reasonable for a group, without going beyond their powers of comfortable endurance (one and a half hours). The work period should be part of every day's program unless the children will be away all morning on a trip or other special activity. The important thing is that the children do not feel hurried and frustrated too soon after they have become absorbed and fascinated by what they are doing. At the other end is the teacher's sensitivity in timing to fatigue, high-pitched excitement, and peak of endeavor. Energy and time must still be available for putting things away, and ending on a note of positive achievement is more desirable than ending with a sense of letdown because one did not know when to stop. Play has a way of petering out. A session should stop before this happens.

Records

One last aspect of the organizational activities of the teacher shall be considered, namely the keeping of records. There are two broad types of records involved; the ones a teacher keeps for her own edification, understanding and planning, that deal with the inner life of her classroom; and the ones that form a part of the total administrative records and add to the long-range view of the child's experience at school.

Records of the inner life of the class. Here again we can divide records into two types: those of individual children and those showing the dynamics of group action. For the first, we recommend *Observing and Recording Children's Behavior*[1] which deals in minute detail with the practical techniques of taking the kinds of notes on individual children that will be useful in gaining an objective picture of a child, thereby leading to better understanding of him and to better preparation for conferences with parents.

[1] Dorothy H. Cohen and Virginia Stern, *Observing and Recording the Behavior of Young Children* (New York, Bureau of Publications, Teachers' College, Columbia University, 1958).

For the group as a whole there are several other techniques, some mentioned in the manual referred to above. The records throughout this volume were largely records of groups in action. Such records are an invaluable source to which to refer when one wishes to go back in time and see what has happened to a group or to individuals. Some teachers keep a log or diary and in this way have a check on what has happened to themselves and the children in their class. It is amazing how much one forgets by Christmas of what occurred in September. Reviewing the development of curriculum this way makes one considerably more sensitive to the subtleties of growth in group life. There are check lists a teacher can make to keep track of the nature of the activities and how often certain materials are used by individuals. Spot-checking during free play on a regular basis can be made simple by preparing ahead of time many copies of the room layout and its basic areas of activity. At some point during the work period a quick glance around and an entry onto that day's room sketch of names in the appropriate areas will eventually give a profile of each child's use of the available opportunities. Such records are of course useful, but they are not records in depth as the individual observations are.

Keeping track in an objective way of what is going on in her class heightens a teacher's awareness of what she herself is doing and is therefore a valuable experience for her. The larger school administration however, has a somewhat different perspective on each class and needs facts and figures to do its own kind of evaluation and satisfy local and state requirements that certain procedures established by law are in actuality being attended to at the school. A teacher thus has to fill out and return to the administration a variety of forms relating to her program and schedule, the health and attendance of the children, reports to, and conferences with, parents, trips away from the building, budget data pertaining to supplies and books, and classroom collections of funds. These often become quite a chore and it is a temptation to attend to them during the times when children are quietly at play. The same times happen to be the best times for observing the children and getting to know them better, so that often administrative efficiency interferes with genuine teaching competency. Requirements vary from school to school and not all forms need immediate attention. Part of a teacher's planning, then, should include an allotment of time for attention to the clerical aspects of her job which, if planned for, could probably be handled with a minimum of time taken from the children themselves.

The time with the children is the most precious time, and should be safeguarded by teachers and administrators alike. The planning and organizing aspects of the job come before and after the time with the children. The more carefully these are attended to the smoother will be the time spent with children in action.

V

beyond the kindergarten room

16

Parents and Teachers Learn from Each Other

Entering school, a child brings something of his home with him, including attitudes and even the very language of his parents. But a teacher's first response, and correctly so, is to the child himself as *she* sees him. She works for the establishment of their *special* relationship, and for the integration of this little individual into the new and unfamiliar world of school. Only in time, as a teacher wants to know a child better still or needs help in understanding certain phases of his behavior does she turn to the parents for help in filling in her own picture of the child.

In reality teachers and parents have somewhat different perceptions of the child whose rearing they share, since their experiences with the child emphasize different, although overlapping aspects of his behavior. Parents know their children's detailed history from birth, remember special events and their effects, and know just how the children will react to certain kinds of people and happenings. They are fully cognizant of the child's uniqueness from long, intense, and intimate association. But parents do not know clearly how their children act among strangers and friends, without familiar family faces nearby; how they react to an authority who is not a parent; in short, how they behave when they are on their own. Nor do parents know how their child compares with others of his age in skills and aptitudes of all kinds.

The teacher on the other hand knows how the child fits into a

355

group, what his social techniques are, and how he takes to learning. But she may have no idea of what the child's fears are and the effects which illness may have had on him. Nor has she any knowledge of the successes and frustrations he may face each day before and after coming to school.

Despite the different perceptions of him that teacher and parent have, the child remains himself throughout. He does not leave parts of him inside or outside the schoolroom door. All of him enters, all of him reacts, all of him feels, all of him leaves in one piece. What happens at home comes to school; what happens at school goes home with him. It follows logically that parent and teacher do well to know how the two parts they observe quite separately merge in the one child. Sharing and comparing their perceptions, teacher and parents together can be most effective in providing for the child. For this a relationship of mutual trust and friendship must be established between teacher and parent.

OBSTACLES TO GOOD PARENT-TEACHER RELATIONS

A common obstacle to the establishment of good rapport right from the beginning is the existence of prejudgment on either side. Sometimes the teacher assumes that the parent does not know much about his own child or the educational process, often because the parent's expressed goals for the child seem somewhat different from her own. Conversely, some parents judge a teacher by hearsay: "I hear the teacher in Room 13 is a horror—everybody says so." Or some mother may feel that she is entrusting her child to someone intellectually or socially her inferior, and is barely tolerant of the teacher.

The teacher, particularly a new one, may worry that the parents are going to be critical of her and that she must impress them with results as soon as possible. Parents on the other hand, particularly those bringing a first child to kindergarten, are apt to be apprehensive about whether this stranger will notice, will try to understand and be able to attend to this child who is so special to them.

Teachers, filled with pride and conscientiousness in their role, may become quite possessive toward "their" children. The parent is even seen as a rival whom one would gladly dispense with so as to avoid any interference. How much more likely are parents, with their emotional investment in a child, to see the teacher as a rival for the child's affection?

Young teachers in particular face a peculiarly sensitive relationship which only time can alter. Barely out of a dependency relationship with their own parents, they may project onto parents in general feelings not quite resolved within themselves. Thus, some very competent teachers are afraid of the parents, afraid that all parents will be condemning and critical; others resent parents because they seem to threaten the teacher's independence of action. Still other young teachers are not sure how they are to talk to an older person now that they are themselves in authority.

These are human feelings, and honest self-evaluation helps to dispel them. The teacher must understand that parents too have human feelings, and perhaps have more to lose or gain from the success or failure of their children. Accepting the reality of this human element in the relationship, and with the welfare of the child as the central objective, the teacher must take the first step. This means being relaxed and easy to talk to. By voice and manner she implies assurance that the communication is not an occasion for attack. In such a climate of acceptance, established by the teacher, parents are better able to meet a teacher halfway. Problems that arise can then be worked out much more readily.

THE PARENTS' POINT OF VIEW

Parents are naturally concerned that when a class is very large the teacher cannot possibly take an interest in each, and that their particular child will surely be the one to miss out. It is important for them to learn early in the year that the teacher, with her training and professional awareness, does plan her program so as to supervise different activities and notice many special characteristics and conditions. A mother may be learning quite a big lesson when she relinquishes some of her jurisdiction over her child to a teacher and then sees that the teacher can be friendly and fair to her child and many others at the same time.

The reassurance that the children will be carefully watched and regarded as individuals is sometimes difficult to communicate to parents with language barriers or different cultural backgrounds. In one unpublished study of school relationships with parents, an analysis of the written communications showed heavy reliance on professional terminology and an overbrisk, clipped manner that was too readily interpreted as coldness and disinterest by the parents. In the cause of administrative efficiency, teacher communication can often fail in its major purpose and leave parents feeling alienated. If there is a distance between parents and teachers because of differences in class and educational background, language, or values, it is the teacher's professional responsibility to assume the leadership necessary for closing the gap between home and school.

ORIENTING PARENTS TO SCHOOL

Some schools have an orientation program in the spring of the year when next fall's kindergarten children are invited to the class for short visits in small groups. The parents also visit, either with the children or separately. On such visits they may be a little awed by the big room and uniform furnishings, and they may worry that their own child would be lost in such a place. However, they also do not fail to notice how the children function without being told to behave or being prodded to perform in this or that activity; they are impressed that little kindergartners can be so big. On such a first visit parents are likely to observe some interesting equipment and the presence of materials which they may not be familiar with.

When, after the visit to the kindergarten, there is a meeting of the parents with the teacher, meaningful questions are apt to be asked pertaining to health and to learning in the kindergarten, and the teacher has a chance to give important advance knowledge about regulations and procedure. All of this contributes to mutual understanding and friendly acquaintance.

Making arrangements for visits and meetings takes both time and interest on the part of the teacher, the principal, and some representative group of parents. However, when there is goodwill and active cooperation (not mere politeness) arrangements for early visits and meetings can be successful and the school year can begin with a head start on good adjustment.

GETTING TO KNOW PARENTS

In order to establish rapport with parents the teacher needs from the very start of school to be willing to face them: to exchange brief greetings or pleasantries with those who escort children to school, get in touch with those whose children require special attention, and plan for some informal get-together with the group of parents. If there are many parents in one kindergarten room that has double sessions, the teacher would do well not to meet them all at once, for if there are too many she will only behold a sea of faces without distinguishing anyone to remember.

Sometimes an informal social meeting can be arranged at the beginning of the year when some friendly conversation takes place, and refreshments add to the expression of hospitable welcome. Questions of common interest may be discussed according to plan or may be allowed to come up spontaneously. At such a meeting the teacher might convey her special pleasure in kindergarten teaching, and her thoughts about the forthcoming year. She might relate the importance of kindergarten to later school experience or discuss the nature of adjustment to school at this age. She would listen to parents' comments, questions, or practical suggestions, and of course invite their cooperation in carrying out regulations pertaining to health and orderliness in the class.

When a teacher has met the parents and listened to at least some of them, she can say comfortably to a child in class, "I talked with your mother the other day" or remark with a note of cordiality, "I met your mother and father at the meeting last night." And the children do not miss the implication that parents are important to the school, that communication is taking place, and that somehow this is all done in their behalf!

CONDUCTING PARENT MEETINGS

General meetings with small or large groups of parents are considered part of school work for the teacher, and a program of learning for both teacher and parent. The planning, preparation, and aims of the group parent meeting are different from the individual parent-teacher conference which we will discuss later.

The number of meetings a year that teachers and parents can be involved in depends on the school. If the school is a private cooperative with parent participation in the classroom, meetings may be held as frequently as once a month because of the need to interpret the program and evaluate the techniques of parent participation. In other schools, where teachers have limited time and parents limited availability, two or three meetings a year may be all that can be arranged. In any case, even after careful thinking and extensive planning the meetings themselves do not always fulfill the teacher's expectations for attendance, and she asks, "How do you get parents to come? Those who do get to the meeting appreciate it and are glad they came, but how do you get *everybody* to come?"

There are many, sometimes surprising reasons why parents do not come to school meetings. The easiest assumption is that the parents are not sufficiently interested in their children or the school to make the effort. A small minority of parents do indeed fall into this category, but it is hardly the usual reason for nonattendance. Most parents care very much about their children's welfare; but they may not come to a meeting because they cannot get a baby-sitter or perhaps cannot afford one. Fathers may get home late for dinner and mothers may be just too exhausted after a hard day to get dressed for going out. During the winter months there can be weeks of illness in a family, as one child gets out of bed only for another to get in! Differences in language, clothing, customs, and values cause feelings of discomfort among some parents, and they are self-conscious about appearing at school meetings if they feel inferior because they speak with an accent, have not had much of an education themselves, or are otherwise different from the school personnel. Well-educated parents on the other hand sometimes feel that school meetings are repetitious of what they already know, and not interesting enough to attract them.

Then there are the parents who have not set foot in an elementary school since the day they themselves were graduated. Depending on their own childhood experience as pupils, they may approach reentry into the school in their new capacity as parents with the same feelings of awe, fear, dislike, or nostalgia they had as children. These feelings are often like the feelings with which a student-teacher first meets as colleagues and peers the teachers whom she has revered, respected, or feared as a student.

The last group of reasons has to do with the meetings themselves—their nature and character, and the spirit in which they are planned. Schools that are eager for parent-teacher relationships have tried various techniques to encourage parent attendance at class or school meetings. At one school with a large number of working mothers, the administration arranged for a box-supper meeting right after work, with parents and teachers arriving in work clothes. Coffee was served by the school and the meeting got off to an early enough start for parents to be home in time to see their youngsters off to bed. At another school, located near a new housing development teaming with young mothers and baby carriages, it was realized that provision would have to be made for the toddler and infant brothers and sisters of their kindergarten children if the mothers were to come. An after-school meeting was arranged with baby-sitters from among parents of older grades, and a contribution of toys and play materials from the kindergarten. At still another school with a large percentage of foreign-born parents, the business of the meeting was always translated on the spot by a willing bilingual parent interpreter. Many a seemingly knotty problem can be solved with the assistance of those parents who have already established their relationship with the school and who are only too happy to be of assistance in drawing new parents closer to the school community.

The content and procedure of the meetings themselves are something else again. No one enjoys long-winded speeches or being preached to, and parents are no different from other people in this respect. Meetings can and should be interesting, not too long (forty-five minutes to an hour and a half), and should allow for two-way communication. If a topic is to be explored with the help of a speaker, film and moderator, dramatic presentation, or group discussion, the topic must be one that has meaning and appeal to most parents in that group. Uses and values of creative and scientific materials and activities at school, books children enjoy, pursuit of interests through trips and other experiences, discipline at school as opposed to discipline at home—all these lend themselves to displays, workshops, panel discussions, speakers, films, etc. Resource people for such meetings exist in most communities among the professional personnel (doctors, social workers, psychologists, teachers), in film libraries of universities or state departments of education, little theatre groups, state and local organizations devoted to parent and family education, and of course the parents and teachers themselves who have much to offer.

The most important part of the planning however, is not the speaker or special film, helpful as these are. It is rather the pertinence of the topic chosen for the group for which it is intended. For example, there are general topics having to do with the development and behavior of preschool children which absorb young parents, but these topics may bore mothers of third and fourth children who have been through it all before. Groups vary so much from each other that one group would do well to talk about how children of five can be helped to become more independent, whereas another may need to explore the question of limits for their self-sufficient but much-too-daring five-year-olds. One group may need help in handling brother-sister conflicts at home that are spilling over into school behavior, another may welcome guidance in the selection of good books and play materials for Christmas presents. By observing the children at school, listening to the questions parents ask, recognizing differences in school and home outlook and what these stem from, a teacher can tailor a meeting to fit the needs of her parent group. As a further aid it may be helpful to a teacher to sound out parent representatives before making a final decision on choice of topic. Whatever the decision however, it must be made to fit the needs of a specific group and not be arbitrarily pulled out of a hat.

Announcements of meetings can be genuinely inviting or dutifully correct and uninspiring. For example, a letter to parents which says: "Would you like to know what your children talk about? Then come to hear a report on 'Children's Conversations and Discussions in the Kindergarten' and learn the deeper meaning of children's language" would seem more inviting than an Announcement that "The subject of tonight's parent meeting is a talk on Children's Language." Or, a statement that describes the topic for discussion as: "How to promote good health and natural stamina of young children" would sound more interesting than one that says bluntly: "Health Rules for Your Child to Follow."

One teacher, in planning her workshop meeting for the year, was able to have the school secretary type all the invitations to the parents on post cards (they could easily have been run off on a ditto machine). Then she told the class of five-year-olds about the meeting at which their parents would use the children's materials, and to the great interest of the children the teacher read aloud all the parents' names and addresses on the post cards. Then the teacher took the class to the nearby post office and each child dropped a card in the mail slot. As the teacher expected, this much children's interest resulted in their concern with the meeting which in turn produced strong pressures: "You *have* to come to the meeting, daddy—I sent you a letter." The teacher attributed the unusually good attendance—some 90%—to the children's persuasion.

Some teachers, appreciating the meaning and the effect of children's participation in planning a parents' meeting, help the children prepare a snack for the evening meeting and of course let the parents know about it in the notice. Other teachers arrange to have a committee of parents attend to the invitations and reminders, sometimes by means of a telephone chain. But whatever method is used to summon parents, it must be remembered that tricks to gain attendance do not lead to *consistent* effect. Only sincerity of purpose and the actual development of suitable programs can do that.

BUILDING OVERALL COMMUNICATION

Continued communication between parents and teachers throughout the year goes beyond the establishment of rapport and orientation to include sharing and mutual evaluation of the children's growth. There are several techniques for doing this, some verbal, some written. Traditionally schools have prepared report cards on children's achievement and deportment, indicating the level of a child's performance in subject matter areas. Carrying forward the same idea but adapting it to the curriculum in the kindergarten, some schools enumerate various activities and kinds of behavior, such as language, music, painting, cleanliness, cooperation, and effort, and give a grade for each. Recognizing that such report cards are probably pretentious for the kindergarten and perhaps ambiguous in evaluative worth, other schools limit the grades to Satisfactory and Needs Improvement, which is somewhat more realistic. In a further attempt to remove a tone of judgment and severity, yet aiming to do right by kindergarten parents, some schools adorn the card with charming and colorful pictures and perhaps some wording reminiscent of a first-grade reader.

However, no matter what the format the terms for evaluation used by any school are actually representative of the point of view in that school or school system of what it considers important and appropriate for children to be learning. With this view in mind let us examine one of these adapted cards. It is a four page booklet. The front page has a bright picture of a little red schoolhouse with stick figures of children and a place for dates, the name of the child, school, and teacher. On the inside two pages are twenty-one panels with colorful stick drawings, appropriate descriptions of activities, and space for marks. The twenty-one activities are:

I keep materials from my mouth.
I use a handkerchief properly.
I put on and take off my own wraps.
I follow directions accurately.
I express myself with art materials.
I finish my work promptly.
I work and play well with others.
I speak clearly in a pleasing voice.
I keep my hands to myself.
I sing songs in tune.
I respond well to music.
I share my ideas and evaluate results.
I listen when others are speaking.
I enjoy stories, books, and poetry.
I take responsibility.
I bring in worthwhile materials.
I obey quickly and cheerfully.
I relax at rest time.
I come neat and clean.
I attack simple problems.
I get weighed and measured.

On the third page of this report there are three lines for the teacher's comments for each of the four periods during the year that a child is marked. On the last page is a record of attendance and a reassuring note "To the Parent—Our Partner" stating that no opportunity is ever lost in the development of the child's personality along happy and wholesome channels.

On the surface the report sounds reasonable enough, since a teacher cannot evaluate kindergarten children in academic achievement. But does this list represent an achievable, realistic, or even healthy ideal of behavior for a five-year-old? And are these items the kinds on which one should pass judgment? "I obey quickly and cheerfully," "I finish my work promptly" are exaggerated virtues for children even older than five, aside from their value as end goals in childhood. "I share my ideas and evaluate results" is closer to high school level than kindergarten. And "I keep my hands to myself" sounds confusing. What sort of prohibition does it imply? Also, must a child "sing songs in tune" in order to qualify? Should a child be officially judged for a skill, singing in tune, which is in part physical and developmental and in part experiential? And for a child of five are neatness and cleanliness on arrival at school not his mother's responsibility far more than his?

It is conceivable that some teachers, because they are charitably disposed or for the sake of expediency, will mark "S" (satisfactory) for everything. Parents receiving such a card note the list of "S"'s and may not bother to read the full listing of "subjects," content only that the child is satisfactory in the teacher's eyes. But another parent may take seriously the "attacking problems" and "evaluating results," and may conclude that they have a child who is thoroughly exceptional. On the other hand they may think he is suspiciously good, or they might even wonder if they themselves measure up to such virtues.

It is important to uphold standards for children. But it is somewhat unfair to pass judgment based on long-term objectives on a young child who is still in the process of growth and development. Rate of growth, pace, and pattern, are somewhat different for individual children. The same behavior can mean quite different things when looked at in the light of a child's total growth rather than referred to as an arbitrary adult standard applied undiscriminatingly to all. Thus, hitting may at the moment be a positive step forward for a child who has hitherto been withdrawn, although it is hoped that he will with guidance mature into other forms of self-assertion. Hitting may also express a residue of unhappiness in a child who has suffered, may indicate sturdy self-sufficiency but poor techniques, or may mean frustration and despair. Such differences are hard to indicate in a simple list of desirable virtues and skills which represent high-level functioning for adults, and therefore far-reaching goals for children. Realistic evaluation of young children will show a composite view of how they are functioning, compared not only to long-range ideals but to achievable performance at the tender age of five, with individual variations noted and acounted for.

For this reason many schools encourage the teacher to write brief personal statements on the child's progress and particular needs of that year, which allows them to describe that child as he is without the restricting framework of a rather final-sounding list of virtues and faults. Some private schools with small classes per teacher are able to send a full written report to each parent. Following is one such report:

Jeff has been a joy to all of us in school. It's true he had a poor start: he was tired and whiny and inactive; he had tonsil trouble, and an accident, the outgrowing of his nap at home, plus the operation—enough to wear out a much sturdier being than a sensitive four-and-a-half-year old boy. But Jeff has managed to work through all his obstacles and interferences with remarkable resilience and strength. He seems to be in very good physical shape now, and, considering his past troubles, his attendance has been very good—82%.

Jeff is a happy child: always smiling and telling the teachers and the children about the good things in his life. He talks about his family, and each particular member, and sometimes requests that each one be mentioned alongside his name on his paintings or other creations. He likes to tell of interesting trips with his parents, but especially about going to Temple with grandpa, and hearing the "Rabbi song." He often invites children to share in his activities, and loves nothing better than to pass something out for everybody. Almost everybody is Jeff's friend, and Emily has been devoted to him. He is free in expressing himself with the teachers, and is often affectionate with them. But when something frustrating happens and Jeff loses his temper, he becomes very angry and uses his strong fist. Earlier in the year Jeff would scratch and bite in anger, but doesn't any more. Outside of those tough moments, Jeff is busy working and *learning*.

Jeff made many planned, structured and functional block buildings, which proved to be particularly effective and satisfying to him. Whatever Jeff does he does wholeheartedly and creatively, and often involves and leads other children in the activity—whether it be building, painting, investigating the clock, or finding out the uses and names of the bones in the body. Jeff has actually taught the "Rabbi song" to several children and entertained the class with it. His interest in bones led us to singing "the bones" folk song, and to interest and learning about parts of the body for several children. He so persisted with his inquiry into time and clock inspection that he advanced considerably in his number knowledge.

Though Jeff really appreciates everything we do in school, cooking does hold something special for him. He is very patient about waiting and watching, always eager to find out what happens; and he likes particularly to take home some of the cooking products.

A great deal of thought and care went into the writing of that report on Jeff as well as sensitivity to what is important to a growing five-year-old. It gave encouragement and pride to the parents too because it was honest, it did not hide difficulties and did not overlook real attributes. The report is good; it gives an account of a child's year, it reflects the school and the teacher, and it is a generous communication to the parent. But can we expect many teachers to be able to write at such length? No.

Nonetheless, whether long or short, whether in card form or in the form of a written report, the evaluation of a child must be carefully conceived. Parents hang onto the teacher's word, and school reports mean much to them. Teachers must therefore reconcile two conflicting views as they evaluate a child's behavior: (a) the goals in adult life toward which we are educating children, and (b) the present stage of development of an individual child, with consideration to what he has developed *from*. This puts any child at a point which is transitional. He is in process and therefore should not be judged when evaluated, but described objectively and sympathetically. Does this mean one cannot say unpleasant things? No. If a child is having difficulties the parents must be helped to face them. But one must be sure these are lags in *childhood* behavior and not simply deviations from *adult* norms.

Parents and teachers do need to stop and take account of how a child is growing—how he handles materials, how he takes to those demands necessary for group functioning, what kinds of satisfactions he finds, and what he cannot cope with—because without a realistic look at him they cannot successfully guide his growth. But perhaps it is wise to remember that what appears in writing seems somehow very final. Too often one cannot communicate fully by means of written reports. Where the gap between school and home philosophy is wide, there can be real misinterpretation.

THE CLASS REPORT

One teacher solved this dilemma by sending a comprehensive report to all the parents, entitled *A Review of the Year's Work in Class*. The report had to be prepared by the teacher well before the end of the year. With this class report every set of parents also received a brief paragraph relating to specific interests or strengths of their child during that year, associated with the program described in the class report. One such notation was, "Andy asked many questions about the horse on the farm trip and enjoyed books about horses." Also, "Alice has recently become interested in painting, and is now often the first one at the easel." This is concrete observation of meaningful activity for that child, and adds a personal quality to the class report. But even without the individual statement the objective report in black and white would enable the parents to learn from the teacher what kind of schooling and what kind of activity and learning there is in the kindergarten. If photographs of children in action could be attached the report would be that much more vivid and graphic. The class report could be approximately three to five pages in length, depending on the style of writing. It may be in outline form, organized statements or description, or short essays for each month. If after receipt of this the parents also meet to discuss the report and to ask questions of the teacher, they would really have a chance to learn important facts as well as values in their child's education. As far as the teacher is concerned preparing such a report would require conscious awareness about her own work and special focus on what would be significant to parents. There would be real learning for her as a result of the parents' discussion.

CONFERENCES

Good written reports are so difficult to produce that most kindergartens do not send them out at all, relying instead on personal conferences as a means of communicating with parents. In many school systems time is set aside for such conferences, which are valuable because they lend themselves best of all methods to the two-way exchange so essential to real communication. A great deal has been written in the last two decades by experienced parent educators on the nature, the value, and the problems of parent-teacher conferences, often in the form of well-written and inexpensive pamphlets and articles. Perhaps the most inclusive of these is the book by James L. Hymes, Jr., *Effective Home-School Relations*,[1] which is full of warmth and positive constructive thinking. All writers in the field stress the dynamic nature of the give-and-take involved in a conference, the necessary restraint and empathy needed in good listening, and the importance of purposefulness and objectivity in sharing knowledge on the one hand coupled with the willingness to learn facts and a point of view from the parents on the other. The ultimate purpose of an individual conference is for a teacher and a parent to exhange thoughts and feelings about a child in a direct face-to-face communication with each other. In order for the teacher to be relaxed and open-minded she should not be too determined or set about the outcome. Human beings are full of surprises, and one can never be too sure that one's understanding of another, even a child, is totally correct. Foregone conclusions and pat assumptions may close off the possibility of learning something really vital about a child or his parent's relations with him.

If the teacher is already somewhat acquainted with the parent and has some understanding and interest in the child, the parent will be put at ease and feel disposed both to contribute and to learn from the teacher. On the other hand if the parent is unprejudiced about the teacher and has some appreciation of, and a basic respect for, the school, this will help the teacher to communicate more freely and listen more warmly. In an informal conference lasting from twenty minutes to an hour of talking together, the parent can gain assurance of the teacher's genuine concern for the child, knowledge of the child's status in the group, areas of needed help perhaps, and areas of special satisfaction to the child.

The teacher can learn from the parent a special dimension of the child's worth, his status in the family, some important detail of the child's physical needs, history, or important family event. One teacher learned from a conference that there was an invalid uncle living with the family, which helped her to understand the child's preoccupation with certain medical matters in his play. Another teacher realized from the conference that the mother's anxiety about doing a good job as a parent was causing her to be overly demanding, and the child's tension could reasonably be traced to this.

A common difficulty for a teacher in facing a parent during a con-

[1] James L. Hymes, Jr., *Effective Home-School Relations* (Englewood Cliffs, N.J., Prentice-Hall, Inc., 1953).

ference is a sense of guilt or uncertainty if she does not happen to like that particular parent's child as much as she does the other children. In that case the teacher might ask herself before the conference, "Can I, or anyone, really love *all* children, and love them equally?" The truthful answer would be "no." There may well be children in the class who do not arouse a teacher's love; there may be a nagging one, one with unpleasant mannerisms, an irritating bully, a tiresome whiner, or a sulky or a sneaky one. A child with such a trait may be a challenge and may even arouse sympathy but not admiration, and rarely love, from a teacher. Yet the teacher, both because she is a teacher and because she is an adult, must be *fair* to such a child, must look at him objectively (she can do that better than his mother can), and by all means must notice his good qualities and whatever constructive interests he might have. In this way she can gain some understanding of the child's positive drives as well as the occasions or causes of his distress. Then a teacher may share such observations and understanding with the parent, to whom they can be of vital interest. The teacher would also hear of the mother's worry or interest, impatience, and even burden concerning this child and gain some realization of the life and love this mother has with the child in a continuous way. The teacher might acquire from such a conference a special respect or regard for the mother, and hence added insight into the child. Or the teacher might come out from the conference with added sympathy and respect for the child as she sees him in a very tough spot at home. In any case the teacher's and mother's thinking on the child's behalf and their mutual increased understanding of him is bound to benefit the child and even make him more loveable! Good communication in a conference invariably affects the teacher's attitude towards the child, and thus the child himself.

DIFFERING PERSPECTIVES OF PARENT AND TEACHER

The teacher may have a child whom she regards as fairly average in personality and ability. Then she hears from the parents about his unique gifts and his importance within the family, and she feels the charm of the child as it is shown in the depth and warmth of the parents' expression; the teacher catches some of the parents' glow and adds a line or a word of extra value to her picture of that child. And the mother, having thus expressed herself, is often apt to say, "I suppose all parents tell you their child is just wonderful. I really want to hear about the bad things too." One wonders then whether the standards by which one judges a child as average are sufficiently inclusive!

DO YOU GIVE ADVICE?

One of the common and confusing challenges to a teacher is the matter of giving advice to parents: should you, should you not, and if you do, how much? It is common knowledge that advice is easier to give than to take, and in the parent-teacher relation this is no less true than in human relations in general. Yet parents ask for advice and a teacher is often beseiged with pleas for specific help: "How do you punish a child? What do you do about stubbornness?" "He keeps asking how to spell words. Shall I tell him?" "Exactly what shall I say when he asks . . . . ?" A look at the commonsense understanding in this matter tells us that people do not take advice as a rule because the advice may not exactly fit their own perception of the situation, may not really answer their underlying question behind their obvious one, or may represent a solution impossible to fulfill for that person at that time. The teacher, in giving advice, may have spent years of learning from schooling and experience before she was able to come to an approach to the problem that satisfied her. Yet when she gives the parent the end result of her experience the answer may enter the parent's ears as a mechanical formula to be applied without understanding or flexibility, and will possibly be more damaging than useful as a result. Very few teachers would presume to dictate to a parent about any problem. But few teachers enjoy disappointing a parent and fewer still like to have it appear that they do not know how to solve the parents' dilemma. It is human to take pleasure in revealing wisdom and knowledge to those who look to us for such leadership. True leadership however, also takes into account the ways by which those led can be helped to grow in understanding themselves. It is wise therefore, in response to requests for direct and specific advice, to try to involve the parent in solving the problem so that he can himself see the reasoning behind the solution.

Let us suppose, for example, that a parent asks a teacher for a list of good children's books to read to the child during the summer. An experienced teacher could easily compile a list of her favorites and might even have one readily available for all the parents. The parent would feel safe in the choices and there would be a kind of minimum guarantee that the child would gain from the selections. But suppose that instead of merely supplying a list the teacher asked the mother to browse among the books in the classroom, had a little conversation with her about the subjects in children's books, the styles of writing illustrated in several of the classroom samples, and the particular child's interests and preferences. In this way the mother would herself discover some values in good literature for young children, and would be able to make up part of the list by using her new-found understanding of what to look for. Conceivably, this could be quite stimulating to the teacher and certainly would furnish more far-reaching information than the mother at first asked for.

Or a parent might ask advice about a suitable trip. In that case, along with giving the name and address of a place, the teacher could invite the mother to join a class trip and in this way help to see at first hand the values in good trips for children.

The more complicated question "How do I deal with his stubbornness?" is worthy of more than a technique. For one thing, what does the mother mean by *stubbornness?* What might she be doing that is causing the child to resist her so strongly? Is her concern truly justified? Does the matter call for a shift in the relationship between the two? Only as the mother can look at the problem with the teacher, only as they pull it apart together, can they reach a decision that the mother will be capable of carrying out. Advice in such a case is breath wasted if the mother does not understand the reasoning behind the decision.

A common method of giving advice is the recommendation of suitable adult reading on varying aspects of child growth and child rearing. But too often we see how very well-read parents keep right on reading more and more, and become less and less spontaneous, natural, and effective as parents. There must be self-awareness and conviction along with reading if the books are to become a supplement and stimulation to, but not the chief source of, guidance to parents.

HELPING PARENTS DEVELOP SUITABLE STANDARDS

Although the teacher needs to be judicious and thoughtful in giving advice to parents, she can do an important service by pointing out the value of things which parents may have taken for granted or overlooked. For example, modern urban and suburban parents are often eager to introduce their preschool children as soon as possible to such public cultural institutions as museums, zoos, botanical gardens, and popular spectacles such as Disneyland and Freedomland. In their zeal to give children opportunities, parents act on the naïve assumption that a child is never too young for such public adventure; they overlook the possibilities of suitable education and entertainment nearer home, even within the site of family living. A teacher might point out how various home operations in which a child may be allowed to have some safe part are new and interesting. These could include errands to repair shops, really helping once in a while with cooking and cleaning or animal feeding, taking part in shopping for food, clothes and housewares, or taking a trip to the father's place of work. The mother, having the intimate relation with the child and being herself really involved in all these activities, exerts greater influence than she realizes on the preschool child's attitudes toward responsibility and toward work and workers in ethical as well as material standards. Thus, during daily activities and companionship a mother is the greatest teacher to a kindergartner; she can bring much stimulation to her child if she can be helped to see where the possibilities are. Parents who feel they do not do much for their children because they do not have the time or energy to take them places, are very appreciative of the teacher's recognition of the values of good home experiences.

VISITING THE HOME

Still another way of communicating with parents, aside from the written and oral reports, group meetings, and individual conferences, is a home visit by the teacher. In some situations this might serve as an initial acquaintance, as when the teacher is allowed a certain number of days before school starts officially to call on each of her new kindergarten children for a brief greeting to the child and his family. Such visits give the teacher an impression of each child's home and helps in her later communication with child and parents after school starts. However desirable this practice is, it is practical only when special time is provided, where groups are not overwhelmingly large, and where the visits would be acceptable and welcome in the particular community. For example, one teacher who called on a child of a poor family was regarded with suspicion and self-consciousness as if she were an investigator from the Welfare Department. Another teacher, calling on a child of a very well-to-do family, was "entertained" by the servant. In neither case was there genuine communication during the visit. Although the teacher learned more about the children's environmental background than she might have otherwise, this was not enough for the expenditure of time and energy involved.

Sometimes a teacher visits a child's home at the invitation of the child or mother, or both. This is an individual social visit, for lunch, perhaps, or tea, or even supper, and it usually takes place in the middle of the year when it can be particularly important to the child. By that time the child knows his teacher well enough to want her to come to his house. He is apt to assume that if the teacher is willing to come to his house she not only likes him, but his whole family! To the teacher such a visit may mean the opportunity for more intimate contact with a child who needs just that, or a way of gaining some insight into the child's home life as it affects him (seeing his siblings, for example, or his toys). Usually she gains appreciation of the mother's total responsibilities and influence as well. The social experience with the teacher at home frequently results in a livelier social experience at school for a shy child. Of course the teacher would not have time for many of these visits, nor would she be likely to get invitations from all the children in her class, but the few social visits that she could make would give her and the parents the opportunity to improve communication and relationships.

Actually, a rather special purpose served by a home visit is the possibility of alleviating a troubled situation at school. If a teacher feels by the middle of the year that she is not reaching a child, is not able to cope with a child's apparent tensions or aggressions or unhappiness of some kind, and is not successful in establishing a good communication with the mother, she might well improve things by making a friendly call. In getting a glimpse of the child in his own setting and having some conversation with the mother on a subject other than school and the child, she may gain more in understanding her "problem" child than she realizes. One teacher, for example, learned of the tremendous importance of the family dog to both of the parents, and this enabled her to understand the persistent animal play the child was involved in at school.

Another helpful purpose served by visiting is keeping up a contact with a child who has been out of school for a long while. A five-year-old who is out of school for a lengthy period of time because of ill health responds with pride and pleasure at being remembered and still included in the still novel position of school membership. The consideration and thoughtfulness expressed in this gesture to an isolated child pays rich rewards in his later ability to find his way back again with security and ease.

MAINTAINING HOME-SCHOOL RELATIONS BY MAIL

One other effective and expressive way of communication during a child's prolonged absence is a letter or card written by the teacher or by the children under the teacher's guidance. Such communication with an absent member also provides opportunity for original expression. Some children like to send a drawing, some dictate a proper "How are you? Hope you'll get well soon," and others like to tell some news, such as "Mike the turtle got lost again," or "Guess what happened to Janie—she threw up." But whatever the content of the child's letter, the teacher-initiated communication between school and home impresses the child and it speaks to the parents as well. It speaks of personal interest.

PARENTS COME TO SCHOOL

Let us now consider briefly visits moving in another direction: *from* the home *to* the school. Mothers, so interested in the five-year-old's school experiences, would be the first to benefit from a direct visit. Coming into the kindergarten, a mother could observe how the child actually fares. She could observe his special associates, the atmosphere of the work and play of which her child is a part, and the way the teacher manages the group as well as the way she treats different individuals. The mother may help out here and there or she may remain an observer; she may be shown special things by her own child or by other children; then at the end she may talk briefly with the teacher, ask some questions perhaps, or share impressions.

Although fathers are seldom able to visit school, those whose occupations permit them to bring the child to school and walk into the kindergarten once in a while, or who can take time for an hour's visit in class, find themselves especially appreciated not only by their own child but by the entire class. Many men find small children's work appealing in its earnestness, and genuinely interesting and surprising in purposefulness. If a father happens to be a large man he may at first feel self-conscious in the midst of the crowded heads and bodies down below, but if a teacher can direct his attention to a discussion among several children working on a building, to an expression of opinions by two children looking at a book on flight, to the muscular expression of concentration on the face (including mouth and tongue) of a child using a hammer, or to spirited and abandoned singing, the most likely response from the father will be something such as, "If I were a pupil here I'd never want to leave." Even a brief contact with a visiting father is impressive to the children. And if the father is also able to *do* something in the kindergarten —to show or demonstrate the tools or products of his trade or profession— or if he happens to be a fireman, farmer, plumber, manufacturer, doctor, musician, or whatever, then his status and that of his child will rise to great heights among the kindergarten people. What seems like a mere visit by a father can entail significant communication between teacher, parent, and children, increasing mutual awareness.

THE WHOLE FAMILY IS IMPORTANT

Other members of the kindergarten child's family may have an opportunity and interest in visiting the kindergarten too, and may make their contribution. Grandparents, whether young or elderly, can bring a special affection or friendship; sometimes they bring items or language of a different culture from the one prevailing in the immediate community. The child's grandparent will most likely not be living in the same home but only visiting him, and this makes the grandparent especially important. Grandparents, like parents, may be people of special skills, hobbies, or talents that could be of interest and perhaps even assistance to the class. In one New Jersey town several years ago the principal sent out a questionnaire to grandparents inquiring into their abilities, interests, and available time for help in the kindergarten. The response was substantial and that year grandparents were in the kindergarten classroom, reading to children, sewing doll's clothes, helping with children's clothing, playing the piano, and helping the teacher with materials. What an interesting contact that was for the teacher, meeting and communicating so usefully with members of another generation!

Visits from older brothers or sisters, if an occasion permits, are also a meaningful home-school communication as far as the kindergarten child and teacher are concerned. An infòrmal, sincere welcome from the teacher invariably helps the older child to feel at home and to enjoy surveying or trying out kindergarten play materials, which are always appealing to the bigger children. Then, when the older child says, "You are lucky to have such nice things to play with!" the younger one feels happy and privileged, although he usully does not say anything about it.

PETS ARE PART OF THE FAMILY

Sometimes family pets can visit the kindergarten to add to the communication between home and school, and may help the child to improve his status in the group. When Sheila showed envy of another child who legitimately held attention and admiration from the group, the teacher allowed her to bring her new pet kitten to school. This was rather complicated to arrange, since the mother had to bring the kitten and then return to take it home, but it proved to be so important to Sheila that the teacher allowed the kitten to be brought a second time. The children gave loving and undivided attention to the lively, cuddly kitten, and Sheila was just as pleased as if the attention had been given all to her.

Thus, going to kindergarten need not mean to a child a sharp break with his past and his home at all, but could signify a continuity and extension of the world he knows. When the school invites parents for something pleasant and does not summon them only for trouble, a child enjoys his family's participation and feels secure in the knowledge that all concerned have a strong interest in him.

Bibliography

Baruch, Dorothy W., *Parents and Children Go to School: Adventuring in Nursery School and Kindergarten* (Chicago, Scott, Foresman & Company, 1939).

————, *Parents Can be People* (New York, Appleton-Century-Crofts, 1944).

Bettelheim, Bruno, *Dialogues with Mothers* (New York, The Free Press of Glencoe, 1962).

Beyer, Evelyn, *Sharing A New Level in Teacher-Parent Relationships* (Chicago, National Association for Nursery Education, 155 E. Ohio St., 1959).

Brim, Orville G., *Education for Child Rearing* (New York, Russell Sage Foundation, 1959).

Dept. of Elementary School Principals, *Happy Journey—Preparing Your Child for School* (Washington, 1201 16th St., N.W.).

D'Evelyn, Katherine, *Individual Parent Conferences* (New York, Bureau of Publications, Teachers College, Columbia University, 1945).

English, O. S., and Foster, Constance J., *Fathers Are Parents, Too* (New York, G. P. Putnam's Sons, 1951).

Gilkeson, Elizabeth C., *Let's Talk About Our Children*, Bank Street College Publication No. 88 (New York, Bank Street College, 69 Bank St.).

Grant, Eve H., *Parents and Teachers as Partners* (Chicago, Science Research Associates, 1959).

Hymes, James L. Jr., *Effective Home-School Relations* (Englewood Cliffs, N.J., Prentice-Hall, Inc., 1953).

Kawin, Ethel, *A Guide for Child Study Groups* (Chicago, Science Research Associates, 1959).

Langdon, Grace, and Stout, Irving, *Teacher-Parent Interviews* (Englewood Cliffs, N.J., Prentice-Hall, Inc., 1954).

National Education Association, Dept. of Classroom Teachers, *Parent-Teacher Relationships* (Washington, 1201 16th St., N.W.).

Norton, Edith N., *Parent Education in the Nursery School* (Washington, Association for Childhood Education International, 1949).

Osborne, Ernest, *The Parent-Teacher Partnership* (New York, Bureau of Publications, Teachers College, Columbia University, 1959).

Piers, Maria, *How To Work With Parents* (Chicago, Science Research Associates, 1955).

Rudolph, Marguerita, "A Parents' Workshop," *The Journal of Nursery Education*, Nov., 1962 (Chicago, 155 E. Ohio St.).

Strang, Ruth, *Reporting to Parents* (New York, Bureau of Publications, Teachers College, Columbia University, 1947).

Weill, Blanche C., *Through Children's Eyes* (New York, Island Workshop Press, 1940).

Williams, Irene, *Strengthening Family Life; How Much Can a Teacher Do?* (New York, Welfare League of America, Inc., 1952).

Sources of publications for parents:

Association for Childhood Education International, 3615 Wisconsin Ave., N.W., Washington 16, D.C.

Bank Street College Publications, Bank Street College, 69 Bank Street, New York 14, N.Y.

Bureau of Publications, Teachers College, Columbia University, New York 27, N.Y.

Child Study Association of America, 9 E. 89th St., New York 28, N.Y.

Children's Bureau, Department of Health, Education and Welfare, Washington 25, D.C.

Human Relations Aids, 104 E. 25th St., New York 3, N.Y.

Metropolitan Life Insurance Company, 1 Madison Ave., New York 10, N.Y.

National Association for Mental Health, 10 Columbus Circle, New York 19, N.Y.

National Education Association, 1201 16th St., N.W., Washington, D.C.

Parents' Magazine, 52 Vanderbilt Avenue, New York, N.Y.

Play Schools Association, 120 W. 57th St., New York 19, N.Y.

Public Affairs Pamphlets, 22 E. 38th St., New York 16, N.Y.

Science Research Associates, 259 E. Erie St., Chicago 11, Ill.

17

Kindergarten Is School

Let us review the contents of each of the preceding parts in order to assess what "school" is for our four to six-year-old *preschoolers*.

In Part I we looked at the children who come to kindergarten. We did not see them as pupils in the pedagogical sense, but as immature and tender young beings with physical and psychological dependence on adults. We noticed their many strengths, their need to exercise and experiment with growing muscles, their capacity for developing friendships, their eagerness to nourish the growing powers of their minds. We saw the teacher as one immersed in her work with her heart as well as her intellect, for she appreciates and enjoys the children and feels for and with them, even as she observes and studies them objectively.

We saw the many different ways in which the teacher shares with and relates to the children, and how children's relationships with each other are tested and tried as part of the human group education in the kindergarten. We saw how teacher attitudes in the classroom create a climate of such intangibles as warmth and freedom and how an atmosphere for learning is dependent on physical vigor and adventurous spirit, on the quality of language, movement, intellectual curiosity, and open communication with the teacher.

In Part II we looked more carefully and critically at what the curriculum can offer children. We considered fully the program itself and what the children do in this program. We explored some of the infinite variety of materials in the immediate physical world of the child, the teacher, and the school, a world in which children behave like scientists, with independent thinking and original investigation. We saw good teachers allow for the gradual gaining of concepts through related experience rather than quickly offering finished and remote abstractions and accumulations of fact regardless of comprehension by the children. We saw concern for honest intellectual probing geared to a constant goal of comprehension.

In Part III we saw the children familiarizing themselves with different media and materials, testing and trying, and free to express feelings and communicate ideas through the objective world. We saw the wide range of language usage in the kindergarten, from simple conversation to detailed accounts of events, from mere ideas to an occasional imaginative literary production. We also saw in Part III how the children learn from the teachers and how teachers in turn learn from the growing children each season, each session, each day.

In Part IV we saw the children's dramatic interest in practical work and their readiness for learning responsibility. We considered the controversial, vital question of discipline, ascertained its aims, questioned ineffectual practices, and examined samples of positive, helpful controls. Surely there can be no schooling of any kind unless discipline is understood, practiced, and evaluated. Negative approaches such as restriction, deprivation, and punishment, need to be questioned for their true usefulness in all situations; control of harmful actions, protection, direction, encouragement, and confidence in the power of a child to learn right from wrong were seen to be positive ways of accomplishing our purposes.

What reasonable conclusions, then, can we draw which would clarify the philosophy and improve the daily practices in our kindergartens? What conclusions would give the student, the young starting teacher, or the older practicing teacher an incentive to think for herself and an urge to learn with the children—conclusions that would expand the teacher's confidence in her own human, rational, and even creative powers as a teacher?

The first conclusion, it seems, would be the need to accept every child for what he is and where he stands, to recognize his natural immaturities, his level of experience, his special dependencies—in short, to know and understand clearly how much and what kind of learning is possible and desirable for the full growth of a five-year-old. Perhaps young children today can go farther than we ever thought before. But there is a point at which the natural limitations of development must make us halt if we are not to pressure unwisely. Let us not try to make five-year-olds behave and learn as though they had lived ten years. Let us not aim for impressive, superficial glibness, but instead for a meeting of those needs of children which, when met, lead to emotional stability and social adaptiveness along with the intellectual expansion which five-year-olds so dearly love.

The second conclusion would be the importance of the teacher's listening to the children and being guided in her actions by what she hears.

In the sixteen preceding chapters we saw the energy, the intelligence, the intensity of feeling which young children generate when they are engaged in meaningful work and play. A teacher who is also meaningfully and gainfully occupied is a listener who catches that special warmth, those inimitable words, the wonder, and even the wisdom which make children's expressions often so impressive. As the teacher listens she grows in understanding and sometimes even in the strength to alter her own attitudes. Listening, she becomes a better planner of experiences suitable for the children; listening, she evaluates and reevaluates the effectiveness of her curriculum.

A third and still more important conclusion for the teacher from the preceding chapters is the inescapable one that four to six-year-olds are avid learners and that kindergarten is real school. We see school as a particular place where a group of children meet regularly with a teacher and where special facilities are provided for all necessary areas of growth that affect learning; school is a structured but flexible program of education appropriate to young children's capacities and carried out in a setting in which both the pleasure and the strife of living and learning are expressed. School is a place where learning goes on in groups but is accomplished by individuals on a personal basis rather than uniformly and by imposition. How, then, does kindergarten differ from the grades in a real school?

Good teaching and learning follow the same principles at any age level, but specific practices must vary with the maturity and readiness of the pupils. In regard to practices, there is much confusion abroad as to how best to encourage and develop mental powers in young children. It is popularly reasoned that since school learning is mainly from books and the good readers are the best learners, the earlier a child learns to read the sooner he will taste of the knowledge books contain. If only this were really true! It seems logical enough on the surface, but it is an unfortunately shallow and misleading conclusion that holds true, when it does, for a very small minority of superior children. The rest still need the many, many firsthand experiences that are necessary before vicarious learning can be meaningful. Even for the precocious ones there is the hidden danger that reading skills learned too early may become an avenue of escape from the more trying challenges of daily living, in which, as five-year-olds, even precocious children are still quite unsophisticated. Confidence for a five-year-old rests on physically-based, directly experienced success of a concrete kind with people and things, and not on entry into the values of the adult world. For the vast majority of children who have arrived at kindergarten age and school entry, much growth in breadth and depth is still indispensable for genuine appreciation and good use of the tools of reading. This is so because reading itself is more than the mere recognition of words and sounds. Unless reading is eventually tied to meaning and purpose it can be a self-defeating activity, or at best limited to utilitarian purposes only. Smooth and easy facility in reading does not occur in the first year of learning, or even in the second for the majority of children. There is no sudden, magic entry into the world of imagination and ideas. There is many a hump to be overcome before reading is as natural as breathing, and a pleasure and joy as a result. Children must be mature enough to have the patience, the perspective, and the motivation before they start on a long-range process that can as easily lead to defeat as to success. Studies indicate that an earlier start does not even shorten the process in the long run, just as early maturation studies on physical skills pointed to a proper moment for the most efficiency in learning.[1]

To be able to handle words and concepts of increasing difficulty and subtlety as one moves beyond the primer, a child's oral and concrete experience with the meaning behind new words must be far ahead of his halting technical proficiency. When his skill grows smooth his mind must be ready to absorb conceptually what his skill can lead him to realize technically: he must *understand* what he can recognize. At five, such conceptualization and vocabulary building grow out of firsthand experience. Consequently, in spite of the fact that it may well be possible to teach kindergartners to read at great cost and effort for many of them and their teachers, it is well to question the value of this. Too early withdrawal from sensory learning may prove to be penny wise and pound foolish in the end.

It has been well brought out in this book and elsewhere that most children of kindergarten age are not quite ready for organized, sequential, academic instruction in reading, writing, and arithmetic, largely as a matter of their overall development at age five. The tension and emphasis on drill in early teaching of a skill, and the raising of a hard-to-reach-goal for young children who have barely begun to find themselves as individuals in an adult-directed world, should cause us to question the drive to earlier and earlier tangible achievement. No matter what the social climate or political considerations may be, teachers of young

---

[1] A. Gesell and Helen Thompson, "Twins T and C from Infancy to Adolescence," *Genetic Psychology Monographs*, Vol. 24 (1941), pp. 3–121; Myrtle B. Mc-Graw, *Growth: A Study of Johnny and Jimmy* (New York, D. Appleton-Century Co., Inc., 1935); Mabel V. Morphett and Carleton Washburne, "When Should Children Begin to Read?," *Elementary School Journal*, Vol. 31 (1931), pp. 496–503; Beatrice E. Bradley, "An Experimental Study of the Readiness Approach to Reading," *Elementary School Journal*, Vol. 56 (1956), pp. 262–267.

children are morally bound to protect the rights of children of every generation to normal maturing. We must help them to assimilate the heritage of their culture, certainly, but we must resist forced growth in one narrow direction that eliminates equally significant areas affecting the total learning process and eventually the functioning of the adults our kindergartners will be. All the evidence on the development of young children points to the conclusion that too early and too severe training in controls of any kind takes a toll in unexpected areas.

Yet real intellectual growth can and should proceed apace. Here is where attention to the children's curiosity and hunger for information, their eagerness to find out, and their readiness to examine evidence and open new areas of knowledge, is the path the teacher follows to encourage true intellectual maturing. The *mind* needs cultivation. The *method* must take into account the absorptive capacities of young children and the degree of strain and frustration tolerance that leads to strength rather than despair. Skill learning is not the same as intellectual development.

The teacher must herself be well-read however, so that she is a ready source of direction for finding answers. The teacher must read *to* the children so that they can hear orally words and concepts that they understand but cannot yet decipher for themselves from a printed page. Children must learn to value knowledge and realize fully that books are an unending source of satisfaction, but they must *experience* this and not learn it by rote.

CHILDREN MUST LEARN TO VALUE BOOKS

Practically all children love books. They show curiosity in handling and seeing books, they feel pleasure in looking at pictures, and thrill with excitement to know and to hear the story in the book. Kindergarten children can absorb, remember, enjoy many books, cultivate distinct preferences, remember the content or subject of many, recognize titles by the cover, and be aware of some authors. Kindergarten children can learn the use of a library and learn to respect and care for books they love. All this is basic readiness for the skill of reading, but it needs time and cultivation. Children's appetite for reading must be whetted and a taste for literature instilled in these receptive five-year-olds before they turn to the complex intellectual organization of learning to read. Once they have been well-prepared in attitudes and understanding they will want desperately to read, not for the prestige of themselves or their parents and teachers, but out of a need to tap the rich resources that they know lie in books. Beyond kindergarten, when they are able to sit still, able to see relationships between skills and the end goal, able to concentrate more on the abstract, and better equipped by maturation and learning to handle symbols, their reading progress is far more likely to be significant and unburdened by anxiety and feelings of failure, for they will begin the arduous task of deciphering when they are fully ready, and highly motivated.

INCIDENTAL LEARNING OF THE RELATION BETWEEN MEANINGS AND SYMBOLS

Despite the postponement of formal, consistent reading lessons, the concept that printed symbols have meaning is one which can and should enter the kindergarten child's life, although we are advocating an easy and unpressured admission. Modern children are surrounded with letters and number signs in the home, in the street, in the stores, on the road. Some three-year-olds know STOP and GO signs. Many four-year-olds can spell their name and ask for meaning of printed words. And some five-year-olds are interested in distinguishing words in books and writing their names when they enter kindergarten.

Reading of signs, brief instructions, directions, or names *in relation to experiences*, distinguishing hot and cold water faucets, STOP and GO signs, ingredients in recipes, names on supply boxes, numbers on classroom doors are all examples of reading as the child explores and looks and tries to understand what he is doing at the moment. Incidental, individual learning of reading by children who evidence such interest is not the same as asking all children to follow precise lines in confined areas in order to achieve standard, measurable success. It would be as foolish not to answer the logical questions of such children as it is to try to force others.

HELPING TO STRENGTHEN PERCEPTION OF LIKE AND UNLIKE

Ample experience with pictures in books and other places gives children the opportunity to discern and examine designs and decorations and a variety of orderly shapes. Experiences in listening can mean making fine differentiations in words and tones, in sounds produced by voice, by instruments, by nature, and by innumerable objects in the environment. Familiarity and experimentation with shape and sound tend to sharpen children's eyes and ears; these are necessary prerequisites for learning to read.

LANGUAGE AND READING

Closely related to listening is the speaking. Although this may seem too obvious to be worthy of mention, oral language power needs to be well-established before a child can gain from language in print. It happens that even among children with good verbal facility some do not learn to read easily in first grade. But nonverbal children are definitely slower to develop reading skills. There is a strong likelihood that the still poorly-defined relationship between language and thought functions in the case of culturally inarticulate children. Poor verbal facility is all too often related to limited experience in general; symbol learning rests on an experiential base. Therefore, language as an expression of meaning must be nurtured, both by offering something to talk about and creating the opportunity to express thought. When one is quite familiar with meaning in *oral* language, the symbols for the words one knows are more readily recognized.

At the upper levels of the elementary school there is clear correlation among all phases of language usage: reading, vocabulary, sentence sense, and paragraph sense. The key to all-pervasive success or equally all-pervasive failure, is in *word meaning*. The meaning of words is learned in a total context of experience and relationships, not memorized as for a test. Comprehensible experiences of all kinds through which vocabulary is actually strengthened and built and language is used as a tool for expressing concepts and ideas, constitute time well spent, not only for the immediacy of kindergarten success and pleasure but as a truly fruitful base for academic progress later in the grades.

THE CASE AGAINST A TOO EARLY START

In general, then, the reason for questioning reading instruction in the kindergarten, besides the fact that the greatest majority of five-year-olds are not yet capable of learning to read, is that there are some basic and timely things for kindergartners to learn which promote necessary physical, social, and emotional maturity, as well as stimulate intellectual approaches of the kind that support later reading. There is a proper time for the most efficiency in learning. Let us look carefully at the readiness of children at each stage of life.

WRITING IN THE KINDERGARTEN

Kindergartners, with all their activity, agility, and nimbleness, like to use all their muscles, their limbs, and their fingers. They use fingers for grasping, holding, and controlling, and are interested in using crayons, paintbrushes or fingertips. In the process of painting, drawing, coloring, scribbling or scratching, they are practicing wrist, hand, and finger movement and control, and are becoming aware of the relationship between movement and form. In such activities the children are also discovering and inventing designs, shapes, and spaces and are becoming aware of the differences and similarities in lines, circles, semi-circles, curves and curlicues. Preschool children sometimes even invent "writing" freely, which is fascinating to an observing literate adult.

When four to six-year-olds first become interested in letters and excited by their own ability to produce them, they "write" persistently, diligently, and independently. Here is a child at the easel writing his initial *M* with large strokes of blue paint, then elaborating the sides, then fencing and framing the impressive letter form on the large sheet of paper, and finally filling in the area with bits of color and supporting patterns. He tells the teacher not to write his name on his work because his initial is right there for everyone to recognize. Another child at the easel labors at writing her full name with a paintbrush after finishing her painting. She uses up the space for the first three letters, *A, L, I*, but determined not to stop, finds room for the next letter, *C*, on the side. There is still another letter left to Alice's name; frustrated neither by the lack of space next to the *C* nor by standards and rules of hyphenating, she places her necessary *E* gaily and crookedly on the top of the page. To Alice her name is now happily complete.

Using plasticine at a table, four children are squeezing and rolling it into various shapes; they contract and expand, lengthen and shorten, curve and straighten the shapes. "Look, I made an *O*—isn't this an *O*?" "Yes, it is," the teacher confirms. Encouraged, the child attaches a vertical appendage to the side and exclaims, "I made a *P*—look!" The teacher and the children look in recognition. Another child then says, "I am making an *L*," and he bends his pliable "snake" into an "L for Lewis." So pleased is he with his success, and so impressed with the shape, that while block-building shortly afterwards he uses a large area of the floor and builds a flat structure consisting of two narrow block lines of different lengths perpendicular to each other. He is indeed absorbed in building the letter *L!*

Children enjoy digging letters on crumbly sandy surfaces, tracing them on smooth areas of snow, or even doing "sky writing" with wide gestures of the arms. Feeling the shapes of letters with fingers and muscles and unlimited vision is a way of learning to know them.

All of the children described above—the one embellishing and beautifying the form of the letter, the one determined to write all the letters of her name in whatever place and order happens to be handy, the children stretching plasticine on the table into letter shapes, and the one using floor space to fashion letters—show interest in, and a beginning conception about, writing. But does this interest call for sitting those five-year-olds down, handing them lined paper, and *instructing* them to copy correctly shapes of prescribed dimension? Should the children's practice and concentration be focused on precision and control of minutia at this age and stage? Or should the teacher not conclude that the children are ready to learn that letters are symbols, and that they will be motivated in varying degrees by their own creative initiative and emulation of adults to make letters and words with various materials, in different activities, and in different positions?

Practical as they are, kindergartners are quick to see the usefulness of writing as it enters their activities, as it pertains to their own lives, and as it serves in communication. The following situation illustrates this understanding.

"We don't want the afternoon children to let the spider out," a child in the morning class told the teacher. "Will you tell them that?"

"Yes, I could, but why don't you tell them—it's your spider. You would know what to say."

"Well. We won't be here so how could we?" When the teacher did not answer immediately another child observed brightly, "You mean, we could leave a message?" "Yes, we could leave a message!" exclaimed another one. The teacher wrote down the children's message, using their own words. The children's concern about the effectiveness of the communication was very real and the next day they immediately checked on the results. They were very excited when a responsive message was left for them by the afternoon class. The meaning of exchanging messages became apparent and thus a basic lesson in writing was learned by the kindergartners. Such lessons may be repeated many times under different conditions, and they will never become boring. They give meaning to the mechanics of writing that come later.

PRACTICING ARITHMETIC IN THE KINDERGARTEN

Because of their alertness and practicality, and their interest in order and in physical relationships, kindergartners are keen mathematicians. In their play, five-year-olds are continuously practicing and experimenting with numbers, sizes, dimensions, and units of all sorts. How concerned they are with observing *big*, discerning *bigger*, and finding *biggest*, whether this involves trees, triangular blocks, sticks, stones, mugs, or bugs! A teacher brings a large carpenter pencil for the work bench and immediately children put regular, smaller pencils next to it and compare. She brings three pumpkins to class and at once the children perceive the three different sizes and designate them as Father, Mother and Baby. The teachers would do well to provide materials that allow children to express interest in bigness, littleness, wideness, narrowness, tallness, shortness, heaviness, and lightness. Watch children blockbuilding and note their attention to dimensions in relation to physical structuring.

"Here, you can use these blocks. I don't need them."

"No, I can't use them. They are squares. They are too small; see how big the blocks in my building are."

"But the round one won't fit into the corner. I need a straight one."

"I need five more doubles," a child says confidently, having counted accurately five blocks of a necessary height.

Five-year-olds love counting everything in sight: wheels, light switches, numerals on a clock, buttons on a shirt, objects on pictures, seeds in an apple cut in half. Since the verbal ability to count by rote does not necessarily correspond to a concept of number as quantity, children generally require considerable practice and individual experience before the numbers can have real meaning. There are no prescribed and arbitrarily limited ways of teaching number concepts. The teacher who did not *allow* the kindergarten children to use more than five paper petals for making Mother's Day flowers (because the official bulletin advised that five-year-olds should not be expected to have the number concept beyond five) did not appreciate the individual differences in children and was curbing mathematical (as well as artistic) interests. This teacher, with the intention of doing the right thing, avoided numbers of more than five to the point of absurdity, as if she were avoiding an illness. Yet when one watches and listens to children one learns that fives frequently are concerned with numbers way beyond five, as in the following record of table conversation in the kindergarten.

"I say 'thirty' not 'thirteen'" (in reference to a birthday date).

"My mother is twenty-two."

"My mother is twenty-six, and that's more!"

"Well, my mother is twenty-two, but my *grand*mother is more."

Four-year-old Maggie, in Kenneth Wann's article,[2] was breaking up a cracker into innumerable small pieces, and said to the teacher: "I am making an infinity of crackers." In reply to the teacher's question of what an infinity is, Maggie stated unhesitatingly, "Oh, you know, it just goes on and on and on." And six-year-old Robbie interrupted his mother's reading of ". . . they came from all the four corners of the earth . . ." to protest, "But, mother, the earth is *round,* so how could it have *corners?*"

Kindergartners' practice of arithmetic means more than mere ability to count; it means gaining a sense of relationship, of degree, of

[2] Kenneth Wann, "Children Want to Know," *Childhood Education,* September, 1960, p. 9.

quantity, of one-to-one correspondence through firsthand experience, through spontaneous conversation and discussion. Kindergartners are also interested, in varying degrees, in addition, subtraction, multiplication, and division as well as in fractions, though they do not stop to define the process. "There is a wheel missing on the wagon . . . there are only three here; there has to be four. This has to be fixed because one is missing." "I need one cup for everybody at my table. That means five cups." Learning that half an apple is going to be the allotted portion, Pattie brings the teacher four whole apples as a necessary number for eight children, although neither she nor the teacher use the term *fractions*. Observing the above, the teacher does not conclude that the kindergarten children are ready for arithmetic workbooks; rather she concludes that the children appreciate working with materials which enable them to express and gain mathematical concepts in an immediate and pertinent, rather than an abstract way.

In a sense, then, during the kindergarten year children are not only preparing in a long-range way for academic learning of the three R's, but have some kind of significant experience in all subjects they may encounter in college! Bruner's concept of a spiralling approach to subject matter,[3] in which basic concepts and principles are dealt with in increasing degrees of technicality and detail, supports our conception of curriculum building. Kindergartners can learn a great deal, but the technical level must always be fitting to five-year-old hands, minds, and feelings, to five-year-old muscles and coordination, and especially to five-year-old scope of interest and tolerance for failure.

What, then, is our aim? What are we building? Words of a five-year-old child come to mind.

A group of children are absorbed in building a complex road with several approaches on different levels. The process requires solution of human as well as mechanical problems. But at last the aim is achieved, the last blocks are in place, and the road is built. And one child stands straight with his arms stretched wide; he announces delightedly:

"The road of the World, the road of the World!"[4]

[3] Jerome Bruner, *The Process of Education* (Cambridge, Mass., Harvard University Press, 1961).

[4] Marilyn Chandler, Children Here and Now, No. 4, *Children at Work—Ideas at Work* (New York, Bank Street College of Education, 69 Bank St., 1956).

Bibliography

Biber, Barbara, *Implications for Public Education of Research in Learning; Our Human Potential: Challenge to Education; Premature Structuring as a Deterrent to Creativity,* Bank Street College Publications (New York, Bank Street College, 69 Bank St.).

————, and Snyder, Agnes, *How Do We Know A Good Teacher?,* Bank Street College Publication (New York, Bank Street College, 69 Bank St.).

Bradley, Beatrice E., "An Experimental Study of the Readiness Approach to Reading," *Elementary School Journal,* 1956.

Bruner, Jerome, *The Process of Education* (Cambridge, Harvard University Press, 1961).

Chandler, Marilyn, *Children at Work—Ideas at Work,* "Children Here and Now," #4, Bank Street College Publication (New York, Bank Street College, 69 Bank St.).

Gesell, Arnold, and Thompson, Helen, "Twins T and C from Infancy to Adolescence," *Genetic Psychology Monogr.,* Vol. 24 (1941).

McGraw, Myrtle B., *Growth: A Study of Johnny and Jimmy* (New York, Appleton-Century-Crofts, 1935).

Morphett, Mabel V., and Washburne, Carleton, "When Should Children Begin to Read?", *Elementary School Journal,* Vol. 31 (1931).

Wann, Kenneth, "Children Want to Know," *Childhood Education,* Sept. 1960.

Index